Averting the Old Age Crisis

A World Bank Policy Research Report

Averting the Old Age Crisis

Policies to Protect the
Old **and** Promote Growth

Published for the World Bank
OXFORD UNIVERSITY PRESS

Oxford University Press

OXFORD   NEW YORK   TORONTO
DELHI BOMBAY CALCUTTA MADRAS KARACHI
KUALA LUMPUR SINGAPORE HONG KONG TOKYO
NAIROBI DAR ES SALAAM CAPE TOWN
MELBOURNE AUCKLAND

and associated companies in

BERLIN   IBADAN

Published by Oxford University Press, Inc.
200 Madison Avenue, New York, N.Y. 10016

Manufactured in the United States of America
First printing September 1994

Cover photographs: At the bottom, workers in a television factory in Hanoi, Viet Nam, by Les
Stone/Sygma. Used by permission. Portraits of aged individuals are World Bank photographs
by Curt Carnemark.

Library of Congress Cataloging-in-Publication Data

Averting the old age crisis: policies to protect the old and promote growth.
    p. cm. — (A World Bank policy research report)
    Includes bibliographical references.
    ISBN *0-19-520996-6*
    1. Old age pensions.   2. Retirement income.   3. Aged—Economic
conditions.   4. Old age assistance.   5. Economic security.
I. Series.
HD*7105.3.A94 1994*
331.25'2—dc20   *94-1661*
                                                                            CIP

ISSN *1020-0851*

♾ *Text printed on paper that conforms to the American National Standard for Permanence*
of Paper for Printed Library Materials, Z39.48-1984

Contents

Text figures

Text tables

Appendix tables

Foreword

SYSTEMS PROVIDING FINANCIAL SECURITY FOR THE OLD ARE under increasing strain throughout the world. Rapid demographic transitions caused by rising life expectancy and declining fertility mean that the proportion of old people in the general population is growing rapidly. Extended families and other traditional ways of supporting the old are weakening. Meanwhile, formal systems, such as government-backed pensions, have proved both unsustainable and very difficult to reform. In some developing countries, these systems are nearing collapse. In others, governments preparing to establish formal systems risk repeating expensive mistakes. The result is a looming old age crisis that threatens not only the old but also their children and grandchildren, who must shoulder, directly or indirectly, much of the increasingly heavy burden of providing for the aged.

For these reasons, many economists and policymakers are seeking information and advice about old age security arrangements. But there are still too few who are aware of the impact these arrangements have on such diverse concerns as poverty, employment, inflation, and growth. *Averting the Old Age Crisis: Policies to Protect the Old **and** Promote Growth* is the first comprehensive, global examination of this complex and pressing set of issues. The culmination of a two-year research project, it synthesizes what is known, analyzes the policy alternatives, and provides a framework for identifying the policy mix most appropriate to a given country's needs.

The study identifies three functions of old age financial security systems—redistribution, saving, and insurance. It evaluates the policy options for meeting these according to two criteria: their impact on the aged and their impact on the economy as a whole. It finds that most existing systems provide inadequate protection for the old (because benefits are rarely indexed) and that redistribution is frequently perverse—for example, from poor young families to comfortable retirees. Moreover, as the systems mature, they may actually hinder growth— through high wage taxes, which cause evasion and push labor into the less efficient informal sector; through rising fiscal deficits, which fuel inflation; by squeezing out growth-promoting public spending, such as education or health services for the young; or through a combination of all three.

The study suggests that financial security for the old and economic growth would be better served if governments develop three systems, or "pillars," of old age security: a publicly managed system with mandatory participation and the limited goal of reducing poverty among the old; a privately managed, mandatory savings system; and voluntary savings. The first covers redistribution, the second and third cover savings, and all three coinsure against the many risks of old age. By separating the redistributive function from the savings function, the public pillar—and the size of the payroll tax needed to support it—can be kept relatively small, thus avoiding many of the growth-inhibiting problems associated with a dominant public pillar. Spreading the insurance function across all three pillars offers greater income security to the old than reliance on any single system.

The relative importance of each pillar, and the timing of transitions to a sustainable old age security framework, will vary among countries. The report analyzes these differences and the appropriate reform strategies in detail. The bottom line is that all countries should begin planning for their aging populations now.

This volume is the third in a series of Policy Research Reports prepared by the World Bank Development Economics Vice Presidency. Like the first two reports, *The East Asian Miracle* and *Adjustment in Africa,* it brings to a broad audience the results of World Bank research on key development policy issues. While accessible to nonspecialists, these reports are also meant to contribute to the debate among academics and policymakers about the appropriate public policy objectives and instruments for developing economies. As research documents, they may also provoke debate about the analytic methods used and the conclusions drawn.

Averting the Old Age Crisis is a product of the staff of the World Bank, and the judgments made herein do not necessarily reflect the view of its Board of Directors or the governments they represent.

Michael Bruno
Vice President Development Economics
and Chief Economist
The World Bank

The Report Team

THIS POLICY RESEARCH REPORT WAS PREPARED BY A TEAM LED by Estelle James and comprising Asli Demirguc-Kunt, Louise Fox, Donald Keesing, Robert Palacios, Klaus Schmidt-Hebbel, Anita Schwarz, Salvador Valdés-Prieto, Dimitri Vittas, and Christine Wallich. Jeffrey Nugent had primary responsibility for the chapter on informal systems of old age income support. Meta de Coquereaumont and Bruce Ross-Larson were the principal editors. The study was initiated by Lawrence H. Summers and Nancy Birdsall and was carried out under the general direction of Michael Bruno and Lyn Squire.

The editorial-production team was led by Anthony Pordes. The team was assisted by Paola Brezny, Heather Cochran, Danièle Evans, Audrey Heiligman, Jennifer Keller, Montserrat Pallarès-Miralles, Sushma Rajan, and Elfreda Vincent. Polly Means assisted with graphics. Alfred Imhoff and Lawrence MacDonald provided additional support.

Acknowledgments

MANY INDIVIDUALS INSIDE AND OUTSIDE THE WORLD BANK provided valuable contributions and comments. Particular thanks are due to: Emily Andrews, Anthony B. Atkinson, Nicholas Barr, Zvi Bodie, Gerard Caprio, David Cole, Peter Diamond, Elizabeth Duskin, Colin Gillion, Dalmer D. Hoskins, Michael Hurd, Richard Ippolito, Emmanuel Jimenez, Larry Kotlikoff, Ching Boon Lee, Sean McAlinden, William McGreevey, Olivia Mitchell, Robert J. Myers, Tom Powers, Monica Queisser, James Schulz, Jee Peng Tan, John Turner, and Zafiris Tzannatos. The report drew on background papers prepared by: Patricio Arrau, Mukul G. Asher, Barry P. Bosworth, Gary T. Burtless, Maria G. Cattell, Eric P. Davis, Jane Falkingham, Robert Holzmann, Paul Johnson, Deborah Mitchell, and Olivia S. Mitchell.

Definitions

Economy Groups

FOR OPERATIONAL AND ANALYTICAL PURPOSES, THE WORLD Bank's main criterion for classifying economies is gross national product per capita. Economies are classified as low-income, middle-income, or high-income. The income-based economy groupings used in this report are defined in 1990 U.S. dollars (not adjusted for purchasing power parity) as follows:

- *Low-income economies* are those with a gross national product per capita of less than $600.
- *Middle-income economies* are those with a gross national product per capita between $600 and $8,000.
- *High-income economies* are those with a gross national product per capita of more than $8,000.

Low-income and middle-income economies are sometimes referred to as developing economies. The use of the term is convenient; it is not intended to imply that all economies in the group are experiencing similar development or that other economies have reached a preferred or similar stage of development. Classification by income does not necessarily reflect development status.

Geographical Groups

THE GEOGRAPHIC GROUPING USED IN THIS REPORT ARE NOT intended to be comprehensive lists of all countries in a particular region. Furthermore, complete data may not be consistently available for all countries in each group. Where coverage differs significantly from the standard definitions that follow, those differences are indicated.

- *Sub-Saharan Africa* comprises Angola, Benin, Botswana, Burkina Faso, Burundi, Cameroon, Cape Verde, the Central African Republic, Chad, Comoros, Congo, Côte d'Ivoire, Dijbouti, Equatorial Guinea, Ethiopia, Gabon, The Gambia, Ghana, Guinea, Guinea-Bissau, Kenya, Lesotho, Liberia, Madagascar, Malawi, Mali, Mauritania, Mauritius, Mozambique, Namibia, Niger, Nigeria, Rwanda, Sao Tome and Principe, Senegal, Seychelles, Sierra Leone, Somalia, South Africa, Sudan, Swaziland, Tanzania, Togo, Uganda, Zaire, Zambia, and Zimbabwe.

■ *Asia* comprises Afghanistan, Bangladesh, Bhutan, Brunei, Cambodia, China, Fiji, Hong Kong, India, Indonesia, Kiribati, the Democratic People's Republic of Korea, the Republic of Korea, the Lao People's Republic, Macao, Malaysia, Maldives, the Federated States of Micronesia, Mongolia, Myanmar, Nepal, Pakistan, Papua New Guinea, the Philippines, Singapore, the Solomon Islands, Sri Lanka, Taiwan (China), Thailand, Vanuatu, and Viet Nam.

■ *The Middle East and North Africa* comprises Algeria, Bahrain, Cyprus, Egypt, the Islamic Republic of Iran, Iraq, Israel, Jordan, Kuwait, Lebanon, Libya, Malta, Morocco, Oman, Qatar, Saudi Arabia, the Syrian Arab Republic, Tunisia, Turkey, the United Arab Emirates, and the Republic of Yemen.

■ *Eastern Europe and the former Soviet Union* comprise Albania, Armenia, Azerbaijan, Belarus, Bulgaria, Croatia, the Czech Republic, Estonia, Georgia, Hungary, Kazakhstan, the Kyrgyz Republic, Latvia, Lithuania, Moldova, Poland, Romania, Russia, Slovenia, Taijikstan, Turkmenistan, Ukraine, Uzbekistan, and the Federal Republic of Yugoslavia.

■ *Latin America and the Caribbean* comprise Antigua and Barbuda, Argentina, the Bahamas, Barbados, Belize, Bolivia, Brazil, Chile, Colombia, Costa Rica, Cuba, Dominica, the Dominican Republic, Ecuador, El Salvador, Grenada, Guadeloupe, Guatemala, Guyana, Haiti, Honduras, Jamaica, Martinique, Mexico, Nicaragua, Panama, Paraguay, Peru, St. Kitts and Nevis, St. Lucia, Suriname, Trinidad and Tobago, Uruguay, and Venezuela.

Acronyms and Abbreviations

AFP   Administradora de Fondos de Pensiones (Pension Fund Administrator). A private pension fund manager in Chile.

GDP   Gross domestic product

GNP   Gross national product
IDB   Inter-American Development Bank
ILO   International Labour Organisation
IMF   International Monetary Fund
ISSA   International Social Security Association
OECD   Organization for Economic Cooperation and Development (Australia, Austria, Belgium, Canada, Denmark, Finland, France, Germany, Greece, Iceland, Ireland, Italy, Japan, Luxembourg, the Netherlands, New Zealand, Norway, Portugal, Spain, Sweden, Switzerland, Turkey, the United Kingdom, and the United States).

Glossary

Actuarial fairness: a method of setting insurance premiums according to the true risks involved.

Adverse selection: a problem stemming from an insurer's inability to distinguish between high- and low-risk individuals. The price for insurance then reflects the average risk level, which leads low-risk individuals to opt out and drives the price of insurance still higher until insurance markets break down.

Average effective retirement age: the actual average retirement age, taking into account early retirement and special regimes.

Benefit rate: the ratio of the average pension to the average economy-wide wage or covered wage.

Contracting out: the right of employers or employees to use private pension fund managers instead of participating in the publicly managed scheme.

Defined benefit: a guarantee by the insurer or pension agency that a benefit based on a prescribed formula will be paid.

Defined contribution: a pension plan in which the periodic contribution is prescribed and the benefit depends on the contribution plus the investment return.

Demographic transition: the historical process of changing demographic structure that takes place as fertility and mortality rates decline, resulting in an increasing ratio of older to younger persons.

Full funding: the accumulation of pension reserves that total 100 percent of the present value of all pension liabilities owed to current members.

Implicit public pension debt (net): the value of outstanding pension claims on the public sector minus accumulated pension reserves.

Intergenerational distribution: income transfers between different age cohorts of persons.

Intragenerational distribution: income transfers within a certain age cohort of persons.

Legal retirement age: the normal retirement age written into pension statutes.

Means-tested benefit: a benefit that is paid only if the recipient's income falls below a certain level.

Minimum pension guarantee: a guarantee provided by the government to bring pensions to some minimum level, possibly by "topping up" the capital accumulation needed to fund the pensions.

Moral hazard: a situation in which insured people do not protect themselves from risk as much as they would have if they were not insured.

Old age dependency ratio: the ratio of older persons to working age individuals. The old age dependency ratio used in the text refers to the number of persons over 60 divided by the number of persons aged 20 to 59.

Pay-as-you-go: in its strictest sense, a method of financing whereby current outlays on pension benefits are paid out of current revenues from an earmarked tax, often a payroll tax.

Pension coverage rate: in this report, the number of workers actively contributing to a publicly mandated contributory or retirement scheme, divided by the estimated labor force.

Pension spending: in this report, pension spending is defined as old age, retirement, survivors', death, and invalidity-disability payments based on past contribution records plus noncontributory, flat universal, or means-tested programs specifically targeting the old.

Portability: the ability to transfer accrued pension rights between plans.

Provident fund: a fully funded, defined contribution scheme in which funds are managed by the public sector.

Replacement rate: the value of a pension as a proportion of a worker's wage during some base period, such as the last year or two before retirement or the entire lifetime average wage. It also denotes the average pension of a group of pensioners as a proportion of the average wage of the group.

System dependency ratio: the ratio of persons receiving pensions from a certain pension scheme divided by the number of workers contributing to the same scheme in the same period.

System maturation: the process in which young people who are eligible for pensions, in a new system, gradually grow old and retire, thereby raising the system dependency ratio to the demographic dependency ratio. In a fully mature system all old people in the covered group are eligible for full pensions.

Universal flat benefit: refers to pensions paid solely on the basis of age and citizenship, without regard to prior work or contribution records.

Vesting period: the minimum amount of time required to qualify for full ownership of pension benefits.

Overview

A S WE GROW OLD WE WORK, PRODUCE, AND EARN less, and therefore need a secure source of income to see us through life. Societies and governments have developed mechanisms to provide income security for their older citizens as part of the social safety net for reducing poverty. But these arrangements are a concern for all of us—rich as well as poor, young as well as old—because the arrangements adopted can either help or hinder economic growth.

Today, as the world's population ages, old age security systems are in trouble worldwide. Informal community- and family-based arrangements are weakening. And formal programs are beset by escalating costs that require high tax rates and deter private sector growth—while failing to protect the old. At the same time, many developing countries are on the verge of adopting the same programs that have spun out of control in middle- and high-income countries.

Consider these facts:[1]

- In 1990 almost half a billion people, slightly more than 9 percent of the world's population, were over 60 years old. By 2030, the number will triple to 1.4 billion. Most of this growth will take place in developing countries, over half of it in Asia and more than a quarter in China alone (figure 1).
- Because of the broad diffusion of medical knowledge and declining fertility, developing countries are aging much faster than the industrial countries did. In Belgium, it took more than 100 years for the share of the population over 60 to double from 9 to 18 percent. In China the same transition will take only 34 years and in Venezuela 22 years. As a result, developing countries will have "old" demo-

Figure 1 Percentage of Increase in World Population over 60 Years Old, by 2030

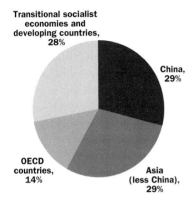

Source: Adapted from the World Bank population data base.

The number of old people will triple by 2030, and most of the growth will be in developing countries.

graphic profiles at much lower levels of per capita income than the industrial nations.

■ The demand for health services increases as countries grow older, since health problems and costly medical technologies are concentrated among the old. Because health and pension spending rise together, pressure on a country's resources and government budgets increases exponentially as populations age.

■ Publicly managed funds set aside for the old are often dissipated by poor management. In Zambia, the public provident fund, invested exclusively in public securities, lost 23 percent per year, on average, between 1981 and 1988. More than half the contributions in 1988 were used for administrative expenses.

■ High payroll taxes distort labor markets and reduce growth. In Hungary, where more than one-quarter of the population are pensioners, the average effective retirement age has fallen to 54 and the payroll tax needed to pay the pensions is 33 percent, cutting the demand for labor, the supply of experienced labor, and national output.

■ Government pensions are rarely fully indexed to inflation, so workers are poorly protected in their old age. In Venezuela, real pension benefits fell 60 percent during the 1980s largely because of inflation without indexation.

■ High government spending on old age security crowds out other important public goods and services. In 1989 Austria's pension fund cost 15 percent of GDP (gross domestic product), and old age benefits absorbed 40 percent of public spending. Without reform these already high percentages will increase further as the population ages.

■ In the Netherlands, Sweden, and the United States, workers retiring in the first thirty years of the public pension scheme received large positive lifetime transfers, whereas many workers retiring in the future will get less than they would from other investments and will suffer negative lifetime transfers.

■ Despite seemingly progressive benefit formulas in the public pension plans of the Netherlands, Sweden, the United Kingdom, and the United States, studies have not found much redistribution from lifetime rich to lifetime poor in these countries. This is partly because the rich live longer than the poor and therefore collect benefits for more years.

Everybody, old and young, depends on the current output of the economy to meet current consumption needs, so everybody is better off when the economy is growing—and in trouble when it's not. In the prime earning years, most people obtain claims on that output by working and earning wages. In old age, when earnings are low, people obtain claims on output through individual action, such as saving during their earlier years, or through informal group action, such as family transfers, or through formal collective action, such as public social security programs.

The choice among alternative arrangements for old age security affects the welfare of the old, because it determines the share of the national pie they can claim. More fundamentally, it affects the welfare of everyone, old and young, by influencing the size of that pie. So this report holds alternative policy options up to a dual test. What is good for the old population? And what is good for the economy as a whole? It analyzes the successes and failures of alternative policies. It evaluates policy options for countries introducing new formal systems of old age security. And it proposes ways to reform existing programs. The idea is to assist in the selection and design of policies that facilitate growth and enable the old to secure an equitable share of that growth.

Old Age Security Problems around the World

INCOME INSECURITY IN OLD AGE IS A WORLDWIDE PROBLEM, but its manifestations differ in different parts of the world. In Africa and parts of Asia, the old make up a small part of the population—and have long been cared for by extended family arrangements, mutual aid societies, and other informal mechanisms. Formal arrangements that involve the market or the government are rudimentary. But as urbanization, mobility, wars, and famine weaken extended family and communal ties, informal systems feel the strain. That strain is felt most where the proportion of the population that is old is growing rapidly, a consequence of medical improvements and declining fertility. To meet these rapidly changing needs, several Asian and African countries are considering fundamental changes in the way they provide old age security. The challenge is to move toward formal systems of income maintenance without accelerating the decline in informal systems and without shifting more responsibility to government than it can handle.

In Latin America, Eastern Europe, and the former Soviet Union, which can no longer afford the formal programs of old age security they introduced long ago, the need to reevaluate policy is even more pressing. Liberal early retirement provisions and generous benefits have required high contribution rates, leading to widespread evasion. The large informal sector in many Latin American countries, for example, reflects in part the efforts of workers and employers to escape wage taxes. The resulting labor market distortions there and in other regions reduce productivity, pushing contribution rates and evasion still higher, even as limited long-term saving and capital accumulation further dampen economic growth. Little surprise, then, that these countries have not been able to pay their promised benefits. Most have cut the cost of benefits by allowing inflation to erode their real value. When Chile faced these problems fifteen years ago, it revamped the structure of its system. Other Latin American countries are now undertaking similar structural changes, and some Eastern European countries are contemplating them. The challenge is to devise a new system and a transition path that is acceptable to the old, who have been led to expect more, while also being sustainable and growth-enhancing for the young.

Countries that belong to the Organization for Economic Cooperation and Development (OECD) face similar problems, as their populations age and their productivity stagnates. Public old age security programs covering almost the entire population have paid out large pensions over the past three decades of prosperity, as poverty declined faster among the old than among the young. But over the next two decades, payroll taxes are expected to rise by several percentage points and benefits to fall. That will intensify the intergenerational conflict between old retirees (some of them rich) who are getting public pensions and young workers (some of them poor) who are paying high taxes to finance these benefits and may never recoup their contributions. Such social security arrangements may, in addition, have discouraged work, saving, and productive capital formation—thus contributing to economic stagnation.

Many OECD countries appear to be moving toward a system that combines publicly managed pension plans designed to meet basic needs with privately managed occupational pension plans or personal saving accounts to satisfy the higher demands of middle- and upper-income groups. The challenge is to introduce reforms that are good for the country as a whole in the long run, even if this involves taking expected benefits away from some groups in the short run.

The Government and Old Age Security

MORE THAN HALF THE WORLD'S OLD PEOPLE ARE ESTIMAted to rely exclusively on informal and traditional arrangements for income security.[2] They receive food, shelter, and care from close relatives or extended family and often provide services or resources to the household in return. Economic development weakens these informal arrangements. Families become smaller and more dispersed. Opportunities for market employment open up for the young. The value of time contributed by old people diminishes. And people live longer, so the proportion of old people in the population increases. Family-provided assistance continues to play an important role in all societies. But in industrial societies, people are likely to withdraw from productive work, to live alone, and to depend on nonfamily sources of income in their old age.

Why Should Governments Get Involved?

When traditional, informal arrangements for subsistence break down in other spheres, they are replaced by formal market arrangements. Why doesn't that happen for old age subsistence? Why do governments everywhere in the industrial world and increasingly in developing countries intervene so extensively in this area?

Depending purely on voluntary actions by individuals to provide for their own old age security leaves several problems:

■ Shortsightedness—some people may not be farsighted enough to save for their old age and may later become charges on the rest of society.

■ Inadequate savings instruments—capital markets are undeveloped and macroeconomic conditions are unstable in many countries.

5

- Insurance market failures—adverse selection, moral hazard, and correlations among individuals make insurance against many risks (such as the risks of longevity, disability, investment, inflation, and depression) unavailable.
- Information gaps—people may be unable to assess the long-term solvency of private savings and insurance companies or the productivity of alternative investment programs, and cannot reverse their choices when large mistakes are discovered late in life.
- Long-term poverty—some people do not earn enough during their working lives to save for their old age, so redistribution is needed to keep them out of poverty.

So government interventions are usually justified on grounds that private capital and insurance markets are inadequate and redistribution to the poor is needed. All too often, however, these interventions have introduced inefficiencies of their own and have redistributed to the rich.

What Have Governments Done?

About 40 percent of the world's workers—and more than 30 percent of its old—are covered by formal arrangements for old age, buttressed by government policy. Public spending as a proportion of GDP has increased closely with per capita income and even more closely with the share of the population that is old. If past trends continue, public spending on old age security will escalate sharply in all regions over the next fifty years (figure 2). The most rapid escalation will occur in countries that may not expect it, because their populations are young today.

Government intervention can take and has taken many other forms besides taxes and transfers. The government may regulate private pension funds, mandate saving, guarantee benefits, offer tax incentives, create a legal system for reliable financial institutions, dampen inflation to encourage voluntary saving, and so forth. So the important policy questions are not: Should spending on the old increase? And should the public sector be involved? They are: How should the public sector be involved? Are public taxes and transfers the best alternative or are other types of public interventions and old age arrangements better?

Figure 2 Projected Public Pension Spending by Region, 1990–2050

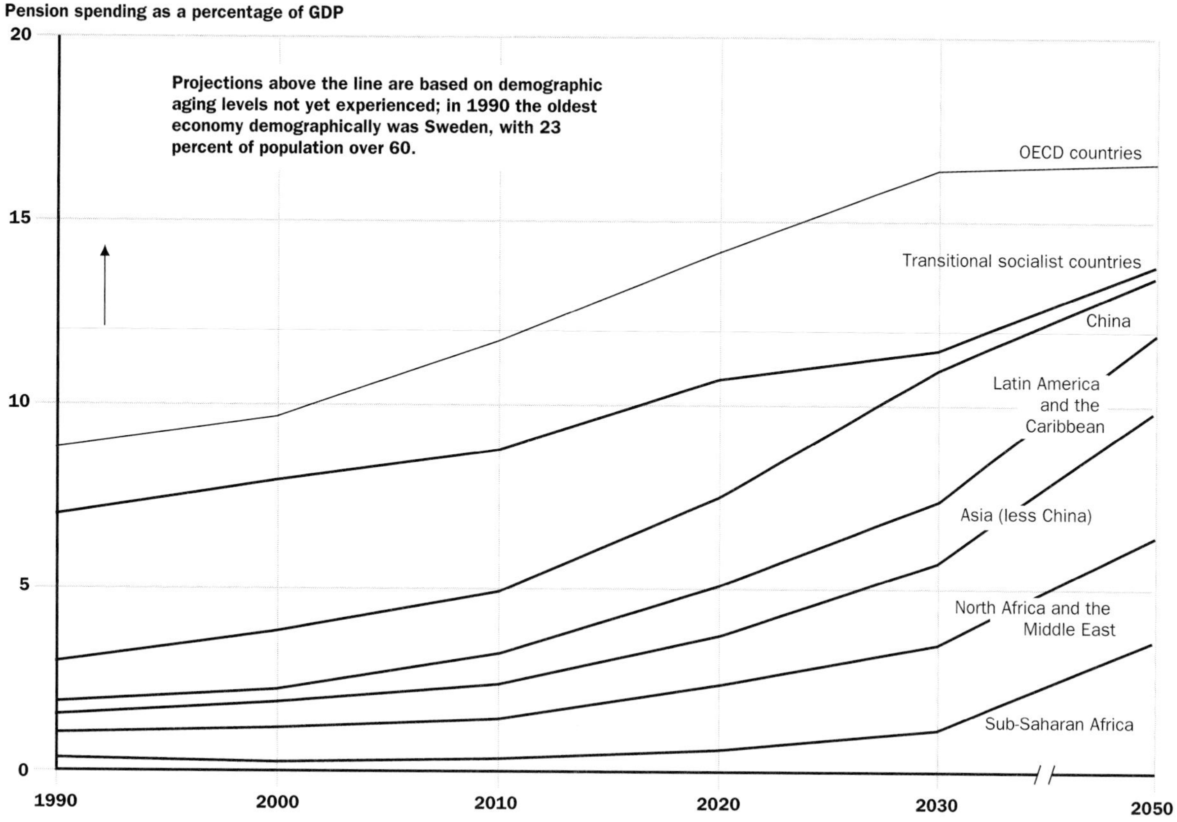
Pension spending as a percentage of GDP
20
15
10
5
0
Projections above the line are based on demographic aging levels not yet experienced; in 1990 the oldest economy demographically was Sweden, with 23 percent of population over 60.
OECD countries
Transitional socialist countries
China
Latin America and the Caribbean
Asia (less China)
North Africa and the Middle East
Sub-Saharan Africa
1990
2000
2010
2020
2030
2050

Note: This projection assumes that the current relationship between demography and spending continues. It applies coefficients of a linear version of the regression shown in figure 1.8 to World Bank demographic projections of the population over 60 by region.
Source: Palacios (1994a).

Formal arrangements also differ in ways that go beyond the type and degree of government involvement. Pension funds may have either redistribution or saving and insurance as important objectives. They may specify either their benefits or their contributions in advance—defined benefits versus defined contributions. And they may be financed on a pay-as-you-go basis—current pensions are financed by taxes on current workers—or on a largely funded basis—current pensions are financed by prior savings, and liabilities don't exceed accumulated reserves.

If trends continue, public spending on pensions will soar over the next fifty years in all regions.

Key Policy Issues

For these reasons, this report does not focus on simple public-private distinctions. Instead, it opens the lens to five sets of questions that distinguish among alternative old age policies and determine their effects:

- Should the system be voluntary or compulsory? And at what levels?
- What should be the relative emphasis on saving versus redistribution? And should these functions be combined or provided through separate financing and managerial arrangements?
- Who should bear the risk of unexpected outcomes—pensioners or others in society?
- Should the system be fully funded or pay-as-you-go?
- Should it be managed centrally—or decentrally and competitively?

Alternative Financing and Managerial Arrangements

Many combinations of answers to these questions are possible but in practice three different financing and managerial arrangements for old age security are most common. They are public pay-as-you-go programs, employer-sponsored plans, and personal saving and annuity plans.

Public pay-as-you-go plans. This is by far the most common formal system, mandatory for covered workers in all countries. Coverage is almost universal in high-income countries and widespread in middle-income countries. As its name suggests, it places the greatest responsibility on government, which mandates, finances, manages, and insures public pensions. It offers defined benefits that are not actuarially tied to contributions and usually finances them out of a payroll tax (sometimes supplemented from general government revenues) on a pay-as-you-go basis. And it redistributes real income, both across and within generations.

Occupational plans. These are privately managed pensions offered by employers to attract and retain workers. Often facilitated by tax concessions and (increasingly) regulated by governments, these plans tended to be defined benefit and partially funded in the past. But the number of defined contribution plans (in which contributions are specified and benefits depend on contributions plus investment returns) and the degree of funding have been increasing in recent years, and these have quite different effects. More than 40 percent of workers are covered by occupational schemes in Germany, Japan, the Netherlands, Switzerland, the United Kingdom, and the United States—but far fewer in developing countries (see table 5.1).

Personal saving and annuity plans. These are fully funded defined contribution plans. Workers save when young to support themselves when they are old. Since benefits are not defined in advance, workers and retirees bear the investment risk on their savings. Voluntary personal saving is found in every country, often encouraged by tax incentives, but some countries have recently made it mandatory. A key distinction is between mandatory saving plans managed by the government (as in Malaysia, Singapore, and several African countries) and those managed by multiple private companies on a competitive basis (as in Chile and soon in Argentina, Colombia, and Peru).

These financing and managerial arrangements are explored in detail in chapters 4 through 6.

Criteria for Policy Choice

The prevalence of these alternative arrangements depends, in large part, on government policies that mandate, encourage, or regulate. The effectiveness of these arrangements depends, in large part, on individual responses, such as evasion, compliance, and the possibility of offsetting actions that reduce other saving, transfers, and work. As a result of these private responses, each arrangement has broad implications for the operation of labor and capital markets, for the government's fiscal balance, and for the income distribution in society.

How are we to evaluate alternative policies? This report argues that old age security programs should be both an instrument of growth and a social safety net. They should help the old by:

- Facilitating people's efforts to shift some of their income from their active working years to old age, by saving or other means.
- Redistributing additional income to the old who are lifetime poor, but avoiding perverse intragenerational redistributions and unintended intergenerational redistributions.
- Providing insurance against the many risks to which the old are especially vulnerable.

And they should help the broader economy by:

- Minimizing hidden costs that impede growth—such as reduced labor employment, reduced saving, excessive fiscal burdens, misallocated capital, heavy administrative expenses, and evasion.
- Being sustainable, based on long-term planning that takes account of expected changes in economic and demographic conditions, some of which may be induced by the old age system itself.
- Being transparent, to enable workers, citizens, and policymakers to make informed choices, and insulated from political manipulations that lead to poor economic outcomes.

Few programs fulfill these criteria. They do not operate the way they are supposed to or the way many people believe they do—a conflict between myth and reality (box 1).

Toward a Multipillar System

ONE OF THE PRIME POLICY ISSUES IN THE DESIGN OF OLD AGE security programs is the relative importance of the saving, redistribution, and insurance functions—and the role of government in each:

- Saving involves income smoothing over a person's lifetime: people postpone some consumption when they are young and their earnings are high so that they can consume more in their old age than their reduced earnings would permit.
- Redistribution involves shifting lifetime income from one person to another, perhaps because if low-income workers saved enough to live on in old age, they would plunge below the poverty line when young.
- Insurance involves protection against the probability that recession or bad investments will wipe out savings, that inflation will erode their real value, that people will outlive their own savings, or that public programs will fail.

A central recommendation of this report is that a country's old age security program should provide for all three functions, but with very different government roles for each. A corollary is that countries should rely on multiple financing and managerial arrangements; that is, they should share responsibility among multiple pillars of old age support.

Box 1 Myths and Facts about Old Age Security

MYTHS ABOUND IN DISCUSSIONS OF OLD AGE SECURITY. Consider some of the most common:

Myth 1: Old people are poor, so government programs to alleviate poverty should be directed to the old.

Fact: In most countries poverty rates are higher among the young than among the old, and families with small children are the poorest of all. The old are even better off when comparisons are based on lifetime income rather than current income. Why? Because people with higher incomes are more likely to live long enough to become old, whereas people with low incomes are more likely to have many children and die young. Targeting young families with children is a better measure for alleviating poverty than targeting the old (see chapter 3).

Myth 2: Public social security programs are progressive, redistributing income to the old who are poor.

Fact: Even if benefit formulas look progressive, four factors neutralize most of the progressive effect. The first people to be covered when new plans are started are invariably middle- and upper-income groups, and they typically receive large transfers. The longer life expectancy of the rich severely reduces or eliminates the apparent progressivity of social security programs when redistribution is calculated on a lifetime rather than an annual basis. Ceilings on taxable earnings keep the lid on tax differences between rich and poor. And when benefit formulas are earnings-related or subject to strategic manipulation, as in many countries, upper-income groups benefit even more, so the net redistributional effect can be regressive (see box 4.6).

Myth 3: Social security programs insure pensioners against risk by defining benefits in advance.

Fact: Benefit formulas are redefined frequently, so substantial political risk remains (see box 4.1).

Myth 4: Only governments can insure pensioners against group risks, such as inflation, and most do so.

Fact: Most developing countries do not index pension benefits for inflation in their publicly managed old age programs. And most OECD countries have skipped some cost-of-living adjustments during the past decade. Failing to index for inflation is the most common method governments use to reduce real benefit levels and escape from unsustainable benefit promises. In countries prone to inflation, the best insurance would be international diversification of pension fund investments—which is more likely when investment decisions are made by private managers rather than government (see box 4.10).

Myth 5: Individuals are myopic but governments take the long view.

Fact: Governments have repeatedly made decisions about old age programs based on short-run exigencies rather than long-run benefits. One example is the use of early retirement programs as a temporary solution to unemployment that in the long run costs the economy in lost labor and the public treasury in large pensions payments. Another is pay-as-you-go financing instead of full funding, allowing generous pensions initially but discouraging saving and growth and lowering pensions in the long run (see box 4.4 and issue briefs 4 and 8).

Myth 6: Government action is needed to protect the interests of generations yet unborn.

Fact: Most public pay-as-you-go pension schemes provide the largest net benefits to workers who are 30 to 50 years old when the schemes are introduced. The unborn children and grandchildren of these workers are likely to receive negative transfers as the system matures and the demographic transition proceeds (see issue briefs 3 and 9).

One Dominant Public Pillar Is Not Enough for Redistribution, Saving, and Insurance

Most countries—including almost all developing countries and some industrial countries—combine all three functions in a dominant public pillar, a publicly managed scheme that pays an earnings-related defined benefit and is financed out of payroll taxes on a pay-as-you-go basis. People with high incomes contribute more and get more, but some of their contributions are supposedly transferred to people with lower incomes. This combination of functions has been defended on grounds that it keeps administrative costs low through economies of scale and scope and that it builds political support for the plan. The savings component encourages high-wage earners to participate, whereas the redistributive component lets them express their solidarity with those less well-off. In industrial countries, these plans have been credited with reducing old age poverty during the post–World War II period.

But the evidence suggests that public schemes that combine these functions are problematic—for both efficiency and distributional reasons.

When populations are young and systems are immature, it is tempting for politicians to promise generous benefits to workers when they retire. But these same benefits require high contribution rates once the population ages and schemes mature. Indeed, any system that is supposed to redistribute to low-income workers while also providing adequate wage replacement to high-income workers will be costly at that point. But the defined benefit formulas do not make benefits actuarially contingent on these contributions. The high contribution rate is therefore likely to be seen as a tax by many workers, not as a price for services received. High tax rates lead to evasion—thereby defeating the purpose of the mandatory scheme. They also lead to strategic manipulation that enables workers to escape much of the tax but still qualify for benefits—thereby causing financial difficulties for the system. And they reallocate labor to the informal sector—causing difficulties for the broader economy. Employers who cannot pass payroll taxes on to workers cut back on employment, reducing national output. Older workers who are eligible for large pensions retire early, reducing the supply of experienced labor. Such unhappy outcomes, of course, vary from country to country and are especially prevalent in developing economies, which have limited tax enforcement capability, imperfect labor markets, and large informal sectors.

The pay-as-you-go method of finance in a single public pillar further separates benefits from contributions for the cohort as a whole. It inevitably produces low costs and large positive transfers to the first covered generations. It also inevitably produces negative transfers for later cohorts because of system maturation and population aging, increasing the labor market distortions and incentives to evade. In some cases, countries may wish to make this transfer across generations. More often, the transfer is unintentional. Ironically, the largest transfers go to high-income groups in earlier cohorts, whereas middle- and sometimes even lower-income groups in later cohorts get negative transfers. The larger and more earnings-related the benefits in the public pillar, the greater are these perverse transfers.

A dominant pay-as-you-go public pillar also misses an opportunity for capital market development. When the first old generations get pensions that exceed their savings, national consumption may rise and savings may decline. The next few cohorts pay their social security tax instead of saving for their own old age (since they now expect to get a pension from the government), so this loss in savings may never be made up. In contrast, the alternative, a mandatory funded plan, could increase capital accumulation—an important advantage in capital-scarce countries. A mandatory saving plan that increases long-term saving beyond the voluntary point and requires it to flow through financial institutions stimulates a demand for (and eventually supply of) long-term financial instruments—a boon to development. These missed opportunities in a pay-as-you-go public pillar become lost income for future generations—and another source of intergenerational transfer.

Additionally, large pay-as-you-go public pillars often induce expenditures that exceed expectations—because of population aging, system maturation, poor design features such as early retirement and high benefit rates, and opportunities for political manipulation that lead to these poor design features. The costs of the system—whether covered by higher contribution rates or subsidies from the general treasury—make it difficult for the government to finance important public goods—another growth-inhibiting consequence.

But ultimately the costs (higher taxes and their distortionary effects) have become too large to bear in many countries. When the public pillar fails to deliver on its promises, old people who depended on it exclusively have nowhere else to turn. Thus a dominant public pillar in a single pillar system increases risk for the old. The most common failure occurs when inflation develops because demands on the national pie exceed its size and pensions, which are not fully indexed, lose much of their value.

For all these reasons, public systems that have tried to do it all have too often produced costly labor and capital market distortions and perverse redistributions to high-income groups while failing to provide security for the old—outcomes that are neither efficient nor equitable nor sustainable.

Problems with Other Single Pillar Systems

Other single pillar systems, too, are problematic. In many countries, especially in Africa, publicly managed funded plans (provident funds) have a record of misuse. Usually they are required to invest solely in public securities, yielding low or even negative returns for the pension funds. Their availability at low interest rates may lead governments to borrow and spend more than they would have otherwise, in unproductive ways. They are, essentially, a hidden tax on labor, subject to misuse precisely because it is hidden. By giving governments control over a major share of the financial assets in a country, they deprive the private sector of access to these funds and thereby inhibit growth. They contain no provisions for redistributing to low-income workers and, in fact, often include nontransparent redistributions to high-income workers—until finally the fund is depleted and can't pay much to anyone.

Privately managed occupational or personal saving plans would also fail as single pillar systems. (No country has ever tried to use them as such.) Occupational plans have better capital market effects than publicly managed plans but may impede the smooth functioning of labor markets. They redistribute in accordance with employer rather than social objectives. They usually do not protect those with limited labor market experience or high mobility. And they are subject to employer or insurance company default, in the frequent case in which they are not fully funded. Privately managed personal saving accounts are beneficial for capital market development, have the least distortionary effects on labor markets, and are relatively immune to political manipulation by governments or strategic manipulation by workers. They do not, however, address the problems of information gaps or of poverty among those with low lifetime incomes whose earning capability is further diminished by old age. Nor do they insure against the risks of low investment returns (because of poor individual choices or economy-wide recession) or high longevity, in the absence of annuities markets.

Tying the Objectives to the Pillars

To avoid these problems, this report recommends separating the saving function from the redistributive function and placing them under different financing and managerial arrangements in two different mandatory pillars—one publicly managed and tax-financed, the other privately managed and fully funded—supplemented by a voluntary pillar for those who want more (figure 3 and chapter 7):

Reliance on individual pillars will vary with a country's circumstances over time, but every country should have a multipillar system.

Figure 3 The Pillars of Old Age Income Security

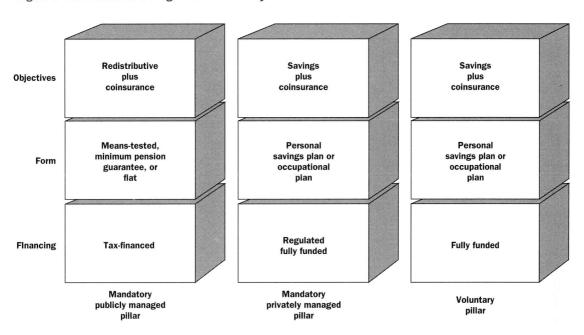

Objectives	Redistributive plus coinsurance	Savings plus coinsurance	Savings plus coinsurance
Form	Means-tested, minimum pension guarantee, or flat	Personal savings plan or occupational plan	Personal savings plan or occupational plan
Financing	Tax-financed	Regulated fully funded	Fully funded
	Mandatory publicly managed pillar	Mandatory privately managed pillar	Voluntary pillar

- The public pillar would have the limited object of alleviating old age poverty and coinsuring against a multitude of risks. Backed by the government's power of taxation, this pillar has the unique ability to pay benefits to people growing old shortly after the plan is introduced, to redistribute income toward the poor, and to coinsure against long spells of low investment returns, recession, inflation, and private market failures. The public pillar could take three alternative forms. It could be part of a means-tested program for the poor of all ages, with eligibility criteria taking into account the diminished ability of the old to work and benefit levels taking into account age-linked needs. Alternatively, it could offer a minimum pension guarantee to a mandatory saving pillar. As still another alternative, it could provide a universal or employment-related flat benefit that coinsures a broader group. But it should be modest in size, to allow ample room for other pillars, and pay-as-you-go, to avoid the problems frequently associated with public management of national provident funds. Having an unambiguous and limited objective for the public pillar should reduce the required tax rate substantially—and therefore evasion and misallocated labor—as well as pressures for overspending and perverse intra- and intergenerational transfers.

- A second mandatory pillar—one that is fully funded and privately managed—would link benefits actuarially to costs and carry out the income-smoothing or saving function for all income groups within the population. This link should avoid some of the economic and political distortions to which the public pillar is prone. Full funding should boost capital accumulation and financial market development. The economic growth this induces should make it easier to finance the public pillar. But a successful second pillar should reduce the demands on the first pillar. The second mandatory pillar could take two alternative forms: personal saving accounts or occupational plans. In either case, mandatory programs require careful regulation.

- Voluntary occupational or personal saving plans would be the third pillar, providing additional protection for people who want more income and insurance in their old age.

- Although the redistribution and saving functions would be separated, the insurance function would be provided jointly by all three pillars, since broad diversification is the best way to insure against a very uncertain world.

Crucial Choices within the Mandatory Pillars

Within each mandatory pillar are numerous policy options—some of which are much better than others. For the public pillar, one important choice is between earnings-related benefits, on one hand, and those that are flat or means-tested on the other. Although earnings-related benefits may have political appeal, the need to pay higher benefits to high-income workers while also trying to alleviate poverty among low-income workers creates numerous problems, including high taxes and excessively large transfers to the first generation of beneficiaries, many of whom are well-to-do. For these and other reasons, earnings-related benefits are a poor choice for the public pillar.

The next choice, between flat and means-tested benefits, is less clear-cut and will depend on such variables as institutional and taxing capacity (flat benefits are costlier but easier to administer) and income distribution (means-tested benefits redistribute to the poor more efficiently, provided that the administrative requirements can be met at low cost). A variant of the means-tested scheme, a minimum pension guarantee, may be the best option for the public pillar in countries that already have a mandatory saving scheme to which the guarantee can be added.

For the mandatory funded pillar, governments must choose between public management and private management. Most publicly managed funded schemes, also known as provident funds, have had poor results. Publicly managed funds are usually required to invest in government securities or the securities of quasi-government entities such as state enterprises or public housing authorities—frequently at below-market interest rates. These funds thus earn less than they would on the open market and must charge higher contribution rates or pay lower benefits than would otherwise be the case. In contrast, private, competitively managed schemes—in which workers or employers choose their fund managers—are rarely required to accept below-market returns and are less likely to be used as disguised forms of government revenue. They have incentives to invest in stocks and bonds that offer the best risk-yield combinations, and can tap the benefits of international diversification and management expertise. The resulting superiority of privately managed funds over publicly managed funds is strikingly apparent from a comparison of rates of return of selected funds in the 1980s.

Higher returns to contributors aside, mandatory, privately managed funded schemes offer economy-wide advantages. They can be part of a national policy to develop new financial institutions and deepen capital markets by mobilizing long-term saving and allocating it to the most productive uses, including uses in the private sector. For these reasons, the report strongly recommends that the funded pillar be privately managed.

For privately managed funded schemes, still another choice must be made between personal saving plans and occupational pension plans set up and run by employers. Occupational plans have the seeming advantage that they can start up on a voluntary basis before the market and the government are ready for a mandatory plan. They can be implemented through payroll deductions with low record-keeping and marketing costs. And they use the financial expertise of employers and prearranged groups of workers to overcome insurance market problems. However, these advantages often prove illusory. Without mandatory participation and adequate regulation, occupational plans tend to be spotty in coverage, to be offered mainly to middle- and upper-income workers, to involve large regressive tax expenditures, to be underfunded and therefore default-prone, and to restrict vesting and portability of benefits, impeding labor mobility and economic restructuring. In contrast, coverage under personal saving plans can be broad, and benefits are fully portable. Because of these distributional and labor market effects, personal saving plans are probably preferable to occupational plans for the funded pillar, except for countries that already have substantial coverage under well-functioning employer-sponsored schemes. A privately managed mandatory personal saving scheme was pioneered in Chile and is now being incorporated into new systems in Argentina, Colombia, and Peru.

Despite the advantages of privately managed, mandatory personal savings schemes, governments should not rush to establish one. Rather, they need to assess carefully market and regulatory capacities before deciding to go ahead. A banking system, rudimentary stock and bond markets, and the capacity to develop these further in response to demand from pension funds are essential preconditions. In addition, because workers may lack the education and experience necessary to choose effective investments, careful government regulation is needed to keep the investment companies financially sound and workers' exposure to investment risk within reasonable bounds. Where market and regulatory capacities are lacking, governments should proceed slowly and cautiously.

How to Get There

HOW SHOULD COUNTRIES START THIS PROCESS? AND HOW can those that already have large public pillars make the transition? Although the ultimate goals are similar for all, the paths and time frame depend on country circumstances (chapter 8).

Young Low-Income Economies

Consider first a country with a young population, a low per capita income, and only a small public pillar or publicly managed provident fund, primarily one covering government sector employees. Many countries in Africa and South Asia are at this stage. The weakening of informal systems of old age support and the absence of reliable capital and insurance market instruments are prompting political pressures for an expanded public pillar. These countries typically do not have the financial markets or regulatory capability necessary to establish a decentralized funded pillar. But they should be creating an enabling environment for voluntary and, later, mandatory saving and pension plans by:

- Keeping inflation down
- Avoiding interest rate and exchange controls
- Establishing reliable savings institutions that are accessible to people in rural as well as urban areas
- Developing a regulatory framework that gives people confidence in banks, insurance companies, and other financial institutions
- Instituting an effective tax policy and tax administration system
- Building the human capital essential for the effective management of financial and regulatory systems.

These basic conditions, important for old age systems, are also necessary for continuing economic growth.

These countries should also be taking steps especially geared to providing old age security, using methods that avoid the problems of large pay-as-you-go plans and that will eventually fit into a multipillar system. They should:

- Keep the existing contributory public pillar small, flat, and limited to urban areas and large enterprises in which transaction costs are relatively small, fraud is easiest to detect, and the informal system breaks down first.

■ Provide social assistance (in cash or in kind) to the poorest groups in society, including the old poor who are not covered by contributory plans, taking into account their vulnerability stemming from their diminished ability to work.

■ Carry out simulations of the long-run impact of alternative public plans (coverage, benefit level, retirement age) on taxes and the distribution of transfers across and within generations. This requires making assumptions about wage growth, interest rates, labor force participation, unemployment, and evasion—and recognizing that the choice of system will affect these parameters (box 8.2).

■ Phase out (or convert to voluntary status) centrally managed provident funds, which are often misused.

■ Set up the legal and institutional framework for personal saving and occupational pension plans, requiring full funding, portability of benefits, and disclosure of information for the latter.

■ Give equivalent tax treatment to occupational and personal retirement plans that meet prudent standards.

■ Avoid crowding out informal support systems and offer incentives to families to continue taking care of their older relatives.

■ Avoid the pitfalls—overgenerous pensions, early retirement, benefit-contribution structures that encourage evasion or discourage saving, perverse redistributions to high-income groups in public plans; and unregulated, unfunded, nonportable occupational plans—that are so tempting, especially in young countries with immature schemes and limited regulatory capability.

Young but Rapidly Aging Economies

The next set of countries, also with young populations, is aging and often growing rapidly—since rapid economic growth is associated with falling fertility rates and rising longevity. Many East Asian economies are at this stage. In addition to accelerating all the actions just mentioned, these economies should:

■ Begin designing and introducing a mandatory decentralized funded pillar. Preconditions for this pillar are government regulatory capability, a banking system, a secondary government bond market, and an emerging stock market—or the ability to develop these institutions quickly in response to demand from new pension funds.

- Start by setting up a strong regulatory framework, determining the required contribution rate, and deciding whether saving or occupational plans should be used for the mandatory funded plan. Establishing this structure and phasing in the second pillar could take several years. Governments should not rush ahead too fast, beyond their institutional capabilities. But if they do not move ahead fast enough strong political pressures will otherwise develop, from middle- and high-income workers, for a dominant earnings-related public pillar—and all its associated problems.

- Gradually expand coverage for the public pillar, keeping it modest and redistributive while satisfying workers' saving or income-smoothing needs through the privately managed funded pillar. Otherwise these economies will face the much more difficult task of restructuring later.

- Initially use a payroll tax for the public pillar, to avoid inefficiencies from excise taxes and transfers from uncovered to covered groups, but shift to a broader tax base as coverage becomes universal, the government's ability to collect general income and consumption taxes increases, and the redistributive function can be emphasized.

Older Economies with Large Public Pillars

The third set of economies comprises those that are already middle-aged, are growing older rapidly, and have substantial public pension programs that provide widespread coverage and whose costs will soar, with dependency rates, over the next three decades. This set includes OECD and Eastern European economies and several Latin American economies. Although the degree of urgency varies, all these economies face imminent problems with their old age systems. Rather than relying on an ever more costly public pillar to do it all, at high tax rates that inhibit growth and bring low rates of return to workers, the time is ripe for these economies to make the transition to a mandatory multipillar system.

- The first step is to reform the public pillar by raising the retirement age, eliminating rewards for early retirement and penalties for late retirement, downsizing benefit levels (in the frequent cases in which they are overgenerous to begin with), and making the benefit structure flatter (to emphasize the poverty reduction function), the tax rate lower, and the tax base broader.

■ The second step is to launch the second pillar by setting up the appropriate contribution and regulatory structures. The transition can be accomplished by:

(1) Downsizing the public pillar gradually while reallocating contributions to a second mandatory pillar or

(2) Holding the public benefit relatively constant (in cases in which it is low to begin with) but raising contribution rates and assigning them to the second pillar or

(3) Recognizing accrued entitlements under the old system and agreeing to pay them off while starting a completely new system right away. This involves designing the new system, calculating the implicit social security debt that is owed under the old system, and figuring out how to finance it all in a way that is both politically and economically acceptable.

Several OECD countries are engaged in the gradual transition (alternative 1 or 2). Several Latin American countries have already introduced a radical transition (alternative 3). And many former socialist countries are trying to decide which way to go.

Conclusion

A MANDATORY MULTIPILLAR ARRANGEMENT FOR OLD AGE security helps countries to:

■ Make clear decisions about which groups should gain and which should lose through transfers in the public mandatory pillar, both within and across generations. This should reduce perverse or capricious redistribution—and poverty.

■ Achieve a close relationship between incremental contributions and benefits in the private mandatory pillar. This should reduce effective tax rates, evasion, and labor market distortions.

- Increase long-term saving, capital market deepening, and growth through the use of full funding and decentralized control in the second pillar.
- Diversify risk to the fullest because of the mix of public and private management, political and market determination of benefits, the use of wage growth and capital income as the basis for finance, and the ability to invest in a wide variety of securities—public and private, equity and debt, domestic and foreign.
- Insulate the system from political pressures for design features that are inefficient as well as inequitable.

The broader economy should be better off in the long run as a result. So should both the old and the young.

The right mix of pillars is not the same at all times and places. It depends on a country's objectives, history, and current circumstances, particularly its emphasis on redistribution versus saving, its financial markets, and its taxing and regulatory capability. The kind of reform needed and the pace at which a multipillar system should be introduced will also vary—from quick in middle- and high-income countries whose systems are in serious trouble to very slow in low-income countries, which should avoid these same mistakes. But one simple recommendation is clear: all countries should begin planning now.

Notes

1. These facts are from World Bank population projections; B. Mitchell (1982); Zambian National Provident Fund (1988–89); Rofman (1994); Marquez (1992); ILO (forthcoming); Nelissen (1987); Stahlberg (1989); Creedy, Disney, and Whitehouse (1992); Aaron (1977); Hurd and Shoven (1985); Boskin and others (1987); additional data from unpublished World Bank documents.

2. Global coverage estimates used in this report c from Palacios (1994a).

CHAPTER 1

Growing Older

MOST PEOPLE EARN LESS AS THEY REACH OLD age, because they work less or less productively (or not at all). So, many governments have programs to provide income security to their older citizens—arrangements that are part of the social safety net for reducing poverty. But the programs directly concern the young as well as the old because, depending on their design, they can either help or hinder economic growth. This concern will sharpen as the number of old people triples over the next 40 years to nearly 1.4 billion—increasing their share in the total population from 9 percent in 1990 to 16 percent 2030 (figure 1.1).

Everybody, old and young, depends on the current output of the economy to meet current consumption needs. Most people in their prime earning years get claims on that output by working productively and earning wages. But few old people can fully support themselves through current earnings. They obtain claims on output in other ways—through such informal group action as family transfers, through such formal market systems as saving and investing, and through such collective action as public social security programs.

The choice among these alternatives and the specific form they take affect the welfare of the old by determining their share of the national pie. These choices also affect the welfare of the young by determining the size of the pie. Alternative policy options should thus be held to a dual standard: what is good for the old population, and what is good for the whole economy? The policies adopted by many countries fail this test. They are beset with problems that spill over from the old age system to the rest of the economy.

Figure 1.1 Percentage of the Population over 60 Years Old, by Region, 1990 and 2030

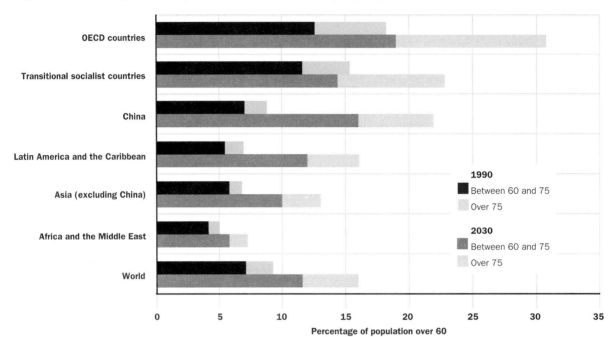

Note: Japan is included with the OECD countries, not with Asia.
Source: Adapted from the World Bank population data base.

Although the old make up a larger share of OECD populations, developing countries are graying faster.

Consider these examples from low-, middle-, and high-income countries.[1]

- The payroll tax rate for pensions in most countries in Eastern Europe is 30 percent or more—and this is sometimes supplemented further by general revenue finance, discouraging employment and deterring investment in important public goods.
- In Hungary only 2 percent of those over 60 are officially in the labor force—the rest are retired and receiving a pension or working in the informal sector to avoid payroll taxes.
- In Argentina, before the 1994 reform, every worker had to support two-thirds of a pensioner, because early retirement increased the number of beneficiaries and evasion decreased the number of contributors.

- In Egypt, Peru, Turkey, Venezuela, and Zambia, the rate of return on publicly managed pension funds ranged between -12 percent and -37 percent in the 1980s.
- In Brazil, during the 1980s, evasion reduced contribution revenues by more than one-third in a typical year. Inflation, with only partial indexation, reduced the government's fiscal burden but made things worse for pensioners.
- By 1990 the average OECD country spent 24 percent of its annual public budget and over 8 percent of its GDP on old age, disability, and survivors' benefits. The average person spent more on social security taxes than on income or value-added taxes. These numbers are expected to increase over the next decade as populations age.
- Studies of old age programs in the Netherlands, Sweden, the United Kingdom, and the United States have found large income transfers to the early generations covered under these plans, at the expense of their grandchildren, but little (if any) redistribution from lifetime rich to lifetime poor.

Because of these problems, calls for policy change are being raised everywhere. Many OECD countries are decreasing their reliance on publicly managed plans and increasing their reliance on privately managed voluntary or occupational plans. Latin American countries are introducing drastic structural changes that include mandatory saving plans. Eastern European countries are considering major reforms of their collapsing systems. And African and Asian countries, with younger populations and small formal programs, must decide which way to go in the years ahead.

The Graying of the World's Population

THE PROPORTION OF OLD PEOPLE IS NOT THE SAME IN EVERY population—nor is the rate at which populations are aging. Moreover, chronological age may differ from functional age—some people can work productively until age 70 or 80, whereas others become unproductive much earlier. A 45-year-old woman might be considered old in Zambia, where life expectancy (at age 15) is 59, but still young in Japan, where life expectancy (at age 15) is 83 (World Bank population data). Some generalizations about the distribution of the chronologically "old" (over 60) around the world:

- Although the proportions of people who are old is highest in OECD and transitional socialist countries, most of the growth in the world's old population—from half a billion people in 1990 to almost 1.5 billion people in 2050—will be in developing countries, particularly in Asia (figure 1.1).
- About one old person in four is "very old" (over age 75)—and of these almost two-thirds are women. The economic position of the very old is very different from that of the younger old, and the position of old women is very different from that of old men (figures 1.1, 1.2, and box 1.1).
- The proportion of the population that is old rises with per capita income. In low-income countries, less than 7 percent of the population is over 60. This proportion rises to 12 to 16 percent in middle-income countries and to 17 percent or more in most high-income countries. The ratio of old people to working age people (the old age dependency ratio) also rises with per capita income—

Figure 1.2 Ratio of Old Women to Old Men in Developing and Industrial Countries, 1990

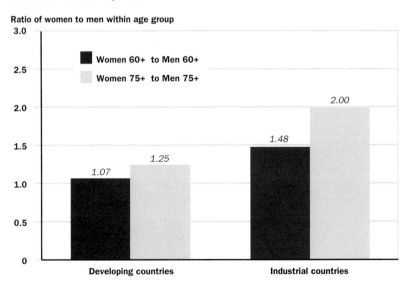

There are more old women than old men in the world—and the difference rises among people over 75.

Source: Adapted from the World Bank population data base.

Box 1.1 The Plight of Older Women

BECAUSE OF DEMOGRAPHIC, CULTURAL, AND IN-come differences between the genders, old age means something quite different—and more troubling—for women than for men. In most countries, women live longer than men. Life expectancy at age 15 is eight years longer for women than for men in the United States, seven years in Canada, and six years in Belgium, Germany, and Sweden. At age 65, women can still expect to live some four years longer than men in these countries. Women in developing countries also have longer life expectancies, though generally less than in industrial countries. For exam-ple, at age 15 the advantage is five years in Mauritius and four years in Venezuela—at age 65 it is three years in Mauritius and two in Venezuela.

Most women marry men older than themselves and are less likely than men to remarry after divorce or the death of a spouse. Since women also live longer than men, a much higher proportion of women end up living alone. Widows outnumber widowers in almost every country. In Africa and Asia, more than half of women over the age of 65 are widows, compared with only 10 to 20 percent of men. Whether through widowhood, divorce, or be-cause they never married, elderly women living alone outnumber elderly men living alone by a large margin. In Australia, one in four elderly women live alone, but fewer than one in ten elderly men do. In Switzerland, four times as many elderly women live alone (40 percent) as elderly men (10 percent), and in Germany, six times as many (37 percent of women, 6 percent of men).

Because of responsibilities for child rearing and caring for elderly family members, women's labor force participation is generally shorter and more ir-regular than that of men. Women are more likely to engage in part-time work and to retire early. For the same type of work, women's wages are usually less than those of men—70 percent of men's in the United Kingdom, 64 percent in Egypt, and 50 per-cent in the Republic of Korea. Women are also more likely than men to work in the informal sector, where wages are lower and access to pensions difficult.

(Box continues on the following page.)

a relationship that stems directly from the lower fertility rate in richer countries and the ability to lengthen life span through med-ical intervention (figures 1.3 and 1.4).

- Most old people live in poor countries (which are also the most populous), a pattern that will intensify toward 2030. By then, more than three-quarters of the world's old people will be in areas not now industrial—more than half in Asia and more than a quar-ter in China alone (figure 1.5). (See appendix tables A.1 and A.2 for additional demographic data.)

With rising incomes and medical advances, families have fewer chil-dren and people live longer. Together, these forces have raised old age dependency in many countries. This "graying of the population" means that a smaller working age population has to support more and more old people. The graying is already well under way in OECD countries, and dependency ratios are expected to rise steeply in much of Latin America,

Box 1.1 *(continued)*

Finally, cultural practices and legal systems discriminate against women in many countries. Women's lower social status, weaker property rights, and more limited access to inheritance strongly influence their economic security in old age. Older widows are most vulnerable (see box 2.2). When a husband dies in Uganda, his relatives claim the household property, often evicting the widow and her children from their home. In some areas widows are part of the property "inherited" by brothers-in-law.

The upshot of all these differences: women are more likely to be poor in old age than are men. In Australia, where the public pension is means- and asset-tested, it is received by 85 percent of old women compared with 65 percent of old men. The disparity is greater in the United States: one in three single women over 65 lived in poverty in 1986, twice the rate for the rest of the population.

Women in developing economies, where public assistance is meager, are even more likely to end up in poverty in their old age. In Chile, 65 percent of old people who receive social assistance are women. In urban China, 41 percent of old women have annual incomes below an extreme poverty line (70 percent of the normal poverty line), compared with 4 percent of old men. In Venezuela, women account for two-thirds of old people in the lowest income decile. Similar data hold historically in the United Kingdom. In 1899, before welfare programs were established, a British House of Commons investigation found that 60 percent of women over age 65 had incomes of less than 10 shillings a week, compared with 40 percent of men.

Old age security schemes to alleviate poverty thus need to take into account the fact that most of the old poor are women, many of whom are very old and have had very limited labor force experience.

Source: Cangping (1991); D. Mitchell (1993); U.K. Parliament (1899); U.S. Department of Commerce (1993); Nordic Countries Statistical Secretariat (1993); Diamond and Valdes-Prieto (1994); International Social Security Association (1993); Falkingham and Johnson (1993).

Eastern Europe, Central Asia, and China over the next two decades. By 2050, only Africa will still be "young."

As a result of the broad diffusion of medical knowledge and lifestyle values, developing countries will age much faster than industrial countries did. It took 140 years for the proportion of old people to double from 9 to 18 percent in France, 86 years in Sweden, and 45 years in the United Kingdom. It will take only 34 years in China and 22 years in Venezuela (figure 1.6).

Developing countries will have old demographic profiles at much lower levels of per capita income—and the numbers will be enormous. China and other developing countries will be much poorer than Sweden and other industrial nations were when their populations aged. Their large old population will need support, but their economic, political, and institutional capabilities may limit their ability to satisfy this need. The problem will worsen if their cultural definition of old age is not re-

Figure 1.3 Relationship between Aging and Income Per Capita, Selected Countries, 1990

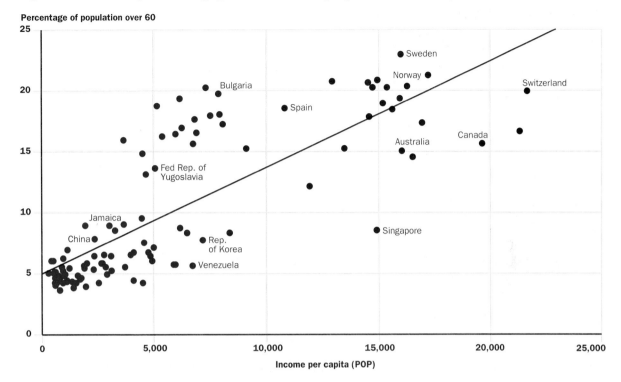

Note: Because of space limitations, not all data points are identified. $R^2 = 0.64$. POP60 = 4.92 + 0.00087 × YCAP90, where POP60 is the percentage of population over 60 and YCAP90 is the income per capita adjusted for purchasing power parity in U.S. dollars for 1990.
Source: World Bank population data base; World Bank (1992d), table 30.

vised to accommodate their people's increased longevity and if their labor productivity does not increase rapidly. The old age policies these countries adopt now will determine whether they will have the ability to support their old populations as the demographic transition takes place.

Some argue that the drop in the child dependency rate caused by the fertility decline will free resources to meet the needs of the growing older population. But careful analysis shows that it won't. Reallocating resources from children to old people is not easy. The extra private subsistence cost of each old person is greater than that of each child. In OECD countries public spending per old person on social services and transfers is two to three times as great as public spending per child, so the resources released are less than those demanded, on average (table 1.1). And as families and societies have fewer children, they are likely to invest more

The old make up more of the population as income rises...

31

Figure 1.4 Relationship between the Old Age Dependency Ratio and Income Per Capita, Selected Countries, 1990

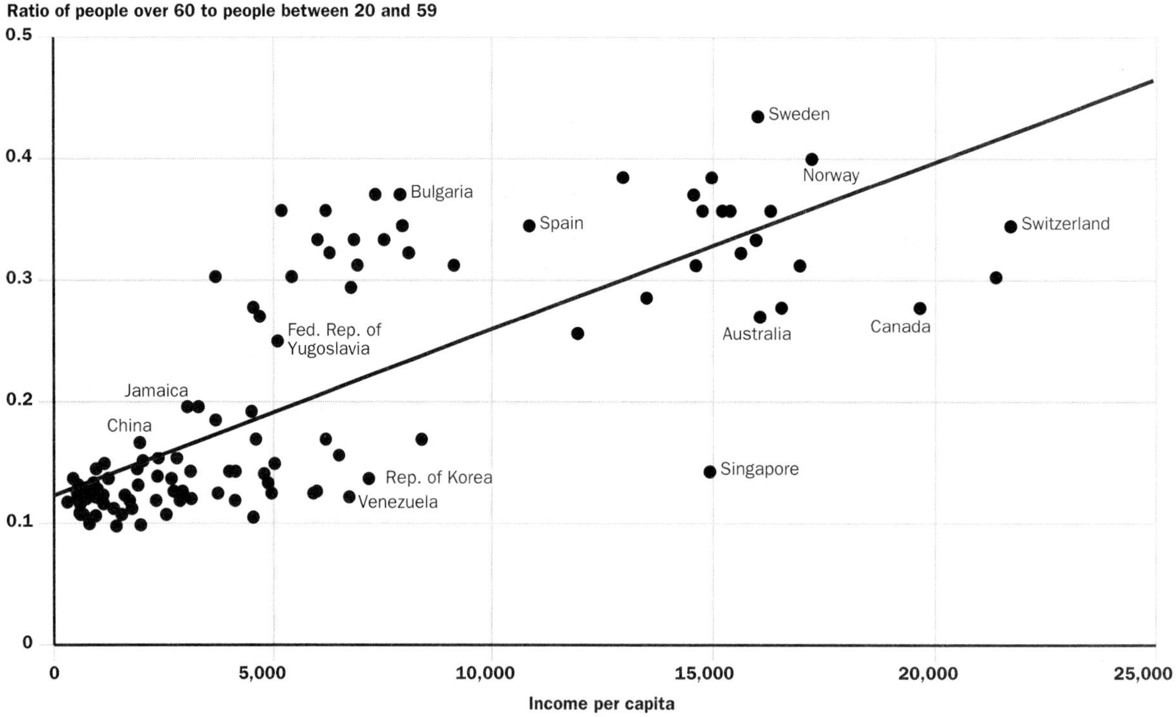

Ratio of people over 60 to people between 20 and 59

Note: Because of space limitations, not all data points are identified. $R^2 = 0.59$. DEP = $0.12299 + 0.0000136 \times YCAP90$, where DEP is the old age dependency ratio.

Source: World Bank (1992d), table 30; World Bank population data base.

...and the ratio of old people to the working age population rises with income as well.

in each child, so even fewer resources become available at the margin. Both the young and the old will need costly services and financial support. Meeting these needs requires careful planning, starting now (box 1.2).

Informal Systems of Old Age Support and Their Breakdown

IN AFRICA AND PARTS OF ASIA, OLD PEOPLE LIVE WITH THEIR children in extended families. All members of the household, even the old, contribute to its productive capacity in some way—working

Figure 1.5 Percentage of People over 60 Years Old, by Region, 1990 and 2030

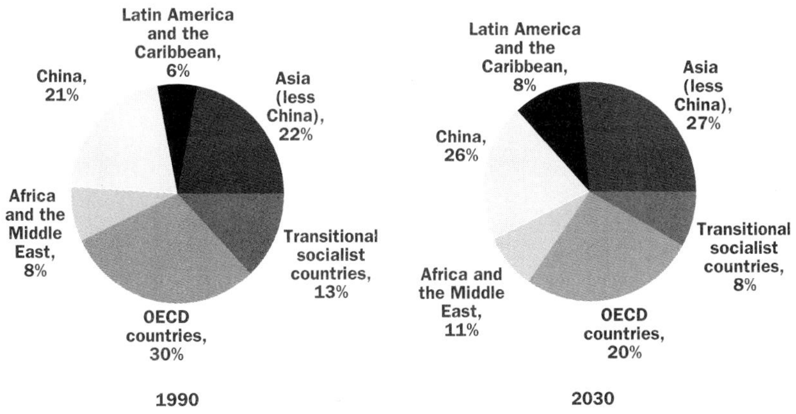

1990

2030

Note: Japan is included with the OECD countries, not with Asia.
Source: Adapted from the World Bank population data base.

Most old people live in poor countries—in thirty-five years four of five old people will live in countries that are poor today.

in the fields, caring for children and grandchildren, giving advice from experience. The family group covers the consumption needs of all members. As the productive capabilities of the old decline, they are supported by the work of their children, just as they once supported their children and parents. Social sanctions in close-knit communities—bolstered by parental ownership of family assets such as land and homes—reinforce these arrangements. Mutual aid societies sometimes extend this informal insurance-redistributional system beyond the family to the broader ethnic or cultural group.

Even when this system works well, some people fall through the cracks—those who never had children, those whose children have died or moved away, and those whose children do not earn enough to support less productive household members. These cracks widen as urbanization and mobility increase, nuclear families replace extended families, medical progress extends life expectancy for the old, and the formalization of jobs makes it difficult for people to continue working as they age and their productivity declines.

In some African countries, informal systems have been subject to additional pressures from famines, wars, and AIDS—which have reduced the size of the working age population. Informal systems in East Asia are under stress because the population is aging at an unprecedentedly high

Figure 1.6 Number of Years Required to Double the Share of the Population over 60 from 9 to 18 Percent, Selected Countries

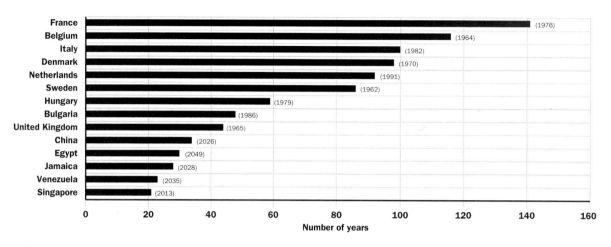

Note: Year in which population doubling was or will be reached is shown in parentheses.
Source: Mitchell (1990); World Bank population projections.

France needed 140 years to double the proportion of its old people from 9 to 18 percent—China will do it in 34 years; Venezuela in 22.

rate. As a result of all these factors, China, Indonesia, Sri Lanka, and several African countries are considering fundamental changes in the way they provide old age security. The challenge is to move toward formal systems of income maintenance without speeding the breakup of informal systems, without shifting too much responsibility to government, and without repeating the mistakes of other countries.

Table 1.1 Relative Per Capita Social Spending, by Age Group, 1980

Country	Age group		
	0–14	*15–64*	*65 and over*
Canada	100	72.0	265
France	100	51.4	263
Germany, Fed. Rep. of	100	59.5	316
Italy	100	110.0	380
Japan	100	44.0	235
Sweden	100	43.0	234
United Kingdom	100	53.3	213
United States	100	66.9	381

Note: This table refers to public social spending as calculated in OECD (1988).
Spending on the youngest age group has index value that equals 100.
Source: OECD (1988b). Cited in Palmer, Smeeding, and Torrey (1988).

Box 1.2 Will the Falling Child Dependency Rate Offset the Rising Old Age Dependency Rate?

THE INCREASING PROPORTION OF OLD PEOPLE IN the population is caused in part by the decreasing proportion of children, during the demographic transition. Does this enable the diversion of resources from the children to the old, solving the old age security problem? Although the long answer to this question is complex, the short answer is no.

■ The marginal subsistence cost is probably less for each child than for each old person (because children live with their parents in nuclear families, while many old people live apart), so the subsistence cost saved by one fewer child would not cover the subsistence cost of another old person.

■ It is not a simple matter to reallocate child social service resources to the old. Children need primary schools, whereas old people need pensions, hospitals, and custodial care. During the transition the child support system may have excess capacity while the old age support system has insufficient capacity. In Thailand, where the fertility rate has declined rapidly over the past decade, average class size and student-faculty ratios have fallen far below the cost-effective point, yet these resources have not been reallocated, in part because the political system lacks feedback mechanisms to make this happen.

■ Families—and societies—with few children have made a quantity-quality trade-off and are likely to invest more heavily in the health and education of each child, both privately and publicly. For example, they send their children on to secondary schools and universities, which are much more expensive than primary schools. As the proportion of children in the population declines, most countries do not "save" large amounts of resources that they could then spend on the old. Instead, they concentrate their spending on the remaining young.

The reduction in fertility rate or family size that is part of the demographic transition has other effects that may ease the old age problem.

First, many more women enter the market labor force, increasing taxable family income and social security revenues. But the other side of the coin is that these women are less available to care for their older parents at home, so larger monetary outlays for nursing and custodial care are needed. These effects partly cancel each other out in their impact on the financial viability of old age support systems.

Second and more important, the greater money spent per child may result in productivity gains that can improve the standard of living of everyone. In East Asia, where fertility has fallen rapidly, productivity and wage growth have exploded. This improvement may stem partly from the larger investments in the health and education of the young people who are now entering the labor force and partly from the increased physical capital per worker as population growth slows. If so, the total wage bill—and contributions to pension systems—may go up rather than down as the demographic transition proceeds.

But the relationship between population growth and productivity has not been clearly established and probably differs across countries. Moreover, many industrial countries set part of their benefits as a proportion of the economy-wide average wage and index pensions to wages, so pension expenditures go up commensurately with productivity. In that case, productivity gains increase the absolute amount of the pension but do not eliminate financial pressures on pension systems as populations age.

Source: Sanderson and Tan (1994); Birdsall and Sabot (1994); Kelly (1973 and 1988); Kling and Pritchett (1994).

Why Should Governments Get Involved?
The Failures of the Marketplace

WHEN TRADITIONAL FAMILY-BASED ARRANGEMENTS FOR production and subsistence break down, formal market-based arrangements often replace them. Why do pure market solutions to the problems of old age often fail? Why don't people simply save or purchase annuities when they are young, so that they can maintain a decent standard of living when they are old and less productive? Why do governments intervene in this area throughout the industrial world and increasingly in developing countries?

Market solutions—such as individuals saving and investing for their old age—help to fill the gaps left by the breakdown of the family system, but they fail to do the job completely. In the simplest case, people may not save enough when they are young because they are *shortsighted*. They may not expect to live long or they may place a much higher value on consuming today than on saving for tomorrow. It is difficult for 30-year-olds to anticipate their needs when they reach 80. Income security in old age requires very long-term planning, and many people *lack the information* for this type of planning (including information about future health, cost of living, lifetime earning capacity, and the safety and productivity of alternative forms of investment and insurance).

Probably every society has some myopic members. But it is hard to prove whether or not people are generally myopic—the evidence points in both directions. Some societies have very high voluntary saving rates, while other societies have low saving rates. Consumer borrowing at high interest rates—10 to 20 percent in industrial countries, 20 to 30 percent or more in developing countries—is consistent with the notion that many people value present consumption much more than future consumption.

Shortsighted behavior becomes a social problem for two reasons. First, as people age they may change their preferences and wish that they had saved more—but then it is too late. Second, if people don't save enough for their old age, the rest of society may feel obliged to support them. (This obligation may even deter people from saving when they are young, a problem known as *free riding* and *moral hazard*.) Insufficient saving may also starve the economy. So, government policies that encourage or require people to save can make everyone better off.

Even if people try to save when they are young, they may find *few reliable savings instruments*, particularly in developing countries. Or workers may not invest wisely, later finding themselves with much lower returns than expected. Or investment returns may be low for the entire economy during long spells. During the Great Depression of the 1930s, many U.S. and European workers saw their life savings go down the drain. And in developing countries experiencing a sudden devaluation or inflation, the savings of many workers have evaporated in real terms, discouraging further saving.

Another set of problems stems from the *absence of insurance markets*. Since people are always uncertain about how long they will live, they may wish to purchase insurance that will pay them an income—a pension or an annuity—over their lifetime. But insurance companies are not well developed in many countries because of informational deficiencies and weak capital markets. When people have more information about their life expectancy than the insurance company does, a problem known as *adverse selection* occurs. Good and bad risks are pooled, and premiums are charged according to the average risk of the group. The good risks (those who expect to die young) find these terms unacceptable. So the insurance company, left with only the bad risks (those who expect to live long), raises its premiums, leading more good risks to opt out. In the end, prohibitive prices put annuities beyond the reach of most people.

Even when annuities are available at a fair price, consumers must commit large sums of money irreversibly before age 65 in return for the promise of a lifetime pension paid out over twenty to thirty years. Many people, for good reason, would doubt the *credibility* of such long-term promises by private insurance companies. Private insurance companies also have a difficult time insuring against risks such as unexpectedly high *inflation,* which hits everyone simultaneously. For all these reasons, private annuity markets are undeveloped in most countries, and annuities that fully insure against inflation and recession are generally not available.

In Western countries, employer-sponsored group annuities developed as one response to the deficiencies of individual annuities. In the late-nineteenth and early twentieth centuries, large companies introduced pensions as a way of rewarding and retaining the loyalty of their long-term employees. Later, unions and tax advantages fostered the growth of these and other fringe benefits. But few employers, especially small employers, have this long time horizon and easy access to insurance or capital markets. And employers who started plans often failed to fund them adequately, limited the number of workers who qualified, disqualified workers who left before retirement, did not index for inflation, or were unable to follow through on their promises because of competitive pressures or bankruptcy.

Thus when systems of communal living in extended families break down and before remedial government policies are firmly established, old people may have a hard time maintaining their customary standard of living because of saving or insurance problems. Furthermore, pockets of severe poverty have developed among those whose lifetime incomes were too low to cover minimally adequate consumption levels during their retirement as well as their working years (the *long-term poverty* problem).

It is clear, then, that governments should get involved when informal old age security arrangements no longer work. And the need for government involvement becomes more urgent as a country's population ages.

How Have Governments Responded?

GOVERNMENTS GET INVOLVED IN OLD AGE SECURITY FOR many reasons, and their policies take many forms. Governments can simply require or encourage families to look after the old, as in China. Malaysia gives a rebate to adult children whose parents live with them and an additional tax deduction for parental medical expenses. Governments can set up savings instruments, such as the postal savings program in Japan. They can also provide information to people about how much they will need to save to attain different living standards when they are old and about the likely effects of alternative investment programs. And governments can give employers tax incentives to provide pensions for their workers—or even require them to do so, as in Australia, France, and Switzerland. In addition, investment and insurance companies providing annuities can be required to meet specified fiduciary standards, as in the United Kingdom and the United States. Going a step further, governments can also offer means-tested assistance to the old, a practice in many industrial and some developing countries. Such assistance can take the form of cash or of goods and services, such as health care and housing.

Moving another step, governments can establish mandatory pension plans into which all the young must pay to provide support for old age, as in every industrial society. Such plans can cover the entire population, the entire labor force, or selected groups that are easier to reach. The plans can be redistributive toward the lifetime poor—or they can be based on savings and insurance principles that closely link contributions to expected benefits. They can be financed out of current contributions on a pay-as-you-go basis or out of funds accumulated from past contributions. If funded, they can be managed publicly or privately. The multitude of long-term risks can be borne largely by the old or shared more generally among all groups in society.

The term "government policies" thus encompasses a multitude of arrangements for financing, managing, regulating, rationing, and delivering income security in old age. The following chapters evaluate how these alternative policies have worked, drawing a sharp distinction between policies that are appropriate to solve the three main problems of long-term poverty, inadequate saving, and insurance market failure.

The Growth of Formal Mandatory Plans

Formal old age programs and public spending on old age support both increase with economic development. At the same time, the variation among countries at similar stages of development shows that policies are to some extent discretionary and that which policies governments choose does make a difference (figures 1.7, 1.8, and 1.9).

Per capita income and coverage by formal mandatory plans. An estimated 40 percent of the world's labor force participates in formal programs of old age income support, most of them publicly mandated and publicly managed. Per capita income is the best predictor of a country's coverage: the relationship is close and explains 94 percent of the variance in coverage rates (figure 1.7). Richer countries have higher coverage by formal plans, in part because informal systems no longer function adequately and in part because richer countries are better able to enforce compliance. In high-income OECD countries, nearly all workers and their survivors are covered. In developing countries, much smaller proportions of workers are covered, usually in privileged occupations such as the civil service or the military. Agricultural workers, domestic servants, temporary labor, and self-employed people—the bulk of the labor force in developing countries—are generally not covered.

Figure 1.7 Relation between Publicly Mandated Pension Plan Coverage and Income Per Capita

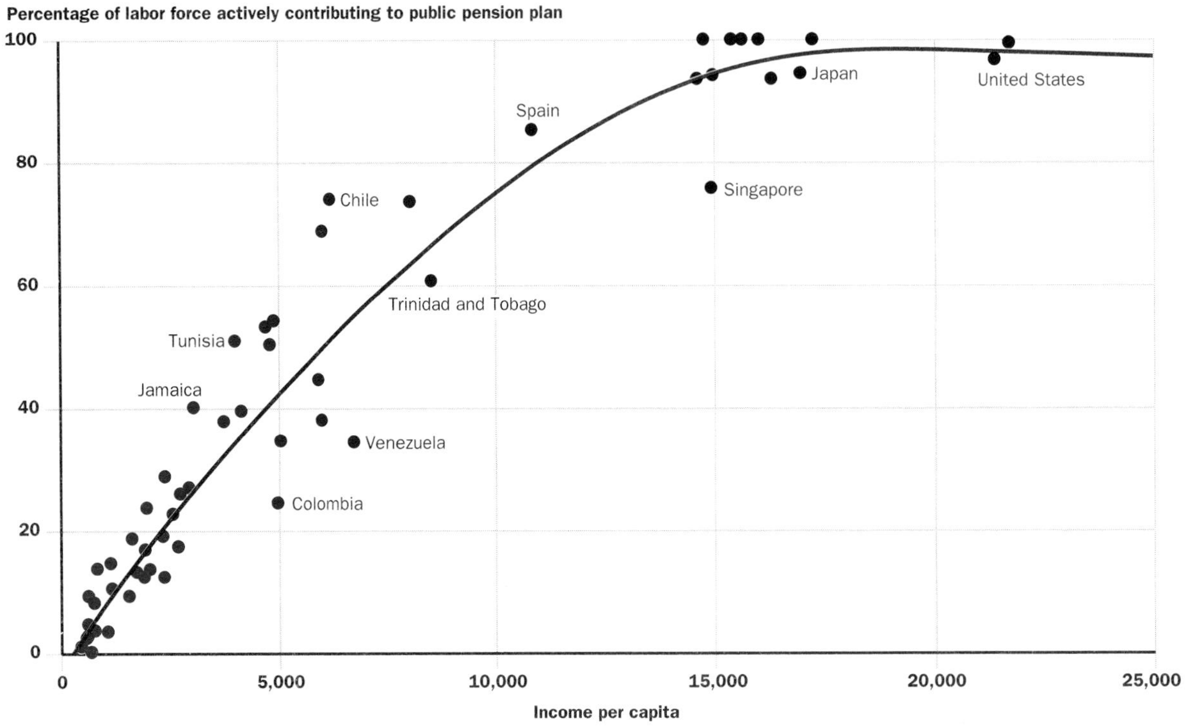

Percentage of labor force actively contributing to public pension plan

Income per capita

Note: Because of space limitations, not all data points are identified. $R^2 = 0.94$. COVRATE $= -1.56 + 0.010664 \times$ YCAP90 $- 0.00000028 \times$ YCAP90^2, where COVRATE is the number of contributors as a proportion of labor force. Sample covers fifty-five countries between 1985 and 1992.

Source: Palacios (1994a).

Richer countries have broader coverage by publicly mandated pension plans.

Extending coverage to the rural population is often impeded by illiteracy, administrative difficulties, and high transaction costs.

Approximately half of the labor force is covered by formal plans in middle-income countries such as Argentina, Brazil, Costa Rica, Malaysia, and Tunisia. Coverage falls to less than 20 percent in lower-income countries such as Indonesia, Morocco, the Philippines, and Sri Lanka—and to less than 10 percent in most of Sub-Saharan Africa. Five of the world's poorest countries—Bangladesh, Malawi, Mozambique, Sierra Leone, and Somalia—have schemes for public employees only, and even these are not always implemented. Coverage usually expands from public sector workers; to employees of public enterprises, public utilities, and large private enterprises; to other employees in the formal sector in

Figure 1.8 Relation between the Percentage of the Population over 60 Years Old and Public Pension Spending

Public pension spending as a percentage of GDP

Percentage of population over 60 years old

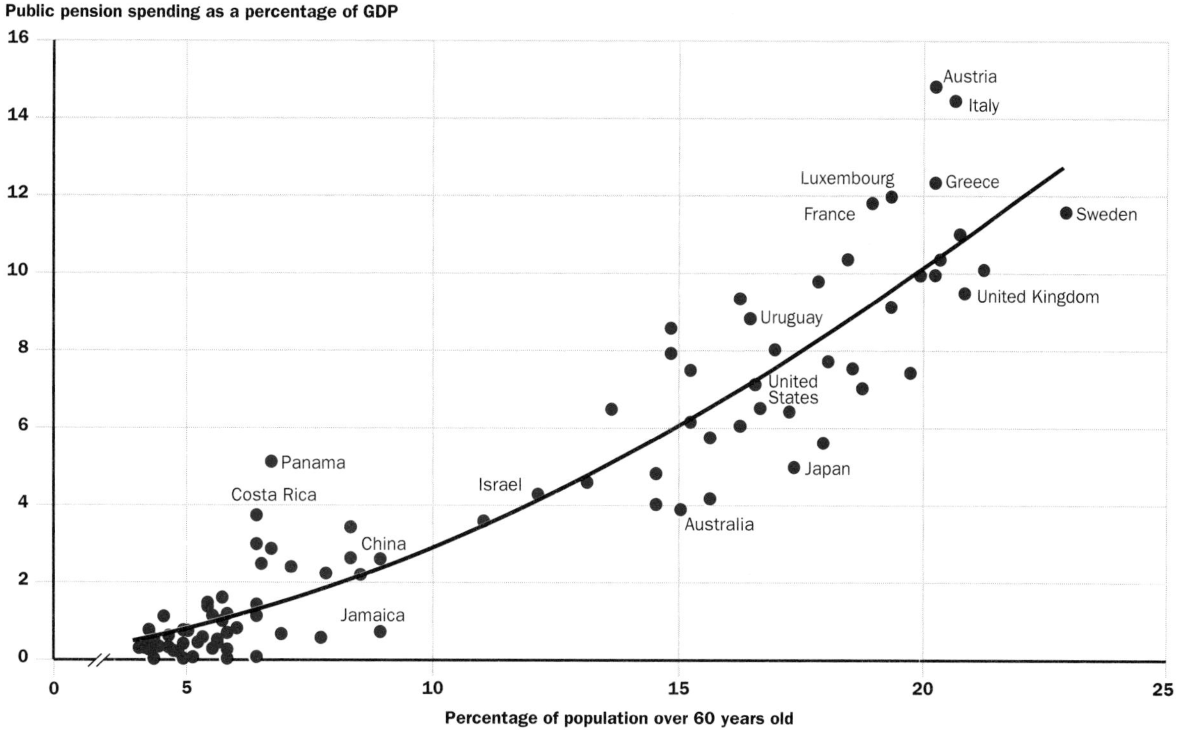

Note: Because of space limitations, not all data points are identified. $R^2 = 0.88$. PS/GDP = $0.6517 + 0.191088 \times$ POP60 + $0.01759 \times$ POP60^2, where PS/GDP is the public pension spending share of GDP. Sample is ninety-two countries for various years between 1985 and 1992.
Source: Palacios (1994a).

Most countries with older populations spend more on public pensions.

urban areas; and much later to agriculture, small business, and the self-employed.

Per capita income, old age dependency, and public spending on pensions. Public spending on old age programs as a proportion of GDP is tied closely to per capita income but even more closely to the proportion of the population that is old (figures 1.8 and 1.9). In fact, spending increases slightly faster than the proportion of the population over 60. Austria has the highest ratio of public pension spending to GDP (15 percent), followed by the other OECD and Eastern European countries, which spend between 6 and 12 percent. Middle-income, middle-aged Latin American countries spend from 3 to 8 percent of GDP, while most young, low-income developing countries spend less than 2 percent of their GDP on

Figure 1.9 Relation between Income Per Capita and Public Pension Spending

Public pension spending as a percentage of GDP

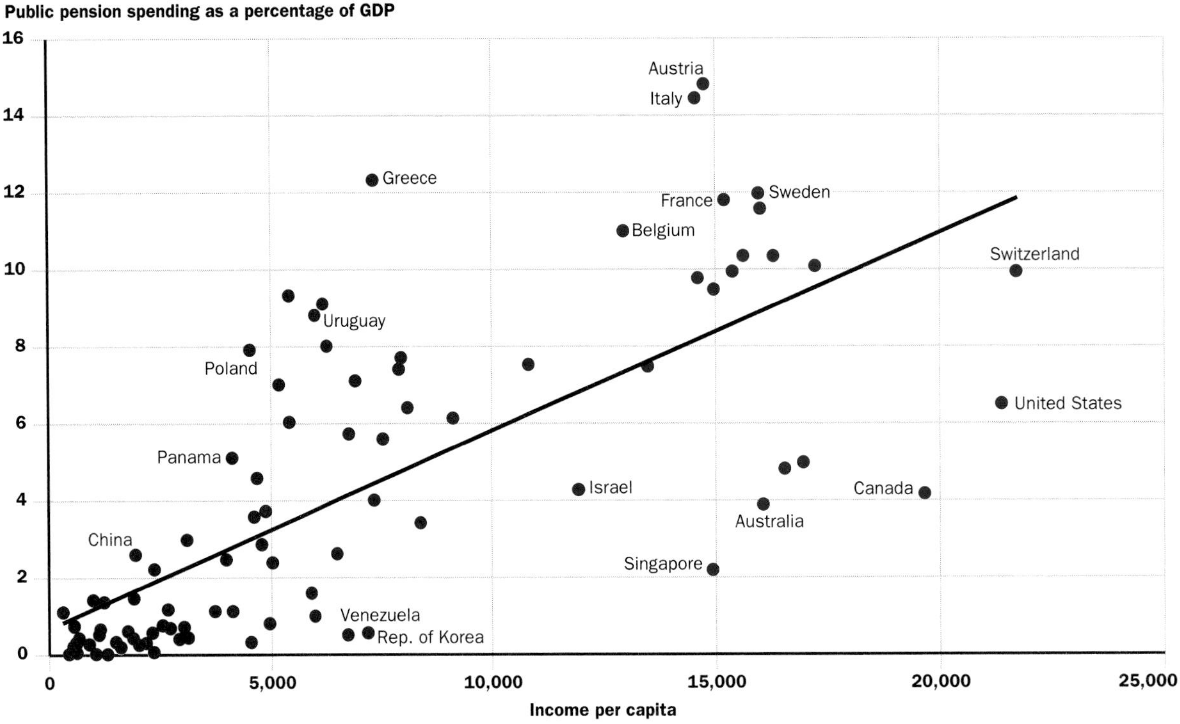

Note: Because of space limitations, not all data points are identified. $R^2 = 0.55$. PS/GDP $= 0.66708 + 0.000519 \times$ YCAP90. The sample comprises ninety-two countries for various years between 1986 and 1992.
Source: Palacios (1994a); World Bank (1992d).

Richer countries usually spend more on public pension plans—but some poor countries also spend more.

formal pensions, mainly on schemes for public employees and other special groups.

Countries can use information on the relation between age profiles and pension spending as a diagnostic tool—to see whether the policies they have adopted have put them above or below average for countries with equivalent per capita incomes and similar demographic structures. For example, as national income dropped in the Eastern European economies during the 1990s, they had the per capita incomes and tax-collecting capabilities of middle-income countries but the old age demography and spending (as a proportion of GDP) of high-income countries—most likely, an unsustainable combination (box figure 4.7).

Per capita income and occupational or personal savings plans. Reliance on formal personal savings and occupational plans also increases with a country's per capita income, but data on total spending is not available for most countries. Coverage by formal voluntary plans is never more than half that of mandatory plans. (In a few countries where employers are required to provide pensions, the occupational plans are thus mandatory and coverage rates are high [table 5.1].) Often tax incentives are involved. The people covered by occupational and personal plans are usually higher-income groups and are almost always covered by publicly managed plans as well; so, voluntary occupational and personal savings plans augment rather than substitute for publicly managed plans.

Old age dependency and public spending on health. The demand for other social services, particularly health services, also increases as countries grow richer and their populations grow older. Richer countries have more expensive health facilities that keep people alive longer, increasing the demands on their pension systems. Conversely, an aging population places increasing strains on the health care system of a country, since health problems and costly medical technologies are concentrated among the old. In Australia, public health spending per person over age 65 is six times that per person under age 15; in Hungary this ratio exceeds ten (Palmer, Smeeding, and Torrey 1988; Vukovich 1991). The proportion of the population that is old explains 92 percent of the variance in public health plus pension spending in a large sample of industrial and developing countries (figure 1.10). The correlation between health and pension spending means that pressure on a country's resources and on government budgets increases exponentially as populations age, underscoring the need for long-term planning (box 1.3).

The Failure of Government Programs

The old age security programs adopted by many governments in the past helped people who grew old over the past three decades. This first generation of beneficiaries received generous slices of the national pie. But these programs are now in trouble, and they may also be causing trouble for the broader economy—keeping the pie smaller for everyone. The big problem:

- Political pressures lead to tax-financed benefit formulas that are not sustainable.
- High payroll taxes that are not closely tied to benefits discourage employment.

Figure 1.10 Public Health and Pension Spending Compared with Population Aging

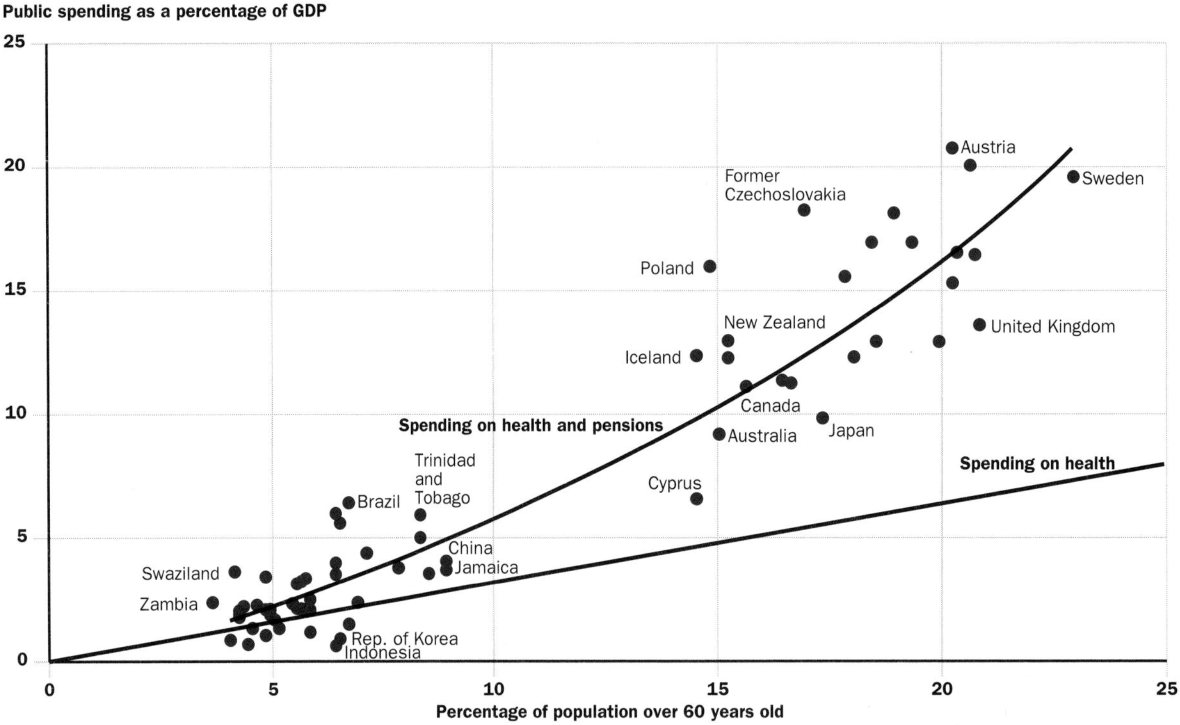

Public spending as a percentage of GDP

Note: Because of space limitations, not all data points are identified. Data points show health plus pension spending data only. For health spending, $R^2 = 0.76$. H/GDP $= 0.069915 + 0.298553 \times$ POP60; for health and pension spending. $R^2 = 0.92$. H + P/GDP $= 0.25449 + 0.369237 \times$ POP60 $+ 0.022744 \times$ POP60^2, where H is public health spending and P is public pension spending. Sample covers sixty-six countries for various years between 1983 and 1992.
Source: Murray, Govindaraj, Chellaraj (1993); Palacios (1994a).

Spending on health and pensions increases exponentially as the population ages.

- Early retirement provisions reduce the supply of experienced workers.
- Financing methods misallocate capital and may reduce national saving.
- Workers often evade contributions but manage to qualify for benefits.
- The failure to index benefits means that pensioners in many countries have not been protected from inflation.
- The growing deficits of old age programs are passed on to the general treasury, requiring higher taxes, higher public borrowing, or less public spending for other important purposes.

- Publicly managed pension reserves are invested unproductively, earning low, even negative, rates of return.
- Large income transfers go to upper-income old people, while many of the lower-income old are not helped.
- Occupational pension plans have not been adequately regulated.
- Today's children and young workers may pay the price of higher taxes, lower pensions, and therefore lower living standards, as old age dependency rates rise and growth declines.

Policy Constraints and Incentives in Developing Countries

These market and planning problems are particularly great in developing and transitional countries. *Capital and insurance markets are more limited* in poorer than in richer countries. This is both a major reason for government intervention and an important constraint on the kinds of policies that can be implemented. One reason the industrial countries chose the policies they did and are now reevaluating was the limited development of financial markets at the time their old age security systems were introduced. But because of their lower levels of income, education, and infrastructure, developing countries also have *less governmental capacity to collect taxes, implement complex programs, and regulate to correct these market failures* than industrial countries. Closely related, the greater *ease of evasion and the larger size of the informal market* in developing countries limit the degree of reliance on mandatory programs, the success of these programs, and the amount of redistribution that can be accomplished through taxation.

Market failures are thus greater in developing countries than in industrial societies. But the government also has less ability to remedy these failures. This explains why *extended family* arrangements continue to play a much greater role in developing countries, why governments should take special care not to drive out informal systems rapidly as they explore formal systems, and why they need to choose these formal systems with great care.

Developing countries have younger populations than industrial countries, and the poorest countries are the youngest. This makes old age security look like a distant problem that can be ignored. It also tempts politicians to promise large pensions today to influential older workers. Both temptations need to be resisted. Within the next thirty to fifty years—that is, within the lifetimes of today's workers—almost every

45

Box 1.3 Health Care and Old Age Security

HEALTH CARE AND PENSION SYSTEMS ARE strongly interrelated. The way health services are provided affects pension costs, both for the individual and for the country. Conversely, aging affects health care costs, and pension funds are often used to finance these costs. Countries need to be aware of these interrelationships and take them into account in their long-term planning for health and old age security.

The Interaction between the Costs of Old Age and Health Care

An individual's health care costs rise with age because physical and mental health deteriorates as people grow older. The kind of medical care required for old people often involves more expensive technology, hospitalization, and long-term nursing care than does medical care for younger people. So, countries spend more on health care as their populations age. The percentage of the population over 60 explains more of the variation across countries in the health share of GDP than does income per capita (see figure 1.10 for the relationship between population over age 60 and the health share of GDP).

For similar reasons, the availability and cost of health services have an important impact on the income needs of old people. The amount of income required to maintain preretirement living standards and therefore the desired size of pension programs is much lower when subsidized health care is available than when people must pay for medical care themselves.

The quality of a country's health services also affects the number of people who reach old age. Medical improvements are responsible for increased longevity in many countries. An efficient system of rural health clinics has helped raise life expectancy in China above that in other countries at a similar income level. These medical successes have increased total pension costs. By raising the health level and productivity of young people, they simultaneously increase the ability of the economy to pay these costs.

Old Age and Disability

Most old age security programs provide disability benefits at an earlier age than pension benefits, so if people approach old age in poor health, they are likely to receive such benefits early, pushing up the cost of the old age security program. This is another example of how spending on the health of the young affects the pension costs of the old.

But disability is a subjective and ambiguous concept. Pension costs are high in countries that interpret disability loosely. Some people who claim to be disabled may in fact be able to work. Some countries use disability programs as a hidden early retirement program, a policy meant to disguise unemployment by creating easy access to disability benefits for people aged 40 to 60. In Costa Rica, 20 percent of all

country in the world will have grayed. Policies that seem harmless now may be regretted later—but will be difficult and costly to change.

Developing countries have one big advantage: someone did it before. Their governments have the opportunity to learn from the mistakes of others and to design old age security systems that can withstand the forthcoming demographic transition as well as the other serious problems that older systems are now facing. We know more now than we did earlier, and new options are available.

pensioners receive disability pensions and more than a third of social insurance spending is for disability payments (Caja Costarricense de Seguro Social 1992). China introduced early retirement through disability programs as a way of shedding excess workers in public enterprises. In one enterprise in Wuhan, 4,312 of 5,612 retirees were put on total disability retirement (World Bank 1990). This may reduce enterprise costs in the short run, but it increases the country's pension costs for many years to come.

Cross-Subsidies from Pensions to Health

Sometimes governments try to hide some of the health costs of an aging population through financial transfers from pension programs to health care programs. Most Latin American countries have a special system of health care for workers covered by social insurance programs. The large surpluses of immature pension programs are often used to pay for the health care of covered workers. This hidden cross-subsidy is poor policy because it impedes good planning for health services and for pensions.

As populations age, these reserves are depleted and the health system must find its funds elsewhere. So too must the pension system, whose reserves have been depleted by this cross-subsidization. In Venezuela, between 10 and 30 percent of pension reserves were "invested" in the hospitals of the social security system during the 1980s (Marquez 1992).

As the pension scheme matured and its fund was decapitalized, it could no longer finance these huge transfers to the health sector. Now Venezuela, whose population is projected to age rapidly in the next 25 years, must cope with an inexorably rising demand for resources for both health and pension programs.

Long-Term Planning and Transparency

When countries are young, they can finance health, pension, and disability spending with relatively low payroll taxes. But these costs rise exponentially as populations age. Future demand for health services and old age pensions should be expected and planned for as a predictable consequence of the demographic transition. To accomplish this:

- Pension and health financing should be separate and transparent to avoid depleting pension reserves and hiding the true costs of each service.
- Eligibility for disability benefits should be carefully defined to avoid cheating and should not be used as a substitute for early retirement or unemployment.
- The complex interrelationship between total health spending and pension spending should be taken into account in planning by households and governments.

Plan of This Report

AFTER DESCRIBING THE INFORMAL SYSTEMS THAT SUPPORT more than half the world's old people (chapter 2), this report analyzes the key policy choices that must be made as countries shift their emphasis to formal systems (chapter 3). It analyzes three common financing and managerial arrangements for old age support—publicly managed tax-financed plans, occupational pension plans, and personal savings plans (chapters 4–6). The final chapters (7–8) outline how these arrangements can be combined in a multipillar system consisting of:

- A mandatory tax-financed public pillar that has primary responsibility for redistribution,
- A mandatory funded private pillar (of personal saving or occupational pension plans) that has primary responsibility for saving, and
- A voluntary pillar that provides supplementary protection.

All three pillars coinsure against life's risks and uncertainties—as the best way to achieve the dual standard set forth at the beginning: doing what is best for the old population and what is best for the economy as a whole.

Note

1. Sources for these examples are IDB (1993); Palacios (1994a); Banco de Prevision Social (1991); World Bank (1994a); Nelissen (1987); Stahlberg (1989); Creedy, Disney, and Whitehouse (1992); Aaron (1977); Hurd and Shoven (1985); unpublished OECD social data base (1993); Boskin and others (1987).

CHAPTER 2

Informal Arrangements

THE INFORMAL SYSTEM FOR INCOME SECURITY— with no governmental and little market involvement— is still the mainstay in most developing countries. The extended family takes care of insurance, redistribution, and even saving—investing in children and in land or housing for the whole family. Although voluntary, this system has been buttressed by strong social sanctions, and an estimated 60 percent of the world's labor force and 70 percent of the old rely on it exclusively.

The remnants of informal systems remain important in industrial countries, as children care for their parents and income transfers flow between generations in both directions. But with economic development, these informal arrangements have given way to formal market arrangements and mandatory government programs, which dominate in industrial countries.

Informal support systems worked because the extended family can pool the work opportunities, income, and risk of all its members—and solve many of the informational problems that plague more formal systems. But modernization—urbanization, migration, secular education, nuclear families, and the breakdown of traditional social norms—lowers the prestige of the old, reduces their control over resources, and diminishes the effectiveness of the extended family in pooling income and risk. Because mandatory formal programs can hasten this process, governments should carefully assess when, where, and in what form to introduce formal programs of old age support. They should use measures to maintain rather than crowd out informal systems that may still be functioning reasonably well.

The Diversity of Informal Systems

INFORMAL SYSTEMS SHOW TREMENDOUS DIVERSITY. THE BASIC system is one of children taking care of their old parents, while other support systems involve local communities, informal clubs, kinship networks, patrons, and religious and other nongovernmental organizations. These institutions generally supplement the support from families in industrial as well as developing countries. Although chronological age is used to define "old age" in this report, in most societies with large informal systems, "old" is not synonymous with chronological age. Instead, old age is defined primarily as the inability to earn, work, and care for oneself. Family members and other providers of informal support are likely to have much better measures of functional inadequacies and needs than chronological age can provide. Indeed, this is one of the big advantages of informal systems.

Informal Systems in Asia

Asia has the most old people—230 million people over the age of 60 in 1990. It also has the highest old age dependency ratio in the developing world and is expected to experience the most dramatic increases over the next thirty years (World Bank population projections). And although it has some of the strongest informal support systems, rapid growth is putting them under stress.

One source of the strength of informal systems of old age security is the deeply embedded sense of filial loyalty in most Asian cultures. Nowhere is this bond stronger than in China, where for at least 3,000 years filial loyalty has been a cultural cornerstone, continuously encouraged except during the chaotic Cultural Revolution, when families were broken up, children were turned against parents, and some members were exiled from urban to rural areas. Chinese parents have reinforced filial loyalty through control of property, marriage age, and choice of marriage partner for their children. The 1954 Constitution continued this tradition by asserting that "parents have the duty to rear and educate their minor children, and the children who have come of age have the duty to support and assist their parents" (Fang, Chuanbin, and Yuhua 1992). Modern China also has unusually strong control of outmigration from rural areas, which helps to protect the informal system from the corrosive effects of massive rural-urban migration.

Several recent changes nevertheless signal a weakening of China's informal systems. In many urban areas, employment-based pensions, community-based health care, and old age clubs are emerging. Small apartments—and changes in the occupational structure away from activities in which experience-based knowledge is important—have undermined extended household living arrangements and the respect of children for their parents. Even in rural areas, the informal support system is feeling stress from such forces as out-migration, education, longer life expectancy, and the official one-child policy—stress that can be expected to increase, as the old double from 9 percent of the population to 18 percent in 2025 (figure 1.6).

Some of the greatest stresses on family support systems are in other East Asian economies with high growth and urbanization rates—such as Hong Kong, Malaysia, the Republic of Korea, Singapore, Taiwan (China), and Thailand. But those systems are demonstrating resilience, which seems to come from flexibility and adaptability (box 2.1). Higher incomes allow for increased monetary transfers between households, so that financial aid is substituting for joint living arrangements. Higher incomes also allow more personal saving by the old, relieving pressure

---

Box 2.1 Caring for Parents in Thailand

THAILAND, WITH ITS RAPID ECONOMIC GROWTH, modernization, and declining fertility, may not long be able to maintain its traditional informal system of old age support. Yet a large percentage of married people in the country cite that support as a major reason for having children, and the pattern of older parents living with their adult children seems to be holding up. Urban young people still expect to live with and support their elderly parents (Knodel and others 1984, 1987, 1992a, and 1992b).

Using a variety of data collection and analytic techniques, Knodel and his collaborators concluded that Thai filial piety reflects myriad influences:

- Deep-seated social norms that still prevail in the absence of large formal social security programs

- The moral obligation of children to support their parents regardless of gender, birth order, marital status, or distance from the parental residence

- The tradition of parents living with a single child, which means that little adjustment was needed when the number of children declined

- Increased education and earnings, which help the smaller number of Thai children to support their parents

- A high rate of remarriage, which increases the opportunities for filial support for those without natural children

- Higher rates of saving than in the past (made possible by reductions in fertility), which complement rather than substitute for help from children (Mason and others 1993).

on children. Another adjustment is the support that daughters provide, offsetting some of the effect of having fewer sons. And the strategic use of inheritance for encouraging support from children seems to be on the rise. In Japan, the proportion of women of childbearing age who expected to leave property to the child who takes care of them rose from 18 percent in 1963 to 32 percent in 1977 (Martin 1990).

In the Hindu, Muslim, and other cultures of the subcontinent, children's responsibility to support their elderly parents also has a long history—still intact. Well over 75 percent of the old live with their children in all these countries—almost 95 percent in Nepal. Even in urban Bombay, more than 80 percent of the old live with their children (Martin 1990; Pathak 1978). As in China, much of the strength of the system rests on parental control over property, inheritance, marriage age, and choice of partner—the last is particularly important because of the vital role of daughters-in-law in providing dowries and care to support parents-in-law.

This does not mean that the old are well taken care of in South Asia. More than in East Asia, responsibility for supporting parents continues to rest primarily with sons and their wives, so parents without male children are considerably more vulnerable. Daughters-in-law are frequently subject to abuse by dissatisfied parents-in-law. And when they become mothers, they are much more vulnerable to income insecurity than are fathers because of their younger age at marriage, longer life expectancy, growing probability of divorce, and lower rates of remarriage, labor force participation, inheritance, and ability to borrow. The problem is greatest for widows, with or without children (box 2.2).

All these problems are increasing. In rural areas, filial loyalty has been weakened by out-migration and poor communication systems. In urban areas, the shrinkage of extended families to their nuclear core and the changing occupational structure are pushing the old out of the labor force and reducing their access to family support. So, although the extended family system is by far the most important old age support system in India and other countries of South Asia, the beginnings of its dissolution is evident even there.

Informal Systems in Africa

Africa's support systems are based on a broader definition of family than Asia's. Households are often extended in many dimensions (for ex-

Box 2.2 In India, the Informal System Treats Widows Poorly

THROUGHOUT SOUTH ASIA, MOST OLD WOMEN are widows, and widows are among the poorest of the poor. Informal systems of providing for the old afford little protection for these women. Indeed, tradition and custom frequently work against them. In India, for example, households headed by widows are by far the poorest group, with an average expenditure per person 70 percent below the national average (Dreze 1990). Dreze identifies five important constraints on Indian widows:

- Their inability to return to the parental home
- Restrictions on remarriage
- The division of labor by gender, which limits a woman's opportunities for self-employment and confines her almost entirely to agricultural wage labor
- Restrictions on inheritance, which is patrilineal
- Lack of access to credit.

Despite laws to the contrary, a widow with living sons is rarely able to inherit anything—purportedly to keep her from abandoning her children to marry again. Yet without inheritance or other property she lacks the collateral to obtain loans, self-employment is largely infeasible, and the possibility of extreme poverty looms large. Support from sons is the primary means of support for 90 percent of the women in Dreze's sample. Widows without sons have a higher rate of remarriage—although it is still remarkably low—than those with sons. Many women complained bitterly about the abrupt change in their treatment by family members after their husbands' death.

A comparison of three villages from different parts of India reveals that widows in villages of West Bengal are better off. Reformers in Bengal have promoted widow remarriage and women's rights. But even in Bengal widows are one of the groups for whom the informal system of old age security is not working well.

ample, adult brothers and sisters may live together, as well as parents and children). Likewise, old age support from siblings is far more common than in Asia. The definition of children is also much more inclusive—adoption, fosterage, and borrowing offspring of other family members are common. In some cases, grandparents raise and are eventually cared for by their children's children. Where polygamy is practiced, several wives and children typically live in a common compound—a very extended household.

Nonfamily institutions—such as kin, community, and tribal support networks—are also more important in Africa. In urban settings, community organizations sometimes spring up around the village or region of origin—often stressing self-help and income-generating activities and providing assistance with burials. But because the ties are weaker than those in families, these community support systems are not very effective insurance. Children are still the main source of support for old age, and being childless is a serious problem for the old.

The old make up only 5 percent of the population in Africa, so informal support systems have not yet felt the stress experienced by those in Asia and Latin America. Africa's much poorer economic performance has made it more difficult for the younger generation to support the old, but it has also blunted urbanization, social change, and modernization. In most African countries more than 75 percent of the population live in rural areas. The old continue to play visible roles in village government, tribal relations, and dispute resolution. Moreover, much of the rural-urban migration in Africa has been circular or temporary, helping to keep intact the informal arrangements for old age support.

Not surprisingly, most surveys show Africa's informal support systems to be working relatively well. A high proportion of old people, including those in cities, live in extended households, and older people frequently receive goods and money from their children. In Nigeria, more than 97 percent of the urban old and 93 percent of the rural old reported receiving some financial or material support from family or kin (Ekpenyong, Oyeneye, and Piel 1986). The provision of lump sum payments to retiring civil servants has allowed many of them to buy land or businesses and to resettle in their villages among their families of origin, bringing them back into the informal system. Even without pensions, the old commonly return to their birthplaces on retirement. And being accepted generally depends on their having been loyal to their parents— by sending remittances or returning to visit from time to time. But some of the fabric of old age support is wearing thin.

Informal Systems in Latin America

Despite substantial diversity across Latin America, several broad differences from the informal systems in Asia and Africa stand out. First, increases in life expectancy, urbanization, and industrialization and other demographic changes occurred earlier in Latin America than elsewhere, although not at the same uniformly high rates as in Eastern Asia. The southern part of Latin America is already aging, while Central America is still quite young. A second difference is the sharply dualistic character of society in several countries that have a relatively large low-income indigenous population, a much smaller well-off European population, and rural-urban migration that is usually permanent.

Third and closely related are the large urban-rural and rich-poor differences in household structure, fertility, occupation—and thus in the importance of informal support systems. In São Paulo, Brazil, the rich elderly have good access to public and private pensions, individual savings, housing and health care entitlements, and life and disability insurance. So, they do not need monetary support from their children. But the urban poor are almost totally dependent on support from children, having few alternative sources of support, and many still live in extended families (Ramos in Kendig and others 1992). The situation is similar for the rural poor, except that indigenous communities stress communal systems of support more heavily than populations of European origin.

A fourth difference is that formal support systems are generally much more developed in Latin America than in other developing countries— perhaps helping drive out informal systems. Some of these formal systems that have been in effect for many years are now near collapse as a result of demographic pressures and design weaknesses. But the informal system is seldom there to fall back on.

What Makes Informal Support Systems Run?

P EOPLE IN TRADITIONAL SOCIETIES USE INFORMAL RISK POOL-ing within extended multigenerational families or village groups to insure against the risk of old age dependency and other vicissitudes of life. The family's size and heterogeneity enable the realization of economies of scale and risk pooling within a diverse group while avoiding the informational costs and asymmetries of formal systems.

Two kinds of old age risks are particularly important—the risk of becoming unproductive through ill health or disability, and the risk of living long and needing income for consumption. Voluntary market-based insurance arrangements against these risks often break down because people who think they have a low risk will opt out of the system, while high risks opt in (adverse selection), making the price that insurance companies must charge prohibitive for the average person. Market-based arrangements also break down because people who are insured may fail to protect themselves against disability or may pretend to be disabled when they are not (moral hazard). Families are different: there is little choice to opt in or out, and the monitoring and knowledge of relatives can distinguish a feigned illness from a real one. Members who do not cooperate can be punished by the head of the household.

By pooling risks, the family can adjust to unforeseen outcomes in a fairly flexible way, in contrast to a formal contract that cannot spell out every contingency, and may therefore end up with unexpected outcomes and unintended sharing of risks. One problem with informal risk pooling is that if the entire family lives in the same village and engages in the same occupation, their risks would be correlated and the gains from risk pooling small. Extended families sometimes solve this problem by spreading risk beyond the village. A satellite family unit might be set up in an urban area, where the wage rate is high enough to raise the joint family's expected income and the activities are sufficiently different to reduce the joint risks. Or the family might marry off a child into another family from a distant village, after researching the resources and reliability of the other family.

The informal system also holds down the cost of old age support. Because of a household's many needs and variety of tasks, it is easy to find useful activities for old members to perform: they can cook, take care of small children, and clean or paint the home, freeing younger members to do the jobs that demand more energy and speed. And because care of the old is within the household, the caretakers can carry out other activities, reducing the opportunity cost of the care.

The Old Age Security Motive for Children

It has long been alleged that one reason people in developing countries have so many children is for old age security (Leibenstein 1957, 1975). Without reliable saving instruments or public pension programs, children are the best bet. People voluntarily save and invest in their children, expecting to reap the return later. And because infant and child mortality rates are high in these areas, having a large number of children helps ensure that at least some children—of the "right" gender—will survive to provide support in old age. A stark example is the persistence of families with more than one child in rural China—despite the official one-child policy—and the steps taken to make sure that at least one child is male (the male-female ratio at birth is 1.2 to 1).

Other analysts (such as Lindert 1980, 1983) have strongly challenged this motive, citing the costs of children, the low returns on children after the first three or four, the long time between fertility decisions and old age, the possibility that children may die and that even surviving children will not support their parents, and the unimportance of old age in societies with high mortality rates.

What does the empirical evidence say? One source of evidence is what people have said about their motives for having children—in surveys conducted in several countries (table 2.1). In almost every developing country surveyed, more than 40 percent of respondents indicate that having help in old age is a "very important" motive for "wanting another child" (Arnold and others 1975; Kagitcibasi 1982). The percentages are generally higher for women than for men, for the urban lower class than for the urban middle class, and for people in rural areas. Similar data are available for many other countries. But evidence based on behavior is limited and inconclusive (box 2.3). There is probably a weak old age security motive for having *some* children, but it is not clear that it is a motive for having *many* children.

How the Old Exact Compliance

What prevents the family head or coalitions of family members in intergenerational households from deciding to shirk responsibility for providing assistance to older members? Why do people "voluntarily" provide assistance? One protection, certainly, is the empathy and altruism of the household members who derive happiness from the welfare of the older members. Another is concern for the family's reputation, particularly in communities or kin networks in which social norms make

Table 2.1 Percentage of Respondents for Whom Help in Old Age Is a "Very Important" Motive for Wanting Another Child

Area	Males	Females	Total	Urban middle class	Urban lower class	Rural
Indonesia (Java)	73	82	78	—	—	—
Japan	—	—	12	2	7	21
Korea, Rep. of	12	18	16	3	26	43
Philippines	77	78	78	49	53	80
Singapore	43	48	46	—	—	—
Taiwan (China)	53	48	50	9	21	35
Thailand	67	71	69	12	55	58
Turkey	37	48	43	—	—	—
United States (Hawaii)	7	9	8	—	—	—

— Not available.

Source: Arnold and others (1975), table 4.16; Kagitcibasi (1982), table 1.

Box 2.3 Is Old Age Security a Motive for Large Families?

WHEN ASKED WHY THEY HAVE CHILDREN, PEO-
ple often say they want someone to provide for them
in their old age. There is little evidence on actual behavior, however, to verify or refute such claims.
Though the old age security motive is likely to be
considerably stronger in developing countries than in
industrial countries, most attempts to test for the importance of the motive have used cross-sectional data
from industrial countries (Friedlander and Silver
1967; Holm 1975; Kelly, Cutright, and Hittle 1976;
Entwisle and Windgarden 1984). Study participants
are usually men living in urban areas, although,
again, the old age security motive is likely to be
stronger in rural areas than in urban ones and among
women than among men (even one of the few studies in a developing country, for a village in India, included only men: Vlassoff and Vlassoff 1980). That
few studies have shown the old age security motive to
be important, then, really tells little about its influence in rural areas of developing countries.

For rural areas in Bangladesh and India, Cain
(1981, 1983) hypothesized that the risks are greater
and the alternatives to children fewer and weaker in
Bangladeshi villages than in Indian villages, partly
explaining the higher fertility rates of Bangladesh.
Nugent and Gillaspy (1983) showed that Mexican
workers involved in sugarcane production, who
qualified for old age pensions, had significantly
lower fertility rates than other agricultural workers
who did not qualify—suggesting that pensions were
viewed as an alternative to children for old age support. But these studies had two important shortcomings: a small number of observations (three and
thirty-six) and the use of village averages rather than
household observations.

Using data from the Malaysian Family Life Survey, Kenney (1988) found that women subject to the
greatest risks preferred to have more children and to
educate them less than other women did. Jensen
(1989) used a two-stage procedure on the same data
and found that old age support motives had a small
influence on early fertility (the decision to have the
first children) but not on later fertility.

The weakest link in the argument seems to be the
assertion that a large number of children are needed
to provide old age support. Data from the Malaysian

much information about a family public. The system is also protected
against breakdown by the social norms of filial loyalty inculcated
through repeated religious and family teachings. Similarly, the adults
who provide such aid to their parents know that they will one day depend on their children.

Perhaps the most important means by which the old protect themselves is by retaining control of the household's resources almost until
death. Savings in traditional societies—in housing, land, cattle, gold,
and jewelry—are a means of inducing support from children. The ability to threaten disinheritance is a strong motivator, and having several
children compete for inheritance helps to strengthen the credibility of
the threat. An aging head of household is often assisted in holding onto
headship and control of household resources by superior knowledge of
the activity in which he (and sometimes she) has specialized. Indeed, in

Family Life Survey demonstrate that for Malaysians aged 50 and older both the probability of receiving some support from children and the amount of that support rose continuously with the number of children, but the relation is clearly one of diminishing returns (box table 2.3).

If people have children to provide security for their old age, the introduction of formal systems of old age security should reduce fertility rates and population growth. By increasing old age dependency rates this process may place unexpected financial strains on formal pay-as-you-go systems. To the degree that this is the case, new public pay-as-you-go plans contain the seeds of their own destruction.

Box Table 2.3 Probability of Receiving Old Age Support from Children, Malaysia, 1988–89

Number of children living elsewhere	1	3	4	5	6	7	8	9	10+
Seniors receiving help from adult children living apart (actual)	0.51	0.60	0.71	0.69	0.75	0.73	0.82	0.80	0.78
Simulated (for people with mean characteristics)	0.66	0.71	0.73	0.78	0.79	0.80	0.83	0.84	0.85
Simulated amount of help received per month (in ringgit)	154	199	207	244	252	303	311	338	426

Source: Setapa (1993). This is based on a weighted random sample of 1,357 persons aged 50 and over in peninsular Malaysia known as the Malaysian Family Life Survey in 1988–89.

some countries and time periods, the balance of power may have favored the old too much relative to the young.

Shortcomings of Informal Systems

Even when the safeguards work well, other shortcomings often keep such informal systems from meeting all the old age security needs. The resources transferred to an old parent may not be enough. The investments in children—or the return to these investments—may be low. The household head may be ineffective and unproductive. The young who move to cities may be less responsive to the social sanctions of the village. Older people in cities may prefer to live alone rather than in extended family households. Informal systems have little ability to redistribute income from rich families to poor families, and even some wealthy family members may be reluctant to share with their less wealthy relatives. As the capabilities of governments and financial markets develop, formal systems can address these deficiencies.

Signs of Breakdown

CHANGES IN THE ECONOMIC, POLITICAL, SOCIAL, LEGAL, AND demographic environments—having already broken down the family systems of old age support in industrial countries—are now weakening those systems in developing countries.

Changes in the Broader Environment

Economic environment. With development, the structure of production changes. Rural activities—such as agriculture, fishing, forestry, and animal husbandry—became less important, and urban-based industry and services, more. As the importance of agriculture diminishes, so do the opportunities for older people to participate in the labor force. And with the growing capital intensity of agriculture, older people are less able to provide their children with employment opportunities, so the children are more likely to move away.

Political environment. Many newly independent developing countries installed activist, interventionist governments that encouraged industrialization through policies of import substitution behind high, protectionist walls, systematically disadvantaging the stronghold of informal support systems. They also invested heavily in education. The wider availability of schools and the growing need for new skills in the labor market encouraged school attendance, but at the expense of family time available for the care of dependent parents. And the fact that children are better educated than their parents or grandparents undermined the respect of the young for the old.

Social and cultural environment. Greater mobility and less communication between rural-based parents and urban-based children reduce altruism, parental control, and social pressure for parental support. Urbanization also undermines the norm that children should live with and care for their older parents. In urban areas housing space is more cramped, so if parents move in with their children they may be blamed for overcrowding the home. Another important cultural change is the gradual erosion of parents' property rights in their children. In almost all countries, children have increasingly assumed the right to choose their own marriage partners, age at marriage, and place of residence.

Legal environment. When bequests are taxed or laws require that property be divided equally among all family members, or rights to rent out or dispose of property are attenuated, parents lose the most important means they have of rewarding children who have treated them well. While such legal restrictions are often justified on grounds of equity, they have potentially serious consequences for the ability of older people to induce support from their children and other relatives.

Demographics. Fertility rates have begun to fall, but life expectancy has continued to increase. Young adults are caught in a squeeze: there are fewer of them to take care of their increasingly long-lived parents. Longevity tends to increase more rapidly for women than for men, creating a growing disparity in widowhood among older men and women. Women live longer as widows and are more dependent on their children for support.

Evidence of Breakdown in Informal Systems

All these changes undoubtedly affect informal systems of old age support. But almost no studies are nationally representative, comparable over time, and sufficiently quantitative to test hypotheses about whether and how much traditional voluntary systems have broken down. The limited evidence shows considerable variation across countries in the importance of children for providing old age support.

The Value of Children project addressed a common questionnaire to more than 20,000 married adults in nine countries in the mid-1970s. To the question "Would you expect your son(s)/daughter(s) to support you financially when you grow old?" the percentage of respondents answering yes varies from a low of about 11 percent (for daughters) in the United States to a high of 91 percent (for sons) in Turkey (table 2.2). Generally, more mothers than fathers answered yes—and more for sons than for daughters. Because the yes rates are much higher for low-income countries than for the United States, with Singapore somewhere in between, findings like these are frequently used to argue that informal support systems fade away as countries develop.

Table 2.2 Percentage of Parents Who Expect Financial Help from Sons (S) and Daughters (D)

	Indonesia (Java)		Rep. of Korea		Philippines		Singapore		Taiwan (China)		Thailand		Turkey		United States	
	S	D	S	D	S	D	S	D	S	D	S	D	S	D	S	D
Mothers	85	83	85	46	86	85	39	31	85	39	89	87	91	78	12	11
Fathers	79	77	78	42	82	80	31	25	76	29	78	75	84	64	12	11

Source: adapted from Kagitcibasi (1982), table 1, p. 34.

Similar patterns are apparent within countries: support from children is generally higher for rural areas than for urban areas and for smaller and poorer communities than for richer ones. Scattered data are available—though not in strictly comparable form—on sources of financial support in old age in a larger number of countries (table 2.3). In low-income regions (except urban China), the most important sources of support in old age are "own work" and "family." Formal support systems (pensions or welfare) play a negligible role. In middle-income regions, "work" and "family" are still important but "pensions/welfare" is even more common. In high-income regions, "pensions/welfare" is an almost universal source of support. Again, the data seem to imply a shift from informal to formal sources of support as a country's economy grows.

In high-income countries (except Japan) fewer than 20 percent of older parents live with their children (table 2.4). The proportion rises to approximately 50 percent in middle-income countries of Latin America and to more than 75 percent in the generally lower-income countries of Africa and Asia. Financial support and joint living arrangements are, of course, not the only ways children help their parents in old age. Helping with housework and in emergencies is common in most countries, and the high number of positive responses in the United States suggest that nonfinancial assistance remains strong even as income levels increase (table 2.5).

Even in Japan, the only high-income country with the majority of old people still living with their children, support from children seems to be on the decline. Between 1974 and 1983, the share of middle-aged children (35 to 49 years old) providing economic support to their aging parents declined from 45 to 40 percent. The percentage of people 65 years of age and older living with their children dropped from 77 percent in 1970 to 65 percent in 1985 (Martin 1990).

Table 2.3 Sources of Income in Old Age, Selected Countries, 1980s

Percentage of persons over 65 receiving income from

	Work	Family	Pension/ welfare	Savings
High-income countries				
Australia	9	—	93	—
Canada	19	—	97	—
France	4	—	96	—
Germany	2	—	98	—
Netherlands	5	—	100	—
Sweden	0	—	100	—
United Kingdom	13	—	100	—
United States	20	—	94	—
Average	**9**	**—**	**97**	**—**

Percentage of persons over 60 receiving income from

	Work	Family	Pension/ welfare	Savings
Middle-income countries				
Argentina	26	8	74	6
Bulgaria	28	5	99	—
Chile	20	9	73	—
Costa Rica	21	23	46	—
Hungary	47	40	99	—
Budapest	34	21	100	—
Villages	58	54	99	—
Korea, Rep. of	24	64	6	8
Singapore	18	85	16	37
Trinidad and Tobago	15	26	77	—
Average	**25**	**32**	**61**	**17**
Low-income countries				
China	45	34	13	—
Urban	15	17	64	—
Rural	51	38	5	—
Indonesia	46	63	10	4
Kenya	—	88	—	—
Malaysia	34	83	14	11
Nigeria	—	95	—	—
Philippines	63	45	13	2
Average	**47**	**58**	**13**	**6**

— Not available.

Note: Averages are unweighted.

Source: United Nations (1992a); Japanese Organization for International Cooperation in Family Planning (1989); Ju and Jones (1989); Pan-American Health Organization (1989b, c, d and 1990a, b); D. Mitchell (1993); Hoddinott (1992); Vukovich (1991); Petrov and Minev (1989).

Table 2.4 Living Arrangements of Older Persons, 1980s

Percentage of persons over 65 living

	With children or family	Alone	Other[a]
High-income countries			
Australia	7	30	62
Canada (Quebec)	16	21	63
Japan	69	8	23
Netherlands	12	33	56
New Zealand	—	39	—
Sweden	—	40	—
United States	13	30	57
Average	**23**	**29**	**52**

Percentage of persons over 60 living

	With children or family	Alone	Other[a]
Middle-income countries			
Argentina	25	11	64
Chile	59	10	31
Costa Rica	56	7	37
Panama	76	10	14
Trinidad and Tobago	41	13	46
Uruguay	53	16	31
Average	**52**	**11**	**37**
Low-income countries			
China	83	3	14
Urban	74	5	22
Rural	89	1	10
Côte d'Ivoire	96	2	2
Guyana	61	2	38
Honduras	90	5	5
Indonesia	76	8	17
Malaysia	82	6	12
Philippines	92	3	5
Thailand	92	5	4
Average	**84**	**4**	**12**

— Not available.

Note: Averages are unweighted.

a. Includes persons living with spouse.

Source: Japanese Organization for International Cooperation in Family Planning (1989); Pan-American Health Organization (1989b, c, d; 1990a, b); Ju and Jones (1989); Keller (1994); Kendig, Hashimoto, and Coppard (1992).

Table 2.5 Expected Help from Children by Economy and Sex of Respondents, 1975–76

Indicator	Indonesia	Rep. of Korea	Philippines	Singapore	Taiwan (China)	Thailand	Turkey	United States[a]
Mothers								
Percentage expecting help from sons								
Help around the house	81	82	83	39	68	73	65	85
Part of salary	60	71	67	38	76	71	77	29
Contribution in emergencies	83	87	88	58	92	92	95	74
Percentage expecting help from daughters								
Help around the house	92	84	94	55	82	96	94	92
Part of salary	56	59	68	32	72	58	60	29
Contribution in emergencies	81	75	88	49	88	89	85	73
Fathers								
Percentage expecting help from sons								
Help around the house	89	82	86	33	67	73	80	87
Part of salary	52	63	61	29	52	53	67	19
Contribution in emergencies	81	81	85	49	86	87	88	66
Percentage expecting help from daughters								
Help around the house	93	80	92	48	79	92	91	90
Part of salary	50	42	61	24	57	49	27	18
Contribution in emergencies	80	66	84	43	80	84	62	65

a. Hawaii only.
Source: Derived from Bulatao (1979), table 4.

Expectations and attitudes are changing, too. In Korea in 1988, 68 percent of people 60 or older said they would rely exclusively on sons, 20 percent on sons and daughters, and 8 percent solely on self-support (National Bureau of Statistics in Martin 1990). Of those 20 to 29 years old, 33 percent said they would rely exclusively on sons and 44 percent on both sons and daughters, with 17 percent expecting to be self-supporting. In Taiwan (China), the share of married women aged 20 to 39 living or eating with their husbands' parents declined from 81 percent in 1973 to 69 percent in 1985 (Martin 1990). In Kenya, 91 percent of the rural old felt that their children did not do as much for them as they had done for their parents (Kinsella 1988).

So once close-knit communities no longer exist to exert social sanctions and older family members no longer control resources or crucial life choices of their children, purely voluntary family-based systems of risk pooling and income sharing may not work well.

Interactions between Public and Private Transfers: Crowding Out and Crowding In

IRONICALLY, THE GROWTH OF GOVERNMENT PROGRAMS to help old people may further undermine the remnants of the family support system. The effects of public support on private transfers depend on the motives for private transfers between family members: are they motivated by altruism or are they part of an exchange? Altruistic transfers are made by well-meaning donors because another family member is in need. Exchange transfers are made by donors who expect to get something in return, such as a bequest. If the state steps in and provides a transfer to a family member, the altruistic donor no longer sees the need to provide the transfer. So the public transfer crowds out the private transfer. But if the donor is motivated by an exchange, the public transfer does not necessarily undermine the private donor's desire to provide the transfer, since the donor expects a quid pro quo. So, the public transfer need not crowd out the private transfer or need not crowd it out completely.

Because of the complementarity of different types of support, properly designed formal support could increase informal support. For example, a son or daughter providing care and money to an elderly parent might be willing to supply more if the parent had access to medical treatment in a government clinic, which could increase the parent's expected life span and therefore the value of the private transfer. Such crowding in of informal support might also occur if the receipt of a public transfer increases the respect for or bargaining power of an older person. Community organizations that support older people often design their programs to minimize the crowding out of family support and, sometimes, even encourage additional family support.

Quantitative evidence on crowding in and crowding out is scarce because data sets providing the relevant evidence are available for only a few countries. Peru is one. Like several other Latin American countries, Peru has a fairly well-developed formal social security system, yet private transfers (mainly from adult children to their parents) still constitute a significant share of the income of social security recipients. For every dollar of social security taxes and benefits, private transfers fall 17 cents. Social security makes elderly pensioners better off, but not as much better off as its expenditures would suggest because it partially crowds out private transfers (box 2.4).

Policies to Keep Family Support Systems Afloat

I T IS INEVITABLE THAT FORMAL SYSTEMS SHOULD EVENTUALLY replace informal systems as the dominant form of old age support. But it is useful to extend the lives of informal systems, particularly in low- and middle-income countries whose formal systems have limited capabilities to do the full job.

Avoid Biases against Traditional Agriculture

The most obvious way to extend the lives of family systems of old age support is to avoid policy biases against traditional agriculture, in which

Box 2.4 Do Public Transfers Crowd Out Private Ones?

OLD AGE PENSIONS, LIKE MANY OTHER PUBLIC programs, could prompt offsetting private responses that need to be taken into account when measuring distributional effects. For example, children might provide less support for elderly parents if the public sector provides more. So raising public pension benefits by a dollar would mean less than a dollar's worth of extra benefits to the elderly. This crowding out can be especially important in developing countries, where the incidence of private transfer giving is higher than in developed countries. Recent studies in Peru (Cox and Jimenez 1992) and the Philippines (Cox and Jimenez, forthcoming) illustrate.

In 1985, 40 percent of Peru's economically active population was covered by the country's pay-as-you-go social security system. A nationally representative household survey also indicated that the public safety net coexisted with a substantial private network. A third of urban households received private transfers in the three months prior to the survey. For net recipients, private transfers constituted a fifth of total household income.

The authors estimated the determinants of private transfers from young to old in Peru, taking into account possible effects that social security could have had on transfers from children to parents. They then used their estimates to simulate how much more private transfers would have been without social security. The answer? Twenty percent higher. (The simulations accounted for both the reduced incomes of parents and the increased incomes of taxpaying children that would have arisen had social security been cut.) This implies that the Peruvian social security system is less effective at delivering benefits than a simple assignment of benefits would suggest. For every dollar of increased benefits, private transfers are reduced by 17 cents, leaving 83 cents for the elderly beneficiaries.

A similar computation was done for the Philippines, where the proportion of the population covered by the social security system is lower than in Peru and the incidence of private transfers is higher. The crowding out effect is larger—a dollar increase in public pensions would be associated with a decline in private transfers of 37 cents, leaving 63 cents for the elderly.

These simulations imply that social security does indeed prompt reductions in private transfers. Although the magnitude of the reduction is significant, it is much less than that predicted by models of purely altruistic transfers among households. Publicly financed pensions still boost the incomes of targeted beneficiaries—but not dollar for dollar.

family pooling of work, risk, and resources works best. Typical among these policy biases are the protective tariffs and subsidized credit and electricity that favor the modern sector. By artificially supporting sectors that compete with agriculture for scarce resources, these policies draw resources away from rural areas and make them less able to hold onto their work force. Avoiding these policy biases is good for many other reasons and also preserves informal networks of information and social sanctions that are based on the frequent contact, close proximity, and long-term residential stability that underpin the family support system.

Improve Communication between Rural and Urban Areas

Rural-urban migration can have a doubly deleterious effect on old age support systems. The older generation of rural residents, who have invested in the education and rearing of their children, see the risks of these investments rise as their children migrate. The children, for their part, are removed from the rural information and support network. Some children earn more and send remittances home to their parents, but some do not, so uncertainty increases. The weaker the communication links between urban and rural areas, the more harmful the effects of migration—both in allowing children to escape their obligations of support to their parents and in cutting children off from future support networks in their communities of origin. Policies that improve communication between urban and rural areas have the side effect of improving the functioning of informal old age support systems.

Consider Special Programs for Widows

Women are especially vulnerable in their old age. Most women eventually become widows because of their younger age at marriage, longer life expectancy, and lower rate of remarriage than men. Women also have lower labor force participation rates and wages than men, and inheritance and property laws often discriminate against them. These factors make women dependent on their children, and women without children are especially disadvantaged. The most direct way to alleviate these problems is through legislation to remove discrimination against women in the labor market and in property and inheritance laws. But change this fundamental cannot be achieved overnight, since pervasive social norms supporting discrimination have to be changed as well.

Encouraging widows to remarry and not penalizing older men and women who live together outside marriage (as many formal old age security systems do) are other options. China apparently has had favorable experience with these policies. But they are less likely to work in other countries where the sexual imbalance is less severe and where remarriage or living together out of marriage violates strong cultural norms. Widows are thus one of the first groups of old people who should be targeted for formal social assistance, in the interest of alleviating poverty among those whom the traditional system fails.

Try to Have Formal Systems Complement Informal Systems

A general principle in establishing government programs is to provide goods and services that complement rather than substitute for those provided by families and other voluntary sources of support. Singapore gives preferred housing assignments and Sweden provides a housing allowance to families willing to take care of an older relative. Respite care is provided in Canada, France, and the United Kingdom. Community clinics, outpatient health facilities, and day care and social facilities for older people are available in Angola, Hong Kong, and Thailand. In Malaysia, a small stipend goes to adult children who live with their parents. Israel and Singapore grant tax deductions to people who provide support for their parents or for other old people in their communities. These policies make it more feasible for families to care for the old within their households, by easing what could otherwise be an intolerable burden (see box 2.5).

Limiting the level and type of public support may also be important. A lump sum payment on retirement may permit the old to buy their way back into the informal system in their village of origin. Targeting social assistance programs to people without adequate income or without family members capable of supporting them is another way to reduce the crowding out of private transfers. An innovative program in the Indian state of Kerala uses this principle in a means-tested pension scheme for agricultural workers. A pension of 45 rupees ($1.50) a month is paid to agricultural workers whose annual income (including income of spouse and unmarried children) does not exceed 1,500 rupees ($50.00) annually. Although this purportedly is a subsistence income, the recipient cannot get by without additional assistance from relatives. The pension has been credited with enabling relatives to take care of the

Box 2.5 Government Programs That Complement Informal Care of the Old

MANY GOVERNMENT POLICIES, BOTH IN OECD and developing countries, complement and therefore encourage family care of old people. These include housing assistance, respite care, community health and day care centers, and financial assistance.

OECD Countries

Housing assistance. Lack of adequate space in the home to comfortably accommodate an older relative can be a major barrier to family care of the old. In Victoria, Australia, prefabricated units called "granny flats" are available as a form of public housing to help solve this problem. This model has now been adopted by New Zealand and by Ontario, Canada, as well. Japan provides low-interest loans to families to remodel their homes to accommodate an older relative and offers public housing with an extra room to low-income persons with older relatives. Sweden provides a generous housing allowance to enable family members to adapt their homes. In Norway, special loans are granted for the purchase of multigenerational houses.

Supportive services for caregivers. One of the services most frequently requested by caregivers is respite care to enable them to perform important errands, have a night away from home, or take a vacation. In France, Germany, Japan, and the United Kingdom, rooms are available in some nursing homes or geriatric hospitals for short-term stays, to give caregivers at home a respite. In-home respite care, in which a family caregiver is relieved for a few hours at a time, is available in many Canadian provinces and in some states in the United States. Day care for the mentally and physically impaired is important in Australia, Canada, France, Japan, and the United Kingdom. "Night-sitting" services, in which a social service person helps a family care for an ill older relative by taking care of the old person during the night, are provided in parts of Sweden and the United Kingdom.

Low- and Middle-Income Countries

Housing assistance. In Malaysia, public housing authorities allocate ground-floor flats to families with aged or disabled members. In Singapore, families willing to live next door to older relatives are given priority in housing assignments. Families in Cyprus whose older relatives live with them are given priority in housing, are offered units, and can apply for financial assistance to add an extra room.

Supportive services. Day care and counseling services are provided throughout East Asia and Southeast Asia. In Thailand multipurpose day centers provide health care, day care, family assistance, and counseling. Hong Kong and Singapore provide home help and nursing care at home, as well as day centers. In Angola, existing organizations such as churches, clubs, and local collectives are used as sites for day care and other supportive services. In Argentina *clubs de ancianos* provide social, health, and recreational services to the old.

Financial assistance. In Malaysia, adult children who live with their parents have received a tax rebate, and an additional tax deduction is available to help them cover medical expenses and supporting equipment for disabled parents. The Republic of Korea, the Philippines, and several African countries are also considering such arrangements.

Some of these services are provided directly by public agencies and some are delivered by nonprofit or for-profit organizations, subsidized by the government. These forms of public spending are complementary to family services and therefore tend to crowd in rather than crowd out the informal system of old age support.

Source: Most of these examples are taken from United Nations (1985) and Kendig, Hashimoto, and Coppard (1992).

elderly by subsidizing the cost of home care—and thereby encouraging, or crowding in, traditional informal support (Nair and Tracy 1989).

Go Slow with Formal Systems

In rural areas in low-income countries, informal systems may work better than formal ones. Given limited taxing and administrative capabilities, governments in Africa and Asia should be cautious about ambitious formal programs, which might fail, after crowding out family arrangements that function reasonably well. Family investments in education or small businesses may provide better old age security than would required contributions to public pension programs.

Public programs in the rural areas of poor countries should concentrate on social assistance for the neediest of all ages, while every effort is made to develop the capacities that will enable more complex formal systems to work well. Mandatory contributory programs should be introduced first in the formal labor markets of urban areas, where the informal system is most likely to have broken down.

CHAPTER 3

Policy Choices for Formal Systems

I N INDUSTRIAL COUNTRIES AND MOST LOW- AND MIDDLE-income countries, governments have developed formal arrangements for old age support. An estimated 30 percent of the world's old people are covered by these formal arrangements, and 40 percent of the world's workers are contributing with the expectation of being covered when they grow old. The key policy questions that must be answered in setting up the formal arrangements are:

- Should the primary reliance be on voluntary or mandatory mechanisms? When should mandatory coverage be phased in, and at what level of pensions and contributions?
- What should be the balance between the objectives of poverty alleviation and redistribution versus saving and income smoothing? And what role should the government play in satisfying each objective?
- Who should bear the many risks that beset people in old age, what kinds of insurance should be provided, and how?
- Should the system be financed on a funded or a pay-as-you-go basis?
- Should it be managed publicly or privately?

The answers to these key policy questions determine how a country's old age security system affects the economy and how its benefits and costs are divided between old and young, rich and poor. This chapter introduces these issues, and chapters 4 through 6 discuss the answers that are provided by public, occupational, and personal saving plans.

Voluntary or Mandatory Mechanisms? How Much Mandatory Coverage?

INFORMAL SYSTEMS OF OLD AGE SECURITY RELY ON VOLUNTARY actions, buttressed by strong social sanctions. When a government decides that such systems do not suffice, it must also decide whether to reinforce voluntary actions or install a mandatory plan.

Voluntary actions—such as personal saving plans and employer-sponsored occupational pension plans—can be encouraged by macroeconomic stability, reliable saving instruments, and favorable tax treatment to long-term saving and annuities. This approach to old age security has the lowest evasion and disincentive costs. It also provides the greatest accommodation of diverse tastes. And it places the lightest administrative burden on government. These are big advantages everywhere, especially in developing countries. But there also are disadvantages. This simple approach may not reach some people. It does not fill the gaps in the insurance market. It will not eliminate the vestiges of lifetime poverty among the old. And it involves hidden—probably regressive—tax costs. Low-income workers may not respond to tax incentives, while many high-income workers who receive the tax advantages might have saved anyway.

If the goals are to cover everyone, to prevent people from becoming a charge on the public treasury, and to redistribute income to the old who are long-term poor, a mandatory scheme with broad coverage is required, one that does not permit people to opt out. Compulsory schemes have the further advantage that they can save the treasury money, since they do not require tax incentives, although incentives are often included to facilitate enforcement and political acceptability. All industrial countries have mandatory schemes as the core of their old age security systems—usually financed by worker or employer contributions and buttressed by tax provisions that encourage voluntary saving through personal or occupational plans.

Mandatory schemes require extensive government management or regulation, which may strain the capabilities of many developing countries. They also incur administrative costs that tend to be particularly high in relation to per capita income and total contributions in low-income countries. For these reasons, they should be phased in and expanded cautiously, after careful analysis of the long-term impact on costs, benefits, and their distribution within and across generations. Policymakers must decide which groups to cover first—and at what level of pensions and contributions.

In practice, coverage has been extended first to workers in the public sector and in large private sector firms, where enforcement is easier and transaction costs are low relative to wages and pensions. Almost every country has a mandatory plan that covers these groups. Employees of small firms, the self-employed, and agricultural workers—the bulk of workers in developing countries—are added later, as government tax and administrative capabilities grow and income levels rise.

This phasing in of mandatory coverage poses three potential dangers. Costs are high because the plans do not benefit from economies of scale. Low-income workers not covered may be taxed to subsidize the retirement plans of higher-income workers who are covered. And some informal sector or rural workers may find themselves in poverty when they grow old. Countries can guard against these dangers by starting with administratively simple systems, avoiding subsidies from outsiders to insiders by minimizing general revenue financing at the beginning, and supplementing contributory retirement plans with social assistance for the poor of all ages.

How generous should the mandatory contribution and benefit rates be for covered workers? Some households might wish to replace 75 percent or more of their gross average lifetime wage on retirement. Others might prefer a lower wage replacement rate so that they can consume more when young. Forcing the second group to contribute enough for a high replacement rate would make them worse off rather than better off. Divergent tastes can be accommodated and evasion minimized, while avoiding poverty, by setting a target replacement rate (through mandatory public and private plans) of, say, 60 percent of the gross average lifetime wage for the average worker, with a floor at the poverty line for low-income workers. Survivors' benefits should be required to protect dependents who do not have income of their own. These mandatory pensions could be supplemented by voluntary saving by households that have higher wage replacement targets (see issue brief 1).

Saving or Redistribution—and the Link between Benefits and Contributions

I N AN OLD AGE SECURITY SYSTEM THAT EMPHASIZES SAVING OR income smoothing, people shift their income over their lifetimes, spending less now to spend more later. The lifetime expected value of benefits and contributions are equal for each individual. In a system that emphasizes redistribution, one group receives greater expected lifetime benefits than its lifetime contributions, and another group receives less. Income is shifted across groups.

A system that emphasizes saving has several advantages. By making benefits directly contingent on contributions according to market principles, it discourages evasion, labor disincentive effects, and political pressure for design features that lead to inefficient, inequitable outcomes. But it has one major disadvantage: It fails to alleviate poverty among old people who did not have sufficient resources to save or reliable financial institutions in which to place their savings.

In choosing its old age security system, each country must decide on the relative emphasis on saving versus redistribution. The link between the contributions workers make and the benefits they receive will vary accordingly. The assumption throughout this report is that poverty elimination is an important goal, although the degree to which it can be achieved will depend on costs and country circumstances. Policymakers must also decide whether the saving and redistributive objectives will be satisfied through one unified program—or through separate financing and managerial arrangements.

Should Income Be Transferred to the Old?

Three arguments are often put forth for emphasizing the redistributive objectives of old age security programs:

- The old tend to be poor in current income, so it makes sense to use old age as a criterion for targeting income transfers.
- Younger generations will benefit from economic growth, so they should make income transfers to older generations whose lifetime income is less.
- Poor people who are old should receive more generous income transfers than other groups who are poor.

Are these arguments valid? Are old age programs an effective way to reduce poverty? And should that be their primary objective? To evaluate these arguments one must distinguish between poverty measures based on current income and those based on lifetime income (the present value of total or average annual income generated over an individual's lifetime). Also to be considered are the relative claims to redistribution of the old versus other groups, such as young families with children.

Are the old poor in terms of current income? If old people are disproportionately poor in the absence of extended families or government programs, redistribution from younger to older cohorts will help equalize current incomes. But empirical data suggest that, in current income, the old are not disproportionately poor in many countries. Data for developing countries such as India and Nigeria in the 1970s and Côte d'Ivoire and Thailand in the 1980s show that households with old people do not have lower average incomes than young households, particularly when urban-rural differences are taken into account (Deaton and Paxson 1991; Gaiha and Kazmi 1982; Hill 1972). Extended family arrangements in these countries are an important explanatory factor. But they are not the full explanation, since findings are similar in middle- and high-income countries where the nuclear family is more important. While the incidence of poverty can be quite sensitive to the choice of poverty line, to the relative costs of living imputed to large and small families, and to the time period under consideration (Förster 1993), it appears that:

■ In countries such as Brazil and Chile, poverty rates among children are higher than among old people (figure 3.1).

■ In Hungary, Poland, and Russia, families with young children are more likely than old pensioners to be poor (van de Walle, Ravallion, and Gautam 1994; Fox 1994; World Bank data).

■ In Poland the poverty rate among old people is half the national average, whereas the poverty rate among children is almost 50 percent higher than the national average (World Bank data).

■ In most OECD countries, current income is lower and poverty is higher among working age adults and children than among the old (figure 3.2).

How can this be? There are several explanations. Young workers are at the bottom of their age-earnings profiles, whereas older workers are at the top; those who continue to work may receive high wages. Old peo-

Figure 3.1 Relative Poverty Rates for Children and for Persons over 60 Years Old, Selected Countries in Latin America, 1980s

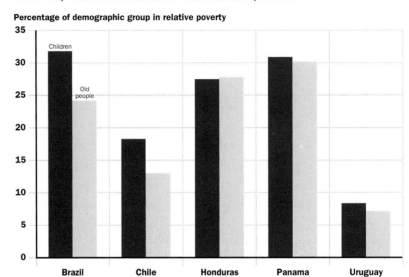

Percentage of demographic group in relative poverty

More children than old people live in poverty in some Latin American countries.

Note: Relative poverty is defined as 50 percent of median income per capita, with children weighted: those under 5 are 25 percent of an adult; those between 5 and 14 are 45 percent of an adult. Children are defined as persons under 15 years, old as over 60 years.
Source: Calculations by World Bank, using Household Survey Data; Keller (1994).

ple have also had an opportunity to save and accumulate assets—including, in some cases, homes that reduce their need for monetary outlays. Those who have retired also have considerable leisure time as a reserve, which they can use to make their money go farther. So, their consumption capacity exceeds their current earnings. In contrast, children are born disproportionately to low-income families, further depressing the per capita income of these families. Targeting transfers or services to families with children may be a more effective way of alleviating poverty than targeting to the old.

Do the old have lower lifetime incomes than the young? If an economy is growing rapidly, the average member of a young cohort will have a higher lifetime income than the average member of an older cohort. Then, equity considerations could motivate redistributions from working age cohorts, who will benefit from growth, to the old, even though the old have a higher current income than the young (the young will earn more later on).

Figure 3.2 Relative Poverty Rates by Age Group for OECD Countries, Mid-1980s

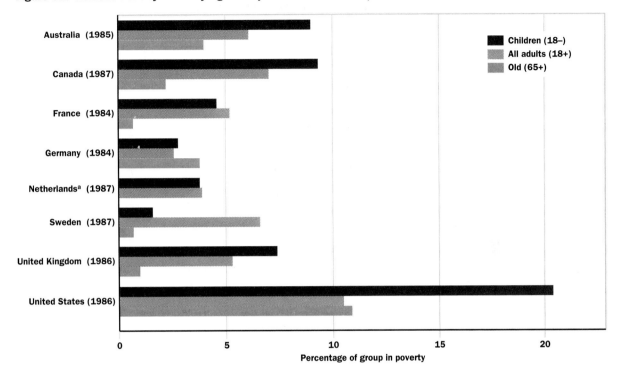

Note: The poverty line is defined as 40 percent of adjusted family income after tax and transfers, adjusting for family size, using the U.S. poverty line equivalence scale.
a. For the Netherlands, the poverty rate for persons over 65 is zero.
Source: Luxembourg Income Study, as presented in Smeeding (1992).

Two countering forces weaken this argument. First, economies do not always grow rapidly. Over the past two decades, real per capita income has declined in many African countries, and real wage growth has slowed down in OECD countries (appendix table A.3). In Latin America, real wages have been subject to wide swings. When economies are sluggish, average lifetime earnings are not much higher for younger than for older cohorts. Second, people who survive to old age are not a random sample of their cohorts. They generally come from higher socioeconomic groups, whose expected longevity is high. People who are poor for most of their lives are much less likely to survive to old age.

In some OECD countries, old people have lower poverty rates than children or other adults.

- In the United States, the mortality rate of working age persons in the lowest income group is five times that of workers in the high-

79

est income group, and the differential has increased over the past three decades (Pappas and others 1993).

- In Argentina, high-income public workers are estimated to live ten years longer than low-income industrial workers (Rofman 1994).
- In the United Kingdom workers in high-paid occupations have substantially lower mortality rates than workers in low-paid occupations (Creedy, Disney, and Whitehouse 1992).

Given this difference, a large proportion of people who are young will have shorter lifetimes and lower lifetime annual incomes than people who are old.

Should poor old people be treated differently from others who are poor? To the degree that old age poverty has been caused by inadequate saving, it can be prevented by forcing people to save when they are young. Thus a remedy is available for old age poverty that is less appropriate for other groups and does not involve transfers—but it requires advance planning. Redistributive old age policies should be carefully structured to encourage saving and not to crowd it out. For example, providing a minimum pension guarantee as part of a retirement saving program may encourage saving, while stand-alone income and asset-tested programs may have the opposite effect.

Even if saving and work are encouraged, some low-wage workers will simply not earn enough income to keep out of poverty for their entire lifetimes. If forced to save for old age, they may be plunged into poverty when young—these are the long-term poor. Rather than expecting them to save, which would push them below the poverty line throughout their lifetimes, it may be more efficient to concentrate redistributions to this group in their older years. When people are young the presumption is that they are able to work, but when they are old the presumption is that they cannot work, or at least not productively, especially in urban industrial economies. Thus the labor disincentive effect of transfers is smaller for the old than for the young, as a group—providing the retirement age is set high enough. In addition, it may be more politically acceptable to transfer to the long-term poor after they have "paid their dues" by working, when they are no longer able to work because of old age. Therefore, both economic and political forces suggest that the long-term poor may receive larger transfers when old than when young.

There are also identifiable subgroups of old people whose current income is particularly low. In many countries, these subgroups include women living alone and the very old—nearly the same groups, since women live longer than men. In OECD countries, very old people living alone are more likely than other groups to be in the bottom decile of the income distribution, and most of them are women (figure 3.3). In urban areas in China 41 percent of old women but only 4 percent of old men live below an extreme poverty line (Cangping 1991). In India, households headed by widows are by far the poorest group, with an average expenditure per person 70 percent below the national average (Dreze 1990). Many of these people have not participated steadily in the labor market, had few resources of their own to save when young, and are not likely to be reached by pension plans tied to employment. While giving them joint ownership of their spouses' pension rights is a part of the answer, this is not always feasible. These pockets of old age poverty might be targeted for redistribution.

Figure 3.3 Percentage of All Persons over 65 and Females Living Alone with Incomes below Subsistence, Selected OECD Countries, Early 1980s

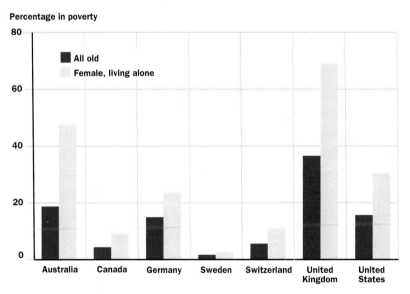

Old women living alone are more likely to be poor than are other groups.

Note: Poverty thresholds are those employed by the U.S. Bureau of the Census, taking into account the number and ages of persons within the household and adjusting for economies of scale in consumption.

Source: Adapted from Palmer, Smeeding, and Torrey (1988), table 5.8, p. 105. Data source is Luxembourg Income Survey for various years between 1979 and 1982.

For all these reasons, it may be efficient to use different types of programs and eligibility criteria, reliance on saving as a preventative as well as redistribution as a cure, and more generous transfers to reduce long-term poverty among the old than among the young.

What Should Be Done?

Taxing and transferring income should be done with great care because of the distortions and evasion they engender and because poorly targeted transfers can be perverse. In considering whether to emphasize the saving or redistributive aspect of old age security programs, countries should evaluate the relative positions of the old and other groups in their income distribution. In many countries, this evaluation will lead to the conclusion that the old are not disproportionately poor in current income or lifetime income. In these countries, targeting transfers to young families with children (through public spending on primary education and health care, among other ways) is likely to have a more equalizing effect on income and on stopping the intergenerational transmission of poverty. Poverty among the old could be substantially alleviated by encouraging or requiring people to save when they are young.

At the same time, there are some pockets of extreme poverty among the old. In industrial countries, old women living alone who had little labor market experience earlier in life are one such group. Another consists of people who were low-wage workers when young, had no surplus funds to save, and despite the odds survived to old age. More generally, the labor disincentive effect is a lesser concern when people are old. The old are less adaptable, more vulnerable to economic shocks, and unable to reverse mistakes they made earlier in life, and their lifetime incomes are low relative to those of younger cohorts in periods of rapid economic growth. For all these reasons, this report makes the value judgment that redistribution and saving both have an important role to play in old age security programs, although their relative importance will vary across countries. Furthermore, both the criteria for and amount of redistribution may be different for the old and for the young. The potential and actual roles of public, occupational, and personal saving plans in achieving these saving and redistribution objectives are discussed in chapters 4 through 6. Whether these dual functions should be provided through one mechanism or through separate managerial and financing arrangements is a central issue in the design of pension systems.

Bearing the Risks: Defined Benefits or Defined Contributions?

PLANNING FOR OLD AGE INVOLVES ENORMOUS UNCERTAIN-ties. People can become disabled, die young, require expensive medical care, or live long and healthy lives. Firms can go bankrupt, and new industries emerge. The economy can stagnate or flourish. There can be major demographic changes, revolutions, wars, droughts, floods, famines, inflation, depressions—and governments good and bad. These vicissitudes affect the amount of goods and services available in the economy for consumption and the claims of different people on these goods. They thus affect the viability of young people's plans for their old age.

Who should bear these long-term risks, and how should they be shared between the old and the rest of society? In informal systems, the old share in the fortunes of the extended family with whom they live. In formal systems, old people bear different kinds of risks, depending on how old age security is provided. Among the many risks are the risks of investment, disability, longevity, political disruption, company insolvency, and inflation. Broadly speaking, the risk faced by old people versus young depends on whether the plan is set up as a defined benefit or defined contribution plan and whether it is publicly or privately managed. Public, occupational, and personal saving plans each pose different sets of risks and offer different kinds of insurance (chapters 4–6).

Defined Contribution Plans—and Investment Risk

When people save for their own old age, as in personal saving plans, contributions are specified and ultimately determine future benefits. But there is considerable uncertainty about future rates of return, the duration of working and retirement periods, and therefore about future annual benefits. So, workers bear considerable investment, disability, and longevity risk. This kind of arrangement is known as a defined contribution plan, because the annual contribution is defined in advance but the benefit—which depends on how well the investments are managed and how long workers contribute and collect—is not. To a large extent, investment returns depend on the economic health of the country—and that of other countries in the case of foreign investments. For privately managed funds, the inability of workers to evaluate the competence of investment companies and the possibility of outright fraud further increase investment risk. For publicly managed funds, the government may intervene to limit investment options and returns, so political risk is intertwined with investment risk.

Defined Benefit Plans—and Political and Insolvency Risk

In defined benefit plans, the pension formula is defined in advance. Often benefits depend on years of employment and salary over some period, such as the final three years or the lifetime average. The rest of society bears the risk that the economy will not do as well as expected or that people will live longer than expected. The sheltering of old people from these risks—on grounds that they are less able to adjust and recoup than the young—is considered one of the big advantages of defined benefit plans.

In reality, workers continue to bear important risks in defined benefit plans. For one thing, their pensions depend directly on their wages, especially their wages in the last few years of employment. If wages fail to rise as rapidly as expected, the pension amount will be commensurately less. In occupational defined benefit plans, workers bear the risk that they will lose their pensions because of employer insolvency or worker mobility. In public defined benefit plans, workers bear the risk that the taxing ability of the government will decline or the political regime may change, with the new government repudiating the arrangements made by a previous government.

Disability and Longevity Risks

Disability risk arises because some people are unable to work productively and contribute as long as expected. Longevity risk comes of living longer than expected and outlasting savings. These risks can be handled by covering them in defined benefit plans or by purchasing disability insurance and annuities from insurance companies in defined contribution plans (in effect this converts part of the defined contribution into a defined benefit).

One problem with disability insurance is that workers may claim to be unable to work even when they can work, raising costs for everyone; this is known as the *moral hazard* problem. Another problem is that because of the informational failures described in chapter 1, disability insurance and annuities may not be available at an actuarially fair price;

this is the *adverse selection* problem. In addition, if the insurance is provided privately, workers face the risk of insurance company insolvency. And if it is provided publicly, they face political risks, given the long periods involved.

Inflation Risk

Inflation poses a particularly important risk. Inflation averaged 7.7 percent a year from 1965 to 1980 and 4.5 percent from 1980 to 1990 in high-income countries. In middle-income countries it averaged 21.1 percent and 85.6 percent over the same periods, and in low-income countries, 17.3 percent and 15.1 percent. Annual inflation exceeded 200 percent in Argentina, Bolivia, Brazil, and Peru during the 1980s and recently exploded in the former Soviet Union (World Bank 1992d). Wages usually rise with prices, albeit not always as fast. But pensions are often fixed in nominal terms, so their real value declines precipitously during inflationary periods, leaving the old in poverty. With annual inflation at 10 percent, the real value of a pension that is fixed in nominal terms is cut in half in seven years. And with inflation at 100 percent, it takes just one year (figure 3.4).

Figure 3.4 Effects of Different Rates of Inflation on Unindexed Pensions

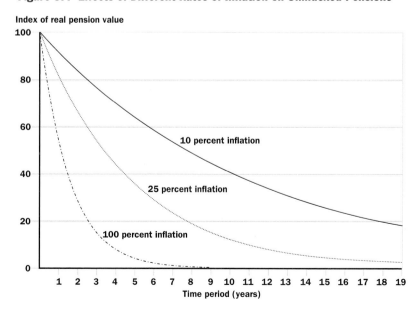

The real value of unindexed pensions slides down a slippery inflationary slope.

Policymakers need to decide whether indexation of pension benefits should be required in mandatory plans, and if so, whether the indexation should be full or partial—and be to wages or to prices. Under price indexation, pensions move with the price level: their absolute real value remains unchanged, and the risk that aggregate demand exceeds the country's output is borne by other groups in society. Under wage indexation, pensions rise and fall together with wages. The relative position of old people is protected, but their absolute standard of living is not.

In general, indexation by either method requires a higher contribution rate or lower initial benefit rate than a nonindexed plan, since indexed pensions are likely to rise nominally over the retirement period. Workers and citizens unaccustomed to high rates of inflation may be reluctant to pay this price, but they may be disappointed later on if inflation accelerates and the real value of benefits declines. Indexed pensions can be and have been provided by private annuity companies or by public defined benefit plans.

How Should People Share the Risks?

In view of the uncertainties and long periods involved, it is difficult to predict which risk-bearing arrangement is best for the old—or for the rest of society. Clearly, older age groups cannot be insulated from all these economic and political risks. Nor is this the most desirable outcome. But a variety of techniques can and should be used to reduce the social costs of risk. Risk can be reduced through pooling or neutralized through diversification or shifted to those more willing and able to bear it. As countries make their choices about the best risk-sharing arrangement, the following principles might be observed:

- Certain risks that are uncorrelated across individuals, such as longevity risk, are minimized by pooling across the largest number of people—including everyone in a single insurance pool or reinsuring across several smaller pools—since the average outcome for the group is much more certain than the experience of any particular individual.
- Other risks, such as disability risk, are subject to moral hazard problems, which should be constrained to keep costs down.

- Some degree and type of indexation, shifting part of the inflation risk to younger workers, is needed to prevent the very old from living in poverty during inflationary periods.
- Investment, insolvency, and political risks are real and potentially large, but they cannot be reduced through risk pooling because they are correlated across individuals and subject to moral hazard problems. Diversification is the solution here. Diversification across several managerial and financing mechanisms protects pensioners against exposure to extreme failure of any one arrangement, reducing overall risk for the old.

Financing the Plans: Funded or Pay-as-You-Go?

OLD AGE SECURITY PLANS CAN BE FULLY (OR PARTIALLY) funded—or financed on a pay-as-you-go basis. Under pay-as-you-go financing, workers today pay pensions to retirees today, expecting that their pensions will be paid by future workers. A plan's current revenues cover its current obligation, and there is no stock of savings to pay future pensions. A low ratio of retirees to workers (the system old age dependency ratio) and a high rate of productivity and real wages permit high benefits or low contributions.

In a fully funded scheme, a stock of capital accumulates to pay future obligations so that aggregate contributions plus investment returns are sufficient at any time to cover the present value of the entire stream of future obligations. The current generation of workers supports itself through wages and saves part of its output for support after retirement. A low ratio of retirement years to working years (the passivity ratio) and a high rate of interest enable high benefits or low contributions.

Defined contribution plans are by definition fully funded, since people are entitled only to the proceeds of their individual accounts. It is also possible for defined benefit plans to be fully funded. But the concept of full funding is ambiguous in defined benefit schemes (whether public or private) because of uncertainties about the future rate of return, worker longevity, and age-earnings profiles. If the actual rate of return turns out to be lower than expected or if people live longer than expected or retire earlier, a defined benefit plan that appeared to be fully funded might not be. Most privately managed defined benefit plans in industrial countries have substantial funding. Most publicly managed defined benefit plans are pay-as-you-go or only lightly funded.

Which Financing Method Requires Lower Contribution Rates?

In the early years of an old age support program—when the system dependency rate is very low because there are few eligible beneficiaries—pay-as-you-go will always appear cheaper than a fully funded plan. But as the system matures, more retirees are eligible for benefits—so this temporary advantage disappears. Pay-as-you-go will continue to have a cost advantage or higher rate of return in the long run if the earnings growth rate plus the labor force growth rate exceed the interest rate (Samuelson 1958; Aaron 1966). In this case (providing the pension system does not affect the growth rate), pay-as-you-go could make all generations better off: each generation could get back a higher present value of pensions than it paid in as contributions.

But if the rate of earnings growth plus labor force growth falls below the rate of interest, the long-run cost advantage and the higher rate of return go to fully funded programs. This can easily happen in plans tied to particular firms or industries. It also happens for a country as a whole if its population and earnings cease to grow rapidly. Data from several countries show that when the time period for investment is long, the rate of interest on a combination of debt and equity has generally exceeded the rate of earnings growth by approximately 2 to 3 percent. This means that because of the productivity of capital, the same benefits can be paid to each generation with a lower contribution rate under full funding, unless the population is growing by 2 to 3 percent. If population growth is less than 2 percent and pay-as-you-go funding is used (or if pay-as-you-go funding has a negative impact on growth—see below), each generation gets back in benefits a lower present value than it paid in as contributions (issue brief 2).

Intergenerational Transfers and the Demographic Transition

To many, a high rate of population growth seemed inevitable three or four decades ago, in which case pay-as-you-go seemed a good way to finance old age programs. But today, birthrates are falling or projected to fall everywhere, while the longevity of the old is increasing rapidly. During the demographic transition that industrial countries are going through now and developing countries will go through in the next half century, population growth falls toward zero. Unless there are large off-setting productivity gains, tax rates must rise or benefit levels must fall under pay-as-you-go plans. With the growth rate of average earnings below the interest rate, as in most countries, workers will get back in pensions a lower present value than they put in as contributions. So, early cohorts of pensioners who retired while the covered population was growing rapidly will have gained lifetime income. But later generations will lose, as a result of the initial choice of pay-as-you-go.

Suppose that China decides to use pay-as-you-go financing to pay a flat benefit equal to 40 percent of average wages to all people over the age of 60, starting in 1995. The contribution rate needed to pay those pensions would be less than 7 percent in 1995 but would rise to 18 percent in 2035 and 23 percent in 2065. When allowance is made for unemployment, evasion, strategic manipulation of benefits, survivors' benefits, ceilings on taxable earnings, and administrative costs, the required tax rate could easily exceed 35 percent—on top of income taxes charged for other purposes. Cohorts retiring in the early years of the plan would get back much more than they paid in, but later retirees would get back much less. In effect, today's children and their children would be making large transfers of their lifetime income to today's middle-aged and old people (figure 3.5 and issue brief 3).

What would happen under a fully funded plan? Such plans require a start-up time of twenty years or more to build retirement savings. So, earlier cohorts of retirees would not get large pensions because they would not get large positive transfers from younger generations. But later cohorts would fare better, as they have not lost lifetime income. Either their benefit rate would be much higher or their contribution rate would be much lower. (Although saving by large cohorts of young people and dissaving by large cohorts of old people during the demographic transition could cause swings in the interest rate that also have distributional consequences, these effects would be substantially mitigated by international diversification, since different countries are aging at different rates [Reisen 1994].)

Policymakers need to know that when a population and earnings are not growing rapidly, the financing method chosen affects the distribution of lifetime income between present and future generations. If they want to favor the present generation of workers, pay-as-you-go has an advantage. If they want to be distributionally neutral, full funding is preferred.

89

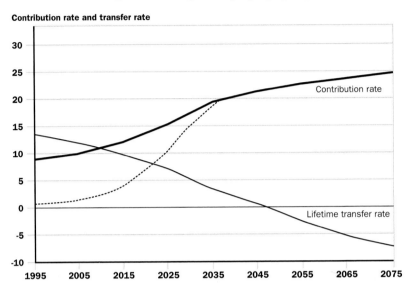

Figure 3.5 Contribution Rates Required to Finance a 40 Percent Flat Pension for a Country with a Young but Rapidly Aging Population

Contribution rate and transfer rate

In the early years of a pay-as-you-go plan, retirees get back much more than they paid in, but later retirees will get back much less.

Note: Demographic projections for China are used. This figure is based on the following assumptions: The average benefit rate is 40 percent of the economy-wide wage. The required contribution rate is expressed as a percentage of wages (a payroll tax). The transfer rate is a percentage of the lifetime wage for a cohort retiring in a given year. The solid line assumes instant maturation, that is, all old people are immediately eligible for full benefits. The dotted line assumes gradual maturation, that is, there is no credit for service prior to 1995, and the pension equals 1 percent of the economy-wide wage for each year of work after 1995. For other assumptions, see issue brief table 3.
Source: Schwarz (1994).

The Implicit Public Pension Debt

Because of its emphasis on current cash payouts, pay-as-you-go finance hides the true long-run cost of pension promises. The current situation is only the tip of the iceberg. When workers pay their social security taxes, they expect to get a specified benefit in return. The present value of this future stream of expected benefits is known as the "implicit public pension debt." This liability for the government, corresponding to the "entitlement" people believe they have acquired, is the iceberg underneath the tip. Although this implicit debt varies by country and depends on the coverage of the pension system, the age distribution of workers, the level of benefits, and the discount rate used in the calculation, in many countries it is two or three times the value of the conventional explicit debt (figures 3.5 and 3.6). In simulations using China's demography and two alternative discount rates, the pension debt starts low as the hypothetical system described below is introduced but rises to 100 to 200 percent of GDP (figure 3.6).

But an implicit debt is a hidden liability, of which many citizens and policymakers are unaware. In the early years of a pay-as-you-go pension plan, costs may look very low because required contribution rates are low, but the implicit pension debt is building up surreptitiously and will have to be paid off through higher taxes, as the system matures and population ages. Policymakers should take this into account from the start, through simulations of the debt and tax rates required in the long run, before choosing the system and the target benefit rate.

Figure 3.6 Growth of the Implicit Public Pension Debt, 1995–2075

Public pension debt as a percentage of GDP

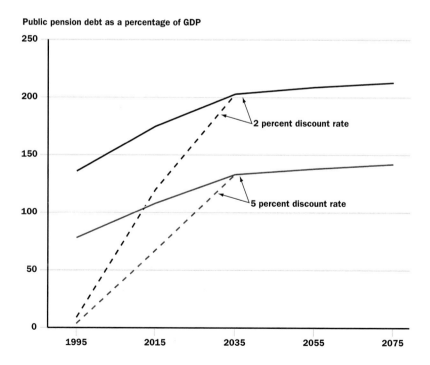

The benefits people expect to receive from public pension programs becomes a large hidden debt for the government.

Note: Projections are based on the demographics of China. See the assumptions in issue brief table 3. The solid line assumes instant maturity—that is, full service credit to workers and retirees in 1995. The dotted line assumes gradual maturation (see figure 3.5 for assumptions).

In contrast, in fully funded schemes, contribution rates are higher from the start, accumulating assets sufficient to pay the pension debt. The simulated pension debt line in figure 3.6 is also a measure of the assets that would build up over time to pay an equivalent benefit stream in a fully funded scheme. Governments will not be hit by exploding liabilities later on. This is a much more transparent situation for citizens and policymakers.

How Financing Affects Saving and Growth

Increasing productivity is the only way a smaller working age population can support a larger retired population without a fall in the overall standard of living, regardless of which funding system is used. A crucial question: Are productivity and GDP growth likely to be higher under one system than the other?

Since pay-as-you-go funding breaks the market link between benefits and contributions, it may lead to evasion and labor supply distortions, especially in developing countries with large informal sectors and weak tax enforcement capabilities. In addition, many economists argue that pay-as-you-go schemes reduce saving, capital accumulation, and therefore growth. The reasoning is that the first few cohorts reap a windfall gain in the form of pensions that enable them to consume more without having saved more. Unless the government compensates by increasing public saving, total national saving will decline, with harmful consequences for productivity and growth. This negative effect on growth is another potential source of intergenerational transfer.

Numerous empirical studies have tried to determine whether this savings effect held for social security systems in the United States and elsewhere during the 1950s and 1960s. Some studies claim to have proved negative savings effects, whereas others claim to have proved their absence. The results are inconclusive, in part because it is so difficult to determine what people would have saved otherwise. (See issue brief 4 for a fuller discussion of the impact of pay-as-you-go plans on saving.)

Nevertheless, even if a mandatory pay-as-you-go plan does not reduce saving relative to a voluntary scheme, it seems likely that a fully funded mandatory plan will increase saving relative to pay-as-you-go. Although never tested empirically (because of the paucity of empirical cases), this effect seems inevitable—providing people are required to contribute more than they would otherwise have saved, consumers do not evade these constraints by borrowing or dissaving other assets, and government does not react to the greater availability of household savings by running a larger deficit. The first and second requirements remind us that small funded plans (say, less than 5 percent of wages) will be ineffective as a means of capital accumulation because they will simply crowd out voluntary saving or induce consumers to borrow offsetting amounts. The third requirement warns that if government consumes the extra pension savings, national saving will be unchanged even if household consumption falls. Full funding has the added advantage that its accumulated savings are committed for the long term, may flow through financial institutions, are largely invested in financial assets, and can therefore be an instrument of capital market development (for empirical evidence see chapters 5 and 6).

The bottom line is that a funded pension plan, if appropriately managed, has a strong saving and capital market advantage over pay-as-you-go. A credible funded plan may be an important part of a national savings policy that includes fiscal discipline by the government and inducements against consumer borrowing or dissaving other accumulated assets. Under these conditions, a pension system with a large funded component may be part of a country's strategy for increasing capital accumulation and growth. Although increased saving may not be desirable everywhere and at all times, many analysts would argue that it would be growth-enhancing for most countries and for the world as a whole today. For these reasons, many capital-scarce countries are becoming increasingly interested in funded old age security arrangements.

Should Pension Reserves Be Publicly or Privately Managed?

LARGELY FUNDED PLANS HAVE THE POTENTIAL TO CHANNEL savings into capital market institutions for long, well-defined periods—facilitating financial intermediation and long-term investment. The process also concentrates substantial capital market power in a small number of large pension funds. Examples are the pension funds in Chile, the national provident funds in Malaysia and Singapore, and the social security reserves in Japan, Sweden, and the United States. The investment policies of the fund managers strongly influence the allocation and productivity of capital, with important effects on the economy. Since centralized public managers chosen by political leaders and decentralized private managers chosen by individual savers in a competitive environment face different incentives and, more important, very different constraints, the investment outcomes may be very different under these two arrangements. The choice between public and private management of pension funds is thus crucial.

Public Management

Publicly managed funds are usually required to invest in government securities or the securities of quasi-government entities such as state enterprises or public housing authorities—often at below-market interest rates that become negative in real terms during inflationary periods. This imposes a hidden tax on contributing workers. The fund earns less than it could have on the open market and must charge higher contribution rates or pay lower benefits than it would have otherwise (figure 3.7 and chapter 4).

The impact of publicly managed pension funds on capital accumulation and its allocation depends on how the government responds to the availability of these cheap resources. Suppose that access to these funds does not change the spending and tax policy of the government: it simply sells its bonds to the pension fund instead of to other buyers (albeit at lower rates of interest). In this case, an increase in household saving channeled through funded pension plans increases private sector investment, because other bond buyers now shift their resources to the private sector.

But in some cases, as government gets privileged access to large pension reserves, it may be induced to spend and borrow more. Borrowing from the pension fund is less transparent than that from the open capital market. It is often not reported as part of the public debt, and the interest cost is generally lower. This may tempt governments to increase deficit spending and therefore deter private investments that might otherwise have been made. The danger is that this choice among uses can be made without an explicit productivity comparison, without a market test based on interest rate and risk, and without citizens and policymakers being fully aware of the expenditures and trade-offs (see chapters 4 and 6 for fuller discussion).

If the publicly managed funds are partially invested in the private sector another problem arises: fund managers may be motivated by politi-

Figure 3.7 Average Annual Investment Returns for Selected Pension Funds, 1980s

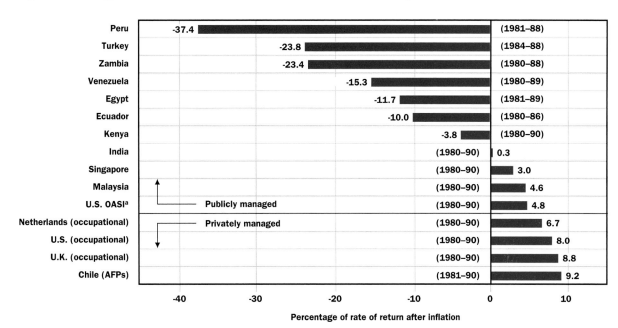

Note: Simple annual averages are computed for countries with at least five years of data. India, Kenya, Malaysia, Singapore, and Zambia are provident funds. Rates reported are returns credited to worker accounts. Ecuador, Egypt, Peru, Turkey, the United States, and Venezuela are publicly managed reserves of partially funded pension plans. Rates reported are not adjusted for administrative costs. For privately managed occupational plans in the Netherlands, the United Kingdom, and the United States, estimated average net returns have been reported by subtracting one percentage point from simulated average gross returns. Actual average net returns, after expenses, are reported for the Chilean AFPs; average gross returns were 12.3 percent. For the occupational plans and AFPs, actual returns and expenses varied by fund.

a. Old-Age and Survivor's Insurance.

Source: Mesa-Lago (1991a); Davis (1993); Marquez (1992); Asher (1992a); Acuña and Iglesias (1992); India Employees Provident Fund (1991); U.S. Social Security Administration (various years); Palacios (1994b).

cal rather than economic objectives. In general, central planning has not been the most efficient way to allocate a country's capital stock. Pension funds hold a large part of the financial assets in a country, especially if the funds are mandatory. The net impact on growth may be negative rather than positive, if public fund managers allocate this large share of national saving to low-productivity uses.

Privately managed pension funds beat publicly managed funds hands down.

Private Management

Privately managed schemes—in which workers or employers choose their fund managers—are usually not required to accept below-market returns and are less likely to encourage deficit spending by government.

In general, private managers have invested much more heavily in private securities and have earned much higher rates of return than their public counterparts (figure 3.7 and chapters 5 and 6). They have incentives to allocate capital to stocks and bonds that offer the best risk-yield combinations, whether these securities are public or private. They can benefit from international diversification of investments and international managerial expertise. Governments can and do borrow from these funds but very transparently, as part of the national debt, and by paying the market interest rate.

Of course, these arrangements too are not trouble-free. Some countries simply do not have well enough developed financial markets to allow such schemes to function. Demand from pension funds will eventually stimulate the supply of financial instruments, but this process may take a long time. Another problem is that workers and employers might not have enough information to choose capable investment managers, misallocating capital and leaving some old people with inadequate pensions. To avoid this problem, privately managed pension funds must be regulated by government—but many governments do not have this capability. A third problem is that privately managed funds may have higher marketing costs and may not benefit from economies of scale as much as publicly managed funds; but by contrast public funds may have less incentive for cost efficiency than private ones (issue brief 5). Chapters 5 and 6 discuss in detail how countries can solve these problems and continue to get the benefits of private management of mandatory pension funds.

Which Pillars, Which Design Features?

THIS STUDY ANALYZES THREE FINANCING AND MANAGERIAL arrangements for old age security that give different answers to the five key policy questions (table 3.1).

- *Public plans* are by far the largest and most pervasive in the formal system. They are used in all OECD and Eastern European countries and in most Latin American countries. They are mandatory and redistributive, offer defined benefits that are largely financed on a pay-as-you-go basis, and are publicly managed.

Table 3.1 Alternative Financing and Managerial Arrangements for Old Age Security

	Formal			Informal
Characteristic	Public plans	Occupational plans	Personal savings	Extended family
Voluntary or mandatory	Mandatory	Voluntary or mandatory	Voluntary or mandatory	Social sanctions
Redistribution	Yes	Yes	Minor	Family
Benefits closely linked to contributions	No	Mixed	Yes	Within family
Defined benefits or defined contributions	Defined benefits	Mixed	Defined contributions	n.a.
Type of risk	Political	Job mobility, company insolvency	Investment	Joint family risk
Pay-as-you-go or fully funded	Pay-as-you-go	Mixed	Fully funded	Mixed
Public or private management	Public	Private	Public or private	Private
Examples	Eastern Europe Latin America OECD countries	Australia Brazil France Netherlands South Africa Switzerland	Mandatory: Chile Malaysia Singapore Voluntary: United Kingdom United States	Most of Africa and Asia

n.a. Not applicable.

- *Occupational plans* are also found in many countries and cover about 40 percent of the labor force in OECD countries (table 5.1). They are sponsored by employers, are usually voluntary—but in some countries have become mandatory—have some redistributive effects based on the employer's objectives, can be a defined benefit or defined contribution, and are largely funded in industrialized countries but unfunded or only partially funded in developing countries. Private sector plans are privately managed, whereas schemes for government workers, which are quite common, are publicly managed.

■ *Personal saving plans* are usually voluntary but have become compulsory in several countries. They are defined contribution, generally not redistributive, and fully funded. When mandatory, they can be publicly managed (Malaysia, Singapore) or privately managed and regulated by the government (Chile).

The choice among these arrangements for old age support—public, occupational, and personal savings—has major implications for the efficiency of labor and capital markets, the fiscal balance of government, and the distribution of income in society. In making this choice, governments should aim to maximize the national income and to distribute it equitably among old and young, rich and poor. Old age security programs should thus be an instrument of growth and a social safety net.

They should help the old by:

■ Facilitating people's efforts to shift some of their income from their active working years to old age (the saving or income-smoothing function).
■ Redistributing income to the old who are lifetime poor but avoiding perverse intragenerational and unintended intergenerational redistributions.
■ Providing insurance against the many risks to which the old are especially vulnerable, including longevity, disability, and inflation risks.

They should help the economy as a whole by:

■ Minimizing hidden costs that impede growth, such as reduced employment, reduced saving, heavy fiscal burdens, misallocated capital and labor, heavy administrative expenses, and evasion.
■ Being sustainable, in the sense that expected revenues cover expected payouts in the long run after taking account of expected changes in economic and demographic conditions, some of which may be induced by the old age system chosen.
■ Being simple and transparent, to enable workers, citizens, and policymakers to make informed choices, and insulated from political manipulation that leads to poor economic outcomes.

In the following chapters, each arrangement is evaluated according to these criteria—showing its strengths, its weaknesses, and the complementarities among them. The conclusion: a multipillar system, including two mandatory pillars—a publicly managed pillar concentrating on redistribution and a privately managed (personal saving or occupational) pillar concentrating on saving—supplemented by a third, voluntary pillar, may be the best way to achieve the many objectives of an old age security system.

CHAPTER 4

Public Pension Plans

P UBLIC PENSION PLANS—MANDATORY, PUBLICLY MAN-aged, defined benefit, largely pay-as-you-go, and backed by the power of taxation—have the unique capability to redistribute income to the lifetime poor and to poorer generations as a group. This is their big advantage over other financing arrangements for old age security, and their success in achieving this poverty alleviation objective may be taken as the litmus test of a well-functioning public plan.

Public pension plans have indeed improved the well-being of the first old generations covered in many countries. But their redistributive potential has sometimes been used to benefit rich rather than poor individuals or to help one generation at the expense of another even when not justified on equity grounds. And the social costs—evasion, forgone and misallocated labor, capital, and public resources—have been large.

In both developing and industrial countries, public old age schemes are beset with contradictions and myths. This chapter sorts out myths from realities, analyzes the sources of problems, and proposes solutions. The public pillar is supposed to:

- Redistribute to the poor. *But many rich people get back in pensions more than they contributed, while many poor people do not collect any benefits.*
- Augment the income of the old who can no longer work productively. *But many recipients are middle-aged and still capable of working.*
- Protect the old from risk by defining the benefits in advance. *But these benefits are redefined frequently, so considerable risk remains.*
- Protect the old against inflation. *But many governments have failed to index fully, using inflation to reduce their real costs.*

- Be a remedy for myopia among workers. *But the program's implementation often demonstrates the myopia of politicians, in some cases causing the old age system to collapse.*

The problems facing public pension plans stem partly from poor design features such as early retirement and overgenerous wage replacement rates that favor high-income groups—features that seemingly can be fixed without jettisoning the basic structure. But more basic problems stem from the separation of benefits from contributions that induces evasion, labor and capital market distortions, wasteful use of pension reserves—and political pressures for poor design features. The dilemma facing policymakers is how to achieve the redistributive objectives that only the public pillar can fulfill—while avoiding perverse transfers and inefficiencies that impede growth.

The Evolution of Publicly Financed Old Age Pensions

PUBLICLY MANAGED PENSION SCHEMES WITH DEFINED BENE-fits and pay-as-you-go finance, usually based on a payroll tax, have become the most common way for governments to provide income support for the old. Coverage currently ranges from virtually universal in industrial countries to about 50 percent in middle-income countries and 10 to 20 percent in lower-income countries. For many countries, old age security programs are the largest single item in the consolidated government budget, exceeding 20 percent of the total (table 4.1 and appendix tables A.4 and A.5).

Industrial Countries

Until the advent of industrialization and urbanization, families were the main means of support for the old in most European countries. But these methods were rendered obsolete by the mass migrations to urban centers by the end of the nineteenth century and much earlier in the United Kingdom. Economic change, uncertainty, and the absence of reliable financial instruments made it difficult for people to plan and save for their old age. A growing number of old poor

Table 4.1 Public Pension Spending and Coverage

(national averages by income group)

Income level	Pension spending as percentage of GDP	Pension spending as percentage of government expenditures	Coverage of public pension scheme
Low	0.7 (32)	3.9 (18)	10.2 (19)
Lower-middle	2.9 (29)	10.1 (16)	27.9 (16)
Upper-middle	6.7 (20)	23.8 (13)	50.7 (7)
High	8.2 (23)	23.1 (20)	95.8 (12)

Note: Number in parentheses indicates number of countries for which data are available.

Source: World Bank staff.

filled poorhouses ill equipped to deal with their special problems (Weaver 1982).

The industrial working class began to demand new ways to deal with old age income security. One response was the friendly society, a mutual relief fund to which workers contributed a nominal sum and which was used to provide assistance in the event of injury, death, or declining income because of old age. But these funds were often mismanaged, their coverage was limited, many people did not join, the amounts involved were small, and their membership was too restricted for adequate risk pooling. In 1889 German chancellor Otto von Bismarck seized a political opportunity to mollify industrial workers and lure them away from the socialists by creating the first national contributory old age insurance scheme, giving workers a stake in the central government (Kohler and Zacher 1982).

At the turn of the century European countries were debating whether to provide broadly based contributory old age social insurance as in Germany—or narrower means-tested noncontributory schemes for the old to complement the poor laws that applied to everyone (Petersen 1986). Arguments for the contributory schemes were the universality of the old age problem, their self-financing aspect, and the disincentives to work and saving posed by means-tested programs. Arguments for the noncontributory schemes were their lower cost (since not all the old needed public intervention) and their greater efficacy at alleviating poverty. These arguments—pro and con—are still heard today. In 1891 Denmark put in place a means-tested program, and means-tested old age schemes were subsequently adopted in Australia, France, Iceland,

Ireland, New Zealand, and the United Kingdom. But social insurance schemes were becoming increasingly common. By the start of World War II, national contributory schemes, partially funded and partially pay-as-you-go, had been created in Austria, Belgium, Bulgaria, Czechoslovakia, France, Greece, Hungary, Italy, Luxembourg, the Netherlands, Poland, Portugal, Romania, Spain, Sweden, the United Kingdom, and the United States (Weaver 1982).

Whatever the type of scheme, all publicly managed pensions before World War II were modest, providing no more than 15 to 20 percent of the average wage, with most workers expected to live only a few years after retirement (table 4.2). These modest benefits—combined with the predominance of means-tested old age pensions in the British Commonwealth and the Nordic countries—reflected the original goals of public schemes: to provide a bare subsistence and to reduce poverty.

In 1942 the Beveridge Report in England called for a new and larger public sector role in old age security. Confident in the government's ability to compensate for private market failures, Beveridge saw publicly financed pensions as a way for the emerging social welfare state to

Table 4.2 Ratio of Average Pension to Average Wage in Selected OECD Countries, 1939 and 1980

Country	1939 (actual) (1)	1980 (synthetic)[a] (2)
Australia	19	—
Belgium	14	—
Canada	17	34
Denmark	22	29
Germany	19	49
Italy	15	69
Netherlands	13	44
Norway	8	—
Sweden	10	68
Switzerland	—	37
United Kingdom	13	31
United States	21	44
Average	15.4	45.0

— Not available.

a. Synthetic replacement rates are simulated percentages of final salary for single workers with average wages in manufacturing for 1980.

Source: (1): replacement rates for 1939 from SSIB data files, Esping-Anderson (1990). (2): Aldrich (1982).

guarantee a minimum income to all older citizens. Although the amount of the pension Beveridge had in mind is still a matter of dispute, it was clearly meant to provide a more generous pension to a greater percentage of the old than had the earlier means-tested schemes (Atkinson 1991a).

How could these ambitious goals be financed? With funded pension schemes discredited by the financial disarray of the interwar and wartime periods, public pension plans increasingly became contributory, payroll-tax-financed, and pay-as-you-go. Conditions for the success of such a scheme could not have been better. The two crucial variables for a pay-as-you-go pension system—population growth and real wage growth—were at historically high rates (Maddison 1987). A *Newsweek* editorial by Paul Samuelson in 1967 (February 13) captures the enthusiasm:

This in the post WW2 period.

> The beauty of social insurance is that it is actuarially unsound. Everyone who reaches retirement age is given benefit privileges that far exceed anything he has paid in…. How is this possible? It stems from the fact that the national product is growing at compound interest and can be expected to do so for as far ahead as the eye cannot see. Always there are more youths than old folks in a growing population. More important, with real incomes growing at some three percent a year, the taxable base upon which benefits rest in any period are much greater than the taxes paid historically by the generation now retired…. A growing nation is the greatest Ponzi game ever contrived.

The result was the creation of new social insurance schemes or tiers in Switzerland (1949), the Netherlands (1957), Sweden (1960), Norway (1966), and Canada (1966), and the dramatic expansion of schemes in the rest of Europe, Japan, and the United States. All public pension systems were expanded and made more generous, usually by adding a large earnings-related tier to the existing, smaller means-tested or flat tier (table 4.2). Australia and New Zealand were the only industrial countries that refused to make pensions dependent on prior earnings and contributions. These new, expensive, pay-as-you-go plans produced massive lifetime transfers to the generations retiring in the 1960s and 1970s—substantially reducing old age poverty.

But it is not clear that much thought was given to their long-run consequences. Today, just as OECD plans are beginning to mature, the conditions conducive to a successful pay-as-you-go scheme are fast disappearing. Population growth is coming to a halt. Mortality rates are decreasing among the old, raising their share in the population. Wage growth is slowing dramatically, and public pension plans are in trouble in industrialized countries.

Developing and Transitional Countries

The enthusiasm for public pension schemes soon spread to developing countries. Even before World War II, countries such as Argentina, Brazil, Chile, and Uruguay had contributory schemes with substantial coverage, schemes that initially were supposed to be funded. When low investment returns and rising benefits hit the funded schemes, these countries switched to pay-as-you-go financing, allowing them to pay more generous pensions to greater numbers of old people. After World War II, a few former British colonies—India, Singapore, and later parts of Africa—opted for funded provident schemes. But most developing countries, some of them newly independent and newly establishing their social policies, established contributory pay-as-you-go plans. In the republics of the Soviet Union and Eastern Europe, old age pensions were included as part of the cradle-to-the-grave security that communism was supposed to provide all workers.

Developing countries created public pension plans at a much earlier stage of economic and demographic development than industrialized countries. These countries were poorer when they started these plans, their populations were younger, and they had less ability to tax and administer complex public programs. More than 8 percent of the German and U.S. populations were over 60 years old when their first national pension schemes were instituted. In contrast, dozens of developing countries established such programs when only 4 percent of their population was over 60, and most of the old lived in rural areas.

Developing countries also promised higher income replacement rates than industrial countries had when they started. As a result, many developing countries today spend more on pensions than industrial countries did at a similar stage of development. A cross-section of ninety-two countries today shows much higher pension spending as a percentage of GDP than occurred historically in the United Kingdom, for comparable demographic conditions (figure 4.1). Yet, with a few exceptions (Mauritius and Trinidad and Tobago), little of this money is going to poverty

Figure 4.1 Pension Spending during the Demographic Transition: United Kingdom Historical Pattern versus Current Global Pattern

Public spending as a percentage of GDP

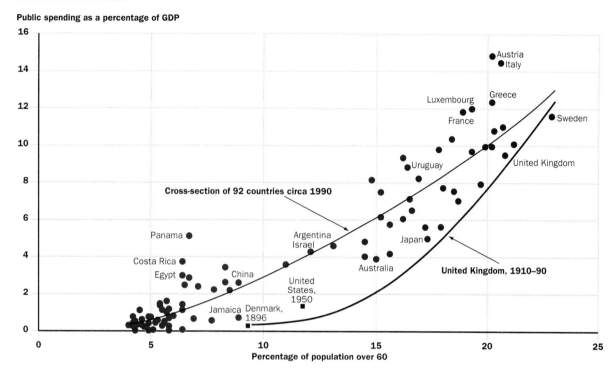

Note: Because of space limitations, not all data points are identified. For the United Kingdom, data show fitted line for fifteen observations between 1910 and 1990. For cross-section of ninety-two countries circa 1990, see figure 1.8. See text for further explanation.
Source: Palacios (1994a); Johnson (1985); United Kingdom (1899); U.S. Social Security Administration.

alleviation and noncontributory social assistance. One result is the juxtaposition of a formal public pension system for a privileged minority of workers with an informal system for most of the population. A second result, most obvious in Latin America and Eastern Europe, is that many developing and transitional countries can no longer afford their pension arrangements.

Developing countries spend more on pensions than did industrial countries at the same stage of the demographic transition.

Why a Dominant Public Pillar? The Politics of Social Security

Public management and financing are clearly needed to address the redistributive side of old age security programs. But the saving and insurance side could be addressed, in large part, through private plans—mandated and regulated by government. Some believe that this would be a more efficient system. Others believe that if government is going to redistribute and to mandate and regulate saving and insurance, it would be more cost-effective for government to provide the entire package in the first place. A major question analyzed by this report is whether combining these functions in one dominant public pillar is an efficient way to go.

Besides this normative question is the positive question of why dominant public plans have evolved in most countries. Why have these combined programs won widespread public support, and why did citizens and policymakers choose to finance them out of payroll taxes on a pay-as-you-go basis? One explanation is that workers who pay the taxes to support the program view it as an implicit, ongoing intergenerational contract. Current workers pay for the pensions of current retirees and expect to receive pensions that others will pay for in the future—very much like an extension of the informal system. But there is much to throw doubt on this explanation. These implicit contracts are not enforceable. They have frequently been changed. Evasion and strategic manipulation are common problems. And predictable lifetime redistributions among generations are involved, so not all cohorts gain.

Another explanation is that workers may not pay much attention to old age security programs when they are young, but once they reach middle age they have accumulated substantial entitlements in existing pay-as-you-go programs. At that point, they are better off if the program continues—even if they would have been still better off with a fully funded defined contribution plan from the start. This does not explain why a country chooses pay-as-you-go in the first place. But it does explain why, once in motion, these plans are very difficult to change. They have a built-in constituency, which is at its most politically influential stage of life.

Still another political explanation is that middle- and high-income workers realize that a basic income floor is necessary to prevent old age poverty, but they want to achieve this with a minimum amount of redistribution. The financing method used by public plans typically contains many provisions that limit redistribution. For example, contributory programs help only people who have worked most of their lives. The payroll taxes generally used are based on earnings from labor, not income from capital. There is a ceiling on taxable earnings. Pensions are usually higher for people with higher wages. Rich people live longer than poor people and so receive more annual payments. The design of the public pillar thus limits redistribution to the poor, making it more acceptable politically to the rich.

Perhaps the most plausible political explanation for the popularity of public pension plans comes from the demographic transition and the life cycle of a typical program (see chapter 3 and issue brief 6). Pay-as-you-go schemes have generally been instituted during periods of rapid population growth, initially paying large benefits to old people who have contributed relatively little. In countries with young populations (many workers), an immature old age security system (few retirees), and expanding coverage, current and promised benefits can be generous while costing little in current taxes. Under these circumstances, practically everyone—young and old, rich and poor—benefits in the early years. The appearance of a high rate of return is intensified by the fact that employers usually pay part of the tax, and workers may not realize that much of the cost has been shifted to them in the form of lower wages.

Problems develop later, as systems mature, birthrates taper off, and life expectancy increases—reducing the returns and transfers for future generations. These effects are worse if growth in labor productivity has been dampened, perhaps as a consequence of the old age system itself. Those who support the pay-as-you-go public plan at the beginning may fail to realize that their grandchildren will pay a high price. Many years later, however, they may regret the fact that they have gone:

> down the primrose path of unfunded employee pensions and in-adequately funded social security programs…. When population growth slows down, so that we no longer have the comfortable Ponzi rate of growth or we even begin to register a decline in total numbers, then the thorns along the primrose path reveal themselves with a vengeance (Samuelson in Wise, 1985, p. 442).

How Public Pension Plans Work

ALTHOUGH MOST PUBLIC PENSION PLANS ARE LARGELY PAY-as-you-go, are financed by a payroll tax, and pay a defined benefit, there are many variations on this theme. Some countries build up large reserves. Some use general revenue finance. The defined benefit may change often. And it may be flat, means-tested, or earnings-related. (Publicly managed plans that are fully funded and based on defined contributions, known as provident funds, are discussed in chapter 6.)

Pay-as-You-Go versus Partial Funding

Under a pure contributory pay-as-you-go plan, the benefits received by current retirees determine the taxes paid by current workers. If the system is financed by a payroll tax (as it usually is), the contribution or payroll tax rate C depends on the benefit rate B (average benefit/average wage) times the dependency ratio D (beneficiaries/covered workers), or $C = BD$. For example, if there is one retiree for every four workers and if beneficiaries have been promised an average pension equal to 40 percent of the average wage, a 10 percent contribution rate will cover system costs (table 4.3).

If the dependency ratio rises to one retiree for every two workers, either the contribution rate must be raised to 20 percent or the benefit rate must be slashed to 20 percent of the average wage. Important factors left out of this equation—such as administrative costs, unemployment, early retirement, survivors' benefits, ceilings on taxable earnings, and evasion—could raise the required contribution rate to 30 percent or more. This is the situation many countries are in today—or will be tomorrow.

Pure pay-as-you-go plans are rare in the real world. Most public plans accumulate a current cash surplus in their early years, but as the systems mature and populations age their reserves disappear and the plans shift into current deficit. The initial cash surplus is an illusion, since it is only a partial offset to the implicit pension debt that is building up, and the later deficit means that some of this debt is being covered by broader tax (or bond) revenues. This is the life cycle of a pay-as-you-go system (issue brief 6 and figure 4.2). Today, partially funded (or scaled premium) systems are common in countries with young populations, such as Egypt,

Table 4.3 Contribution Rates Required for Different Benefit and Dependency Rates under Pay-as-You-Go

Benefit rate (percent)	Dependency rate				
	1/2	1/3	1/4	1/5	1/10
100	50	33	25	20	10
80	40	27	20	16	8
60	30	20	15	12	6
40	20	13	10	8	4
20	10	7	5	4	2

Source: World Bank staff.

Figure 4.2 Pension System Surplus or Deficit as Share of System Revenues (1986) and Old Age Dependency Ratio (1990)

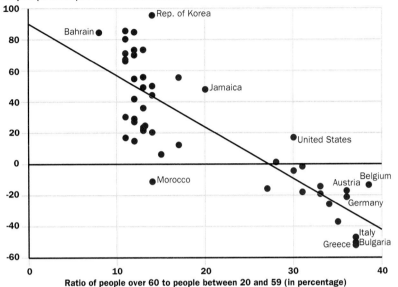

Surplus (or deficit) as share of total revenues

Ratio of people over 60 to people between 20 and 59 (in percentage)

Early pension system surpluses are an illusion—they soon become a deficit nightmare.

Note: Because of space limitations, not all data points are identified. $R^2 = 0.68$. SUR/REV = $89.0086 - 327.688 \times$ OADEP, where SUR/REV is the ratio of system surplus or deficit to total system revenues and OADEP is the old age dependency ratio.

Source: Calculated from data from ILO (1992a). World Bank population data base.

Guyana, Honduras, Jordan, Mexico, the Philippines, the Republic of Korea, and Tunisia. A few industrial countries, such as Canada, Japan, Sweden, and the United States, also have partly capitalized systems, accumulating substantial reserves in preparation for the pension liabilities they will soon have to pay off. But most industrial countries and older Latin American and Eastern European countries rely primarily on pay-as-you-go finance, supplemented by growing payments from the national treasury.

Defined Benefits and Risk

Public pension plans use a defined benefit formula that promises a specified pension to retirees. Most also include disability and survivors' benefits. The most important characteristic of defined benefit formulas is that they supposedly reduce the risk of income uncertainty in old age;

risk is transferred to younger workers, who are considered to be more resilient in the face of unexpected change. This freedom from risk is somewhat illusory, however, since most governments change their benefit promises many times over a typical worker's lifetime (box 4.1).

The second important characteristic of these formulas is that they break the link between benefits and contributions. Annuities sold by private insurance companies make defined benefits contingent on contributions according to actuarial, market-based principles, but defined benefit formulas used by public pension plans virtually never do so. To maintain such a connection the public plan would essentially have to

Box 4.1 How Defined Are Defined Benefits?

ADVOCATES OF PUBLIC DEFINED BENEFIT schemes argue that governments should shield pensioners from the vagaries of capital markets and other risks. Contribution rates are adjusted to cover the defined benefit, which transfers risks to younger workers, who are considered to be more resilient in the face of unexpected change. Just how defined are the benefits in pay-as-you-go public pension schemes? In most countries benefit levels fluctuate less from year to year than stock market prices do, but over the longer run defined benefits change frequently, so substantial risk remains.

Calculating the defined benefit. When the defined benefit is flat, workers know just what pensions they will receive. But when benefits are earnings-related, the value of the benefit depends on the wage base used to calculate the pension, marital status, and other aspects of the worker's personal and employment history. Often benefit formulas are so complex that few people can calculate their expected pension. Some of the complexity may serve a useful purpose by building flexibility into the system so that pensions can adjust to different circumstances. Higher benefits for workers with dependents are an example of an efficient contingent benefit. But some contingencies may increase risk or be prone to strategic manipulation. Tying pension benefits to wages during the last few years of employment is an example.

Changing the rules of the game. Even if workers have enough information to calculate their pensions, the attempt would be meaningless, since benefit formulas change so frequently. Not one public defined benefit scheme has held to the same benefit formula over lifetimes of a cohort of members. When public schemes were running surpluses and the fiscal environment was favorable, governments frequently raised benefits. The average replacement rate doubled in Japan between 1969 and 1980 (OECD 1988b). In the United States the ratio of average pension to average wage rose from 0.14 to 0.37 between 1950 and 1980 (U.S. Social Security Administration, various years). France raised its replacement rate 50 percent and lowered the retirement age to 60 in the 1970s. But when public pension schemes run into deficits, whether because of maturation of the scheme, aging of the population, or general fiscal pressures, governments cut benefits.

- Germany, Sweden, and the United States have scheduled increases in the retirement age; France and the United Kingdom are considering doing so.
- France recently increased the number of years used to calculate the wage base and the number of years required to qualify for a full pension.

"sell" a small annuity to the worker each year in exchange for the contributions made that year. The price of the annuity would depend on the worker's age (young workers would get better terms) and life expectancy (which raises problems concerning pooling of risk categories, discussed in issue brief 10), as well as the expected future interest rate in the economy and the retirement age at which the payments could begin. Each year the worker would purchase a somewhat different annuity, as the size of the annual contribution and the variables determining the annuity price change. When the worker retired, all these small annuities would be added together to determine the total pension.

- The United States effectively reduced the defined benefit for higher-income retirees by making 50 percent of the pension taxable in 1984 and raising the taxable share to 85 percent in 1994. The average wage replacement rate also declined over this period.
- Japan's defined benefits were made less generous in 1986.
- In 1992 Iceland shifted from a universal flat benefit to a means-tested benefit, and thousands of pensioners had their benefits reduced or eliminated.
- Turkey is considering a higher retirement age, lower replacement rates, and more radical reforms to deal with a nearly insolvent pension system.
- Benefits have been severely eroded by inflation and in a few cases by outright cuts in the formerly socialist economies, as declining per capita incomes, aging populations, and early retirement left them no alternative.

While many of these changes constitute desirable reforms, workers who planned for their retirement under the old rules of the game have not been protected from risk. By far the most common tool for downgrading defined benefits is inflation without indexation (box 4.8).

Undefining defined benefits. In several countries people have brought suit to determine whether defined benefit promises are enforceable by law. The United States Supreme Court ruled in 1960 that social security beneficiaries do not have a legally enforceable contract and that the government can cut off benefits at any time (Ferrara 1985). The Brazilian Supreme Court ruled to the contrary in 1992, finding that the government must honor promises made to pensioners. A year later the Brazilian government still had not paid these benefits, which would have required raising benefit levels by 147 percent at a cost of US$10 billion (Lloyd-Sherlock 1992). In 1994, after long-standing litigation, the constitutional court in Italy ruled that the government had to make good the difference between the full benefits owed and the reduced benefits it had paid, dating back as far as 1983, which would cost the government more than US$3.8 billion in arrears plus more than US$380 million annually (*Financial Times,* June 1994). It is not clear when or how the Italian government will raise the money; possibly some of it will come from reducing future pension promises. Thus experience has taught members of most public schemes around the world, especially in developing countries, that their defined benefits are, to a large extent, undefined.

While it would be possible for public pension plans to operate in this manner, none of them do so, possibly because it would entail detailed records and interest rate projections, but more likely because it would require that all redistributions become explicit. Instead, public pension plans rely on defined benefit formulas that fail to make benefits actuarially dependent on contributions and imply substantial redistributions that are implicit and nontransparent.

Flat, Means-Tested, or Earnings-Related Benefits

The defined benefit formula takes different forms in different countries:

- Universal flat, with the same benefits for everyone above a certain age, regardless of income and work history
- Employment-related flat, with the same benefits for everyone per year of covered employment
- Means-tested, with higher benefits for those with lower income or smaller assets
- Minimum pension guarantee or top-up to a mandatory saving scheme
- Earnings-related, with higher benefits for those who have earned and contributed more.

Flat and means-tested benefits are more common in industrial than in developing countries, possibly because they work best where coverage is widespread and tax collection effective (table 4.4). A flat benefit is the mainstay of the public pension plans in Canada, Iceland, Mauritius, the Netherlands, New Zealand, and South Africa. In Japan, the flat benefit is both contributory and universal: workers and the self-employed pay flat contributions for themselves and their dependent spouses, and all contributors receive a flat benefit at age 65. Jamaica, Switzerland, and the United Kingdom use an employment-related flat formula as an important part of their plans. Broadly based means-tested benefits predominate in Australia, Hong Kong, and Trinidad and Tobago. Canada, Denmark, Norway, and Sweden offer a generous combination of flat, means-tested, and earnings-related benefits. In countries that have a mandatory saving plan, as in Chile, the public plan can take the form of a top-up or minimum pension—designed to get the individual to a specified level if the savings are not enough to do the job. This is a special variation of a means-tested scheme. In most OECD countries with

Table 4.4 Spending on Universal Flat and Means-Tested Old Age Benefits, Selected Countries, 1986–92

	Spending on universal flat or means-tested pensions as percentage of total spending on old age pensions	Number receiving flat or means-tested pension as percentage of number of persons over 65	Universal flat and/ or means-tested benefit as percentage of non-agricultural wage		Spending on universal flat or means-tested pensions as percentage of total spending on old age pensions	Number receiving flat or means-tested pension as percentage of number of persons over 65	Universal flat and/ or means-tested benefit as percentage of non-agricultural wage
More than U.S.$11,200 purchasing power per capita				*Less than U.S.$11,200 purchasing power per capita*			
New Zealand[a]	100	100	39	Mauritius	94	100	10
Hong Kong	100	73	21	Trinidad and			
Australia[a]	100	80	28	Tobago[b]	57	56	—
Netherlands	100	100	38	Costa Rica[b]	16	20	11
Iceland	73	93	30	Jamaica	8	16	—
Denmark	72	89	29	Portugal	8	16	15
Canada	64	97	27	Latvia	5	6	—
Norway	57	88	30	Uruguay	5	16	17
Sweden	39	100	28	Venezuela	5	12	7
Ireland	33	39	17	Brazil	4	22	—
Finland	32	100	22	Greece	1	2	—
United Kingdom	7	20	13	Egypt	0	7	—
France	6	17	19	Romania	0	11	—
Luxembourg	4	7	—	Argentina[b]	—	3	6
Germany	4	—	—	China	—	4	—
Italy	4	9	25				
Belgium	3	5	33				
Spain	2	3	16				
United States	1	7	13				

— Not available.

a. Not including spending on government employees' scheme.

b. 1983 for column 2.

Source: Eurostat (1992); Nordic Countries Statistical Secretariat (1993); U.S. Social Security Administration (various years); Banco de Prevision Social de Uruguay (1991); D. Mitchell (1993); Pan-American Health Organization (1989b and 1990b); Holzmann (1992); Mauritius (1987); Jamaica (1993); Palacios (1994b).

flat or means-tested benefits, the basic pension is typically about 20 to 30 percent of the average nonagricultural wage. The share is much lower, more variable, and difficult to define in developing countries.

Most countries feature earnings-related pensions, supplemented by smaller means-tested components. In theory, contributions and benefits, both tied to prior earnings, are thereby tied to each other, reducing the incentive to evade. In practice, however, this connection is very loose. The higher contribution rates required by earnings-related schemes may, in fact, raise the incentives to evade.

Two types of earnings-related formulas are used. In the more common type, used in practically all developing countries, eligible retirees receive a benefit equal to their wage base times an accrual rate for every year of covered service. The pensionable wage base is usually the last one to three years of earnings, which strongly favors high-wage earners whose income rises steeply with age.

In some OECD countries, such as the United States and Switzerland, the pension is based on average annual lifetime earnings over a thirty- to thirty-five-year period, with early year earnings revalued upward according to inflation or average wage growth in the economy. In these countries, a higher proportion of average earnings is paid to lower-income workers. This progressive formula is difficult to apply in developing countries, where workers move in and out of covered status and underreporting of incomes is relatively easy.

The choice among flat, means-tested, and earnings-related benefit formulas goes to the heart of system design. Flat and means-tested schemes have a limited poverty alleviation goal and more readily permit a separation between the redistributive and saving functions through a multipillar system. Earnings-related schemes, to a large extent, combine these functions and facilitate the growth of a dominant public pillar (boxes 4.2 and 4.3). (See appendix table A.7 for more detailed data on benefits and other characteristics of public pension plans.)

Payroll Taxes or General Revenue Finance

Public pension benefits—especially earnings-related benefits—are mainly financed through an earmarked payroll tax, usually with a ceiling on taxable earnings. The tax, generally shared between workers and employers, ranges from 3 percent in a few African and South Asian countries with very young populations to more than 25 percent in older countries with mature schemes, such as Brazil, Bulgaria, Hungary, Italy, Poland, Russia, and Uruguay (figure 4.3). The ceiling on taxable earnings varies widely, but often it is two or three times the average wage. The lower the ceiling the narrower and less progressive is the tax structure and the higher the tax rate required to cover expenditures.

Universal flat and means-tested benefits are often intentionally financed out of general revenues, in keeping with their redistributive in-

Box 4.2 Pros and Cons of Flat versus Means-Tested Benefits

MEANS-TESTED PLANS HAVE TWO KEY ADVAN-tages. They:

■ Incur lower costs or allow larger benefit payments for the same expenditure, thereby having a stronger poverty alleviation impact. (Australia's means-tested pension reaches 70 percent of the population but costs only half as much, as a proportion of GDP, as New Zealand's universal flat benefit.)

■ Keep the rich from collecting larger lifetime transfers than the poor. This is especially important in countries where coverage is usually limited to higher-income groups and where life expectancy is much greater for the rich than for the poor.

Means-tested plans also have three key disadvantages. They:

■ Incur administrative costs plus stigma and take-up problems. (In the United Kingdom 21 percent of people eligible for the income-tested supplement don't apply for it.)

■ Set up perverse incentives for people not to save when young or work when old and near the income threshold (the poverty trap).

■ May become politically unpopular in times of budgetary stringency, since middle-income groups do not benefit.

In contrast, *flat benefits*:

■ Involve minimal record-keeping and transaction costs, important considerations when administrative skills and work records are scarce.

■ Avoid the high marginal tax rate, disincentives to work and save, and stigma and take-up problems that come with means-tested programs.

■ And they provide a basic income floor (say, 20 percent of the average wage) to all old people, thereby coinsuring and possibly winning wider political support.

The big disadvantage of flat benefits is their higher cost, requiring higher tax rates, much of which goes to upper-income groups. Some of these costs can be "clawed back" by subjecting benefits to income taxes—which, in a progressive tax system, would re-

(Box continues on the following page.)

tent. But even in earnings-related schemes that are supposed to be contributory, the payroll tax frequently fails to cover burgeoning benefits, and the unplanned deficits are met by transfers from the general treasury (figure 4.2). Australia, Hong Kong, New Zealand, and South Africa finance flat and means-tested benefits out of general revenues. Chile pays for the minimum pension guarantee through the public treasury. Canada and Denmark finance flat and means-tested benefits out of general revenues and the earnings-related component out of payroll contributions. In France, Greece, and Italy, despite high payroll taxes, contributions are lower than promised benefits, and large deficits are covered by general tax revenues. (See appendix table A.6 for more comprehensive data on sources of revenue.)

Box 4.2 *(continued)*

sult in lower net benefits for the rich. However, this would not work effectively in developing countries that have little capacity to collect income taxes. The disadvantages probably outweigh the advantages in countries with very low incomes, where the transaction costs of paying small pensions to every old person would be relatively high, and in countries with disparate income distributions, where a small flat benefit would have little value to the rich and targeting public transfers to the poor is particularly important.

A variant, the *employment-related flat benefit*, provides a specified flat benefit (say, 0.75 percent of the average wage) for every year of employment. It has many of the same advantages as the flat benefit but to different degrees and may be the preferred option in situations in which administrative and fiscal resources do not permit universal coverage. Compared with universal flat benefits, employment-related flat benefits:

- Cost less or enable higher pensions for long-term employees.
- Require more record-keeping (on years of covered employment).

- Are less likely to reach the poorest groups, such as old women or people who have been unemployed for long periods of their adult lives, making it a weaker measure for alleviating poverty—that is their big disadvantage.
- But are more likely to deter evasion—that is their big advantage.

A *minimum pension guarantee* or *top-up scheme* may be used in conjunction with a mandatory retirement saving scheme. Workers who fail to accumulate enough savings to purchase a minimum pension when they retire could receive the difference from general tax revenues. This:

- Is the cheapest way to eliminate old age poverty.
- Eliminates transaction costs and stigma and take-up problems because it is automatic and based on records maintained by the mandatory saving scheme.
- Minimizes negative effects on work and saving.
- Provides less protection to people who are well above the minimum pension level than a flat benefit would.

Which tax is a better source of finance—the payroll tax or general revenue taxes? In industrial countries, general income or consumption taxes are more efficient because they have a broader base. They are also more progressive since all forms of income are taxed (labor's share of income is about 60 to 70 percent).

In developing countries, the situation is more complex. On the one hand, payroll taxes have an even narrower base (typically only 30 to 40 percent of national income) and thus require a much higher rate than income taxes, making them more distortionary. And wage rigidities may force employers to bear more of the payroll tax, reducing employment and output (see next section). But on the other hand, developing countries may not have the capability to collect income taxes. And the other general taxes (excise or import taxes) that they can collect are also distortionary (World Bank 1991b). In addition, general taxes in develop-

Box 4.3 Pros and Cons of Earnings-Related Benefits

EARNINGS-RELATED BENEFITS ARE SOMETIMES supported on the grounds that they:

- Take advantage of economies of scale and scope by combining the saving, insurance, and redistributive functions in a single public plan.
- Improve pension adequacy and reduce longevity risk for the middle classes by forcing them to contribute more when they are young and paying them a higher pension when they are old.
- Offer a closer link between contributions and benefits than flat or means-tested pensions, thereby deterring evasion.
- Generate broad popular support that sustains benefits for all, including the poor, in the long run.

The opposing argument is that combining these functions in one earnings-related public plan increases labor distortions and evasion while reducing redistribution to low-income groups:

- Paying higher benefits to high-income workers while also trying to alleviate poverty among lower-income workers requires a high contribution rate that is not closely linked to benefits. If the contribution is perceived as a tax, it may encourage workers to evade and withdraw from the formal labor force and may lead employers to cut back on employment.
- The high public spending implied by earnings-related schemes adds to the government's fiscal burden and may prevent spending on other important public goods.

- Such schemes are complicated and lead to strategic manipulation and political pressures for unrealistic pension promises and early retirement opportunities that mainly benefit privileged groups.
- Even when earnings-related benefit formulas appear to be progressive, careful empirical studies show they are not (box 4.6). Often the rich get larger transfers than the poor. OECD countries with large flat or means-tested components to their public pension plans (Canada, the Netherlands, Sweden) have lower old age poverty rates, relative to poverty rates in other population groups, than countries with predominately earnings-related plans (Germany, the United States [see figure 3.2]).
- Since access to earnings-related benefits is based on employment history, these plans are of limited help to women and others who have had little or low-paid labor market experience. In OECD countries with earnings-related benefits, old women living alone have a much higher poverty rate than other groups.
- High contribution rates and generous benefit promises reduce the supply of funds and the demand for supplementary plans, diminishing the opportunities for building a strong funded pillar. Lack of diversification increases risk for the old. Many countries have eventually defaulted on their pension promises, failing in particular to protect pensions against inflation. By the time people realize they cannot count on these promises, it is too late to arrange for alternative sources of old age support.

ing countries are often regressive, drawing heavily from low-income rural areas, whereas formal old age security programs usually limit coverage to relatively high-income urban workers. Using general tax revenues to finance pensions under these circumstances could perversely redistribute benefits from the rural poor to the urban rich.

Figure 4.3 Payroll Tax for Pensions versus Old Age Dependency Ratio, Selected Countries, 1990

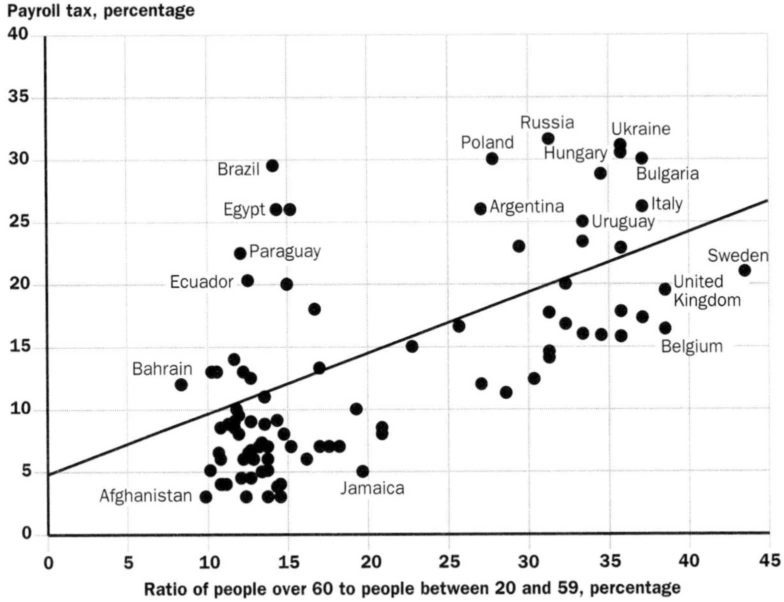

Note: Because of space limitations, not all data points are identified. $R^2 = 0.46$. PTAX = $1.7035 + 57.34 \times$ OADEP, where PTAX is the payroll tax for pensions.
Source: Calculated from data from U.S. Social Security Administration (1993); World Bank population data base.

Payroll tax rates rise steeply as populations age and pension systems mature—but some countries are way above average.

So, the choice between tax methods is not clear-cut on efficiency or equity grounds in developing countries. Most important, these considerations limit the amount of taxation that is efficient and make it all the more important to use the scarce tax revenues wisely.

How Public Pension Plans Affect the Economy

AS COUNTRIES AGE, PUBLIC PENSION PLANS HAVE CONSUMED a large share of their GDP and a much larger share of total tax revenues. These plans thus have major effects on labor and its productivity, on capital accumulation and its allocation, on the ability of government to finance public goods and services—and therefore on the growth of the economy.

Impact on Labor Markets

A public scheme that is financed through a payroll tax provides incentives for employers to reduce their hiring of labor, for workers to escape to the informal sector, and for covered workers to retire early. Therefore, it may lower the employment of trained workers and the productivity of labor—and these effects may be greater in developing than in industrial economies.

Employer and worker response to the payroll tax. If benefits were truly contingent on contributions and valued as much, the payroll tax would be viewed as a price, not a tax, and would have few distortionary effects on the labor market. This was part of the reason for most countries to opt for contributory social insurance schemes. But the defined benefit formula and pay-as-you-go method of finance break this link between benefits and contributions—benefits to some are not as great as their contributions, whereas others can get the benefits even if they do not contribute. So, workers who bear the tax may try to evade it by reducing their labor supply or escaping to the informal sector, whereas employers who bear it may reduce the quantity of labor they demand.

Who bears the tax earmarked for old age security? In most countries, the payroll tax is nominally shared by workers and employers. But the ultimate impact of the tax depends on the relative elasticities of demand and supply. In industrial countries, the supply of labor is relatively inelastic with respect to wages: most workers, especially prime age males, continue working when a tax lowers their disposable wage. In that case, workers pay not only their share but their employers' share as well, in lower wages, since wages fall enough to keep everyone employed. Although wages fall, output does not fall and the tax is not inefficient.

In the few situations in which wages cannot fall any further because a legal or social minimum has been reached, employers pay the tax and may cut back on employment and output as a result. This is inefficient. This line of thought suggests that the rise in payroll tax rates in OECD countries over the past two decades may be one possible explanation for the rise in unemployment and the more general slowdown in the growth of real wages. This process redistributes income away from workers but in an opaque way (less employment, slower wage growth) that may lead workers to pressure for a larger public pension plan than they would want if they realized its full cost.

Wage rigidities may be more common in developing and transitional economies, making it more difficult for employers to shift the tax to workers. One possible employer reaction is to substitute capital for labor, employing fewer workers as they become more expensive. But the scarcity of capital in developing countries limits the degree (and efficiency) of this adjustment. A second reaction is for employers to try to pass some of the tax on to consumers in higher prices. But in a competitive product market, especially one facing international competition, employers will be unable to raise prices. A third reaction is to cut back on production or go out of business. If the payroll taxes cannot be passed on to consumers in higher prices or to workers in lower wages, the result is likely to be unemployment, as is occurring in Eastern Europe today.

A policy conclusion: in the presence of wage rigidities, the efficiency loss is smaller if workers pay most of the tax directly. In the absence of wage rigidities, the ultimate economic effect is very similar regardless of who initially pays the tax. But the political effect may be quite different—if workers pay they are more likely to be aware of the cost and less likely to support overly generous public pension programs.

Escape to the informal sector. Another difference between industrial and developing economies stems from the lax tax enforcement in low-income countries, where workers can readily escape to the informal sector. Evasion is particularly easy in countries where labor force coverage is low and the informal sector is large. Employers, too, often move into the informal sector to avoid taxes. Even large companies can contract out some of their work to microenterprises that operate informally. Indeed, the informal sector is made up largely of workers and employers escaping payroll taxes and other regulations. A recent study in Caracas, Venezuela, found that payroll taxes accounted for one-third of the costs of becoming formal (Cartaya 1992). Roughly half the workers in Bolivia, Costa Rica, Guatemala, Honduras, and Paraguay are in the informal labor market (figure 4.4 and issue brief 7 on evasion).

The growth of the informal sector defeats the main purpose of the public pension scheme—to see that workers contribute in their youth to financial security for their old age. It also hurts the government's fiscal capacity, labor productivity, and national output. Workers and employers in the informal sector generally try to avoid taxes of all sorts, reducing government revenue. And workers in the informal sector may have lower productivity because they have less access to capital, on-the-

Figure 4.4 Percentage of Labor Force in the Informal Sector, Selected Latin American Countries, Late 1980s

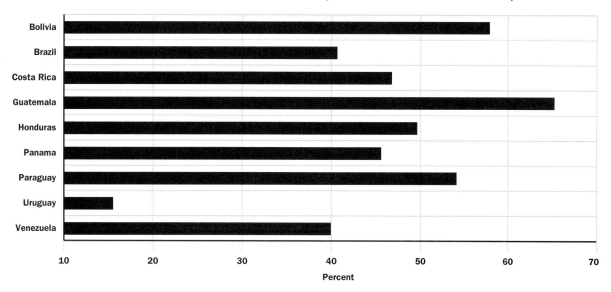

Source: Psacharopoulos and others (1993).

job training, and broad product markets. If marginal output per worker in the informal labor force is 20 percent lower than in the formal sector and if the payroll tax causes 20 percent of workers to operate informally, labor's contribution to annual GDP would be cut by 4 percent. The efficiency loss in the labor market from high payroll tax rates may thus be more substantial in developing than in industrial countries.

Early retirement. In developing and transitional countries, the legal retirement age is lower than in high-income countries. The effective retirement age and the labor force participation by older men has been declining almost everywhere (issue brief 8 and issue brief table 8).

The legal retirement age in public pension plans in developing countries is typically 60 for men and 55 for women, compared with 65 for men and women in most high-income countries. One obvious explanation is shorter life expectancy. But the higher incomes and above-average longevity of covered workers suggest an alternative explanation: provisions for early retirement are secured by politically influential groups who use this as a nontransparent way to gain from public pension plans.

A large informal sector makes tax evasion easier—and defeats the purpose of a public pension scheme.

123

Figure 4.5 Expected Duration of Retirement for Men, Selected Countries, Late 1980s

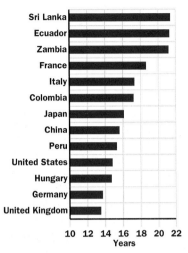

Note: This refers to life expectancy at the legal retirement age.
Source: United Nations (1992b); U.S. Social Security Administration (1993).

Males retiring at the normal retirement age often live longer in developing countries than in industrial countries.

Consistent with the latter explanation, the average person lives longer after retirement in many developing countries than in industrial countries. For example, the average male in Ecuador who retires at the standard retirement age can expect to have eight more years of retirement than his counterpart in Germany (figure 4.5).

The effective retirement age is even lower than the legal retirement age in many countries because public schemes offer multiple opportunities for early retirement—but no rewards, and often penalties, for late retirement. In some transitional socialist economies, the actual average retirement age is under 55, because many young people qualify for disability or other special benefits. China and Romania have tried to encourage enterprise restructuring by encouraging early retirement (box 4.4).

The low and declining retirement age shows up in the low and declining labor force participation rate among 55- to 64-year-olds. These rates have been declining almost everywhere over the past three decades, but faster in richer than in poorer countries. Many forces are at work, but public and private pension plans bear part of the responsibility for this decline. Public pension plans in most industrial countries have an earnings test that strongly induces older people to stop working—otherwise they would lose their pensions. The slower decline in poorer countries may be due to the light coverage rate of public plans, the absence of an earnings test in some cases, and the large informal sector that allows people to continue working unofficially after retirement (appendix table A.10).

The decline in the supply of experienced workers has reduced the labor force by about 1 to 2 percent in developing countries and by 3 to 6 percent in industrial countries. This becomes inefficient if the cost of lost output exceeds the value of the increased leisure that retired workers get in return. In Slovenia, the steeply rising age-earnings profile observed after the market transition signals the high return to experienced labor and the high social cost of early retirement (Orazem and Vodopivec 1994). Raising the normal retirement age and equalizing it for men and women, making early retirement available only with actuarially reduced pensions, and rewarding those who work beyond the normal retirement age by increasing the expected lifetime pension are important steps to take to reduce the negative effect on employment. If this lost output could be recaptured, it would cover a large portion of total pension spending in many countries (see issue brief 8 for a fuller discussion of early retirement).

Impact on Saving and Capital Markets

Some economists believe that pay-as-you-go systems have reduced national saving. Others argue that they have had no such effect. Briefly, a pay-as-you-go system can hurt savings because of the unanticipated increased consumption of the first generation of eligible retirees and the anticipated income transfer in the form of high pensions to the first

---

Box 4.4 Is Early Retirement a Good Way to Reduce Unemployment and Facilitate Privatization?

SOME GOVERNMENTS VIEW EARLY RETIREMENT as a painless remedy for unemployment, arguing that the vacancy left by the retiree can be filled by a younger worker who would otherwise be unable to find work. In Spain early retirement is allowed only if the retiring worker is replaced by a young person just entering the labor force. Socialist economies in Eastern Europe and the former Soviet Union have long disguised the true rate of unemployment and underemployment by encouraging people to retire early, a practice that has intensified in recent years with enterprise reform and privatization. Romania eased eligibility requirements for retirement in 1990 as part of its restructuring program, increasing the number of pensioners by 40 percent between 1989 and 1992. China has done the same. Some countries are considering "buying out" workers who oppose privatization, and paying them pensions out of the public coffers, in order to reduce the liabilities of state enterprises and make them more attractive to potential investors.

Early retirement, though appealing in the short run, is a costly and shortsighted way to reduce unemployment and facilitate enterprise reform. It reduces the country's labor force (especially its experienced labor force), shrinks potential output, reduces political pressures to cut unemployment, and results in regressive redistributions. Pension benefits are often much higher than unemployment benefits, and these costs continue for many years. The government is stuck with a large liability as a result of privatization combined with early retirement. And provisions for early retirement may be difficult to change when the apparent short-term need is gone.

There is little evidence that early retirement reduces unemployment. Many of the vacancies created by early retirement are never filled, perhaps because of permanent reductions in labor demand in certain industries. Younger workers are imperfect substitutes for older, more experienced workers; they have different skills, which, in some cases, are complementary rather than substitutes. The productivity of some young workers may be less than the going wage. Some of the younger replacement workers possess special skills that would have made them employable in any event, while workers without these skills remain unemployed. When Bulgaria and Romania tried to increase the employment of younger workers in public enterprises by lowering the retirement age, enterprises did not take on new inexperienced workers but instead reduced employment. And to encourage workers to retire early, the government must increase current and future levels of pension spending, leading to higher payroll taxes, which, in turn, may lead to higher unemployment.

Rather than being painless, early retirement is a costly solution to the unemployment problem and an expensive way to restructure enterprises. Unemployment should be attacked in other ways, while pension plans should be aimed at the truly old.

generation of working age members. However, empirical studies of this issue in industrial countries have come to very different conclusions, depending on the data, the period, and the model. A major problem is the difficulty in estimating the counterfactual—what saving would have been in the absence of social security. Although very few empirical studies have been done in developing countries, it appears likely that the negative effect of pay-as-you-go plans on saving has probably been small, for at least four reasons: coverage is not widespread, the absence of reliable savings instruments means that savings and assets are small to begin with, private intrafamily transfers may offset the public transfers, and the new pension system may lack credibility, so young people go on saving for their own old age. (Issue brief 4 discusses the impact on saving of pay-as-you-go and fully funded plans in greater detail.)

But even if existing pay-as-you-go systems have had little negative impact on saving relative to the no-pension state, they are an opportunity lost to increase long-term saving through large mandatory funded plans. This could be significant, in view of the capital scarcity in many industrial and developing countries today.

From this vantage point, partly funded public plans may have more positive effects on long-term saving and capital accumulation than pure pay-as-you-go plans. But this effect depends crucially on how the funds are managed and how they affect government spending. If they are used to increase current government spending and deficits, national saving does not rise even if private saving does. If they are allocated exclusively to public investments, some of the potential private capital market development is lost. And if these investments have low productivity, some of the growth-enhancing effects are lost. Although not conclusive, observations from many countries are consistent with these scenarios.

Pension funds in young countries with immature systems, as in Africa, Central America, and South Asia, often accumulate reserves, which almost always are required to be invested in government securities or the securities of state enterprises. Usually the nominal rate of interest on these securities is less than the inflation rate, and devaluation lowers the returns further. International diversification is rarely allowed. The ultimate uses of these funds are not known, since data are unavailable and money is fungible in the government budget. But the large negative returns to many public pension funds in the 1980s suggest that capital was being misallocated in capital-scarce countries. Developing countries need to be particularly careful about this issue because their unstable political environments, lack of private financial markets, and large number of loss-making state enterprises make misuse of publicly managed old age security reserves more tempting (box 4.5 and figure 4.6).

Box 4.5 How Do Pension Reserves Fare in the Public Pillar?

LOW NOMINAL INTEREST RATES, HIGH INFLATION, weak accountability, and prohibitions on international diversification have resulted in negative interest rates being earned on the reserves of most public pillars. The funds are used exclusively to purchase government or public enterprise bonds or to finance housing loans at low rates of return. This is a non-transparent tax on workers whose contributions will not be there to pay pensions when they retire.

Real returns averaged -23.8 percent in Turkey between 1984 and 1988 (ISSA 1990c) and -12 percent in Egypt over the last decade (World Bank data). The National Investment Bank of Egypt credits the pension fund with negative real interest rates, in effect transferring the funds to the government's coffers. More moderate rates of inflation in Tunisia held returns to about -3 percent in recent years, but equipment bonds and social housing loans to the government threaten the medium-term financial outlook of social insurance funds (Vittas 1993a). Probably the worst case is Peru, whose public pension reserves had negative annual returns of -37 percent during the 1980s (figure 4.6).

Russia has recently used pension reserves to keep public enterprises afloat and to buy government bonds, which in 1992 had real monthly interest rates of -20 percent. Hungary used the first surpluses of its reformed pension scheme to make housing loans on concessional terms. Pensions funds began to accumulate in China after the reforms of the mid-1980s, as new contract workers were required to contribute to funds managed by enterprises or state agencies. These funds are often kept in bank accounts earning negative real interest.

In many Latin American countries the decapitalization of pension reserves is even more pronounced (Mesa-Lago 1991a). In Ecuador mortgage and personal loans to members of the elite accounted for 19 percent of the loan portfolio of the Social Security Institute. Low-income workers and peasants had little access to these funds. In 1988, these loans yielded returns of -42 percent—this at a time when borrowers were able to deposit the money in commercial banks and receive positive real interest rates. Real estate and mortgage loans also helped shrink the institute's assets from 2.8 to 1.4 percent of GDP between 1986 and 1989.

Pension reserves were channeled to housing subsidies in Mexico and Venezuela during the 1980s, with similarly dire financial consequences. Venezuela used pension funds to cover the deficits of failing public enterprises—in 1989 stock in these enterprises accounted for more than half the portfolio of the Social Security Institute (Marquez 1992). That year alone, real pension reserves shrank more than 70 percent. The pension fund averaged a -13 percent return on investment during the 1980s. Several Latin American countries are responding to this pension fund crisis by planning a complete restructuring of their old age security systems.

Figure 4.6 Average Annual Real Investment Returns for Selected Publicly Managed, Partially Funded Pension Schemes in the 1980s

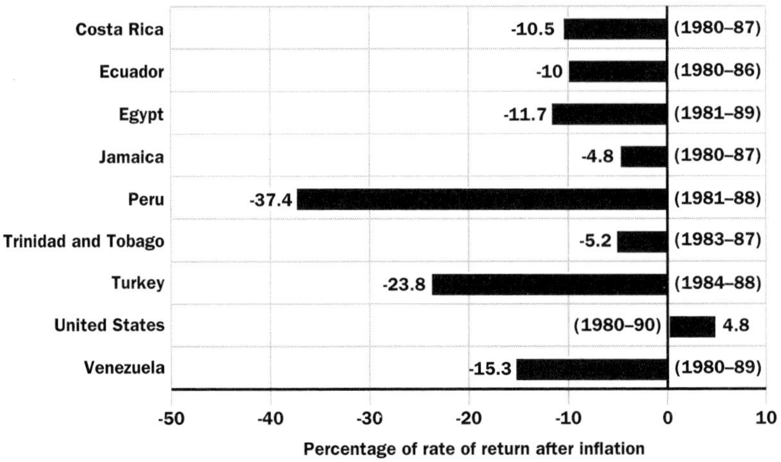

Most publicly managed pension funds lose money.

Note: Countries were selected on the basis of data availability for at least five years. Simple averages of inflation-adjusted annual returns are shown.

Source: Mesa-Lago (1991a); ISSA (1990c); Marquez (1992); Palacios (1994b).

Impact on the Provision of Public Goods

In countries with young populations and immature systems public pension funds run surpluses that can finance the provision of public goods. The problem is that since the tax is not transparent, the wrong public goods with low social value may be chosen. In countries with older populations and mature systems, public pension funds may reduce the provision of important public goods, because they run deficits covered by the general treasury.

In most OECD countries, older Latin American countries, and transitional socialist economies, pension payments are the largest item in the consolidated government budget. Most of these plans began as self-supporting contributory schemes that ran a current surplus, but the surplus was soon dissipated. As the social security debt built up behind the scenes and eventually came due, large current deficits became common. In 1990 Uruguay spent one-third of the consolidated government budget on old age security, including 10 percent of general revenues that covered 27 percent of all pension payments (Szalchman and Uthoff 1992). Italy spends 37 percent of its total government budget on pensions (OECD data). And in Turkey, current pension deficits are almost 2 percent of GDP (World Bank 1993).

These high expenditures on public pensions have contributed to fiscal crises in many countries. With tax revenues limited by economic and political considerations, countries with large pension obligations find it difficult to finance growth-enhancing public goods, such as education, infrastructure, and health services.

It might appear that countries should use partial funding of the public pillar in the early years to build up reserves for paying off the pension debt in later years. But the danger is that these reserves might make things worse, because they might tempt governments to spend more— and to spend it on consumption rather than investment, while dissipating the reserves through negative real interest rates. The funds would not be there when needed and would have induced wasteful public spending in the interim.

With public pension reserves required to be invested in government bonds at low interest rates, some analysts argue that this encourages the government's proclivity toward deficit finance, absorbing saving that would otherwise be available for productive private investment. Others argue that these reserves simply buy government bonds that private savers would otherwise have bought. In that case, a low interest rate implies a hidden tax on workers but does not discourage private investment. The issue hinges on whether pension saving reduces private household saving and whether the government's monopsonistic access to pension reserves encourages it to spend more on current consumption. It is difficult to resolve this issue, since empirical studies lack an unambiguous counterfactual.

One study explored experiences with pension fund surpluses in Canada, Japan, Sweden, and the United States. Pension reserves did not seem to increase government spending in Japan but did seem to facilitate public spending at the provincial level in Canada, where pension funds were obliged to buy government bonds (Munnell and Ernsberger 1989). If there are social security reserves it might be best to keep them separate from the rest of the budget, have them managed by an autonomous institution, and invest them in private as well as public securities. But this could result in lack of accountability, political manipulation, or backdoor nationalization of the private sector, particularly if the reserves are large. In any event, the fact that this is rarely done suggests it is not a politically plausible option.

The United States has a unified government trust fund budget, and usually the net deficit is reported. The trust funds of the social security system and the government employees' pension system are the largest purchasers of government bonds, holding one-quarter of the explicit debt, which is netted out of the total reported debt. The trust funds are paid the market interest rate and in this sense fare better than public pension reserves elsewhere. But the market rate for government bonds might have been higher if all bonds had to be sold on the open market and the trust funds earned less than privately managed occupational pension plans over the same period (figure 3.7). The U.S. national debt has grown concurrently with the trust funds since 1983, and some believe that the large trust funds enabled the government to increase the deficit, perhaps in turn depressing private investment (Marlow and Crain 1990). In about twenty years, the U.S. government will have to begin redeeming its unreported debt to the trust funds—to pay benefits to the baby boom generation. It will then have to raise other taxes or cut other important public spending far beyond current levels (Weaver 1993).

Who Benefits and Who Loses?

PAY-AS-YOU-GO SCHEMES ALWAYS INVOLVE REDISTRIBUTIONS across generations. Defined benefit schemes always involve redistributions within generations as well, since benefits are not linked to contributions in an actuarially fair way. The ability to redistribute to low-income individuals and generations is the big advantage of public pension plans. But if the defined benefit formula is not carefully devised or if the total wage bill in the economy does not grow fast enough, the result may be perverse redistributions from poor to rich.

What does the evidence say about the actual lifetime redistributions brought about by public, defined benefit, pay-as-you-go schemes? The first step in this calculation is to measure the present value of contributions paid and the expected present value of benefits received over the course of a worker's lifetime (and even beyond, since benefits usually include payments to survivors). The difference between these two is the expected net transfer or lifetime redistribution to the worker. This is positive if expected lifetime benefits exceed contributions, and negative otherwise.

Sometimes the rate of return that would equate benefits to contributions is calculated. If the redistribution is positive, the rate of return exceeds the market interest rate, implying that the worker got a better return through the pension system than would have been possible in an alternative investment. Usually, the net transfer or rate of return is calculated across groups of people—poor and rich, males and females, married and single, early and later cohorts of retirees. Because of the heavy data requirements, few studies have measured lifetime redistributional effects. These studies indicate that the first generations of pensioners are indeed helped, but at the expense of later generations, and there is little redistribution from rich to poor within any generation.

Intragenerational Redistribution

Intragenerational redistribution refers to transfers of expected lifetime incomes of individuals born at about the same time, especially redistribution among income classes. In the Netherlands, Sweden, the United Kingdom, and the United States, the main countries where studies have been done, it has been found that there is little redistribution from rich to poor despite progressive benefit formulas, minimum and maximum pensions, and similar devices ostensibly designed for this purpose. Such devices have failed because upper-income people enter the labor force later in life and live longer after retirement, so they contribute less and receive more than lower-income people over a lifetime. They have failed, too, because of policy choices such as low ceilings on taxable earnings and the common use of earnings-related benefit formulas, in which pensions rise with earnings. These studies have also found "capricious" redistributions within generations, that is, redistributions that most citizens may not be aware of and may not approve. For example, public plans often redistribute from dual-wage-earner families to single-wage-earner families and from women working in the market to those who stay at home.

Studies of lifetime income redistributions are generally not available for developing countries, but indirect evidence shows that intragenerational redistribution is even less progressive there. Usually, high-income formal sector workers in urban areas are the main group to be covered, but the schemes may be financed, in part, by lower-income taxpayers (figure 4.7). In addition, privileged groups are often eligible for better benefit formulas and earlier retirement, income-related differences in longevity and age-earnings profiles are strong, and the pension depends

Figure 4.7 Access to Social Security in Latin America, by Income Quintile, Late 1980s

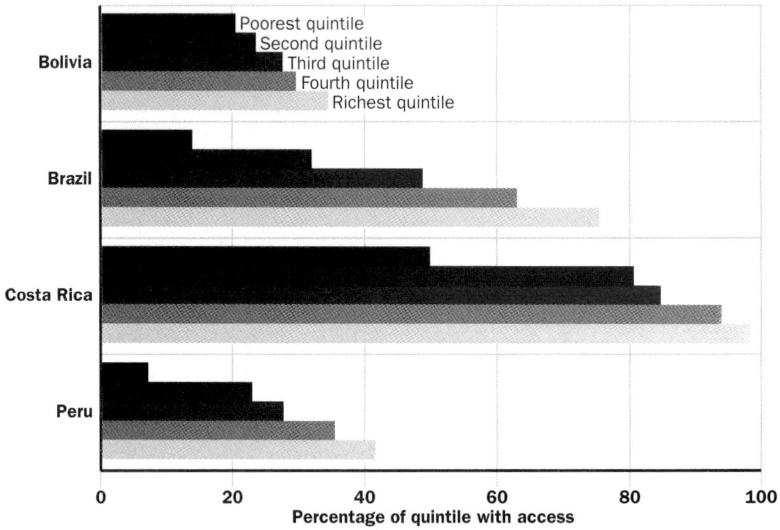

Note: Quintiles ordered by per capita income; "access" refers to members of households with at least one active participant in a social security program.
Source: Psacharopoulos and others (1993).

Social security programs are supposed to help the poor, but they usually help the rich more.

mainly on final year salary. In their present form, public pension plans in both industrial and developing countries do not seem to be effective at redistributing to the old in lower-income groups (box 4.6).

Intergenerational Redistribution

The second type of transfer—intergenerational—occurs in all unfunded schemes. It is measured by comparing the difference between lifetime benefits and costs for successive generations of retirees in a country. All empirical evidence to date shows such transfers to be much larger than intragenerational transfers, especially during the first few decades of unfunded schemes. In all cases, earlier generations have done better than later generations, regardless of income. That is, covered workers aged 30 to 50 at the inception of the scheme always gain, whereas their children and grandchildren lose. In the United States, real rates of return were more than 15 percent for workers retiring in the 1950s and 1960s and about 8 percent for workers retiring in the 1970s, signifying large positive transfers to these workers from the social secu-

Box 4.6 Redistribution within the Same Generation

PAY-AS-YOU-GO PUBLIC PENSION SCHEMES HAVE the capacity to redistribute lifetime income from the rich to the poor. From that objective comes the rationale for public management and pooled finance with complex benefit formulas instead of separate accounts with actuarially based risk categories. To achieve redistributive objectives, the United States and the Philippines provide higher wage replacement rates for individuals with lower lifetime wages. The Netherlands uses a flat benefit and Switzerland a combination of employment-related flat and progressive earnings-related benefits (box 4.9). Many developing countries use explicit minimum or maximum pension levels for the same purpose. None of these mechanisms seems to work as expected.

Why the poor don't benefit more than the rich. Empirical evidence indicates that once certain income-specific characteristics of workers are taken into account, public schemes redistribute little lifetime income to the poor. For one thing, the well-off live longer than the poor and so collect pensions over a longer period (chapter 3). Many poor people contribute but die before they become old enough to collect benefits. People who live longer than average require larger lifetime incomes to maintain their standard of living, and pensions are designed to insure against this eventuality. Nevertheless, the longevity differences between rich and poor are predictable, not random, so the differences in benefits received because of these longevity differences are expected and constitute redistribution rather than insurance. Does society wish to transfer income to the rich because they live longer? We do not know whether well-informed citizens and policymakers would consider this equitable—yet that is exactly what many societies do.

Besides drawing a pension over fewer retirement years, lower-income workers usually enter the labor market earlier because they leave school earlier. Yet they often fail to accrue much extra pension credit during these extra contributing years. Germany and Hungary grant pension credit to university students, who thus earn pension benefits during those years without contributing for them. Pension benefit formulas that give more weight to earnings in the years just before retirement also penalize low-income workers, as compared with more educated, higher-income workers whose earnings rise with age. Such formulas are quite common in developing countries.

Financing mechanisms introduce another regressive element to most public pension plans. In OECD countries, where coverage is nearly universal, systems are financed via payroll taxes instead of general income taxes, and taxable earnings are usually capped. In developing countries, where coverage is sparse, the regressive effect comes from using general revenues to subsidize pension plans for the better-off. Guatemala pays a third of the costs of its public pension plan out of general revenues collected from the entire population even though its pension program covers less than a third of the population. Tax deductibility of contributions, a common feature of public pension plans, also favors higher-income workers over low-income workers.

Empirical evidence. Considering all these forces of regressive distribution, it is not surprising that studies for the Netherlands, Sweden, the United Kingdom, and the United States show little if any redistribution from the lifetime rich to the lifetime poor. The public pension scheme in the Netherlands was found to have redistributed income primarily from unmarried to married individuals, regardless of income (Nelissen 1987). A study of the Swedish system detected no intragenerational redistribution and suggested that the scheme might be regressive if mortality differences were taken into account (Stahlberg 1990). Income-related differences in mortality rates and earnings profiles in the United Kingdom offset progressive benefit features (Creedy, Disney, and Whitehouse 1992). In Italy intragenerational redistribution has regional implications as well. One study found a pattern of transfers from the poor

(Box continues on the following page.)

Box 4.6 *(continued)*

South to the richer North, the result of steeper age-earnings profiles, longer lifetimes, and a higher old age dependency ratio in the North (Schioppa 1990).

Several studies have looked at the intragenerational effects of the U.S. social security system and found little support for the contention that the lifetime poor have received significantly higher rates of return than others. Four studies found little or no difference in the rate of return to lower- and higher- (lifetime) income workers retiring in the same year, particularly after adjusting for mortality rate differences and other income-based factors (Aaron 1977; Hurd and Shoven 1985; Burkhauser and Warlick 1981; Steurle and Bakija 1994). Three other studies found small progressive effects (Meyer and Wolff 1987; Rofman 1993b; Leimer and Petri 1981). Some of these studies do not take into account benefits received by surviving children; this would probably increase the degree of progressivity. But they also do not take into account the fact that poor workers probably have a higher discount rate than rich ones, which makes the system less progressive. Studies have

also shown a variety of other nontransparent redistributions that may not have been intended or widely desired: from single workers to married couples, from dual to single wage-earner families, from women in the work force to other women (Feldstein and Samwick 1992; Boskin and others 1987).

Developing countries. Indirect evidence for developing countries suggests that intragenerational redistribution in public pension schemes is strongly regressive. Typically, only formal sector workers in urban areas are covered by the plans; the very poor are usually excluded (figure 4.7). Income-related differences in mortality rates, age of entry, and age-earnings profiles are even more pronounced than in OECD countries. Many developing countries have multiple plans that provide more generous terms to privileged groups of workers with more political clout. In Brazil higher-income workers have an easier time documenting their covered employment, so they are eligible for generous length-of-service-related benefits. Civil servants in Egypt and Mexico receive better inflation protection than private sector workers, and in Colombia they contribute at a

rity system (Moffitt 1984; Hurd and Shoven 1985). But the return is expected to fall to about 2 percent for workers retiring after 2000, less than they could have gotten in other investments (figure 4.8).

The redistribution from younger to older generations may be equitable if the younger generations have much higher incomes than older ones. But if national income is not rising rapidly, young workers with average or below-average wages may find themselves subsidizing the pensions of retirees who are better off. In the United States, the largest transfers during the 1960s and 1970s went to the old, who were wealthy—because of their greater earnings, pensions, and longevity—(Hurd and Shoven 1985; Steurle and Bakija 1994). Middle- and even some low-income workers today and tomorrow will pay the price and get less than they put in. In developing countries, where upper-income groups are the first to be covered, this regressive intergenerational effect is likely to be accentuated.

lower rate than private sector workers, yet get the same wage replacement rate. In Brazil, Hungary, Turkey, and many other countries, white collar workers are more likely than blue collar workers to retire at age 40 or 50, increasing their rate of return relative to those who continue working. In Colombia, though all current retirees receive net transfers that constitute approximately the same proportion of benefits for all income groups, the absolute value of the transfer is eight times as large for a high-income worker as it is for a minimum wage worker (box table 4.6).

Misuse of pension fund reserves contributes further to regressive intragenerational transfers. In Ecuador and the Philippines pension fund reserves are lent to high-income workers at negative real interest rates of as much as 40 percent a year. In Trinidad and Tobago well-off workers borrowed pension reserves for mortgages at below-market rates.

Not a single study for any country has presented strong evidence that the public pension scheme has substantially redistributed income from the lifetime rich to the lifetime poor once mortality differences

Box Table 4.6 Distributional Effects of Colombian Public Pension Scheme

	Present value of benefits	Present value of taxes paid	Present value of transfer	Transfers of benefits (percent)
Minimum-wage worker	12.8	3.1	9.8	76.5
Worker making five times the minimum wage	51.8	15.4	36.9	71.3
Worker making ten times the minimum wage	102.0	30.7	72.8	71.4

Note: Married male worker contributes for thirty years and retires at age 60 without children.
Source: Fernandez Riva (1992).

are taken into account. In fact, in some countries the redistribution goes from the poor to the rich.

Before adopting or expanding old age security systems, countries should carefully calculate the likely intergenerational transfers over long periods, by establishing a system of intergenerational accounts that tracks benefits received and costs paid by each generation (Auerbach, Gokhale, and Kotlikoff 1994). Policymakers will then be better able to evaluate whether the expected transfers are desirable—and if not, how the system should be changed to make it more equitable (see issue brief 9 for further evidence on intergenerational redistributions).

Poverty Reduction

Even if public pension plans have not redistributed significantly across income classes, they have probably alleviated poverty among the old. The large intergenerational transfers found in all pay-as-you-go schemes would be expected to have this effect temporarily. But that

Figure 4.8 Rates of Return to Generations Retiring Twenty-five to Forty-five Years after the Start of a Public Pension Scheme

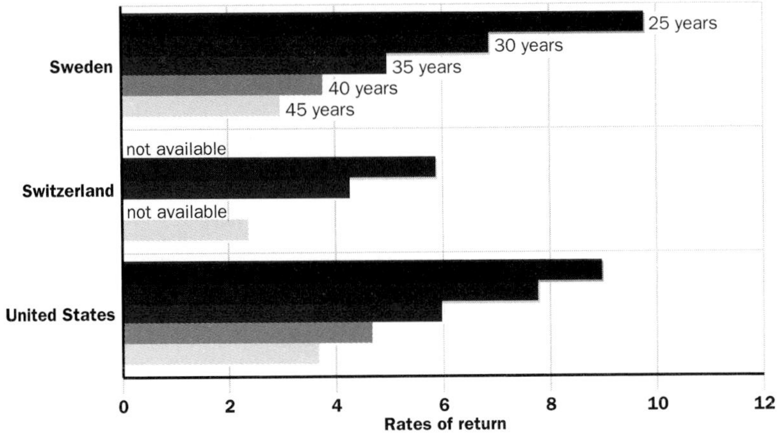

As public pension programs mature, returns to new retirees shrink.

Note: Starting dates of earnings-related public pension schemes are: Sweden 1960, Switzerland 1949, United States 1935. Swedish rates are for men only; Swiss rates are for single, high-income males, and data are not available for twenty-five and forty-year cohorts.
Source: Stahlberg (1989); Hauser and others (1983); Moffitt (1984).

transfer is now coming to an end and becoming negative in many countries, so it will no longer alleviate poverty. Dependents' and survivors' benefits should help reduce poverty among older women—but their poverty rates remain higher than those of men in OECD countries with large public pillars, just as in informal systems. Public plans could also alleviate old age poverty more permanently by shifting people's consumption from younger to older years (the saving function) or by developing risk-pooling opportunities (the insurance function) that would not otherwise have been available. These saving and insurance effects would reduce the incidence of poverty among the old, even if the lifetime incomes of different income classes were unchanged. A mandatory saving pillar would reduce old age poverty for exactly the same reasons.

There is even less empirical evidence about the effects of public schemes on old age poverty than there is about its lifetime redistributive effects. Fragmentary evidence indicates that the old are not particularly poor in developing countries, including those with and without large public pension plans (chapter 3). Evidence from OECD countries suggests that poverty among the old was disproportionately high during the

Great Depression and shortly after World War II but has fallen substantially over the past four decades. In York, England, the old made up more than two-thirds of the poor in 1950 (Crowntree and Lavers 1951), but in the 1980s they made up less than one-quarter nationwide (Luxembourg Income Study). In the United States, the absolute poverty rate among the old fell from 35 percent in 1959 to 12 percent in 1991 (U.S. Bureau of the Census, various years). Today, in Australia, Canada, France, the Netherlands, Sweden, and the United Kingdom the relative poverty rate is lower among the old than among the working age population (figure 3.2). Most of these countries have large flat or means-tested components in their programs.

Clearly the vast expansion in old age security programs during this period deserves some of the credit for the drop, but it is difficult to know how much—because other factors were at play. The prolonged prosperity of the 1950s and 1960s in OECD countries enabled people to save for their old age. The rapid rise in real estate prices benefited workers who owned their own homes. There was some improvement in the general status of women. Moreover, social security transferred income to all older cohorts over this period, but this effect was only temporary. Countries will have to target their benefits and costs much more carefully in the future to achieve the same poverty alleviation effects.

If poverty reduction and income redistribution toward the lifetime poor are the objectives, countries should be wary of earnings-related pay-as-you-go pension systems that produce large intergenerational transfers from later to earlier cohorts but few equalizing intragenerational transfers. They should also be wary of nontransparent systems that make it difficult to figure out who is gaining and losing. To reduce the likelihood of inequitable transfers, public pension systems should:

- Avoid paying benefits that exceed contributions to middle- and upper-income classes at the start of the scheme.
- Use a progressive benefit formula such as a flat or means-tested formula or minimum pension guarantee.
- If an earnings-related formula is used it should be compressed, with the maximum and minimum not far apart.
- Be sure to tax either benefits or contributions and imputed returns.
- Impose a floor but no ceiling on taxable earnings.
- Finance benefits through general revenues once coverage is widespread.

■ Use other financing arrangements—such as mandatory saving plans—to provide higher pensions to higher-income groups.

The Financial Unsustainability of the Public Pillar

PUBLIC PENSION SCHEMES ARE UNDER INCREASING FINANCIAL pressure. The problem is three layers deep. First, some are on the verge of insolvency, particularly in Latin America and Eastern Europe. Second, pension deficits are straining already strained public treasuries, which can no longer bail them out. And third, behind the government's fiscal crisis lies the deeper crisis of labor and capital markets that are malfunctioning, preventing the growth that is ultimately the only way out of these difficulties. This multilayered problem threatens the financial sustainability of pension plans, which may not be able to keep their promises to workers.

The situation is worst in Latin America and Eastern Europe. Argentina tried to deal with the fiscal crisis and inflation of the late 1970s by raising contribution rates and indexing pensions. The increased contribution rates led to greater evasion, the indexation raised costs, and when the unemployment rate also rose in the mid-1980s, the result was an even larger deficit. To avoid insolvency Argentina arbitrarily reduced pension benefits below legally determined targets and increased transfers from general revenues. The arbitrary reduction in benefits was successfully challenged in court, leaving the government with unpaid pension liabilities and a crippled pension system. After a prolonged political debate, Argentina has scaled back its public pension and is now radically restructuring its old age security system by shifting to a multipillar system.

Of Hungary's 10.3 million people, 2.9 million were receiving a pension in 1993 (including 100,000 orphans). The result was one of the highest system dependency rates in the world, with an estimated 0.75 beneficiary to every contributor. To cover the system's huge outlays, 10 percent of GDP in 1993, the payroll tax for pensions has risen to more than 30 percent, increasing evasion and making it difficult for Hungarian firms to compete in international markets. By 1993 the accumulated arrears plus interest penalties owed by Hungarian firms had reached 3 percent of GDP and was expected to grow. Hungary is now trying to decide which way to go—how to restore its pension system in a way that helps rather than hurts the economy (World Bank data).

Things seemingly are better in OECD countries, but they, too, face looming problems, which can be summed up by examining the size of their implicit social security debt. Countries with public pension plans owe an implicit debt to retirees and workers who have accumulated large social security entitlements. The present value of this implicit debt depends on the number of covered workers and retirees, their age distribution and expected life spans, the size of the average benefit, the retirement age, and the discount rate used to calculate present value. In OECD countries, the social security debt varies from 90 percent to more than 200 percent of GDP (van der Noord and Herd 1993). Although not well known because it is implicit, the implicit social security debt for all countries is much larger than the explicit debt (figure 4.9). Adding both components would in most cases triple the total national debt.

Current payroll tax rates are not nearly large enough to pay off this debt. The gap between expected revenues and expenditures over the next 150 years (much of it in the next 50 years) exceeds 200 percent of

Figure 4.9 Explicit Debt versus Implicit Public Pension Debt in Seven OECD Countries, 1990

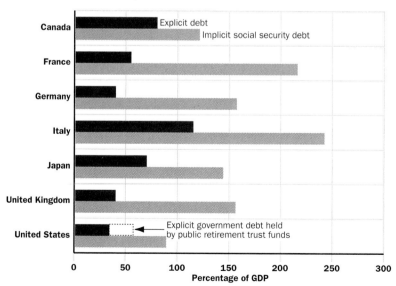

Hidden public pension debt—which needs to be paid off to reform pension schemes—often dwarfs the explicit national debt.

Note: The assumed discount rate is 4 percent.
Source: Van der Noord and Herd (1993).

GDP in most countries. A much larger tax will have to be imposed to pay off these obligations—unless the promises themselves are not kept. Figure 4.9 also indicates the debt that countries will have to make explicit if they decide to move away from a pay-as-you-go system. The prospect of making such a large implicit debt explicit and transparent is likely to deter efforts to reorganize the pension system.

In developing countries the implicit debt is smaller because of their lower coverage and younger populations. But estimates for Argentina, China, Colombia, and Turkey indicate that the public pension debt already exceeds one-third of GDP because of generous benefit promises— and it is increasing rapidly (IDB 1993; Lora and others 1992; World Bank 1993).

How did these countries get into so much trouble, and what can they do to get out of it? The public pension plans of many middle- and high-income countries are in crisis today because:

- Populations are aging.
- Pension systems have matured.
- Coverage can no longer be readily expanded.
- Early retirement and easy access to disability benefits have raised the system dependency rate.
- Increasing numbers of workers and employers are evading the high contribution rate.
- Wage replacement rates are too high.
- Ceilings on taxable earnings are too low.
- Pension reserves are earning low, even negative, returns.
- Productivity is not increasing fast enough.

Box 4.7 describes these problems in the Eastern European and transitional countries.

Pension system reform is always painful and sometimes politically impossible. The strong message for countries whose systems are still young is to avoid these costly and irreversible mistakes.

The Temptation of Young Populations and Immature Systems

Pay-as-you-go schemes are deceptive. When populations are young, systems are immature, and coverage can easily be expanded to younger groups, it is tempting for countries to offer generous benefits, since the costs are low. But these low costs will not continue indefinitely. The pension debt is building up. As populations age, systems mature, and coverage can no longer be expanded, these same benefit levels may become unaffordable.

Aging population. The aging of the population is due to falling birthrates and to falling mortality rates. Although in the past the biggest drops were in child mortality, many demographers believe that in the future the most rapid drops will be among the old, putting great strain on old age support systems. A two-year-per-decade improvement in life expectancy among retirees—less than today's trend in many countries—could double both the dependency and required contribution rates over the lifetimes of today's young workers. This process is already well under way in Eastern European, Latin American, and OECD countries (see issue brief 3).

System maturity. Although it is possible for a new system to mature instantly by giving all old people full pension rights, most countries have chosen not to give benefits to people who retired before or shortly after the scheme was introduced. Many countries in Africa and Central America with young pension schemes have a system dependency rate much lower than the demographic dependency rate for this reason. But the system dependency rate rises rapidly as the system matures. Ineligible retirees die and are replaced by new retirees who qualify for pensions. Even though Mexico is still a young country that is aging slowly, its system dependency rate tripled over the past thirty years, rising much faster than the population rate (figure 4.10).

Expanding coverage rates. Worker coverage in public pension plans usually starts from a narrow base. As the system matures and costs rise, governments frequently finance the generous benefit promises made earlier by expanding coverage to new occupations with young workers. Since the old people in these occupations are not eligible for benefits but the young workers are contributing, system dependency ratios fall and the system remains immature. Many Latin American countries increased their coverage substantially in the 1960s and 1970s. Although the increases in coverage are presented as egalitarian measures to help the newly covered low-income workers, it is often the high-income workers who benefit. Ecuador had 29 percent coverage in 1982, but only 15 percent of those covered were rural peasants. By 1991 coverage had increased to 43 percent, with almost half rural peasants. Most peasants are not yet eligible for pensions, but their contri-

Box 4.7 Pension Problems in Eastern Europe

THE WORLD HAS TURNED OUT TO BE DIFFERENT from the one that the old had expected and grown accustomed to in the transitional socialist economies. For citizens who followed the rules, the old command economy had promised cradle-to-grave income security: support for families with children, a job with a modest and relatively undifferentiated wage, and compensation for these relatively low wages through a generous pension after retirement. But now that pensioners have come to collect, the coffers are bare.

Old age security systems are part of the problem, not the solution. The transitional countries have only a single pillar, a publicly managed, pay-as-you-go scheme financed by payroll taxes. Occupational pension plans and voluntary saving did not emerge under central planning, as they had in OECD countries. Private financial intermediation and competitive financial markets never developed and personal saving was small. Though a dominant public plan with high tax rates could function in an authoritarian command economy, it is dysfunctional in a market economy that depends on incentives, compliance, decentralized capital mobilization, and competition in world markets on the basis of costs and price.

Eastern European economies spend much more on old age benefits than their income or demography would predict. And this share has been rising rapidly (box figure 4.7 and appendix table A.11). As GDP has fallen, the share of GDP captured by the old, through public spending, has increased. In many countries pensions are the largest single item in the government budget, accounting for more than 15 percent of spending or some 10 to 14 percent of GDP in Bulgaria, Hungary, Poland, and Slovenia. This is as large a share of GDP as in the OECD welfare states, where the proportion of old people, per capita income, and

tax collection capacity are much greater. How did this come about and what are the consequences?

High statutory replacement rates. Most Eastern European economies have set statutory replacement rates at about 80 percent of wages. Although inflation has eroded these values, the average pension is still a very high percentage of the average wage—67 percent in Hungary, 70 percent in Poland, and 85 percent in Slovenia.

High dependency rates and early retirement. Because of declining birthrates, dependency ratios are higher in transitional economies than income levels would predict. And the system dependency rate is higher still because of early retirement, unemployment, and evasion (many workers and employers simply do not pay). The average effective retirement age is 57 for men and 53 for women, pushing the ratio of beneficiaries to contributors up to 0.6 in Romania, 0.7 in Hungary, and 0.87 in Bulgaria, where every worker has to support almost a full pensioner.

High payroll taxes. Payroll taxes required to support these benefits are enormous—typically about 30 percent for pensions plus 20 percent for other social insurance. Firms are squeezed from both sides: administered wages prevent them from fully shifting the payroll tax to workers, while partial shifts lead to low and falling real wages. This situation drives evasion to the growing informal economy, stirs up conflict between workers and employers and between workers and retirees, discourages private entrepreneurship, makes it impossible for firms to compete in international markets, and deprives the government of revenues to invest in much-needed public goods that might enhance growth. Shifting to a broader tax base would release some of these pressures, but the institutional capacity is not yet there.

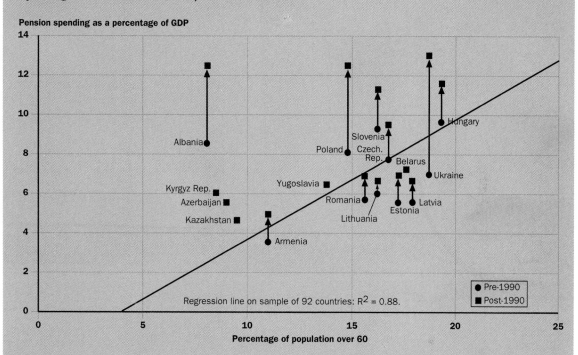

Box Figure 4.7 Relationship of the Percentage of the Population over 60 Years Old and Pension Spending: Transitional Economies, Pre- and Post-1990

Pension spending as a percentage of GDP

Regression line on sample of 92 countries: $R^2 = 0.88$.

Percentage of population over 60

Source: See Palacios 1994b for details.

Lack of indexation. Real benefits and expenditures are being reduced implicitly because of high inflation without indexation. Indexation is not viable unless these countries cut benefits explicitly. While real pensions are not falling faster than real wages, young workers at least can hope for a better future. For older retirees the future is now.

In sum: The transitional economies offer old age benefits that the old find unsatisfactory and the young cannot afford. Too much money goes to transfers to early retirees who could still work, while the truly old receive pensions that are barely adequate. High tax rates and excess government spending on pensions encourage evasion, distort employment, deter private enterprise, and crowd out public investments in productive infrastructure that could boost economic growth. Overhaul of the system is clearly needed.

Figure 4.10 Maturation of the Mexican Pension Schemes, 1960–92

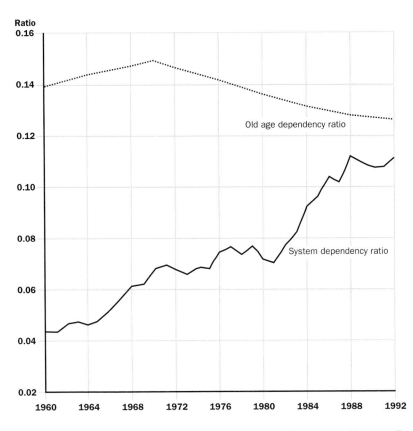

Mexico has a young population but a maturing pension system, so the system dependency ratio is rising fast while the old age dependency ratio is still falling.

Source: Instituto Mexicano de Seguridad Social (1993); B. Mitchell (1983); World Bank staff calculations.

butions (albeit small) are helping to finance the retirement of urban workers.

During the past two decades, the finances of public pension plans in OECD countries have been helped by the increased number of women who contribute. Concomitant with the declining fertility rate, many women have made the transition from home work, not subject to the old age security tax, to market work, increasing contributions to the system. Although this increased the number of contributing workers by 10 percent or more, it did not increase the number of beneficiaries by nearly as much, since many women would have been eligible for pensions as dependents of their spouses. The incremental return that households receive from these social security contributions is thus low, even negative, decreasing their lifetime disposable incomes. But the contributions have enabled the old age security systems of several OECD countries to stay afloat without raising taxes more transparently.

Coverage cannot expand indefinitely. Nor can it always bring in new young workers. As the rate of coverage expansion slows and newly covered workers age, the system dependency rate rises. Contribution rates must then rise or benefits must be cut—or the difference will have to be made up by the treasury. When the pension plan runs into financial trouble, the latest groups to get coverage, who tend to be from lower-income groups than the initial entrants, are likely to get a lower rate of return than they expected.

Policy Choices That Raise System Dependency Rates above Demographic Rates

The aging of the population and the maturing of systems are part of the reason for old age programs to be in trouble. But they are not the whole story. In Argentina, Brazil, Hungary, and Turkey, among others, system dependency rates are much higher than demographic dependency rates because of policy choices in their public pension schemes (figure 4.11). The main culprits are early retirement, lenient disability benefits, unemployment, and evasion stemming from high contribution rates that are not closely tied to benefits. Not surprisingly, the same design features that cause problems for the economy as a whole also cause problems for the financial sustainability of the public pension system.

Early retirement. Early retirement—in addition to its drag on growth—doubly threatens the financial viability of public pension plans by reducing the number of workers making contributions and increasing the number of retirees drawing benefits. Suppose that there are equal numbers of people in each age category and that workers enter the labor force at age 25, retire at 65, and die at 85. The dependency rate is then one retiree to two workers, and a contribution rate of 20 percent will cover a pension paying 40 percent of the average wage. If the retirement age is increased to 70, the required contribution rate falls to 13.3 percent. But if the retirement age is lowered to 55, the dependency rate becomes one to one, and the required contribution rate soars to 40 percent. This has been the trend in many countries. For example, in France pension spending as a proportion of GDP more than doubled over the

Figure 4.11 System Dependency Ratio versus Old Age Dependency Ratio, Selected Countries

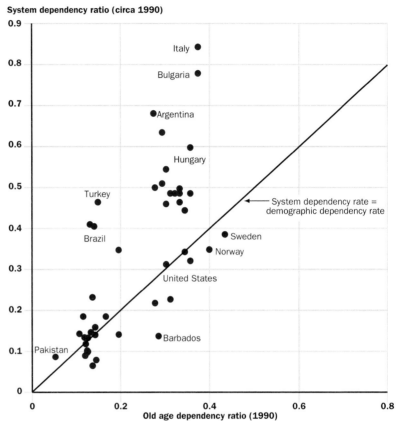

Policy choices can boost system dependency rates high above demographic dependency rates, spelling trouble for public pension schemes.

Note: Because of space limitations, not all data points are identified. The old age dependency ratio is the number of persons aged 60 or over divided by the number of persons aged 20 to 59. System dependency rates are for years ranging from 1987 to 1992 and refer to the number of pensioners divided by the number of active contributors.
Source: Palacios (1994b).

past two decades, and one-third of the increase was due to earlier retirement spurred by the lowering of the retirement age from 65 to 60 in the early 1980s (Guillermard 1991). Although Brazil has demographic characteristics similar to Mexico's, its system dependency rate is three times as high, in large part because workers can retire earlier. In Turkey, some workers retire in their forties, and more than half retire before 55. The system dependency ratio for the main public pension scheme is three times as high as the demographic dependency rate.

Raising the retirement age—regularly, as longevity increases—is probably the single most important reform to improve the financial prospects of the public pension plan. It will also raise the supply of experienced labor in the economy. Because of the early retirement age in many public pension plans, these plans now pay out generous benefits to middle-aged workers and may not have the resources to continue paying as pensioners grow older or to pay young workers when they retire. When Chile faced this problem fifteen years ago, it drastically raised the retirement age in its public pillar shortly before introducing a multipillar system. Argentina also raised its retirement age as it introduced major reforms in 1994. Benefits should be reduced on an actuarially fair basis for people who retire early, while people who continue to work after normal retirement age should get actuarially fair increases in benefits.

Disability benefits. In many countries easy eligibility conditions for disability benefits have been a major route to early retirement. In the Netherlands, 20 percent of all retirees are on disability, and in Hungary, 27 percent. This raises the dependency rate and, because disability benefits are relatively generous, the required contribution rate even higher. As the normal retirement age is raised, more people can be expected to apply for disability benefits and more will qualify—thereby offsetting some of the gains of the higher retirement age. Disability benefits should be retained for those who are truly disabled but not be used to disguise unemployment or early retirement by those who are able to work. Therefore careful application of the disability criteria is needed. To prevent abuse by healthy workers, some countries put truly disabled people on the boards that review applications for disability benefits.

Unemployment and withdrawal from the labor market. Unemployed workers do not contribute to the pension system although they eventually become eligible for benefits. Dependent spouses, who do not work in the labor market, may also become beneficiaries. Although coverage for the unemployed and for dependents and survivors is important, it raises the dependency rate and cost of the system, particularly in countries where unemployment is high and labor force participation is low. This points up the strong interaction between the health of the overall economy and the health of the pension system.

Strategic manipulation and evasion. If escape to the informal sector is easy and the eligibility period is short, workers may respond to a high tax rate by opting out as contributors as soon as they become eligible for benefits. As required payroll tax rates rose in Uruguay, the proportion of contributing workers fell from 81 percent in 1975 to 67 percent in 1989, largely because of evasion (Szalchman and Uthoff 1992). Workers in Brazil are eligible for a pension equal to 75 percent of their wage base after only five years of contributions, making evasion highly profitable thereafter. During the 1980s, the rates of evasion and delayed contributions were 60 percent in Brazil, 44 percent in Barbados and Jamaica, and 33 percent in Peru (Schulz 1992). Arrears were 29 percent of total social insurance revenues in Estonia in 1992 (Cavalcanti 1993) and more than 20 percent in Hungary (World Bank data). In many cases the noncontributing workers had already become eligible for pension benefits. (See issue brief 7 for a fuller discussion of evasion.)

Informal systems of old age security, in which contributions and benefits are shared within the family, avoid evasion and strategic manipulation by close observation of family members and strong social pressures to cooperate (chapter 2). But in formal systems these social sanctions and mutual monitoring are lacking, so people may exploit the system. Evasion and strategic manipulation increase the dependency rate and preclude the option of raising revenues by boosting the contribution rate, thereby undercutting financial viability. The pension system should close off these opportunities and get the incentives right. Taxes for the public pension plan should be kept as low as possible, while part of the responsibility for old age support is shifted to a second mandatory scheme, run as a defined contribution plan—which workers have less reason to evade because benefits depend directly on contributions and the costs of evasion are borne by the individual directly involved rather than the rest of society.

Other Design Flaws

Flawed benefit formulas, high administrative costs, and low ceilings on taxable earnings add further to the financial difficulties faced by many public pension plans and their negative effects on the economy.

Unsustainable benefit rates and inefficient benefit formulas. Many countries have set statutory wage replacement rates unrealistically high. And because the benefit formulas usually are earnings-related, the highest payoffs go to upper-income workers. In Costa Rica, the average old age pension was 68 percent of the average economy-wide gross wage in

1992 (Caja Costarricense de Seguro Social 1992). In Hungary, Poland, and Slovenia, the average pension in the early 1990s was, respectively, 67 percent, 70 percent, and 85 percent of the average net wage. When other European countries were at a similar stage of development before World War II, they paid a replacement rate 15 to 20 percent of average gross wages. Even now, most pay only 35 to 50 percent of gross wages, or 40 to 50 percent of net wages (table 4.2), although Austria, Italy, and Sweden pay much more. High replacement rates imply correspondingly high contribution rates, which, in developing and transitional countries, lead to evasion, which requires still higher tax rates—a vicious cycle that may eventually lead to a breakdown of the entire system. Lower and flatter benefit rates in the public pension plan are more consistent with system sustainability and with its poverty alleviation and basic income goals. This also allows room for the development of complementary pillars that raise overall replacement rates in a less distortionary way (boxes 4.8 and 4.9).

High administrative costs. In many developing countries, a big part of total expenditures goes for administrative costs—10 to 15 percent in Brazil and Turkey, compared with 1 to 2 percent in most OECD countries. Administrative costs per worker (or pensioner) tend to fall as per capita income rises, because of improved education, infrastructure, and communication systems. They also fall as the number of plan members rises, because of economies of scale (issue brief 5). So, to some extent, it is inevitable that immature schemes in poor countries will have high expense ratios. They lack the human and physical infrastructure. They have limited coverage. And they must incur the fixed costs of building a new system. But inefficient practices add to this burden. Good records are absent in many countries. When Peru recently reformed its pension system and tried to pay off its old social security debt, it had almost no records of prior employment or contributions on which to base these payoffs. In Brazil, the only records are kept on social security cards in the possession of workers—and easily subject to loss or fraud. The absence of such records makes it possible for people to collect benefits without having made commensurate contributions. One advantage of a flat benefit system is that it puts the least burden on record-keeping capacity and reduces the opportunities for corruption and fraud. Countries should be wary of establishing complex pension systems before they have the critical size and administrative skills to run these plans effectively and with low transaction costs.

Box 4.8 Earnings-Related Benefits: How Not to Do It

MANY COUNTRIES HAVE GOTTEN INTO SERIOUS financial difficulty by making the wrong choices about earnings-related benefit formulas. These wrong choices lead to unsustainably generous benefits that go disproportionately to high-wage workers. They also encourage evasion, strategic manipulation, and early retirement; and governments often escape from these obligations by not indexing benefits for inflation.

The Problems in Brazil

High replacement rate. Statutory replacement rates are 75 to 100 percent of the calculated wage base. Such rates are common in Latin America but much higher than rates used in most OECD countries.

Short averaging period for the wage base and inadequate employment records. Because of high inflation and no public tracking of work records, most developing countries count only the last three to five years in calculating the pensionable wage base. Brazil counts the last three years; China and Sudan count only the last month. Tying pensions to recent earnings is a simple way to correct for rapidly rising inflation and absence of work records, but it leads to high costs, strategic manipulation (working double time for the last three years to double pensions, for instance), and disproportionately high benefits going to higher-income workers, with steep age-earnings profiles.

Falling accrual rates. The accrual rate (the proportion of the wage base to which a worker acquires pension rights for each year of covered employment) is 15 percent a year for the first five years (75 percent total) and 1 percent thereafter, up to 100 percent of the wage base. After the first five years extra contributions add only a small amount to benefits, and after thirty years they add nothing. This sets the stage for strategic manipulation—for instance, staying in covered employment just long enough to qualify for generous pensions and then evading further payroll taxes.

Early retirement. Although 65 is the nominal retirement age, workers can retire early on the basis of years of service or disability. Many early retirees

Low ceilings on taxable earnings and unprofitable reserves. Almost all public pension plans include a ceiling on taxable earnings. In some cases, the ceiling is not much higher than the average covered wage, so a large proportion of the total wage bill is not subject to the payroll tax. This mitigates the possible negative effect of the tax on the supply and evasion of high-wage workers, but it also reduces the redistributive impact of the plan and the revenues of the system. In many cases the ceiling on taxable earnings should be raised—and eventually the burden should be shifted to a broader tax base.

The revenue base of the public plan is also depressed by the low earnings on pension reserves. A higher competitive interest rate would improve the financial balance of the system. But this does not seem to be politically feasible. An alternative is to spend down public reserves by financing pension benefits and making a downsized public plan truly are middle-class workers who enter the informal sector while collecting their generous pensions from the formal sector.

High contribution rate. The current contribution rate is about 30 percent, but this is not enough to cover the promised benefits. In 1992, the government was ordered by the courts to come up with additional funds.

Incomplete indexation. Until 1991, only two of the three years used to calculate the wage base were revalued upward for indexation, so this lowered benefits by 25 to 30 percent. The minimum pension was supposed to be indexed for inflation to help low-income workers, but the government often delayed—or refused to make—inflation adjustments. Pensions above the minimum were only partly indexed, so their real value fell to the minimum level, and replacement rates plummeted in inflationary periods.

Evasion. The short averaging period, the falling accrual rates, and the high contribution rate encourage evasion—which averaged well over 25 percent for the past decade.

The Solutions

Brazil, like many other developing countries, has allowed inflation without indexation to do the job of cutting real benefits that it could not do more explicitly because of political obstacles. This is inefficient because it creates uncertainty for workers—and inequitable because its effects are capricious and unpredictable.

A better way would be to lower promised replacement rates, reduce early retirement, shift to a constant or rising accrual rate structure, use a longer averaging period for the wage base, and index the resulting pension fully to wages, prices, or a combination of the two. These reforms could cut costs in half after they are fully phased in. A more radical approach would introduce a reform similar to that recently adopted by several Latin American countries—downsize the public pillar, flatten its benefits, and supplement it with a defined contribution plan in a privately managed pillar.

pay-as-you-go while creating a second mandatory pillar that is fully funded and privately managed.

Inflation, Indexation, and Productivity Growth

Protecting pensions against erosion by inflation is one of the major arguments for having a strong public pillar in an old age security program. When the cost of living rises, old people on fixed pensions are especially vulnerable. Private insurance plans sometimes offer indexed annuities—backed by indexed bonds, equities, and other assets whose value is expected to rise with inflation. But such plans may be unable to honor their promises in times of hyperinflation. In theory, the government can guarantee the real value of pensions by using taxation to shift the cost of inflation to younger generations, which are better able to

Box 4.9 A Better Way: Flat and Means-Tested Benefit Formulas in OECD Countries

SWITZERLAND. THE SWISS PAY-AS-YOU-GO PUBLIC pension scheme has a two-part benefit structure. The first part is an employment-related flat benefit based on years of covered employment, and the second part is based on each worker's average lifetime earnings. For a full career worker, the two parts together pay a pension varying from 20 percent to 40 percent of the average economy-wide wage—a relatively compressed benefit schedule. The required contribution rate is only 8.4 percent (split evenly between worker and employer), supplemented by a government transfer of 20 percent of total system expenditures.

The system has several safeguards to minimize labor market distortions, strategic manipulation, and perverse redistributions. The relatively low contribution rate dampens the effect on labor supply or demand. The absence of a ceiling on earnings subject to the payroll tax and the use of general revenue finance help keep the tax base broad, the required rate low, and the redistributive impact positive. There are few opportunities to retire early (below age 65 for men, 62 for women).

The employment-related flat pension provides basic income insurance to most old people. Since it is proportional to total years of employment, it avoids the problems of workers who never qualify because the eligibility period is too long and workers who escape contributions by entering the informal labor market but are still entitled to large pensions. Making average lifetime earnings the pensionable wage base in the earnings-related part discourages workers from understating earnings when they are young or evading when they are old—and minimizes perverse redistribution to higher-income workers whose wages rise steeply at the end of their careers. Pensions are indexed to the arithmetic average of price inflation and wage growth. This protects pensioners against inflation—but only partially, which helps put a brake on an inflationary spiral that is accompanied by real wage declines—and lets pensioners share in the country's economic growth.

The Netherlands. A more redistributional benefit formula in the Netherlands pays a universal flat benefit of about 38 percent of the average gross manufacturing wage to a single person and 54 per-

adapt and recoup. In practice, many public old age security schemes do not include indexation for inflation—or they index inadequately, so the real value of pensions paid after a few years of retirement is quite different from the initial value. Inflation without indexation is the way that most countries have scaled back unrealistic benefit promises.

Inflation needs to be taken into account both when setting the initial benefit and when adjusting benefits after retirement. In earnings-related schemes, the initial benefit level is calculated as a percentage of wages during some averaging period. Many OECD countries use a long averaging period of twenty to forty years and revalue earnings upward for wage inflation during the period. Instead of revaluing for inflation, developing countries shorten the averaging period. But this method does not adequately resolve the inflation problem. For example, during the 1980s Mexico used as the base wage a simple average of nominal wages over cent to a couple, indexed for inflation and supplemented by special means-tested benefits. The system is financed by a payroll tax on earnings, with a ceiling on taxable earnings 1.7 times the average wage—a financing method that is less progressive and probably also less efficient than that in Switzerland. The low tax ceiling and higher benefit rate lead to a higher required contribution rate of 15.2 percent. This is augmented by payments from the general treasury (about 15 percent of system expenditures) to cover the contributions of very low-income workers. The high tax cost of this program could have distortionary effects.

Australia. The Australian system, more redistributive and less costly than the Swiss or Dutch systems, pays a means- and asset-tested pension to those whose other income is not sufficient to bring their standard of living to the specified level. About 70 percent of the population gets at least part of the public pension, financed out of general revenues.

In Sum. These benefit structures, unlike the one in Brazil (box 4.8), minimize perverse redistribution and opportunities for strategic manipulation.

They also leave ample room for development of supplemental privately managed funded pension plans.

None of these systems is problem-free. The generous benefit structure in the Netherlands almost completely eliminates old age poverty, but it is also very costly and could be contributing to early retirement of old workers and unemployment among young workers. The Australian system is much cheaper, but many old people are clustered just above the threshold for support, whereas some middle-class retirees may give away their income and assets to qualify for benefits. As in all pay-as-you-go plans, intergenerational transfers have been large, especially in the Netherlands. Costs will escalate sharply as the population ages, and preliminary efforts to deal with this problem have provoked intense political controversy. To relieve the pressure on the public pillar, Australia and Switzerland recently made occupational pension plans mandatory, and in the Netherlands they are virtually mandatory as a result of collective bargaining (see chapter 5).

the preceding five years. A high rate of inflation over this period reduced the real base for new beneficiaries to a small fraction of what its revalued amount would have been.

Most countries with high rates of inflation periodically adjust the level of payments to current retirees. In OECD countries, this process tends to be largely automatic, although sometimes cost-of-living adjustments have been skipped. In developing countries, the adjustments typically are not automatic, and they are usually delayed and perhaps only partial, reducing pensioners' real incomes. The public pension plans of the transitional socialist economies have no automatic indexing provision because prices were stable under central planning. Now that shortages are showing up in price increases rather than queues, pensioners living on fixed incomes are at a disadvantage. In Mexico, only minimum pensions are indexed—so, all pensions quickly gravitate to the minimum. In Venezuela, the average real pension fell 80 percent between 1974 and 1992 because of inflation without indexation (figure 4.12 and box 4.10). Ninety-nine percent of pensioners received the minimum in 1993 (Instituto Venezolano de Seguro Social 1993).

When political obstacles prevent policymakers from reaching an explicit decision to cut spending, inflation cuts real benefits implicitly, as in Eastern Europe and the countries of the former Soviet Union. If these countries reduce inflation, they will have to find some more explicit way to deal with the high benefits and escalating costs of the public pension plan—politically difficult but fairer and more efficient. Workers who expect the real value of their pensions to be maintained do not make offsetting plans to save when they are young and are not able to compensate when they are old. Workers who are more realistic discount the

Figure 4.12 Real Pension Levels in Venezuela, 1974–92

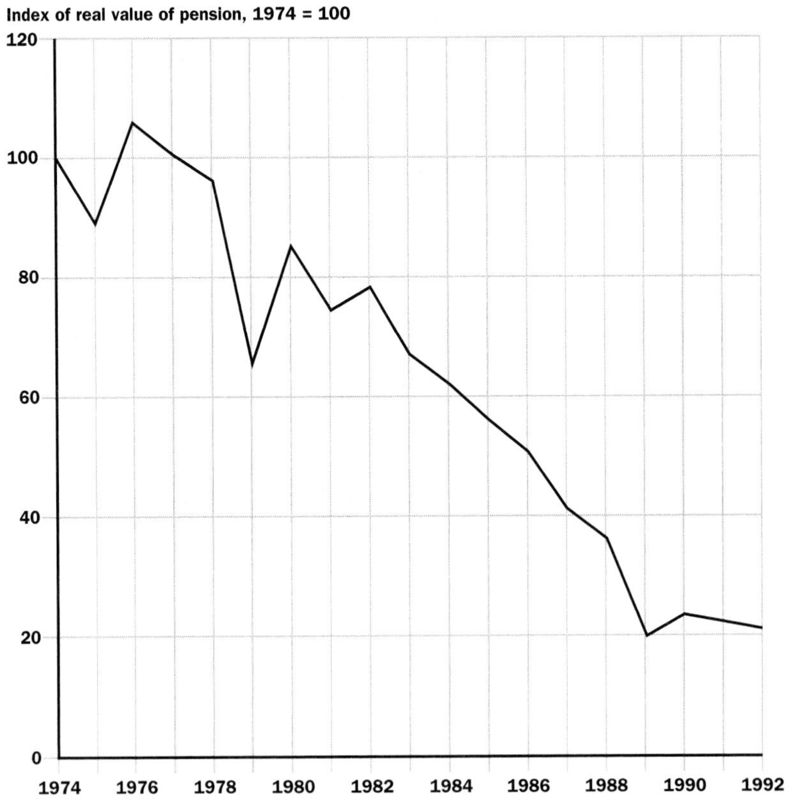

Index of real value of pension, 1974 = 100

Inflation destroyed the value of unindexed pensions in Venezuela.

Source: Marquez (1992).

promised benefits and try to avoid making contributions when they are young. Inflation affects different cohorts in capricious ways. In the interest of minimizing evasion and maximizing equity, the government should make modest, credible pension promises to begin with and should index pensions to adjust automatically to inflation. In an earnings-related benefit formula, the earnings used to compute the wage base should be fully revalued for inflation.

Pensions can be indexed to wages or prices or to some combination of both (as in Switzerland). Wage indexation maintains the relative position of pensioners. It allows them to share in the fruits of productivity growth, but it also subjects them to the risk of falling real pensions. If payroll taxes are expected to increase, countries may wish to use net wages rather than gross for the index, to hold the relative after-tax position of workers and pensioners constant. This is done in Germany and Japan (box 4.11). Price indexation holds the real value of benefits con-

---

Box 4.10 Inflation and Indexation under Public Pension Schemes

ALTHOUGH AUTOMATIC INDEXATION OF PUB-lic pension benefits is now common in most industrial countries, the majority of developing countries adjust pension levels for inflation only irregularly, on an ad hoc basis. Many Latin American countries and transitional socialist economies index only the minimum pension. High rates of inflation have driven average real pensions down toward the minimum, with as many as 40 to 70 percent of pensioners in these regions now receiving only the minimum pension. Industrial countries also did not index pensions before World War II. For example, real pension levels fell drastically in Germany during the hyperinflation of the 1920s.

Inflation affects public pension benefits and reserves in other ways as well. In earnings-related defined benefit schemes, high inflation rates reduce the real value of the pensionable base salary, if past wages are not revalued upward in this calculation. Many countries have multiple schemes, with those in higher-income occupations typically receiving better inflation protection than the general labor force. In

Mexico, for example, the scheme covering private sector workers averages the last five years of wages to determine the pensionable base, while the civil service scheme looks only at the last year's wages, yielding a much higher base in inflationary periods. Publicly managed pension reserves in Tunisia, Turkey, and many other countries are invested in public bonds denominated in nominal terms. The bonds earn negative returns, and the funds become decapitalized during inflationary periods.

The average real pension fell 80 percent in Venezuela between 1974 and 1992, 30 percent in Argentina between 1985 and 1992, and 40 percent in Hungary during the 1980s (figure 4.12). These and other public pension schemes failed to protect the old from inflation. Because uncontrolled inflation tends to be a country-specific risk (and is often accompanied by devaluation), a private scheme with some international diversification of pension fund investment (and some investment in stocks and real estate) would provide better protection to the old.

(Box continues on the following page.)

Box 4.10 *(continued)*

Even when written into law, indexation is not a solid guarantee. When inflation is particularly high, the government may decide to ignore indexation provisions, introducing the issue of political risk. Brazil delayed implementing indexation provisions during periods when the price level soared by 1 percent a day. The United States suspended inflation indexation for one year in 1984. The "index skip" lasted three years in Belgium in 1983–85 and two years in New Zealand in 1992–93. Suspensions like these may be warranted when they are part of a package of reforms designed to reduce everyone's claims on the national budget, but they are not a good substitute for real reform.

When governments reduce real benefits to solve a fiscal crisis, they default on their implicit promise of income security for pensioners—and in a way that is most harmful to the old. Older retirees end up being treated differently from newer retirees, current workers lose faith in the system, evasion increases, and the financial problems of public pension programs intensify.

What's to be done:

- Index pensions automatically to price inflation or to a combination of wage growth and inflation, taking care to set a real value of pensions that can be maintained under difficult fiscal conditions.
- Pursue complementary policies to protect savings from inflation, say by issuing inflation-indexed bonds and encouraging the development of financial markets.
- Avoid the temptation to require pension funds to invest in government bonds, often at negative real interest rates, and thus to decapitalize the funds.
- Encourage international diversification of pension fund investments.
- If earnings-related pensions are used, base them on lifetime average earnings, revalued for price inflation or wage growth, before applying the benefit formula.

stant, protected from price increases or wage declines, but their relative value will fall when real wages rise. If a country expects real wages to rise over long periods, indexing to prices or partially to wages and partially to prices will hold costs per pensioner down and help cover the rising costs of the demographic transition. It will also help countries garner the resources for the shift to a multipillar system.

Conclusion

AS A RESULT OF POLICY CHOICES BY GOVERNMENTS AND RE-sponses by individuals attempting to get the most while paying the least, the actual contribution rate required for system solvency is often much greater than the rate determined by demogra-

Box 4.11 Should Public Pensions Be Indexed to Prices or Wages?

MOST OECD COUNTRIES AND SOME DEVELOP-
ing countries adjust pensions for inflation, but they
differ as to whether they tie these adjustments to
price or wage changes. Under price indexation pensions move with the price level; their absolute real
value remains unchanged. Price indexation means
that the risk of changes in the standard of living that
sometimes accompanies inflation is borne by the
young, whose contribution rate would have to increase if the economy slowed. The insulation of the
old may make it more difficult for governments to
cut back on the high aggregate demand that caused
inflation in the first place. Price indexation also
means that the old do not share in any productivity
growth that occurs after they retire. The argument
for price indexation is that old people are less able to
adapt to falling real incomes than young people and
are less concerned about rising real incomes, since
their consumption habits are already established.
Canada, the United Kingdom, and the United States
index pensions to prices.

Under wage indexation pensions move with
wages. Old people share in higher real income when
wages rise and in shrinking real income when wages
fall. The argument for wage indexation is that young
families should not be expected to bear the full brunt
of drops in real per capita income and that old people should share in the fruits of any economic
growth. Wage indexation also helps keep pensions
equal for all beneficiaries in systems that pay a flat,
means-tested, or minimum pension, where pensions
for new beneficiaries are likely to rise with average
wages. Moreover, since most public pension programs are financed through a payroll tax, wage indexation makes the system as a whole relatively re-

silient to external shocks that alter real wages. Austria
and Mexico are among the countries using wage indexation. Germany and Japan index to disposable
wages; when payroll taxes increase to cover the rising
costs of social insurance, old people share the burden
with workers by getting lower pensions. Other countries may also move in this direction in the future.

If productivity is unchanged, indexation to the
wage level is equivalent to price indexation. But if
productivity changes—whether because of random
shocks, cyclical decline, or growth—wage and price
indexation will yield different real pensions, contribution rates, and degrees of old age security. Which
method people prefer depends on whether they care
more about their relative or their absolute position
and whether they are willing to pay a higher payroll
tax now for the possibility of a higher consumption
level after retirement.

When productivity is rising, wage indexation
holds the required contribution rate constant if all
else remains unchanged, while price indexation allows the contribution rate to fall. Policymakers may
wish to use the fruits of productivity growth for other
purposes—for example, to offset the rising dependency rates that are expected during the demographic transition or to provide the resources for a
shift to a multipillar system. Using price rather than
wage indexation would help to dampen the contribution rate increase needed to meet these other challenges. If people care about both their relative and
absolute positions, while governments want to capture some savings from productivity growth, the best
position may be a fifty-fifty combination of wage
(possibly the after-tax wage) and price indexation, as
in Switzerland.

phy alone. But the high tax rates lead to still higher evasion. Ultimately,
the system has become unsustainable in many countries. More basi-
cally, the system has become unsustainable because it has impeded economic growth.

In Latin America and the transitional economies of Eastern Europe, high payroll taxes have increased business costs, pushed labor into the informal sector, led to widespread evasion, and diverted spending away from important public goods. A number of Latin American countries are now making radical changes in their bankrupt pension systems as part of an overall reform of their crippled economies. In the transitional countries, too, the pension systems and the broader economies have broken down, but policymakers in these nations have not yet decided how to repair either. In virtually all of the developing countries, even though retirees frequently start out with generous pensions, these benefits have not been well protected from the ravages of inflation and other economic shocks. In addition, pension reserves have been depleted by inflation combined with government borrowing at low nominal rates. The old remain insecure.

OECD countries are seemingly in less trouble because of better functioning labor markets, greater ability to collect taxes, and lower inflation rates. But public pay-as-you-go schemes may have dampened long-term saving and capital accumulation relative to what would have occurred under fully funded schemes. And early retirement ages combined with earnings tests for pensions have helped diminish the labor force participation rates of older workers. As the baby boom generation retires, OECD countries will face tough choices between raising tax rates, cutting benefit rates, or diverting spending from other important public goods—choices that will be all the more difficult if old age policies have impeded growth (box 4.12).

Have the insurance and redistributional gains been worth the price? Despite their poverty alleviation goals, the intragenerational redistributions by public pension plans have not been very progressive, are often capricious, and are sometimes perverse, favoring upper-income groups. The biggest redistributive effect has been intergenerational, toward the first few cohorts of retirees and away from later cohorts. In industrial countries, this positive transfer probably deserves much of the credit for reducing poverty among the old and providing longevity insurance in the last three decades. But these transfers are about to end—and turn negative.

For developing countries tomorrow, just as for OECD countries today, the demographic transition and system maturation will create severe financial and intergenerational strains for public pay-as-you-go plans. To improve their financial sustainability, efficiency, and equity, these plans

Box 4.12 Tough Decisions in OECD Countries

AGING POPULATIONS AND MATURING PENSION schemes in OECD countries are widening the gap between expected future pension contributions and payouts. The present value of benefits scheduled to be paid between now and 2150 exceeds the present value of expected contributions by two to three times the value of present GDP for most OECD countries (box table 4.12, column 1). The fiscal burden implied by this shortfall has opened up heated debate in many OECD countries about the correct balance of real pension cuts and higher taxes needed to cover the growing pension deficits. But until now countries have come up only with quick-fix measures that have eroded benefits and raised payroll taxes without fixing the long-term deficit.

Thus, over the past decade:

- In the United States pensions of high-income retirees have become taxable, inflation indexation was skipped for one year, payroll taxes were increased, and a schedule for raising the retirement age was established.
- In the United Kingdom public pension entitlements were reduced in 1988 from 25 percent of the best twenty years of earnings to 20 percent of earnings over the entire working life.
- France increased the number of contribution years used in calculating pensions and introduced a new income tax earmarked for the country's huge social security deficits.

(Box continues on the following page.)

Box Table 4.12 Alternative Scenarios for Financing OECD Pension Liabilities

Country	(1) PAYG[a] pension gap (percentage of GDP)	Required tax increase as percentage of GDP under:		(4) Required partial wage actualization (percent)	(5) Required increase in retirement age
		(2) PAYG no changes[b]	(3) Partial funding		
Canada	250	6.3	4.4	20	16
France	216	5.5	4.0	60	8
Germany	160	6.2	3.6	50	11
Italy	233	11.9	5.3	40	10
Japan	200	6.8	4.3	30	9
United Kingdom	186	4.8	3.5	50	12
United States	43[c]	4.4	1.1	50	4

Definition of columns:
(1) Gap between expected revenues and expenditures.
(2) Pay-as-you-go continues without major modifications.
(3) Once-and-for-all increase in contribution rate from 1990.
(4) The extent to which a worker's real lifetime earnings are actualized to real wage growth.
(5) Required increase in retirement age assuming current age is 60.
a. Pay-as-you-go.
b. If financed by a payroll tax, this would imply a tax increase of 15 to 20 percentage points. Labor income is only two-thirds of GDP, and earnings above a specified ceiling are usually not taxed, so the covered wage bill is only about one-third of GDP (appendix table A.4).
c. The figure for the United States is based on the assumption that the government bonds in the social security trust fund are redeemed to cover part of the future obligations.
Source: Adapted directly from table 9, page 26 , Van der Noord and Herd (1993).

Box 4.12 *(continued)*

- Belgium reduced real pension levels through several "index skips" in the early 1980s.
- Germany has been gradually reducing its replacement rate formula, linking to post-tax rather than pretax wage.
- Italy announced a planned five-year increase in the retirement age.
- Japan reduced the benefit accrual rate.

These ad hoc adjustments are far from sufficient. A recent OECD report calculated the revenue gap for seven countries and evaluated the contribution rate that would be required to cover projected deficits over 1990–2150, if current benefit policies were unchanged (column 2). This no-change scenario was compared with three hypothetical reforms—each to start immediately—to balance pension finances: partial funding, partial wage indexation in benefit formulas, and later retirement. The simulations use a 4 percent discount rate for the period 1990–2010, reducing it gradually thereafter to 3 percent, and assume real wage growth of 1 percent in the United States and 2 percent in the other OECD countries.

The partial funding option entails a one-time hike in the current contribution rate to amass a temporary surplus to be used to pay the rising pension benefits (column 3). Public pension schemes in Japan and the United States currently use partial funding but not enough to cover the shortfall. The second option, reducing wage indexation, would work by cutting back on the upward revaluation of the pensionable wage base; pension benefits would be smaller because they would no longer reflect the full productivity gain that has taken place over the worker's lifetime (column

4). The last option shows how many years would have to be added to the present retirement age to eliminate the pension revenue shortfall (column 5).

If no changes are made in current pension programs, contributions would have to be gradually increased by 5 to 6 percent of GDP in most countries and by almost 12 percent in Italy (column 2). This implies a gradual payroll tax increase of about 15 to 20 percentage points, depending on the country. If partial funding is used, taxes would have to rise by 3 to 4 percent of GDP, requiring an immediate payroll tax increase of about 9 to 12 percentage points in most countries. At least part of the burden would probably fall on pensioners, in a continuation of the process of benefit erosion that began in the 1980s. Achieving pension fund balance through wage revaluation for pensions would require cutting the adjustment for economy-wide wage growth by at least half. Raising the retirement age would require postponing retirement for eight to twelve years, a politically impossible option in the short run but much more likely in the long run. In fact, later retirement is both probable and efficient.

These options do not exhaust the possibilities, but they illustrate some of the choices OECD countries will have to make. Tough decisions lie ahead. Will pension benefit levels fall, and how will that affect the old, whose incomes are already low? Will rising payroll and other taxes be accepted by workers whose wages are growing slowly or not at all? Will other government programs be cut in order to cover pension deficits? Will government pension promises lose credibility? In short, will public pension systems survive in their present form?

should be reformed in a number of ways, depending on their starting point (box 4.13):

- Raising the retirement age, reducing opportunities and incentives for early retirement.

Box 4.13 Key Features of a Reformed Public Pillar

THE PUBLIC PILLAR OF AN OLD AGE SECURITY program should offer benefits that are fairly distributed, adequate as a safeguard against poverty, yet affordable and therefore sustainable in the long run. The following elements of a public pension plan are essential on their merits and as a prelude to a more basic reform—a transition to a multipillar system that also incorporates a decentralized funded retirement plan:

- *A flat or a means-tested pension* or a *minimum pension guarantee* to a mandatory saving plan is the simplest, least costly way of providing a minimum level of security to all. For high-income countries flat benefits could be universal and financed from general revenues. For lower-income countries benefits could be tied to years of service in covered employment and financed through payroll taxes. Countries with significant flat or means-tested components to their public pension plans spend less than other countries on old age security, and this spending is better targeted toward the poverty alleviation goal.
- Benefits should be set at a *realistic level* that insures people against poverty and should be *indexed* (to prices or to a combination of prices and after-tax wages) to retain their value through time.
- While an earnings-related scheme is not recommended, if one is used, the *wage replacement rate should be based on lifetime earnings*, with an accrual structure that rewards workers for staying in the system. Short-term workers should get a reduced pension but should not be excluded entirely.
- The *retirement age should rise regularly with life expectancy* for the country as a whole. Early retirement schemes have been a major source of financial problems in public pension schemes and a negative force in the economy. Early retirees should have their benefits reduced and late retirees should have their benefits increased in an actuarially fair way.
- Measures to *reduce the costs* of the old age security system can be complemented by measures to increase revenues, such as increasing or eliminating the ceiling on taxable earnings, shifting to a broader income or consumption tax base, and investing the reserves of partially funded schemes to maximize returns.
- *Pension reserves should be kept separate from general government funds*, and *investments should be diversified.* Forced investment in government securities, which often results in negative returns, should be avoided. Better still, because such changes may not be politically feasible and pension reserves will continue to be diverted to low-yielding government projects, the public pension plan should be run on a strictly *tax-financed basis.* Pension reserves should be accumulated in a privately managed pillar that is more sheltered from political influence.

- Lowering statutory replacement rates in cases where they are now too generous.
- Making the benefit formula relatively flat, means-tested, or a minimum pension guarantee.
- Tying the earnings-related component (if there is one) to long-term wages.
- Reducing contribution rates but raising ceilings on taxable earnings.

- Eliminating pension reserves that invariably earn below-market interest rates.
- Indexing for inflation or wage growth.

Nevertheless, because commitments to retirees and workers nearing retirement dominate the total costs of the system, the short-run impact of many reforms is limited. These commitments were easy to make but are difficult to reverse—a reminder that initial costs in pay-as-you-go schemes are misleading and old age security requires very long-term planning. To avoid future shocks, countries currently formulating or expanding their old age systems need to calculate the long-term financial viability and intergenerational implications of their plans, taking projected demographic changes into account (see chapter 3 and issue brief 3). In the past, few countries have done so.

Are these problems endemic weaknesses or incidental design mistakes? Their universality suggests the former. The problems are greatest in countries where the public pension plan is supposed to do the whole job of providing old age security, with little if any help from other plans. In this situation, the public plan is inherently in conflict because it is asked to meet multiple but incompatible goals.

If the system is actuarially fair it provides a form of insurance and saving for workers but does not meet the redistributive objective. If it meets its redistributive goals, it fails to link benefits closely to contributions, encourages distortionary evasion, and is not a good instrument for saving and insurance. The combination of multiple conflicting goals leads to an expensive, complex, and nontransparent system that is open to political manipulation and ultimately unsustainable.

The complexity of a dominant public pillar enables influential groups to exert political pressures for design features that are neither equitable nor efficient—from which they benefit while passing the hidden costs on to others in their own or future generations. Such a strategy is especially tempting when populations are young, systems are immature, and politicians are concerned about today more than tomorrow. This political perspective helps explain why the design flaws described in this chapter—early retirement, high contribution rates that are evaded, low ceilings on taxable earnings, overgenerous pensions for the first generation of retirees, and greater benefits for the rich than for the poor—are so widespread in both industrial and developing countries.

A multipillar old age security system reduces these adverse political pressures. The saving function and part of the insurance function can be turned over to a mandatory, funded, privately managed competitive scheme in which benefits are directly tied to contributions, so reducing the incentives for evasion and the opportunities for manipulation. This scheme is likely to have a more positive effect on national saving, labor productivity, and growth. Planning for tomorrow is built-in. The extent and direction of redistribution and the degree of coinsurance needed from the government will then become much clearer and more explicit, and these functions can be carried out through a redesigned and more carefully targeted public pension plan.

CHAPTER 5

Occupational Pension Plans

I N MOST COUNTRIES THE FIRST PENSION SCHEMES WERE both occupational and public—set up by the government to cover its military and civilian employees. In some low-income countries these are still the only groups covered. But in middle- and high-income countries, even as public sector employees kept their superior benefits, the concept of pensions tied to employment was gradually extended in two directions: publicly run plans were established to cover all formal sector workers and supplementary occupational plans were established by many private employers. Today, occupational plans cover about one-third of all workers in OECD countries but far fewer in developing and transitional countries.

Unlike public pension plans (chapter 4) or personal saving plans (chapter 6), occupational schemes are sponsored by employers, usually voluntarily or as a result of collective bargaining. Their big advantages are that they can be launched with little direct government involvement and relatively low administrative costs—and their contributions are unlikely to be viewed as taxes that people try to evade. But their coverage is uneven, their benefits are not always trustworthy, they differ significantly from one employer to another, and they often are not transferable. This last feature distinguishes them from the other kinds of old age plans and raises efficiency and equity questions.

Both occupational and personal saving schemes enable workers who earn more during their active years to accumulate larger pension rights for their retirement years. Countries must decide which is a better complement to a redistributive public plan that provides a floor to retirement income.

Brief History

ONE OF THE FIRST OCCUPATIONAL PENSION PLANS WAS SET up in the United States in 1776 (the year of independence), providing half-pay for life for soldiers disabled during the Revolutionary War with England. Old age benefits for those in military service were added in 1780. By the early nineteenth century, civilian public sector workers in the United States, the United Kingdom, and other countries were receiving pensions from their employers, the government. Within the private sector, employers paid lump sums to retiring employees on a discretionary basis—to reward them for their long and faithful service—long before formal pension plans were established. This practice is still found among family-owned firms in developing countries (Williamson in Turner and Beller 1992; Schieber 1989; Hannah 1986).

Formal pension schemes became popular in many industrial countries in the second half of the nineteenth and the beginning of the twentieth centuries as a tool of personnel administration for large corporations—to encourage retention of workers with valuable job skills and to ease older workers, whose productivity had declined, into retirement. The offer of deferred payment also deterred fraud and embezzlement among money-handling clerks in banks, railways, and gas companies and induced loyalty among personnel with access to confidential information about new competitive technologies. In these situations, pension plans may have raised productivity, which in turn supported a higher level of compensation. Some workers may have preferred pensions to wages because group plans overcame adverse selection problems that limited their access to annuities markets.

Employers treated pensions as discretionary benefits, not as employee rights. Most plans were defined benefit, largely unfunded, skewed toward senior workers and managers, and lost by workers who left the company before retirement. Thus, besides the efficiency reasons for offering pensions instead of simply offering wages, employers also offered pensions because they did not have to pay until much later and perhaps not even then. Before World War II, these plans had few financial problems because of their limited coverage, modest benefits, small number of pensioners, and fast-growing industry.

Increases in income tax rates and changes in tax rules in the decades following World War II encouraged the expansion of pension plans and the creation of separate trust funds. Most countries made contributions to occupational pension funds tax deductible and deferred taxes on their investment income. Thanks to these tax advantages not available to personal pension plans, workers and employers alike considered occupational plans a desirable substitute for higher wages, so their coverage and assets grew in most OECD countries. Further growth occurred more recently as occupational plans became mandatory in Australia and Switzerland and quasi-mandatory as a result of collective bargaining in Denmark and the Netherlands. Japan and the United Kingdom allow employers to opt out of the earnings-related part of their public plans and into occupational plans (box 5.1).

Currently, about one in every four old persons and more than one-third of the working age population in OECD countries are covered by an occupational pension (table 5.1). As such pension plans grew in importance, problems and pressures to regulate them also grew. Although social security pensions are larger than occupational pensions for low-income workers, occupational pensions are more important than social security for high-income workers in industrial countries. They also are heavily regulated.

In developing and transitional economies, this move toward occupational plans is at an early stage. In most cases, employer-sponsored pension plans cover public sector workers, and the coverage of private sector workers has been growing in such countries as Brazil, India, Indonesia, Mexico, South Africa, and Zimbabwe. These countries and others must decide whether to adopt policies that encourage, constrain, or regulate the spread of occupational pension plans—as a mechanism for achieving the saving or consumption-smoothing function of old age security systems (box 5.2).

How Occupational Plans Work

WHETHER SPONSORED BY SINGLE OR MULTIPLE EMPLOYERS, occupational pension plans can be defined benefit or defined contribution or partially or fully funded, and their economic impact varies accordingly.

Box 5.1 Recent Developments in Occupational Pension Schemes in OECD Countries

IN OECD COUNTRIES THERE HAS BEEN A SLOW trend toward making occupational plans mandatory, to reduce the burden on the public pillar, while regulating them to impose minimum standards of vesting, portability, and funding. Also increasing the role of occupational plans are provisions that allow employers to opt out of public plans, if they meet certain minimum conditions.

In Switzerland, a constitutional amendment, passed in 1972 and implemented in 1985, imposed on all employers the obligation to provide pension benefits to their employees. The law requires separate funding and imposes minimum conditions akin to defined contribution schemes (although defined benefit schemes offering greater benefits can also be established). The pension law expanded coverage among employees of small firms, but in many respects it simply reaffirmed existing practice among large employers. Minimum contributions are vested immediately, while employers' contributions beyond the minimum vest gradually. Two problems remain:

limited portability beyond the minimum amount may restrict mobility, and low returns are earned on these pension funds. More recently, Australia introduced mandatory provision of funded occupational pensions (the superannuation guarantee charge) (see chapter 8). In Denmark and the Netherlands, many occupational plans are established on industry-wide lines and coverage is extensive, with participation often compulsory as a result of collective agreements. These, too, are funded and they vest quickly.

In the United Kingdom, where the state offers an earnings-related benefit and an employment-related flat benefit, employers are allowed to contract out of the former but not the latter. An employer who contracts out must provide either a defined benefit scheme with a pension at least as generous as the earnings-related public pension would have been or a defined contribution scheme with a minimum contribution rate at least as great as the contribution that would otherwise have been paid. Contracted-out benefits are indexed (partly by the company and

Single Employer or Multiemployer

Occupational pension schemes can be industry-wide or company-based. Industry-wide schemes, which are common in continental Europe, facilitate transferability of benefits. Company-based schemes predominate in Anglo-American countries, supplemented by multiemployer plans in sectors with high labor mobility, such as construction. Occupational plans in developing countries tend to be single-employer, covering workers in civil service, public utilities, financial institutions, large corporations, and local subsidiaries of multinationals. For both types, administrative and marketing costs tend to be low, since they can easily be added to existing payroll systems.

partly by the government) and are insured by the government. Almost half the work force is now covered by benefits contracted out to occupational schemes. As a result, annual contributions, pension benefits, and assets of occupational plans have become a larger share of GNP in the United Kingdom than in Canada or the United States (table 5.1). But more recent provisions allow workers to opt out of both the public and occupational earnings-related plans and into their own personal pension plans; about a quarter of the labor force has done so, and this may diminish the importance of employer-run schemes in the future.

These provisions diminish the redistributive potential of the public earnings-related scheme, since workers who think they are losing can simply opt out. A recent study in the United Kingdom found that the redistributive effect, although small before, got even smaller after opting out was permitted. In particular, young workers have tended to contract out; the public system will be in financial trouble if they opt back in as they grow older and find the accrual rate formula more attractive. To prevent this, the United Kingdom has given larger rebates to workers over 30 who stay out of the state system and has raised its contribution rate for those who stay in (Disney and Whitehouse 1992).

Opting out of the earnings-related part of the public scheme is also permitted in Japan, but the conditions are more stringent. Only large employers are eligible. They must provide a pension that is more generous than the state pension, they get a smaller reduction in required social security contributions, and the funds must be turned over to a trust bank or an insurance company approved by the government. Contracted-out benefits are insured (and also indexed) by the government, a service that is paid for by premiums levied on the employer (Turner 1993a). As a result, the occupational pillar in Japan is large, but not as large as that in the United Kingdom.

Defined Benefit or Defined Contribution

Occupational defined benefit plans provide an annuity based on a specified formula, as in public pension plans. The benefit usually depends on years of service and the worker's salary over the last few years of employment. Sometimes workers are required to contribute a percentage of their salaries to the pension plan, with the employer making up the difference. Employers usually retain the right to fire workers, terminate plans, and convert accrued benefits to a defined contribution plan. Most important, benefits are vested (or owned) and portable (to another plan) after a qualifying period of employment; if workers quit or are dismissed before vesting, they lose the rights to

Table 5.1 Occupational Pension Coverage for Selected Countries, 1980s

Country	Percentage of labor force covered by occupational pension	Occupational pension recipients as percentage of persons over 65	Occupational pension assets as percentage of GNP (1990–91)
Austria	less than 10	—	—
Australia[a]	60	13	39
Belgium	5	—	—
Brazil	3	—	4
Canada	45	42	35
Costa Rica	4	2	—
Denmark[b]	—	3	60
France[a]	80	—	3
Germany	65	18	4
Greece	40	—	—
Hong Kong	35	—	—
Ireland	50	—	—
Italy	5	—	—
Japan	38	10	8
Netherlands[b]	82	72	76
New Zealand	22	—	—
Norway	25	—	—
South Africa	70	—	57
Spain	3	—	—
Switzerland[a]	92	28	70
Trinidad and Tobago	—	8	—
United Kingdom	50–60	33	73
United States	55	25	66

— Not available.

Note: Private sector labor force coverage is less than 3 percent for most other countries.

a. Coverage by occupational pension is compulsory. In France most occupational pensions are pay-as-you-go.

b. Coverage quasi-compulsory, arranged by collective bargaining.

Source: Data for varying years in 1980s.

Column 1: OECD countries from OECD (1992), except Japan and Switzerland, which come from Turner and Dailey (1991); Brazil from internal World Bank files; Hong Kong government (1992); South Africa (1992).

Column 2: Australia, Canada, Netherlands, and United States (1985) from Luxembourg Income Study; for Germany and Denmark (1988) from Eurostat (1992); France (1988) and Switzerland (1987) from Turner and Dailey (1991); Japan from Yumiba (1990); United Kingdom (1986) from Daykin (1990). Data for Trinidad and Tobago (1983) from Pan-American Health Organization (1989d).

Column 3: from Davis (1993). Brazil from internal World Bank files. Mouton Report, South Africa (1992). See table 5.2 for notes.

Box 5.2 Occupational Pension Schemes in Developing Countries

IN DEVELOPING COUNTRIES, AS IN INDUSTRIAL countries earlier, occupational pension plans are few in number and mainly cover employees of governments, public enterprises, financial institutions, and local subsidiaries of multinationals. Publicly managed plans for public sector employees are the most common, and they tend to be more generous than other public plans.

Company-based schemes are found in some countries formerly under British rule, such as Cyprus, India, South Africa, and Zimbabwe, and in countries in which multinational corporations have a strong presence, such as Brazil, Indonesia, and Mexico. Such plans are rarer in countries with extensive social security systems, such as Tunisia and Turkey, or with well-developed national provident funds, such as Malaysia and Singapore. Company-based pension schemes are often established to meet a country's obligatory seniority and severance payment rules. In Mexico, companies use pension schemes to avoid layoffs: employees are induced to retire voluntarily by the promise of a pension equivalent to—but receiving more generous tax treatment than—the severance pay to which they are entitled.

Since regulations do not require full funding, pension schemes are frequently unfunded or only nominally funded through book reserves. In many countries most interest and capital gains are tax-free, so concentrating investment income in pension funds offers little tax advantage. But unfunded pension plans may not be able to keep their benefit promises.

The limited coverage of occupational pension schemes and the absence of regulations have enabled companies to impose stringent vesting and portability restrictions. Vesting of ten to fifteen years is common for pension schemes that offer only minimal benefits—and as many as twenty-five to thirty years when benefits are more generous. Moreover, the benefits have limited portability, posing possible equity and efficiency problems if the plans should grow. Workers with many years of service may be reluctant to move to jobs in which their wages and productivity may be higher if this means they will lose their accumulated pension rights. Some who move may be uninformed and may lose their pensions unexpectedly. Normal retirement age varies considerably and is as low as 50 to 55 years in many countries. Workers who join a company at age 20 or 25 and remain until age 50 or 55 fare well under these plans. Others get little or nothing.

South Africa, which has long had well-developed and well-regulated private pension funds, in lieu of a large public pension plan, is an exception to this pattern. So is Indonesia, whose national provident fund has operated with very low contribution and benefit rates, allowing company pension schemes to fill the gap. Indonesia recently passed legislation to regulate occupational pension funds, which is likely to lead the way for regulatory reform in other developing countries (box 5.6).

their pension benefits. Even those who are vested normally lose some of their benefits.

The employer thus bears the investment risk, but workers bear the risk of employer insolvency and job mobility. Workers also bear the risks that their wages will fail to rise late in their working years, which will reduce their pension as well, and that inflation will erode their benefits after retirement, since benefits are rarely indexed.

Defined benefit plans can be funded or operate on a pay-as-you-go basis. Pay-as-you-go plans are self-administered, whereas fully funded plans, especially those of small employers, are often administered by life insurance companies. Plans covering civil servants and military personnel are usually pay-as-you-go. Unregulated plans in developing countries are largely unfunded. The mandatory private occupational scheme in France is also pay-as-you-go. Many German companies use a "book reserve" system in which pension obligations appear as liabilities on the books of the companies, deductible for tax purposes, but are used internally rather than being placed in a separate trust. This facilitates corporate financing out of retained earnings but is otherwise very similar to pay-as-you-go.

With the foregoing major exceptions, most defined benefit schemes in the private sector in industrial countries are substantially funded. Tax provisions often encourage funding, and regulations sometimes demand it. In a competitive world economy, with an aging labor force, the risk of employer default is substantial in pay-as-you-go schemes (see below). Funding reduces this risk but also raises the cost of pension plans to employers.

In defined contribution plans, the worker or the employer or both contribute, with retiring workers getting a lump sum or annuity that depends on the contributions plus the investment income. Thus, defined contribution plans are fully funded by definition—and easily integrated with a national mandatory saving plan. Often, they are administered by life insurance companies or other financial institutions. Workers sometimes have some choice about how their contributions are invested, but usually the choice is limited to selecting among bond, equity, and money market funds specified by the employer. There are relatively few vesting and portability restrictions, especially if the plans are financed primarily by worker contributions. In other words, employer solvency and mobility risk are less than in defined benefit plans, and workers also benefit from diversification—the pension is not tied to their wages or place of employment—but they bear the remaining investment risk. If the accumulated capital is insufficient to pay them their expected pension, the employer has no responsibility to bail them out.

Economic Impact

UNLIKE PUBLIC PENSION PLANS, OCCUPATIONAL PLANS, when funded, have important positive implications for the operations of capital markets. Their impact on labor markets, income distribution, and public finance is more ambiguous and problematic.

Impact on Capital Markets

Long-term saving and capital accumulation. Current regulations in most OECD countries require that occupational pension plans be fully funded. Such plans should raise long-term saving unless households cut back on their personal saving or borrow to offset the increased pension saving.

Evidence from the United States indicates that each dollar of occupational pension savings reduces individual savings by 60 cents, so total private savings increase by 40 cents (Munnell and Yohn 1992; Pesando 1991). In Switzerland, a crowd-out effect of about 20 percent was found, so the net positive effect is 80 percent of occupational pension savings (OECD 1988c). In Australia, government projections assumed that half the contributions to the new mandatory occupational scheme would be offset by declines in voluntary saving, so net national saving would increase by 16 percent (Bateman and Piggott 1992b, 1993). These estimates are all consistent with the argument that funded schemes increase saving moderately relative to the no-pension state and more substantially relative to pay-as-you-go plans. Furthermore, the increased saving is committed for the long term, which should enhance the financial backing for long-term investments (chapter 3 and issue brief 4).

Besides increasing total long-term saving, occupational plans concentrate these savings in a small number of institutional investors. In Denmark, the Netherlands, Switzerland, the United Kingdom, and the United States, the assets of private pension funds, including pension funds run by banks and life insurance companies, are equal to more than half of GNP and are rapidly increasing (table 5.2). In the United Kingdom and the United States, this growth is due to the spectacular recent rise in stock market prices. In Denmark, the Netherlands, and Switzerland, it is due to a substantial expansion in coverage as plans became mandatory or quasi-mandatory. In developing and transitional countries, the capital accumulation by occupational plans is much less, both because their coverage is much lower and because they tend to be largely unfunded, as in the early years of plans in OECD countries. As occupational plans spread to these countries, they might become a mech-

Table 5.2 Pension Fund Assets as Percentage of GDP, 1970–91
(including estimated pension fund assets managed by insurance firms)

	1970	1975	1980	1985	1991
Australia	—	—	—	—	39
Canada	14.2	14.2	18.7	25.3	35
Denmark	18.8	18.8	26.3	45.0	60
Germany	2.6	2.6	2.6	4.0	4
Japan	0.0	1.6	3.2	6.4	8
Netherlands	29.0	36.0	46.0	68.0	76
Switzerland	38.0	41.0	51.0	59.0	70
United Kingdom	20.7	18.3	28.1	57.3	73
United States	29.3	34.6	40.7	50.6	66

—Not available.

Note: For 1970–85, the share of total pension funds managed by life insurance firms is assumed to be the same as it was in 1991. Book reserves are important in Germany and Japan, representing 3 and 7 percent of GDP, respectively, in 1991. These are not included here. Bank-run pension funds are a large share of the total in Denmark; the share is assumed to be the same for 1970–85 as it was in 1991.

Source: Davis (1993, 1994); Brankato (1994).

anism for capital accumulation and capital market deepening—if they require funding.

Capital allocation. Occupational pension funds in OECD countries have become a major source of long-term capital in their own economies and beyond. Unlike public pension reserves, these funds have been invested relatively free of political ties. As a result, most investments have been in private sector assets, including equities, and they have earned much higher returns than publicly managed pension funds and reserves (Davis 1993; figures 3.7, 4.5, and 5.1; appendix table A.12).

The United Kingdom led the way: pension funds hold almost two-thirds of their reserves in stocks and own about half of all domestic corporate equity, as well as considerable foreign equity. The move to equities was spurred by high rates of inflation and a booming stock market at varying times over the last three decades, plus the absence of regulations restricting investment choice. Although the equity share is much smaller in continental European countries, private sector securities and loans (some of them to the sponsoring employers) still make up the largest part of European pension fund assets. The United States stands somewhere in between, with about half of all pension funds in the stock market (see figure 5.1 and appendix table A.12). Pension funds own a

Figure 5.1 Share of Occupational Pension Fund Assets in Domestic Equities and Foreign Securities, Selected OECD Countries, 1970 and 1990

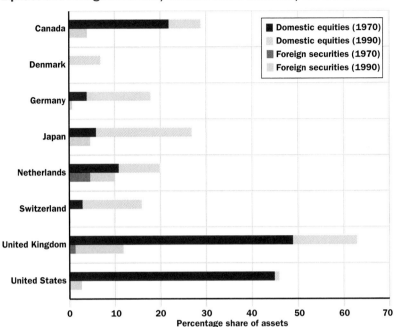

Legend:
- Domestic equities (1970)
- Domestic equities (1990)
- Foreign securities (1970)
- Foreign securities (1990)

Countries: Canada, Denmark, Germany, Japan, Netherlands, Switzerland, United Kingdom, United States

Percentage share of assets

Source: Davis (1993).

Unfettered by political investment criteria, occupational pension funds have become a source of long-term capital for the private sector, at home and abroad.

quarter of all equities and more than half of all corporate bonds in the U.S. economy. To the degree that occupational pension funds have increased long-term saving or directed savings toward productive investments, they have enhanced growth in their countries and in the broader world economy.

Simulated real annual returns to occupational schemes averaged 3 to 5 percent in a sample of OECD countries between 1970 and 1990 and exceeded 7 percent during the 1980s (table 5.3). The highest returns over the period were in the United Kingdom in the 1980s because of its strong stock market and large proportion of equity investments. Occupational plans in the United States did very well in the 1980s but not as well as other institutional investors, such as equity mutual funds (Lakonishok, Shleifer, and Vishny 1992)—a result that has been variously attributed to high risk aversion, lack of competition, agency problems, and public management of civil service plans. The lowest returns were in Switzerland, where interest rates and equity proportions are low.

Table 5.3 Simulated Real Rate of Return to Private Occupational Pension Funds in Eight Industrial Countries, 1970–90

	1970–75	1975–80	1980–85	1985–90	1970–90
Canada[a]	-1.8	-1.1	5.2	7.7	2.2
Denmark[a]	-2.0	0.8	16.9	—	4.1
Germany	3.3	3.2	7.6	6.2	5.1
Japan[a]	-1.0	-1.6	10.9	13.6	4.4
Netherlands	-1.5	1.9	10.4	6.2	4.2
Switzerland	-1.4	3.7	2.7	-0.2	1.2
United Kingdom	-0.5	5.0	12.4	8.0	6.1
United States	-1.6	-2.0	7.7	9.6	3.3
Average	**-0.8**	**1.2**	**9.2**	**7.3**	**3.8**

— Not available.

Note: Figures are compounded annual averages rounded to first decimal. Average is unweighted simple average. These rates of return are based on portfolio allocations among asset types and annual data on yields and prices by asset type, since direct data on rates of returns are not available. These rates of return are very sensitive to the base year chosen. For example, the rate of return in the United States is 3.3 percent for the period 1970–90 but is only 1.8 percent for 1966–90 and would be much higher for 1961–90 or 1981–90. Administrative costs are not subtracted from returns.

a. Data through 1987 (Denmark), 1988 (Japan), 1989 (Canada).

Source: Davis (1993).

In defined benefit plans, sponsoring employers choose the investment manager and bear the investment risk, since they will have to cover any shortfall. They therefore take both yield and risk into account in their decisions. Occupational defined contribution plans—in which employers choose (or limit the worker's choice of) the investment manager but workers bear the investment risk—pose a potential agency problem that may distort capital allocation decisions. Employers might make risk-yield trade-offs different from those preferred by workers. Or they might hand investment management over to financial institutions that will cover the firm's administrative costs rather than maximize net returns to the pension fund. (This contrasts with personal saving plans, discussed in the next chapter, in which workers who bear the investment risk get to choose the investment manager.) Although disparities might be expected in the investment performance of defined benefit and defined contribution plans, data from the United States show little difference (Turner and Beller 1989).

Overall, occupational plans, whether defined benefit or defined contribution, have more investment freedom than publicly managed schemes and greater incentives to maximize yield for a given level of risk.

This is so because the workers who bear the risk don't choose the management

As a mechanism for allocating long-term saving productively, with rates of return as an indicator, decentralized occupational plans appear to be far superior to centralized funds.

Institutional investors and financial innovations. In the United States, pension funds and life insurance companies became the main forces behind financial innovations after the Employee Retirement Income Security Act (ERISA) of 1974, which imposed minimum funding requirements and sharply increased the demand for hedging instruments. New instruments have been tailored to the needs of pension funds (such as zero-coupon bonds, collateralized mortgage obligations, mortgage-backed securities, indexed futures and options, and guaranteed income contracts). These financial instruments have transformed illiquid loans into highly liquid and tradable securities and enabled new forms of risk sharing, facilitating both business investment and housing finance. U.K. pension funds make active use of financial instruments in their international investment strategies, increasing liquidity and lowering transaction costs. So, one reason for encouraging private funded pension plans in middle-income developing and transitional countries is they might become an instrument of financial innovation and capital market deepening.

Concentrating savings in large pension funds, rather than leaving them in the hands of individual investors, can also have undesirable effects on financial markets. Institutionalizing savings and formalizing procedures may make it harder for small firms and new ventures to get financing. This may be particularly relevant in developing countries where small firms predominate and informal information networks often work better than formal ones. Pension funds have difficulty researching firms without track records. They minimize costs by dealing with larger companies, preferably those traded on exchanges. They lack expertise in supplying venture capital. And they face prudential limits on the proportion of a company's equity that they may hold. Pension funds have also been accused of contributing to stock market volatility by their herd behavior and overly rapid response to price changes.

Pension funds and corporate governance. When pension funds have a big stake in corporate equities, they are in a better position than individuals to overcome "free rider" problems, demand improved accounting and auditing procedures, and get information. They are also better able to use that information to assess company managers and press for changes if management is not performing effectively—thereby lessening problems stemming from diversified ownership and separation of ownership from control.

When, however, pension funds have only a small stake in a company, it is easier for them to vote with their feet (by selling company shares) than with their voices—a strategy they have used for many years. Pension fund managers have been criticized for focusing too much on the short term and failing to monitor managerial performance, especially long-term performance. This has left company managers unconstrained, except by the threat of merger and takeover, a socially costly route. Only recently, as ownership stakes have increased, have occupational plans begun to monitor the governance of the corporations in which they invest—developing long-term relationships and bringing about changes in the structure of corporate boards and managerial compensation (box 5.3).

Although problems arising from separation of ownership from control and corporate governance are not yet on the agenda in low-income countries, they are coming to the fore in some middle-income and transitional economies. Can pension funds solve this problem for them? In many of these countries, large occupational pension plans are found mainly in the public sector and state enterprises, so control over corporate management by plan sponsors would be tantamount to government control—precisely what they are trying to move away from.

Private sector schemes are emerging slowly, few of these schemes (aside from those in multinationals) are large enough to serve as monitors, and the sponsoring employers would probably be reluctant to interfere in the affairs of other companies that might reciprocate. In addition, most occupational plans in these countries are largely unfunded, so they do not even have substantial assets. Until funding is required by regulations, and the regulations are enforced, occupational pension schemes will not play a constructive role in corporate governance—or, for that matter, in capital market deepening.

Impact on Labor Markets

Occupational plans, especially defined benefit plans that limit vesting and portability and encourage retirement at an early age, have potentially important effects on labor force participation, training, and mobility—and therefore on the efficiency of labor markets.

Vesting and portability. Where job-specific skills are important, compensation schemes that attract stable workers and discourage labor mobility allow employers to recoup hiring and training costs and raise labor productivity, serving a useful economic role. Wage schedules that rise

Box 5.3 Are Pension Funds Good Monitors of Corporate Management?

ONE OF THE MOST IMPORTANT FUNCTIONS OF financial institutions is to monitor the corporate sector in which their funds are invested. In Germany and Japan, commercial banks play this role. They maintain long-term relationships with their customers, monitor corporate performance, and intervene when necessary to replace managers and restructure operations. Some analysts argue that banks are too conservative as monitors, since their primary concern is loan repayment rather than profit maximization.

The United Kingdom and the United States have a different monitoring system, with such specialized institutions as credit rating agencies, stockbrokers, and—indirectly—securities markets. When investors lose confidence in a corporation's managers, they sell its stock, driving down the price of the stock relative to the value of the corporation's assets and making it an attractive target for a buyout or a takeover. Some analysts maintain that this is a costly monitoring mechanism and argue for a more constructive and direct system of evaluation and control: sticking with corporate managers whose prospects for long-term performance are good and replacing others. Pension funds that own large blocks of stock obviously are in a better position than individual investors to exercise this supervisory oversight, but in the past they have failed to do so.

Part of the problem is the fragmentation of the pension fund industry and the diversification of its holdings. There are a million pension funds in the United States, each with many small holdings. Diversified institutional investors have little incentive to monitor and strengthen the long-term performance of individual companies. It is easier to sell the shares of failing companies and walk away from the problem.

Recently, however, pension fund representatives on the boards of some leading U.S. and U.K. corporations have begun to press for significant changes in corporate governance: electing outside directors, eliminating directors who are company suppliers and therefore might have conflicts of interest with shareholders, opening up the proxy process to allow greater communication among shareholders, using confidential voting at board meetings, expanding the roles of committees that are independent of the directors, disclosing the amount of and rationale for managerial compensation, and opposing costly measures designed to protect existing managers in the event of a takeover. In the United States, the California Public Employees Retirement System and the New York State Common Retirement Fund have led the way. As institutional investors grow in size and find it increasingly difficult to sell their large holdings without disrupting the market, they will exert greater pressure on corporate boards.

In developing and transitional economies, if occupational pension plans grew and were funded they would own a large share of the country's financial assets and could play an even larger role in corporate governance. In fact, the concentration of ownership could become a problem. Ten years ago Sweden considered allowing the funded part of its pension plan to invest in private corporations, but the idea was dropped for fear that the unions that controlled the fund would end up controlling Swedish industry. The bigger problems in developing countries are that most plans are underfunded or only partially funded and equity investments are often restricted; so, they do not even have a foot in the door.

with tenure and long-term labor contracts could serve this purpose. But collective bargaining agreements or other legal or cultural factors sometimes prevent the use of such contracts. Pensions with limited vesting are then a less transparent way (and, because of tax advantages, a privately cheaper way) of encouraging investment in job-specific skills that boost productivity.

Occupational pension plans in OECD countries historically had restrictive vesting periods (after which pension benefits are owned by the worker), some as long as twenty to twenty-five years, and no provisions for portability. Workers who switched jobs before vesting lost all their accumulated pension rights. Actuarial calculations in early occupational pension schemes built in the expectation that few workers would ever qualify for pensions. Employers even had a perverse incentive to fire workers just before their pensions vested. Many schemes in developing countries today impose similarly long vesting requirements.

Although long vesting requirements may encourage the employer to provide on-the-job training, which is valuable, they have three major disadvantages.

- First, workers may not understand the details of the pension program, particularly the vesting and portability restrictions, so they may impute a value to the pension that is higher than its true expected value and therefore may choose a job in which their compensation package and productivity are not maximized.
- Second, nonportable pensions may impede labor reallocation even when reallocation would be efficient, as when economic conditions change unexpectedly. In both cases, labor ends up allocated to low-productivity uses as a result of the vesting restrictions.
- Third, some workers who lose their jobs late in life, shortly before vesting, may suffer from poverty and become a burden on social assistance programs.

As a result of these criticisms, most industrial countries have passed regulations that limit vesting periods and require preservation and portability of pension rights (see below). But even if these regulations are effective, labor mobility in midcareer may still be discouraged because of benefit formulas that give a higher present value of pension compensation to older workers as they age and approach retirement—a process known as "backloading." Defined contribution schemes have the big advantage that they are inherently portable and therefore should not discourage mobility.

The empirical evidence is ambiguous about the degree to which occupational defined benefit plans have actually impeded mobility. In the United States, where turnover is lower in firms that offer pension plans than in those that don't, studies have shown an association between reduced mobility and restrictive vesting or backloading. Part of this association, however, may be due to the higher overall compensation packages of these firms, their ability to attract stable workers, and their reluctance to fire long-term workers—not to reduced mobility among workers anxious to retain their pension rights. It is difficult to disentangle the magnitude of these effects (Schiller and Weiss 1979; Kotlikoff and Wise 1987a; Gustman and Steinmeir 1990; Wolf and Levy 1984).

In developing and transitional economies, where legislation does not require vesting, where labor markets are very imperfect to begin with, where uncertainty about the future is great, and where major restructuring is currently going on, the negative effects on mobility and efficiency may be much greater if occupational plans grow. These countries need to strike the right balance between encouraging employers to invest in the workers they have versus avoiding misinformed workers and inefficient barriers to reallocating workers in a rapidly changing economic environment.

Retirement age. In OECD countries, the labor force participation rate of older workers has fallen in recent decades, and private pension plans have contributed to this change. In most occupational plans, the value of the pension wealth ceases to increase after the worker reaches a specified age such as 60 or 65, encouraging workers to retire. Sometimes special early retirement schemes have encouraged retirement before age 60 (issue brief 8). These incentives for retirement are often rationalized as attempts to deal with the declining productivity of older employees, especially those whose wages rise with tenure. Although employers would prefer to hold on to workers who remain productive and to let the others go, they may be prevented from making that distinction by unions, laws, or cultural factors. If so, companies may use pension plans to encourage older workers to leave because, as a group, their wages exceed their productivity.

Early retirement schemes are also used as a substitute for layoffs when a firm is reducing its labor force. This policy cuts current production costs but raises long-run pension costs. When workers retire early, the firm's total labor cost (of retirees plus workers) may increase—but in a hidden way. The cost is passed on to the pension scheme. Funded plans based on expectations of later retirement become actuarially unsound. Eventually, the pension plan may not be able to pay the promised benefits. The government may be left with the debt, if public subsidies or guarantees are involved. And the country's labor force, a major productive resource, declines. If younger workers are laid off instead, this would be painful in the short run—but in the longer run they are more likely to find new jobs and continue adding to national output. Early retirement plans need to be introduced with extreme caution and with commensurate additional funding of pension plans by employers to ensure that they take into account the full social cost. (See box 4.4 for a discussion of early retirement under public pension schemes.)

Fiscal Effects

Occupational pension plans can reduce government spending and tax rates if they dampen political pressures for large earnings-related public plans. This may be their most important fiscal effect, albeit one that is difficult to quantify. The other side of the coin is that they usually involve large current tax expenditures. And when government guarantees are involved, occupational plans may have large future explicit costs for the government as well (guarantees are discussed in the next section).

Most countries allow workers and employers to deduct pension fund contributions from their taxable income and exempt investment income from tax, but treat pension benefits like any other taxable income. Tax deferral is especially valuable to high-income workers in countries with progressive income tax systems. Such workers may be in a much lower tax bracket when they retire and pay taxes on their pensions. Australia, Ireland, Japan, and the United Kingdom go beyond tax deferral and allow tax-free payments at retirement, subject to specified limits. The resulting tax expenditure has been estimated at 20 to 40 percent of explicit public pension expenditures in some OECD countries. It is 1 percent of GDP for the United States, 3 percent for the United Kingdom (which has broader coverage and more progressive tax rates), and 2.5 percent in South Africa (table 5.4). These figures may be overestimates, because they do not take into account the fact that returns to saving are often taxed more lightly than other sources of income, nor do they fully recognize that, in immature systems, taxes will be recaptured later when the worker retires and receives the pension benefits. But to compensate for these deferred revenues, in the interim, higher taxes must be imposed elsewhere, government spending must be cut, or government borrowing must be increased.

To contain the negative budgetary impact, some governments have set limits on the deductibility of contributions to pension plans. Den-

Table 5.4 Tax Expenditures in Selected Countries

Country	Year	Percentage of public pension expenditures	Percentage of GDP
Australia	1984	25	1.0
Ireland	1985	22	1.3
United States	1989	20	1.1
United Kingdom	1989	40	3.3
South Africa	1992	—	2.5

—Not available.
Source: OECD (1992); for South Africa, from Vittas (1994b).

mark imposes a special 44 percent tax on pension asset returns when real returns exceed 3.5 percent a year, an obvious disincentive to risk taking. This may help explain the low returns over the past two decades. In the Netherlands, a special tax applies to surpluses that exceed indexed pension obligations by more than 15 percent. Some analysts have proposed using tax credits rather than deductions to reduce the fiscal impact and the advantage given to high-income workers. Going a step further, in 1988, New Zealand made all contributions and investments taxable, but left most pensions untaxed, treating pension savings roughly the same as other savings. Removing the tax exemptions sharply reduced the popularity of occupational pension plans (Davis 1993).

Preferential tax treatment for occupational pension plans may be justified by the importance of encouraging people to save for their old age rather than rely on public transfers or private charity—and because it encourages the growth of group annuities that help solve the adverse selection problem. Tax deferral is also a way of recognizing that part of the nominal return on long-term saving is simply an offset to inflation. But the evidence is inconclusive on whether tax preferences stimulate people to save more—and if so, whether these benefits exceed the costs.

Tax deferral is a less important benefit in developing countries that do not tax other forms of investment income, such as interest on bank deposits, government bonds, and capital gains. In addition, income tax enforcement is very weak in many developing countries—being allowed to deduct pension contributions is worth little to workers who do not intend to pay their income tax in any case. The absence of large tax advantages may be a major reason why occupational plans have not gotten off the ground in these countries.

As the tax enforcement capability of developing countries improves and as the transitional economies develop new tax systems, policymakers need to think about the role of occupational pension plans and how to use tax policies to provide appropriate incentives. It is unclear why occupational pensions should receive better tax treatment than personal long-term saving or pension plans. To encourage capital accumulation, some economists have argued that consumption rather than income should be taxed, so all saving would be tax deferred. Others have proposed that real rather than nominal investment returns should be taxed. Extending equivalent tax advantages to all long-term saving schemes, whether personal or employer-sponsored, would probably retard the future growth of occupational pension schemes.

Who Benefits and Who Loses?

LIKE PUBLIC SCHEMES, OCCUPATIONAL DEFINED BENEFIT PENsion plans also have redistributional effects. But in occupational plans, the direction of the redistribution is determined by the employer operating within the labor market rather than by policymakers operating within the political process. As a result, the direction of redistribution may be quite different.

Who Benefits?

Coverage in occupational defined benefit plans is usually limited and tilted heavily toward high-income workers and workers in large unionized firms. Sometimes, companies cover only senior employees or provide different benefits for different groups of workers. Women and others who have had uneven employment histories are more likely to be left without pension coverage. Among covered workers, early leavers lose and long stayers gain—and some of these workers may not have correctly calculated the odds early on. Workers with high salaries in their last few years of employment gain relative to workers whose salaries have not increased rapidly, because occupational pensions are often based on final salaries rather than average career earnings. Managers may have the power to award themselves large salary increases in their last year of employment, increasing their pensions substantially.

Differential benefits also occur in defined contribution plans. For example, employer contributions may be lost by early leavers. Some workers may fare badly because their employers do not choose capable investment managers. And (as in public and mandatory saving plans) low-income workers lose out because of their shorter life expectancy if they are thrown into the same annuity pool as high-income workers. In general, however, defined contribution plans provide more equal treatment to all covered workers than do defined benefit plans.

As a result of these factors, occupational pensions are often more skewed toward high-income groups than are public pensions or wages (table 5.5). Some governments have tried to curtail such practices through tax and pension regulations but have not eliminated them entirely. And except in countries where they have become mandatory, occupational pensions are not particularly effective at alleviating poverty or resolving capital market failure—since their beneficiaries are more likely to have saved voluntarily and have access to alternative saving instruments for their old age. But occupational plans probably help remedy insurance market failures. To that extent, they may prevent sharp

Table 5.5 Distribution of Occupational Pensions among Households with Heads Age 65 or Over, by Income Quintile, Selected OECD Countries

	Australia, 1985	Canada, 1987	Netherlands, 1987	United Kingdom, 1986	Average
Percentage of households with occupational pension income					
All income levels	12.4	41.9	72.1	49.9	44.1
Poorest quintile	4.0	20.1	54.8	35.3	28.6
Quintile II	8.7	42.4	52.0	40.0	35.8
Quintile III	8.6	60.1	91.0	65.6	56.3
Quintile IV	25.8	54.1	90.4	65.6	59.0
Richest quintile	25.2	38.2	73.0	45.9	45.6
Percentage of gross income from cccupational pensions					
All income levels	5.4	11.7	23.6	14.5	13.8
Poorest quintile	0.8	3.9	2.6	6.3	3.4
Quintile II	3.2	9.1	12.3	7.7	6.8
Quintile III	2.1	13.0	20.2	13.7	12.3
Quintile IV	11.5	16.3	39.8	24.0	22.9
Richest quintile	9.1	16.2	42.9	24.0	23.1

Source: Luxembourg Income Survey; calculations made by Deborah Mitchell (1993).

deteriorations in the standard of living of the very old, who otherwise may not have been able to purchase annuities at a fair price.

Do Occupational Plans Redistribute?

Economic theory would argue that pensions are deferred compensation, that total compensation packages reflect differences in productivity, and that pay scales are adjusted to compensate for the value of pension benefits (the theory of "compensating wage differentials"). So, occupational pensions would affect the mix of wage and nonwage components in the total compensation package. But they would not affect the individual's total income or the distribution of income overall.

Several observations suggest, however, that wages don't fall to offset occupational pensions, so pensions do affect the income distribution.

- Employers who pay high wages are also more likely to provide pensions than those who don't (Gustman and Steinmeir 1990). If workers at these firms receive both higher wages and higher pensions than equivalent workers at other firms, pensions have helped skew the total income distribution. (But if workers at these firms have superior productivity and if, without pensions, their employers would have paid still higher wages to attract them, the theory of compensating wage differentials would still hold and access to pensions would not have changed the overall income distribution.)
- A stronger argument about the distributional effects of pensions stems from social or legal obstacles to raising wages. Public employees may receive a disproportionate share of their compensation in the form of pensions because higher wages would be more visible and less politically acceptable. Similarly, top managers in private companies may be rewarded with large pensions because higher wages would be more transparent and less acceptable to stockholders. In these cases wages would not rise commensurately if pensions were unavailable.
- In most countries contributions to and investment income of pension funds are tax deductible, so their recipients impose a cost (a heavier tax burden or fewer services) on wage earners, who are taxed.

In all these cases, access to generous occupational pensions increases the real income of the favored recipients and influences the overall distribution of income and welfare—in an inefficient and probably a nonequalizing way.

Regulatory Issues

ALTHOUGH OCCUPATIONAL PENSION PLANS WERE INITIALLY unregulated, substantial regulations have developed in every country where they are important. A basic reason for regulating complex pension schemes is that workers may not fully understand the schemes and may as a result make decisions that are best neither for themselves nor for the broader economy. For example, in occupational plans workers may not correctly evaluate the probability of being fired or of quitting before retirement. Or they may not realize that pension promises are underfunded and therefore not trustworthy. Since employers control the degree of underfunding and the firing of workers, they have more information about these probabilities and an incentive to understate them to prospective employees. Along similar lines workers may not know if their defined contribution plan engages in risky investments. To prevent informational deficiencies of this sort from inducing workers to enter into agreements that benefit neither them nor the economy, governments need to establish regulations requiring full disclosure and restricting the actions of pension plans.

Also, once governments encourage the use of occupational plans through special tax concessions or guarantees, they bear some responsibility for ensuring that these concessions are not abused. A first wave of government policies favorable to occupational pension schemes expands their use. But it may also have some unintended effects that necessitate a second wave of more restrictive policies. For example, granting tax advantages to pension funds could make them a haven for upper-income groups. Or government guarantees could prompt excessively risky investments by some pension plans, since if the investments fail the burden will eventually be passed on to the government. Regulation thus prevents companies from taking advantage of tax concessions and guarantees in inefficient or inequitable ways. A basic problem is that developing and transitional economies may lack the institutional capacity to regulate effectively.

Ensuring Financial Soundness in Occupational Defined Benefit Plans

In a funded defined benefit plan, the employer's required contribution depends on the investment performance of the pension fund. The employer chooses the investment policy and bears both the investment risk and the longevity risk, providing insurance to the worker. In an unfunded or partially funded plan, the employer must pay the pension out of current revenues. The worker bears the risk that the employer will be unable to do so, a very real risk given the long-term nature of pension obligations.

When occupational schemes were started, the number of beneficiaries was very low relative to the number of active workers, so it was easy to run them on a pay-as-you-go or partly funded basis. Rapid growth of the labor force and output for much of the last century in industrial countries helped keep the dependency rate low—in defined benefit occupational schemes as in public schemes. This meant that a small wage reduction for workers could finance a large pension for retirees. Or pension costs could be passed on to consumers in slightly higher prices in industries in which competition was limited.

But the conditions required to make unfunded occupational plans viable no longer exist. Many firms in industrial countries have large numbers of retirees, their labor forces are no longer growing, and they face intense competition, often from younger firms in other countries. In a competitive economic environment, firms have serious problems covering unfunded pension obligations. Companies with many retirees that try to pass their higher pension costs along to workers through lower wages will be unable to attract employees if the labor market is competitive. And those that try to pass these costs along through higher prices will be unable to attract customers if the product market is competitive. These problems also occur in some developing countries with aging populations. As one example, the heavy reliance on unfunded plans run by enterprises in China, in the past, is putting companies with older workers at a competitive disadvantage now (Friedman 1994).

Although public plans can operate on a pay-as-you-go basis because they are backed by the power of taxation (so long as the taxes are not so high as to stimulate evasion), companies with private defined benefit plans ordinarily cannot force workers and consumers to deal with them. Newer firms with a younger work force will have lower costs that give them a competitive advantage if pension schemes are unfunded. This also means that pensioners with unfunded plans constantly face the risk of employer default. Although cases of outright default have so far been few, many occupational plans (like some public plans) have escaped financial difficulties by failing to index pension benefits, downgrading real benefits without an explicit default, as inflation takes place (box 5.4).

Box 5.4 Are Underfunded Occupational Plans Viable?

THE AUTOMOBILE INDUSTRY IN THE UNITED States shows the problems caused by underfunded plans and the difficulties in calculating whether a plan is fully funded. The industry has declined over the past two decades, in part because of increased international competition, and its work force has grown older. The number of retirees is now as large as the number of workers and will grow larger still in the years ahead. Pension obligations are largely but not fully funded; some were incurred in the 1960s before funding became mandatory and some were incurred unexpectedly in the 1990s when early retirement plans were introduced to avoid layoffs. Health insurance coverage for early retirees has been another unexpected escalating cost of the retirement program for automobile companies. Even plans that appeared well funded in 1990 now appear less well funded as rising medical costs and falling interest rates have further increased the gap between revenues and expenditures. This illustrates the difficulty in establishing whether or not a defined benefit plan is fully funded, since future costs and returns may turn out to be different from those that were assumed in the actuarial calculations. And eventually the government may be pressured to pick up the tab for part of the higher health insurance costs.

Recent labor negotiations have tried to determine the share of labor expenditures that should go to young workers in the form of wages, to new retirees in the form of pensions, and to old pensioners in the form of cost-of-living adjustments. The choice was dictated by three considerations: labor leaders want to satisfy the majority of union members (many of whom are old and about to retire), employers want to induce early retirement as a substitute for layoffs (which are restricted by the union), and alternative employment opportunities in the surrounding areas are relatively low paid.

The outcome in the U.S. automobile industry has been to protect the real value of pensions for new retirees and, to a much smaller extent, for old retirees, while passing costs back to new workers in lower starting wages and the use of temporary rather than permanent jobs. The higher pension levels exacerbate the underfunding problem, but the lower wages help companies cover these obligations. This tactic can work only in a depressed area with few alternative employment opportunities, or where industry-wide or occupation-wide collective bargaining makes it difficult for workers to escape to higher-wage firms. In the long run, in a competitive product and labor market, it would be difficult for unfunded defined benefit plans to raise the money to cover their pension promises. Under current conditions, the automobile industry might have been able to sell more cars, hence to increase employment, if it had lower pension costs and therefore lower prices. Thus young workers have lost both wages and jobs.

As another example of the dangers of underfunding: When states and municipalities in the United States ran into fiscal difficulties in the late 1980s and early 1990s, some of them revised their assumptions about rates of return on their pension funds. Pushing these assumed rates up a notch or two allowed state and local governments to conclude that funding was more than adequate and therefore they could cut their contribution rates. In fact, interest rates fell sharply shortly after these optimistic forecasts were made, and many plans are now underfunded. Estimates indicate that almost one in three public plans has less than 75 percent of the assets needed to meet its liabilities (O. Mitchell in *Wall Street Journal*, April 5, 1994). Although this tactic saved states and localities considerable money yesterday, the bill will come due tomorrow, to be paid through lower wages to civil servants, reduced benefits to pensioners, or higher taxes to citizens.

Fears that companies would default on their pension promises, and some actual defaults, have led governments in several industrial countries to require funding that covers the estimated liabilities of defined benefit pension schemes. Canada, the Netherlands, the United Kingdom, and the United States require substantial advance funding. In France, where funding is not required, mandatory nationwide contributions to occupational plans enable pension costs to be passed back to current workers—so long as workers do not protest the slow growth of net wages.

Requirements of full funding do not completely solve the default problem. Full funding requires a complex calculation that involves actuarial assumptions. The future rate of return on assets determines the growth rate of the fund, whereas projected salary growth, inflation, turnover rates, and years of retirement determine future obligations. None of these variables is known with certainty. The values that employers and their actuaries use in these calculations strongly influence the contribution rate deemed necessary for an actuarially sound fund.

Many occupational plans in the United States raised their estimates of expected returns in the early 1990s, just before interest rates fell and just as many companies instituted early retirement plans. Some of these pension plans are now underfunded. This behavior may lead to a new round of regulations, covering the actuarial assumptions themselves. In the Netherlands, where funding is compulsory, the government specifies the expected wage and the maximum real interest rate of 4 percent to be used in these calculations. But so far, political forces have prevented other countries from implementing such actuarial standardization (box 5.4).

In developing countries, occupational plans are not subject to minimum funding levels, and most plans are unfunded or the funds are held in the form of book reserves (Mexico and the Republic of Korea). In some countries—including Brazil, Cyprus, India, Panama, the Philippines, and South Africa—occupational plans are funded through separate trusts, but the trusts can be controlled by the employer and may not have enough assets to cover promised benefits. In the transitional socialist economies, companies may make promises about the future that they will simply be unable to keep, given the rapidly changing economic environment.

From the start, developing and transitional economies need to establish regulations requiring a sound long-term financial basis, for it is much cheaper and easier to prevent abuses than to correct them. Funding requirements may reduce the temptation for employers to make irresponsible promises and increase the trustworthiness of the promises that are made. And for the funding requirements to have meaning, governments should specify their key actuarial assumptions, such as expected rates of return and wage growth.

Regulating Investments

A closely related question is whether the investment portfolio should be regulated to prevent excessively risky investments and problems of moral hazard. Sponsoring employers have considerable motivation to choose capable investment managers, given their obligation to cover any deficiencies in defined benefit plans. From society's viewpoint, overly strict regulations defeat the capital market advantages of decentralized pension funds. But if investments fail, pensioners may be in trouble—and if there are government guarantees, the burden ultimately falls on the public treasury. The line between under- and overregulating the investment portfolios of occupational pension plans is thus narrow.

In many countries, the line has been drawn to give considerable leeway to occupational funds. In the United States, they are subject to the "prudent person" rule, which requires sensible portfolio diversification but places no limits on portfolio allocations other than a 10 percent limit on investments in securities of the sponsoring employer. In the United Kingdom, pension funds are subject to trust law and the prudent person rule, with a 5 percent limit on investments in the sponsoring company. Similar rules apply to occupational pension plans in the Netherlands. Pension funds have taken advantage of this regulatory freedom to place a larger share of their portfolios in equity investments, yielding a higher rate of return than more restricted financial institutions can achieve. In developing countries, the limits on equity investments are generally stricter.

Most countries, especially developing countries, restrict the foreign investments of their pension funds. Foreign investment entails an exchange rate risk as well as ordinary stock and bond market risks. It may thus seem to increase risk. But it actually decreases risk because markets are not perfectly correlated across countries. Comparisons of returns to actual portfolios, hypothetical domestic portfolios diversified between equities and bonds, and foreign portfolios in OECD countries for 1970–90 show that a higher share in equities raises both rates of return and risk, whereas international diversification generally reduces risk, sometimes at the expense of yield (Davis 1993 and box 5.5). Opening the door to international investments of pension funds would seem to be warranted, to diversify and thereby diminish risk.

Governments often prod private pension funds into investing in such "socially desirable" assets as government bonds, housing, and infrastructure. Usually, but not always, occupational schemes have had the political clout to resist these pressures. In developing countries, minimum investments in government bonds are often required—a form of central control over investments, which generally decreases yield and (because they limit diversification) increases risk. For exam-

---

Box 5.5 Liberating Pension Funds: An Idea Whose Time Has Come?

PENSION FUNDS ARE OFTEN LEGALLY CONstrained from investing in foreign assets. The reasons are varied: general capital account restrictions, a belief that savings "belong" to the home economy and should be invested there, or fear that incomplete information will result in poor investments and pension fund losses.

But there are also strong advantages from international diversification of pension funds, particularly for countries with small or concentrated domestic economies. Lower risk and sometimes higher returns are possible over the long term through international investment, which reduces the exposure of investors to country-specific risks such as inflation and gives them an opportunity to move their capital to countries that offer the highest return. The switch to freer capital flows could be gradual to allow pension managers time to learn about foreign investments and to minimize disruptive effects on the country's capital account.

Any restriction on capital is like a tax. The rich can often avoid the tax by evading capital controls, while middle- and low-income residents with a substantial share of their savings tied up in funded pension plans bear the full brunt of financial repression. Only if part of their funds are invested overseas are they protected from an increase in financial repression at home. Pension reserves that are confined to

domestic markets can be eroded gradually, through modestly negative real rates of return, or more suddenly, through forced shouldering of losses elsewhere in the economy, as, for example, when governments pass large banking system or state enterprise losses on to the pension fund, leaving it insolvent.

Funded pension schemes are often viewed as a means of increasing national saving and long-term domestic capital formation. And outflows of pension funds are considered a loss to society. Governments can minimize this loss by improving the conditions for domestic financial markets and easing capital controls more generally. Easy capital outflow helps stimulate capital inflows, because a prime concern of international investors is to be able to get out of a market quickly when the need arises. Bilateral or multilateral asset pools in which pension funds from two or more countries share investments, risks, and returns in their respective countries might develop as a financial innovation that would permit diversification of country risk without a net loss of long-term capital to either country.

Allowing pension funds to diversify contributes to the credibility of domestic stabilization policies and is an easily controllable way to begin a wider process of opening up the domestic economy to become part of the global economy.

ple, "prescribed investments" in South Africa earned a negative real return of 3.6 percent in the 1970s and negative 0.9 percent in the 1980s, while the real return to equities was strongly positive—13.2 percent and 5.6 percent, respectively (Vittas 1994b). Special investment requirements for pension funds for state and local workers in the United States also decreased yield (Mitchell and Hsin 1994a, b). The lower return constitutes an implicit nontransparent tax on the funds. A better policy would tighten funding requirements but loosen investment restrictions, subjecting all investments to the market test of a competitive rate of return. The costs of social investments would then become more transparent, so citizens could decide if they want to meet these costs—and if so, who should pay.

Protecting Benefits in Defined Benefit Plans

The uneven coverage offered by occupational plans, combined with the lack of worker information about how they function, has also led OECD governments to regulate some aspects of the benefit formula. Typically, all employees at a firm are required to receive equal access to pension coverage, and several European countries require that benefits be indexed. In some countries (Australia, Denmark, France, the Netherlands, Switzerland) almost all firms must offer pensions as a result of legislation or collective bargaining.

Particularly important concerns are that vesting and portability provisions in defined benefit plans are often misunderstood by workers and exploited by employers—and they may inefficiently limit workers' mobility. To overcome these problems, most OECD governments limit the qualifying period for vesting and make it harder for employers to fire workers just before they acquire vested rights to their accrued benefits. The most common vesting period is two to five years, although the range is large. In Switzerland, compulsory benefits vest immediately, but additional voluntary benefits require five to thirty years of service. Vested rights are indexed in the Netherlands, Switzerland, and the United Kingdom but not in Canada, Japan, and the United States. A departing worker whose rights are preserved in nominal rather than real terms is penalized, and mobility may continue to be discouraged, particularly in inflationary environments. Developing countries generally do not regulate vesting, or other aspects of benefits, except in such cases as the Philippines, South Africa, and Indonesia under the new pension law.

Closely related, portability rights have also been strengthened. In some countries (Denmark and the United Kingdom), companies are required to calculate the present value of the vested benefits of departing employees and to transfer that sum to the pension fund of the new employer or to a personal pension plan. In the Netherlands, transfers are effected through industry-wide clearinghouses, and in Japan, through a nationwide clearinghouse. In Switzerland, the mandatory part of the pension is portable, but the voluntary part may not be, so mobility continues to be hampered (Hepp 1990).

Even when portability is required, the employer usually has considerable discretion over the actuarial assumptions and accrual rates that tend to favor workers who stay. For example, the assumption of a high interest rate reduces the present value of future benefits and therefore the amount that must be transferred. Basing the transfer on current rather than expected future salary or assuming a low rate of wage growth has the same effect. If the transfer is small, the new employer may grant only partial credit, compared with the benefit that would have been received had the worker stayed put. In other words, the same factors that make it difficult to define full funding make it difficult to implement full portability, even in a well-regulated defined benefit system. Portability is facilitated by using a defined contribution scheme, which may be part of the reason why this type of plan prevails in the mandatory programs of Australia and Switzerland. In developing countries, even partial portability protection is rare.

Information Disclosure and Monitoring

Full disclosure to workers—as an alternative to regulation—is favored by free market advocates. Employers could set whatever terms they desire, but workers would have to be given full information about the benefits and risks. Those opposed to this approach argue that workers may not be able to evaluate the information properly. Doing that requires estimating the probabilities that they will be fired or will want to leave the firm before retirement, the likelihood of different age-earnings profiles, and the prospect that the firm will still be solvent and able to pay the defined benefits fifty years down the road.

Trade-offs are possible between disclosure and regulation. Standardizing some provisions through regulation simplifies information disclosure, while full disclosure can reduce the need for regulation. In practice, though, requirements for information disclosure have gone hand in hand with investment regulations rather than substituted for them. In the United States, pension funds must provide participants with an annual report outlining the plan, their rights to receive pensions, and the status of individual pension benefits. In the United Kingdom, trustees must provide a statement of individual benefits and audited annual reports covering the number of beneficiaries, level of contributions, distribution of assets, performance ratings, and remuneration of fund managers. Neither regulation nor information disclosure is well advanced in developing and transitional countries.

A promising model for enforcing regulations and information disclosures is in place in the Netherlands. A single statutory authority, the Insurance Supervisory Board, oversees occupational pension plans, in contrast to the fragmented monitoring system in many other OECD countries. Pension funds must provide the board with detailed information on benefit payments and investments. The board ensures that pension fund commitments are adequately covered by assets and that plan rules and conditions are satisfactory. This model of monitoring—one supervisor, specific rules on funding, standardized actuarial assumptions, portability provisions, annual verification, and periodic on-site inspections—has considerable merit for developing and transitional economies, where regulations, disclosure requirements, and enforcement are at an early stage. Such a board could also issue annual statements to workers on their benefits and contributions. Indonesia recently passed a detailed occupational pension law covering these regulatory and disclosure issues that may become the standard for developing countries (box 5.6).

Guaranteeing Occupational Pensions

Even with requirements of funding, prudent management, and information disclosure, risk remains that the sponsoring employer will declare bankruptcy and the pension fund will be unable to meet its obligations. Should the government insure against this? Several countries, including Finland, Japan, Sweden, and the United States, have public pension guarantee agencies for this purpose.

The U.S. Pension Benefit Guaranty Corporation (PBGC) was set up in 1974 to guarantee pension benefits up to a specified ceiling. All private defined benefit plans must participate and full funding is required to limit the government's losses. Until recently, the PBGC was a seriously flawed

Box 5.6 Private Pension Regulation in Indonesia

INDONESIA PASSED AN INCOME TAX LAW IN 1983 that exempted pension contributions of employers and employees, and new pension programs began to spring up. No pension legislation governed the programs, whose policies were set entirely by employers, and there was no clear separation of pension fund assets from the firm's assets. Most funds were invested in bank deposits, real estate, or subsidiaries of the sponsoring enterprise, or put to other uses at the discretion of the sponsoring employer.

The Indonesian government intended to enact a private pension law soon after passage of the new income tax law, but it took nine years to do so. Legislation defining a comprehensive public social security program was passed at the same time. Among major provisions of the pension legislation:

- Firms are free to establish pension plans or not; employees may opt out of plans that require them to contribute.
- An occupational pension program must be operated as a legal entity separate from the employer's business, with the pension fund's assets held by an approved custodian.
- At least 80 percent of total benefits must be paid in the form of annuities (with death benefits for a surviving spouse or minor children).
- Employers may provide different benefits for different classes of employees; but all employees over the age of 18 must be covered if other employees of their class are covered.
- Pension programs must be fully funded.
- Benefits are vested and portable after one year of service.
- The self-employed and employees whose employers do not offer pension programs may join a defined contribution plan run by a bank or an insurance company.
- Permissible investments are specified, with strict diversification standards. Transactions between the pension fund and the employer are restricted.
- Both contributions and pension fund investment income are tax-free, but pensions are taxed as normal income.
- Regular reporting to participants is required, and independently audited financial statements and actuarial opinions must be submitted to the Ministry of Finance.
- Procedures are established for winding up a pension fund and for liquidating hopelessly insolvent funds. The government assumes no responsibility for the obligations of such funds.

Because of concerns about the annuities market, the government plans to impose strict financial and investment standards and rigorous solvency margin requirements on the annuities part of insurance company business. It is also hoped that competition among life insurance firms will be intense and that the government-owned life insurer will set a standard of fair pricing and prudent investment. To add financial market expertise, joint ventures with foreign companies will be allowed. A separate Pension Fund Directorate has been established in the Ministry of Finance, and its enlarged staff has received special training for conducting compliance exemptions. The new law brings Indonesia up to OECD norms and will probably set the standard for developing countries. But it is not clear whether Indonesia has the institutional capacity to supervise and enforce these regulations.

institution—with little control over actual funding levels, the actuarial assumptions behind them, or the investment policies followed by the funds. Recent measures have strengthened the PBGC, but major shortcomings remain, including the accumulation of past deficits totaling billions of dollars in the pension schemes of several large corporations. These shortcomings should serve as a warning to developing and transitional economies to prevent such deficits from the start. It is very difficult to reverse them later on.

The United Kingdom has no pension guarantee plan, although a voluntary compensation scheme was set up to cover beneficiaries of the Maxwell companies following the recent massive losses from fraud. A compulsory guarantee scheme is being considered—but not very enthusiastically, in part because of the fear that it will have the perverse effect of encouraging risk taking.

Developing countries should try to avoid public guarantees of occupational pension plans, although reinsurance through private pooling arrangements might be encouraged (Smalhout 1994). Public guarantees may lead to large future fiscal outlays and may also create moral hazard problems—that is, workers and their employers may take larger risks than before, knowing that their pensions will be protected. But avoiding guarantees may be difficult, especially since many occupational pension plans are offered by public enterprises. And political pressures often make guarantees implicit even if they are not explicit. The best course is to establish strong fiduciary rules and monitoring mechanisms for occupational plans from the start—to minimize the probability that financially unsound schemes will get off the ground.

Employer Response to Regulations

Requirements for equal access, full funding, vesting, portability, and the payment of premiums for public guarantees make defined benefit pension plans more costly and less attractive for sponsoring employers. Regulated companies can no longer use pensions to attract and reward long-service or other selected workers as before. They cannot count on worker mobility to reduce their pension costs. Nor can they use unfunded plans as, in effect, a low-interest loan to the company. The administrative costs of complying with regulations of defined benefit plans are high, especially for small businesses that must spread the set-up costs over a small number of workers. This is particularly important in developing countries, where small businesses predominate.

Employers are likely to react in several ways: They may engage in less on-the-job training because they are less able to identify stable workers or induce workers to stay. They may use wage differences rather than pensions to make desired distinctions in compensation, leading to greater wage inequality. And they may avoid contributing to pension schemes by hiring more short-term or contract workers, so fewer workers get pension coverage. Such employer behavior has been observed in the labor market in the past decade, although to different extents in different countries.

Employers are also likely to shift their emphasis to defined contribution rather than defined benefit plans. In the United States, the use of defined contribution plans has increased dramatically over the past decade. In Australia and Switzerland, where occupational plans have recently become mandatory, most private employers have defined contribution schemes.

This may be efficient, since defined contribution plans are by definition fully funded and portable, so workers face less employer default risk and mobility risk even without government regulation. Portability is particularly valuable in developing and transitional countries, which will be changing rapidly in the coming years. Although workers bear more investment risk in defined contribution plans, they probably come out ahead because the separation of investment risk from employment risk implies risk diversification. The possibility of investing pension funds in stocks, real estate, or foreign assets further diversifies and provides partial inflation insurance. But the fact that employers choose or limit the worker's choice of investment manager poses agency problems that could lower returns for workers. This disadvantage can be overcome by requiring an expanded set of choices or permitting dissatisfied workers to opt out of occupational schemes and into personal pension schemes with equivalent tax advantages.

Conclusion

THE BIG ADVANTAGES OF OCCUPATIONAL PENSION SCHEMES are that they are adaptable to diverse tastes and can be established with little government involvement or incentive to evade—useful features in developing countries with limited governmental capabilities. Their administrative costs tend to be low. When funded and privately managed, they have increased long-term saving, stimulated the modernization of capital markets, and encouraged financial innovation. In recent years, several industrial countries have tried to ease the financial burden on public pension plans by encouraging the growth of occupational schemes, making them mandatory (Australia and Switzerland) or quasi-mandatory through collective bargaining (Denmark and the Netherlands), or permitting employers to opt out of the public plan if they provide an equivalent private plan (Japan and the United Kingdom).

Occupational plans suffer from several shortcomings, however, stemming from their uneven coverage, underfunding, and complexity. When these plans are not mandatory, low-income workers often are not covered; and workers with high final salaries fare the best. Workers who thought they were covered have been left without adequate benefits when their plans turned out to be underfunded. Vesting and portability restrictions, often poorly understood by workers, have penalized early leavers, discouraged labor mobility, interfered with efficient labor reallocation, and created distributional inequities. In OECD countries, the plans have grown at considerable fiscal expense because of generous tax preferences. And failing plans have placed an unexpected burden on the treasury, as the insurer of last resort.

These flaws have led increasingly to regulations over occupational pension schemes, especially defined benefit schemes, as they have grown in size and importance in industrial countries. Government involvement has thus turned out to be essential and inevitable after all. Regulations prohibit companies from offering different pension plans to different groups of workers and from imposing onerous vesting and portability conditions. Adequate funding, indexation of benefits, and information disclosure have been required, and public insurance schemes have been instituted in many countries. These regulations have mitigated the problems but not eliminated them completely. Nor is it probable that they could, given the complex actuarial calculations and inherent uncertainty involved.

Regulations have also changed the nature of occupational plans in OECD countries, making them more costly, more uniform, less adaptable as a personnel tool, and so less valuable to employers—who are therefore less inclined to offer defined benefit plans voluntarily. The costs and disincentives are particularly great for small business. As a result, defined contribution schemes, automatically funded and more easily vested and transferred, have been growing in importance. Occupational defined contribution plans are very similar to the personal saving plans discussed in the next chapter, except that they do not provide complete coverage (unless they are mandatory) and they allow employers to choose the investment manager, although workers bear the investment risk.

In developing and transitional countries, occupational pension schemes are still small. They are likely to spread, however, especially to large domestic corporations and local subsidiaries of multinational corporations. Although occupational schemes should be permitted, it is not clear that they should be encouraged by special tax privileges unavailable to other long-term saving arrangements. If tax incentives are involved, for efficiency they should be given equally and with similar qualifying conditions to personal and occupational plans, so that job choice is not distorted by access to tax advantages. Most important, to prevent the growth of ill-designed plans that ultimately fail, occupational schemes should develop in accord with a regulatory structure in place from the very beginning. These regulations should include requirements of funding (according to specified actuarial standards), vesting, portability, and information disclosure. They might include private reinsurance but should not include public guarantees. Even if the regulations are not fully enforced at the start, they become a standard and a warning of what is likely to be enforced in the future. Such regulations will probably slow the growth of occupational schemes, especially defined benefit schemes. But they will make those that survive more dependable and efficient. Drawing up this structure is a step that developing and transitional economies should take right now.

CHAPTER 6

Personal Savings Plans— Becoming Mandatory?

A STRAIGHTFORWARD WAY TO REPLACE EARNINGS in old age is to save when young—something people have done voluntarily in all countries and all time periods, although to varying degrees and with different instruments. In developing countries, this saving was often part of the informal support system and took the form of investments in land and children. In industrial countries, financial assets and government policies are more likely to be involved.

Governments have encouraged personal long-term saving by creating a stable economic and political environment, by establishing a legal framework for banks and other financial institutions, and by offering tax incentives to savers. Governments in several East Asian countries, including Japan, Korea, Malaysia, and Singapore, have established postal saving systems that offer greater security and accessibility, higher interest (often tax-free), and lower transaction costs than would otherwise be available, especially in rural areas. OECD countries such as Canada, Switzerland, the United Kingdom, and the United States have granted tax advantages to retirement saving and annuity accounts set up in banks, life insurance companies, and mutual funds. Despite favorable tax treatment, these and other voluntary long-term saving accounts tend to be small compared with other sources of income in old age, it is not clear whether tax incentives have increased aggregate saving, and most of the tax benefits have gone to high-income households, many of which would have saved in any event.

In recent years several countries have made retirement saving mandatory. The motivation for mandatory saving schemes is to solve the problem of shortsighted individuals who do not save when they are young and become a charge on the rest of society when they are old. Also, these schemes may include provisions for increasing the reliability of savings institutions—their absence in many countries constitutes another reason why people do not save. Their basic mode of operations is as follows: contributions are deposited in personal accounts, and benefits available in old age depend on these contributions plus the investment income they earn. These schemes are thus fully funded defined contribution plans not sponsored or differentiated by employer. In making them mandatory, countries must confront a host of policy questions. While recognizing the continuing importance of voluntary saving, this chapter is mainly about these mandatory personal saving plans and the policy issues that they raise.

Full funding implies capital accumulation, and a key question is how these funds are managed and invested. Quite commonly, the government determines the use of the mandatory saving accounts and sets the rate of return. This type of plan, usually called a "provident fund," can involve capital and labor market distortions and capricious redistributions similar to those in public defined benefit plans. As an alternative, mandatory saving schemes may be privately and competitively managed, in which case they are likely to have fewer distortions, fewer incentives for evasion, and less political manipulation.

Like funded occupational plans, mandatory saving schemes can foster long-term saving and capital market development. But unlike defined benefit occupational schemes, they are fully funded by nature rather than by regulation. Their coverage can be broad. They do not imply portability problems or inhibit labor mobility. They permit workers to diversify risk. And unlike defined contribution occupational schemes, they allow workers, who bear the investment risk, to choose the investment manager.

Mandatory saving nevertheless creates a new set of problems. Most notably, privately managed schemes fail to insure workers against poor investment performance of the funds, a problem especially great where many workers have had little financial experience or information. In addition, they do not assist workers with low lifetime incomes or provide adequate pensions in the start-up years of the plan. For these reasons, a decentralized mandatory saving scheme requires a regulatory structure that protects workers against ill-informed investment choices. And it must be supplemented by a redistributive public plan that alleviates poverty. Three central dilemmas are posed:

- If mandatory schemes are needed because of shortsighted workers, how can these same workers be counted on to make wise investment decisions?
- If governments have mismanaged their centrally administered pension plans, how can they be counted on to regulate private funds effectively?
- If government regulates and guarantees the schemes, won't it eventually end up controlling these funds?

Brief History

DURING THE PAST FOUR DECADES, SEVERAL COUNTRIES HAVE begun experimenting with mandatory personal saving plans. These plans were not only an alternative to voluntary saving. They were, more important, an alternative to earnings-related public pay-as-you-go systems of old age security that would have been demanded if some other mandatory scheme had not been adopted.

The first nationally mandated provident fund was established in Malaysia in 1951, and the largest such fund is Singapore's Central Provident Fund, created in 1955. India and Indonesia established provident funds in the early 1950s, but with limited coverage. Several African countries followed in the 1960s, and several Caribbean and Pacific island countries did in the 1970s and 1980s. Contributions, which are compulsory, are paid into individual worker accounts in a national provident fund managed by a public agency. Today, some twenty countries, mostly former British colonies in Africa, Asia, and the Pacific islands, have such schemes. These countries had no public pay-as-you-go pillar when they established their national funded plan.

These provident funds have earned positive investment returns in such East Asian and Pacific countries as Fiji, Malaysia, and Singapore, where economic policies have emphasized financial stability and fiscal responsibility. But economic instability, inflation, and devaluation in most African and some Caribbean countries have produced large negative rates of return and widespread dissatisfaction with the performance of the funds. So, several of these countries—including Dominica, Grenada, St. Lucia, and St. Vincent and the Grenadines in the 1970s and 1980s and Ghana in 1991—have replaced their national provident funds with defined benefit pay-as-you-go pension schemes. Several other African countries are considering following Ghana's example.

Until 1994, Chile was the only country that had fully replaced an existing public pay-as-you-go pension scheme with a mandatory saving scheme. Chile was also the only country whose mandatory saving program is privately and competitively managed. Operating since 1981, the Chilean scheme is known as the AFP system, after the private companies, called Administradoras de Fondos de Pensiones, authorized to run it. The public pension system was replaced because of widespread evasion, unsustainably high contribution rates, and an inequitable benefit structure. For similar reasons, other Latin American countries, including Argentina, Colombia, and Peru are now replacing or supplementing their public pension schemes with mandatory competitive saving schemes.

It is curious—although not surprising in view of their age structures and historical experiences—that this transition away from a dominant public pillar toward greater reliance on mandatory saving schemes is occurring in older Latin American countries at the same time that younger African countries are contemplating a transition in the opposite direction. Because Chile's is the only fully implemented decentralized scheme at this point, the discussion here draws heavily on its experience.

How Mandatory Retirement Saving Schemes Work

IN MANDATORY SAVING SCHEMES, THE BENEFITS WORKERS ultimately receive depend on their contributions, investment earnings, and expected longevity. The performance of these schemes depends largely on whether the funds are publicly or privately managed.

The Contribution and Target Replacement Rates

In a mandatory saving scheme, the worker's pension is financed by the savings account that accumulates before retirement, and its size depends on the contribution rate, the growth rate of earnings, the interest rate, and the number of working and retirement years. The required contribution rate rises the higher the target wage replacement rate, the longer the retirement period relative to the working period (the passivity ratio), and the smaller the rate of return relative to the growth rate of real earnings (table 6.1). The required contribution rate is also higher in plans that make poor investments, incur high administrative costs, index pensions to prices or wages, or permit accumulated balances to be used for such other purposes as housing, education, or health care. When rates of return are high because of a scarcity of capital, a mandatory saving scheme enables a high wage replacement rate while making resources available for investment and growth.

Differences in the basic parameters of the plan may explain why the contribution rate is only 13 percent of wages in Chile but 20 percent in Sri Lanka, 22 percent in Malaysia, and 35 percent in Singapore. During the 1980s in Singapore, about two-thirds of fund withdrawals were used for housing purchases, some of which may eventually have found their way back into retirement income. In Chile, about one-quarter of total contributions are used for term life and disability insurance and fund expenses, with all the rest used for retirement savings. Given this and the higher interest rate relative to wage growth in Chile, it is likely that the same replacement rate of final gross earnings—about 40 percent,

Table 6.1 Contribution Rate Needed to Pay Pension Equal to 40 Percent of Final Salary under Mandatory Saving Scheme

	Nonindexed pension				*Pension indexed to prices*			
Passivity rate	*1 / 2*		*1 / 3*		*1 / 2*		*1 / 3*	
Real wage growth	*0*	*2*	*0*	*2*	*0*	*2*	*0*	*2*
Real interest rate								
0	13	18	9	14	20	29	13	20
2	7	11	5	8	11	16	7	12
5	3	5	2	3	5	7	3	5
Real pension rate at death[a]	15	15	19	19	40	40	40	40
Relative pension rate at death[b]	15	10	19	14	40	27	40	30

Note: Plan expenses and disability and survivors' benefits are not included. These would raise the required contribution rate 3 to 5 percentage points in a well-run plan. A 5 percent inflation rate is assumed. The one-half passivity rate stems from an assumption of forty working years and twenty years of retirement. The one-third passivity rate implies forty-five working years and fifteen years of retirement.

a. Real pension in year of death as proportion of final year's salary.
b. Pension relative to average wage in the economy in year of death.
Source: Schwarz (1992a); Vittas (1992).

Table 6.2 Payroll Tax Rates for Mandatory Saving Schemes, 1991

Country	Percentage of wages			Combined as a percentage of wage plus employer tax
	Employees	Employer	Combined	
Africa				
The Gambia	5	10	15	13.6
Ghana[a]	5	12.5	17.5	15.6
Kenya	5	5	10	9.5
Nigeria	6	6	12	11.3
Swaziland	5	5	10	9.5
Tanzania	10	10	20	18.2
Uganda	5	10	15	13.6
Zambia	5	5	10	9.5
Asia				
Fiji	7	7	14	13.1
India	10	10	20	18.2
Indonesia	1	2	3	2.9
Kiribati	5	5	10	9.5
Malaysia	9	11	20[b]	18.0
Nepal	10	10	20	18.2
Singapore	25[c]	10	35	31.8
Solomon Islands	5	7.5	12.5	11.6
Sri Lanka	8	12	20	17.9
Western Samoa	5	5	10	9.5
Latin America (1994) [d]				
Argentina	11	0	11	11.0
Chile	13	0	13	13.0
Colombia	2.9	8.6	11.5[e]	10.6
Peru	13.3	0	13.3	13.3

Note: African and Asian schemes are publicly managed provident funds; Latin American schemes are privately managed.

a. The provident fund is being converted to a social insurance scheme.

b. This was raised to 22 percent in 1993.

c. The contribution varies from 7 to 30 percent of gross wages for workers.

d. For Argentina and Colombia a new plan started in 1994, for Peru in 1993.

e. This will rise gradually to 14.5 percent in 1996.

Source: U.S. Social Security Administration (1993); Colombia (1993); World Bank data.

indexed—will be produced in both countries (tables 6.1 and 6.2). If workers want to have a higher replacement rate, say, 60 to 65 percent of final gross earnings, they will have to save more voluntarily.

The contribution rate could vary with income and age. For example, the rate could be lower for young and old workers—but high in the middle years, which are generally the high point of life cycle earnings. In Singapore, the rate is lower for older workers—40 percent for those under the age of 55, 25 percent for those 55 to 59, 15 percent for those 60 to 64, and 10 percent for those 65 and older—and workers with low annual earnings also pay less. This schedule helps smooth consumption over the worker's lifetime, a major purpose of the scheme.

Investment, Longevity, and Inflation Risk

In mandatory saving schemes, workers assume the investment, longevity, and inflation risks of their retirement funds. Retirement income will be lower if investment performance is poor. And if people live longer than expected, they may outlast their retirement savings. Some schemes require workers to purchase annuities when they retire—to insure against unexpected longevity. Investment risk is particularly high when accumulated assets are used to purchase the lifetime annuity, and the market interest rate on the date the annuity is purchased is critical. It is important that schemes include some method of spreading this risk across time (see below and issue brief 10).

For inflation risk, an important question is whether pensioners should be required to purchase indexed annuities—and if so, whether these should be indexed to wages or prices. In a mandatory saving scheme, individual workers pay the cost of their own indexation in the form of lower initial benefits or higher contribution rates (table 6.1), in contrast to pay-as-you-go schemes, in which workers bear this risk to protect retirees. In reality, however, retirees are never completely protected in either type of scheme (see chapter 4). Mandatory saving plans can reduce inflation risk by investing in equities and real property (whose nominal values generally rise with inflation), foreign assets (avoiding country-specific shocks), and indexed instruments (passing on the risk to those who are most willing to bear it).

Centralized or Decentralized Management

Risks, costs, and rates of return are strongly influenced by whether the fund is centralized or decentralized. Centralized provident funds are run by an agent of the national government. In their ideal state, they invest productively and benefit from economies of scale that minimize operating costs. Malaysia and Singapore are examples of national provident funds with low costs and stable, though modest, returns. However, more typically, managers of centralized provident funds, which are compulsory monopolies, may have little incentive to operate efficiently or earn reasonable returns—and may be subject to political pressures to invest unproductively.

Decentralized competitive plans, by contrast, face market pressures to operate efficiently and maximize returns and are at least partially insulated from political pressures to misallocate capital. Workers choose the fund in which to place their savings, presumably based on its record of returns and risk. But these plans require a complex regulatory structure to ensure the financial soundness and integrity of fund managers and to prevent workers from making big mistakes. Regulating decentralized mandatory saving schemes requires considerable human capital and institutional capacity, including the ability to enact clear rules and penalize malfeasance in predictable ways. Some elements of modern financial markets are also needed, though these are likely to develop in response to the scheme. For countries that satisfy these criteria, privately managed mandatory saving plans deserve careful consideration.

Impact on the Broader Economy

LIKE FUNDED OCCUPATIONAL PLANS, MANDATORY PERSONAL plans can have positive effects on capital accumulation and capital market development—but they attain these effects with fewer labor market distortions.

Implications for Capital Markets

The mandatory saving pillar can be important for increasing long-term saving, accelerating capital market development, boosting investment in productive capital, and monitoring corporate performance. For countries where the current rates of long-term saving and capital accumulation are below optimal levels, such changes have the potential to enhance economic growth. But the allocation and productivity of this capital depend on whether the funds are publicly or privately managed.

Impact on long-term saving. When a mandatory saving rate is set, to some extent it simply replaces voluntary saving. A low mandatory saving rate, say 5 percent or less, is likely to be largely counteracted by cuts in voluntary saving, having a negligible effect on net capital formation. At higher rates, this crowd-out effect may be only partial because people are shortsighted and would not have saved as much voluntarily for old age. Some of their personal saving may be for bequests or precautions, not easily satisfied by mandatory retirement saving schemes. Limits on consumer borrowing may prevent people from dissaving against future pension benefits. And people might have little faith in the new system, treating their contributions as a tax and continuing to save privately for their old age.

Overall, then, it seems likely that a mandatory saving scheme will increase household saving relative to the situation without a scheme (and even more so relative to a pay-as-you-go system). The higher the required contribution rate and the lower the opportunities for offsetting actions such as consumer borrowing, the greater this effect will be. Perhaps more important is the shift it brings about in the composition of savings in favor of long-term financial assets controlled by large financial institutions, instead of real estate, precious metals, and land (see chapter 3 and issue brief 4).

Empirical evidence on the savings effect of mandatory saving schemes is ambiguous. During the 1970s and 1980s, Singapore had the highest private saving rate in East Asia, with Malaysia close behind. In Chile, private saving went up sharply in the decade after the mandatory saving scheme was introduced. But many other factors were at work in all three cases, so it is difficult to pin down how much of the high saving, if any, was due to the mandatory saving scheme. More striking was the large increase in financial assets controlled by the scheme. In Singapore, the resources of the Central Provident Fund rose from 28 percent of GDP in 1976 to 76 percent in 1991 (despite large withdrawals for housing). In Malaysia, the balances of the Employees Provident Fund increased from 18 percent of GDP in 1980 to 41 percent in 1991 (table 6.3). In Chile, resources of the AFP system totaled 35 percent of GDP by 1991, after ten years of operation.

Mandatory saving plans are thus able to generate—in a short time—substantial long-term savings invested in financial assets. Consider the case in which labor income represents 50 percent of national income. A compulsory scheme covering 50 percent of the labor force and imposing

Table 6.3 Assets of Selected National Provident Funds

(as a percentage of GDP)

Country	1983	Most recent year available	
Singapore	53.8	75.6	(1991)
Malaysia	24.4	40.8	(1991)
Solomon Islands	15.4	—	—
Zambia	9.1	5.8	(1989)
Sri Lanka	8.1	15.2	(1990)
Swaziland	6.0	5.4	(1987)
Nepal	3.8	—	—
India	1.9	4.5	(1990)
Indonesia[a]	1.0	1.4	(1990)
Ghana[b]	—	0.6	(1986)
Fiji	—	43.9	(1987)
Nigeria	—	0.7	(1988)
Barbados	—	16.0	(1986)
Kenya	—	11.5	(1989)

—Not available.

Note: Refers to main provident fund in each country.

a. Refers to both public employees' and national provident funds.

b. Provident funds are being replaced by social insurance systems.

Source: IMF, *International Financial Statistics* (various issues); International Social Security Association (1986); Dixon (1989); Astek (1992); Asher (1992a, 1992b); India Employees' Provident Fund (1990); Zambian National Provident Fund (1989); Kenyan National Provident Fund (1990). See Palacios (1994c) for further description of the data.

a 10 percent contribution rate would annually accumulate funds equal to 2.5 percent of national income. If the rate of return on fund balances equals the rate of growth of GNP (and because pension payouts would be minimal in the early years of operation), such a scheme would accumulate resources equal to 12.5 percent of GNP over five years and 25 percent over ten years. After the first ten years, the growing volume of benefit payments would slow the pace of accumulation—though a higher interest rate, broader coverage, and rising share of labor income would accelerate the rate of accumulation.

In the very long run—in a closed economy, and even in an open economy if mandatory funded plans become common—the marginal productivity of capital and the real rate of return may fall as long-term savings accumulate. At some point, the productivity of capital may fall so far that further high saving is no longer warranted. Since the problem in many countries now appears to be a shortage rather than an overabundance of capital, this effect is far off in the future. And it can be forestalled further by international diversification, investment in human capital complementary to physical capital, shifts of labor from the informal to the formal sector, and capital-intensive technological change. But it is well to bear in mind that a mandatory saving rate, if too high, will diminish social welfare—and that the "right" rate may decline as the stock of long-term capital grows.

Impact on capital allocation. Establishing a mandatory saving scheme presents an opportunity to stimulate capital markets and expand the supply of productive capital. Nevertheless, the allocation and productivity of this capital depends on whether the funds are publicly or privately managed. Most centrally managed funds have been invested in the bonds of government or in failing public enterprises at low nominal interest rates that become negative during inflationary periods. If government has exclusive access to the funds, spends them wastefully, and pays workers an arbitrary interest rate, the potential advantages of mandatory saving schemes are lost. In fact, such schemes become very much like pay-as-you-go schemes in their capital and labor market effects.

Because of the fungibility of money once it becomes part of the government budget, the real productivity of these provident funds is not known. The funds may increase government consumption or investment beyond what they would have been otherwise—or they may substitute for explicit taxes while holding government spending unchanged. Each has a different impact on national output and its composition and distribution. It is known, however, that the real returns credited to worker accounts have ranged from around zero (India) to highly negative (Zambia and other African countries) (figures 3.3 and 4.5). So, for the worker, these systems have failed. And for the broader economy, their allocations have not been subject to any competitive market test or even public scrutiny.

Even in Singapore, more than 90 percent of fund assets have been invested in nontradable government securities with an average rate of return of 3 percent in the 1980s (Asher 1992b), similar to that on twelve-month time deposits and less than what long-term contractual savings could have earned in the market. Using revenues borrowed from the provident fund among others, the Singapore government has invested in foreign assets. The authorities claim that returns have been high, but the claims cannot be corroborated, since audited published data are not available. At any rate, the returns go to the government, not to the provident funds. The relatively low interest rate paid to the fund could thus be viewed as a hidden tax on workers to finance general government expenditures and reserves.

Most countries with national provident funds allow employees to use part of their balances for housing and other specified purposes, and Singapore now allows limited investments in approved securities. Members are obliged to redeposit the funds with the provident fund if they sell the houses or other investments (Asher 1992a). This use of funds has a positive effect on home ownership and the housing market but reduces the impact of national provident funds as a source of productive capital investment and retirement income. It is not clear that mandatory saving for housing is justified on efficiency grounds.

By contrast, in a decentrally managed competitive system such as that in Chile, workers pick their management company from a small number of authorized AFPs and can transfer their accounts from one company to another. This gives decisionmaking authority to workers, who are clearly interested in maximizing returns and minimizing risk, and avoids the problem of earning below-market returns and encouraging excess government spending. But workers may not have the information needed to make wise choices. Their investments may be too risky in some cases and too conservative in others, so they may eventually become charges on the rest of society. To counter this problem, the Chilean government has imposed strict regulations to protect the safety and profitability of investments (see below).

Given the decentralized management and the block on personal withdrawals, the Chilean pension system has become a dominant player in the capital market—a force facilitating privatization and growth. Initially the AFPs invested predominantly in government bonds, but gradually they shifted to corporate securities—especially equities, as the Chilean stock market boomed and investment rules were liberalized (Vittas and Iglesias 1992). Now the government must compete for access to funds and pay the competitive market price. The AFP system also invested heavily in the privatization of public utilities in the mid-1980s, accounting for 10 to 35 percent of the equity capital of the privatized utilities—and even more of the domestically held equity capital. By 1991, 38 percent of AFP funds were in state securities, 24 percent in corporate equities, and about 13 percent each in corporate bonds, mortgage bonds, and bank deposits. AFPs hold more than one-third of all public sector bonds, two-thirds of all private sector bonds, and 10 percent of all corporate equities in the country (Superintendencia de AFPs, Banco Central de Chile).

Perhaps more important, the pension system has stimulated the development of other institutions and practices that have deepened Chilean financial markets over the past decade. These include modern bank supervision, new securities and corporation laws, increased disclosure requirements for public companies, risk classification agencies for bonds, a long-term corporate bond market and a second stock market, new types of mortgage bonds, and improved regulation of insurance companies.

The rate of return to workers in the Chilean system has been much higher than in countries with centrally managed mandatory saving pillars. During the first ten years, the gross annual real return averaged 13 percent, and the average net yield to workers, after fees, was about 9.2 percent, albeit with large variations among different funds and individuals (Acuña and Iglesias 1992). Such high gross returns cannot be expected in the long run, but the high start-up costs of the first two years also will not continue; they have already been reduced from 14.7 percent of assets in 1982 to 1.6 percent in 1992. Overall, this experience is consistent with the observation that decentralized funded plans have earned far higher returns than centralized plans—perhaps reflecting their competitive nature and the market tests for their allocations.

Pension fund concentration and corporate governance. Mandatory pension funds, if invested in the private sector, could eventually come to dominate the ownership of financial assets that represent claims on the economy's real assets—land, housing stock, commercial property, and industrial equipment. This ownership structure has implications for corporate governance, since pension funds would become major stockholders and could exercise voting rights and power over corporate management. Although also true for voluntary occupational pension plans (chapter 5), the magnitudes involved can become much greater with a mandatory plan.

The concentration of ownership means that mandatory pension funds could not simply buy and sell shares without disrupting the market. It also makes it worthwhile for them to incur the costs of gathering and processing information. And it allows them to monitor the management performance of corporations. The other side of the coin is that it may give a small number of pension funds an influential voice in interlocking directorates—an anticompetitive force in strategic corporate decisions. Centralized provident funds are even more concentrated. If these funds were to invest in corporate equities, public officials could gain control of corporate affairs, a back door to nationalization.

In Chile, the three largest companies account for more than 60 percent of total funds and a big chunk of total corporate equity. So far, the AFPs have not attempted to monitor or control corporations, and publicly managed provident funds have not invested in private corporations. But funded plans in other countries are doing so. In the United States, funded occupational plans have begun to monitor the governance of the corporations in which they have an ownership stake. Because this channel allows pension funds to have a far-reaching influence on the economy, it becomes particularly important for them to be concentrated—but not too concentrated—and to have incentives that encourage the right performance from corporations (chapter 5 and box 5.3).

Implications for Labor Markets

Mandatory saving plans, unlike public or occupational plans (particularly defined benefit plans), have relatively little impact on the labor market. Since workers eventually recoup their contributions, with interest, they are less likely to see saving as taxes, which they try to evade. And since they "own" their accounts, they can carry them along from one job to another with no penalty for mobility. In this sense, the important story is that there is relatively little labor market story, compared with the other types of plans.

Even so, some distortions remain. First, when contribution rates are much higher than households' desired saving rates (presumably the reason for a mandatory scheme), incentives are created to evade by shifting to the informal market, understating covered wages, and substituting in-kind benefits for wages. When interest rates are below-market, as is often the case for provident funds, this effect is exacerbated. If workers cannot evade they may be induced, by their higher accumulated savings and compulsory savings rate, to retire early. Thus, mandatory saving plans may reduce the supply of labor, especially experienced labor, in the formal sector. In addition, wage rigidities may prevent employers from shifting their share of the payroll tax to workers—and may decrease employment instead. Singapore seems to have experienced this effect in 1984, when it raised the contribution rate to 50 percent of wages, shared equally by employers and employees. The employers' rate was cut in half the following year because of the belief that this had affected employment adversely. Both of these factors imply a tax element that distorts the labor market and limits the efficient contribution rate.

Fiscal Implications

A mandatory saving plan also has fewer fiscal implications than a pay-as-you-go public plan since workers receive only the value of their contributions plus investment earnings. Political pressure to increase public spending on pension benefits is absent. In fact, governments have borrowed from provident funds at below-market interest rates, cutting future pension benefits and current public borrowing costs. But these low rates could increase public deficits if they induce the government to spend more on other goods and services. The danger is that the spending, financed by a hidden tax on workers, may not be productive. (This is similar to the problem posed by large reserves in a partly funded public plan.) Decentralized schemes that charge market rates avoid this problem. But if the government guarantees their benefits, this constitutes another state obligation that could become surprisingly large if strategic manipulation and moral hazard are not controlled.

Another important fiscal effect stems from the tax treatment of pension savings. Tax incentives are not essential for mandatory schemes, but they improve compliance and are therefore common. The tax loss may force the government to reduce spending or to raise other taxes, which could have a high efficiency cost (Valdes-Prieto and Cifuentes 1993).

Contributions to most mandatory saving schemes are deductible for income tax, as is the current investment income from the funds. Workers in Chile are allowed to contribute additional amounts on a voluntary tax-exempt basis. In most schemes, withdrawals are subject to tax, like any other income. The benefits of tax deferral are greater for higher-income workers, because their initial tax savings are higher and they are likely to be in a lower tax bracket after retirement. To avoid this perverse redistribution, limits may be placed on the tax-advantaged benefits or a tax credit may be offered rather than making contributions tax-deductible, as has been proposed for occupational plans (chapter 5).

Malaysia and Singapore exempt both the contributions and the withdrawals—as well as the interest earned in between—from taxation. The total tax benefits of Singapore's national provident fund (and the government tax revenue forgone) are estimated at slightly more than 1 percent of GDP for 1987, roughly the tax expenditures for the U.S. occupational pension system (Turner and Beller 1989). The Singapore fund thus provides a valuable tax shelter for contributors, especially high-income workers who would be subject to higher marginal tax rates on other investment income (Queisser 1991). The higher tax benefits received by upper-income groups may be one reason they go along with the high contribution rates and low interest rates.

Do Mandatory Saving Schemes Redistribute Income and Alleviate Poverty?

IN PRINCIPLE, A MANDATORY SAVING SCHEME COVERS ALL FORmal sector workers, far more than in a voluntary or quasi-voluntary occupational plan. So, everyone should benefit from access to saving and insurance instruments. Moreover, in principle, there is no explicit redistribution: benefits and contributions are directly linked. In particular, the large intergenerational redistributions in pay-as-you-go systems are avoided. But some nontransparent intragenerational redistributions still occur, particularly in centrally managed funds, and these often involve transfers from low-income households to high-income households.

Redistributions

People whose voluntary saving rate was lower than the mandatory rate, as already noted, value their expected pensions less than their current contributions, and in terms of their own evaluation are losers—although others in society may feel they are misinformed, myopic, and therefore winners from the mandatory plan. They are likely to be predominantly from lower-income households. If the government borrows from provident funds at below-market rates, in lieu of increased taxes to finance general public expenditures, this has a further redistributional effect—since the incidence of the payroll tax is not the same as that of the general revenue tax and generally is more regressive. If the borrowed funds are used to finance public expenditures that would not otherwise have been undertaken, income is redistributed from fund contributors to the beneficiaries of the additional government spending. Such transfers are hard to trace, because doing so requires knowing what would have happened if the funds had not been available. That is why the transfers are likely to benefit privileged groups, who are in a position to understand and influence government transactions. This unclear redistribution is far less likely in a decentralized mandatory saving scheme.

Allowing contributors to withdraw funds before retirement also benefits middle- and upper-income groups. Singapore's condition of permitting early withdrawals from the national provident fund for education, home ownership, and alternative investments as long as contributors maintain a minimum balance in the plan is one that few low-income workers can meet. In some countries, plan members are permitted to borrow against their savings at below-market rates for specified purchases—an option again used mainly by high-income groups. A more competitive system for investing pension funds, yielding a higher rate of return, would reduce this perverse redistribution.

Perverse redistribution may also result, in both publicly and privately managed funds, if retiring workers are compelled to purchase annuities that pool people with long and short life expectancies. Public policies that prohibit distinctions among different demographic and socioeconomic groups in setting the terms of annuities and life insurance contracts have this effect. For example, if regulations require retiring mine workers and white collar employees to pay the same price for annuities, the result would be regressive. This effect could be offset by reducing annuity prices for lower socioeconomic groups, by topping up their accounts directly, or by paying larger benefits to their survivors.

Most mandatory saving schemes avoid this problem by paying lump sums instead of annuities on retirement. But this means they do not provide longevity insurance and do not protect the very old against poverty. Chile gives workers a choice between purchasing an annuity or taking phased withdrawals that are scheduled to last an expected lifetime and that avoid the redistribution problem. Chile also requires all employees to purchase term life and disability insurance, in which mine workers get a net benefit if they are in the same pool with white collar workers.

Poverty Alleviation

Mandatory saving schemes have been criticized for their failure to protect low-wage workers or workers with interrupted careers, many of whom are women who spend part of their lives doing household work.

Another criticism is that they may prevent old age poverty among middle- and high-income workers, but low-income workers may never accumulate enough in their pension accounts to support themselves in their old age. A third criticism is that early generations of retirees are not protected by these schemes, because it takes many years for enough pension capital to build up. Along similar lines, pensions may fall below subsistence standards because of inflation or unexpectedly low returns. For all these reasons, mandatory saving schemes can still leave considerable old age poverty.

Some of these possible sources of poverty can be handled without public transfers. In Chile, the purchase of private disability insurance and term life insurance is compulsory. Most provident funds do not provide or require such insurance, leaving survivors and disabled workers largely unprotected and poor. Regulations could require joint contributions and joint ownership of retirement savings accounts between spouses, protecting women whose labor force participation has been interrupted. Beyond that, governments can deal with the problems of long-term poverty alleviation and extreme investment risk by guaranteeing a minimum pension based on years of employment—or by redistributive social assistance programs; this might be considered an accompanying role of the public plan. Chile provides such assistance and guarantees, financing them from general tax revenues.

Regulatory Issues in Decentralized Schemes

DECENTRALIZED COMPETITIVE SYSTEMS ARE MORE LIKELY than centralized provident funds to maximize investment returns and contribute to capital market development. But decentralized plans raise a host of public policy issues related to the fiduciary standards of pension companies, the safety of their investments, the size of fees and commissions, the information disclosed, and the guarantees provided by government. Extensive regulation is needed because workers often lack the expertise to invest wisely and because private pension companies might exploit their ignorance. Some private investment managers might take too many risks to maximize yield and attract affiliates, whereas others might be too conservative to keep up with productivity and inflation. Given the long term of pension investments, it may be too late for workers to recover financially through new saving once the damage becomes evident. Trying to remedy this flaw through government guarantees may create moral hazard and fiscal problems. Regulations are designed to protect both individual workers and society from perverse competition in the face of information deficiencies. This protection is particularly important in a mandatory program.

If governments cannot control centralized pension funds very well, can they be counted on to regulate decentralized systems well? And at what point does a strict regulatory structure wipe out competition and become government control? Chile shows the kinds of regulations that are workable and may—or may not—be advisable.

Ensuring the Solvency of Funds and the Integrity of Managers

Which funds qualify as custodians of mandatory saving accounts? To ensure competent and responsible administration of pensions funds and protect solvency, criteria must be established for entry conditions and minimum capital margins. The shortage of local expertise in many developing countries can be overcome by using foreign fund managers in joint ventures with local firms. Developing countries reluctant to use joint ventures may have a hard time assembling the expertise needed to run pension funds well, especially in the early years.

Chile limits participation in the mandatory scheme to AFPs, the specialized pension fund management companies. The AFPs are regulated and supervised by the Superintendency of AFPs, which has authority over charter approval. Any group of shareholders—including corporations, trade associations, labor unions, and other financial institutions (but not banks)—can establish an AFP. Until recently, the three largest AFPs, serving about two-thirds of the market, were joint ventures (Vittas and Iglesias 1992).

The pension fund is an independent entity, segregated both legally and financially from AFPs. The assets of the pension fund belong exclusively to individual members, are not attachable, and are not affected by any financial losses suffered by AFPs. AFPs are required to maintain investment reserves equal to 1 percent of the total assets of the pension fund they manage. Reserves must be invested in the same assets as the pension fund under the AFP's management to ensure that AFPs apply the same incentives in investing the resources of the pension fund as they do for their own resources.

In Chile, to simplify the workers' choice of AFP and the switch of their accumulated balances to another AFP, regulations impose a strict limit of one account per worker and one fund per management company—regulations that are very restrictive and very controversial. Allowing workers to have accounts with more than one company would let them hedge their bets and reduce their dependence on the performance of a single company. And allowing management companies to operate a wider range of funds would let them develop expertise in market niches and tailor products to different tastes and age groups. For instance, equity growth funds might appeal to younger workers, more conservative stock funds to middle-aged workers, and income-yielding stock-bond funds to older workers. The one-account, one-fund rule reduces variety, choice, and diversification—three potential advantages of a decentralized system.

The restrictions are aimed at preserving the system's simplicity and transparency, features considered important for a compulsory scheme involving large numbers of financially unsophisticated people. Allowing companies to manage a wider range of investment funds and allowing workers to use more than one fund would complicate compliance monitoring. For example, it would become more difficult to prevent withdrawals or a concentration of the worker's portfolio in risky assets. As the system matures and workers gain financial experience, regulations may become less restrictive. But in the meantime, the cost of simplifying regulations is the loss of choice and risk diversification.

Keeping Investment Risk within Reasonable Bounds

Financial regulation aims to protect participants from fraudulent or imprudent behavior by the managers of financial institutions—a task that assumes particular importance in long-term mandatory schemes. One way to provide such protection is through regular disclosure of information. AFPs in Chile are required to provide statements to contributors three times a year—disclosing the last four monthly contributions paid by employers, the financial performance of the pension fund, and the accumulated balance and rate of return on individual accounts.

Participants are further protected through investment rules. Chile started out with rigid investment regulations—and gradually eased them as the experience of workers and funds increased. Initially, investments in equities and overseas securities were not allowed, but they now are, in steadily increasing amounts. Only upper limits are imposed on investments to control the exposure of pension funds to particular risks. There are no floors requiring purchase of government bonds or other "socially useful" investments. Currently, the upper limits are 50 percent on government bonds, 30 percent on corporate equities, 10 percent on foreign securities, and similar limits on bank deposits, mortgage loans, and other assets (Vittas and Iglesias 1992). As discussed above, current portfolio allocations imply that these ceilings are not binding for most AFPs. Ceilings also apply to permissible investments in the securities of individual companies. Ceilings are higher for so-called Chapter 12 companies, which accept severe restrictions on their management independence. So far, only recently privatized utilities have opted to qualify for Chapter 12, which has allowed pension funds to play an important role in their privatization.

The dispersion in returns across AFPs is reduced through the regulation of relative maximum and minimum returns. If a fund's real investment return over a rolling twelve-month period is 50 percent higher or 2 percentage points higher (whichever yields the higher rate of return) than the average for all pension funds, the AFP has to place the difference in a profitability reserve, which becomes an asset of the pension fund, not the AFP. Similarly, if the real investment return for a pension fund is less than half the average of all pension funds or 2 percentage points lower (whichever yields the lower rate of return), the AFP has to make up the difference by transferring funds from the profitability reserve—and if this is inadequate, from its own investment reserves. If an AFP cannot pay the shortfall, it is declared bankrupt, its pension fund assets are transferred to other AFPs, and the government makes up any remaining difference. So far, no profitability reserves have been established, and three AFPs have been dissolved or merged, with no loss to the government or the pension funds they managed.

Maximum and minimum limits on annual relative pension fund returns are designed to avoid wide dispersion across AFPs. But they also induce herd behavior, since funds are penalized for being different from the average, not for being wrong in absolute terms. In addition, using a twelve-month average in calculating returns unduly emphasizes short-term performance, which is undesirable for long-term contracts that may span sixty years or more. Volatile funds that might get higher returns over the long run are penalized, while less volatile funds that persistently perform at the lower end of the permitted range, producing substantially below-average returns over the long run, are not penalized.

An alternative approach would apply narrower limits (say, 25 percent rather than 50 percent) on performance over three- to five-year periods. Another alternative would specify the maximum and minimum returns as two standard deviations away from the average in a given year or one standard deviation over five years. The better informed workers are, the less need there will be for such regulations, as workers will shift their savings away from consistently poor performers.

To protect against inflation, pension fund managers could be required to invest a portion of their portfolios in assets that provide an effective hedge against inflation. Although Chile does not require indexation by AFPs, this position is widespread in Chilean financial markets—a response to demand in an environment in which inflation has historically been a problem. More than 95 percent of AFP investments are in equities, real assets, or indexed bonds, including indexed bonds issued by banks or private firms whose value is tied to the monthly cost-of-living index. This counters the common assertion that the private sector cannot offer fully indexed securities and cannot protect against inflation. Hedging against inflation would be much more difficult, however, in countries with less developed financial markets, poorly indexed financial instruments, and an inflation rate that is high and volatile.

Allowing Investments in Overseas Assets

Allowing pension funds to invest freely overseas permits diversification of country risk. But it also raises fears of institutionalized capital flight, loss of control by monetary authorities, and depriving local markets of the increased availability of long-term funds (box 5.5). Perhaps because of these fears, Chile did not allow the AFPs to invest in foreign securities until 1991 and then only on a gradual schedule, beginning at 1 percent of funds and rising to 10 percent by 1995. Authorizing investment in foreign securities represents a recognition of the maturity of the system, the large size of the pension funds, the saturation of domestic markets, and the growing need for diversification of country risk. It is also a response to the large capital inflow that Chile has experienced in recent years. Conversely, liberalization of capital outflows may encourage inflows by convincing foreign investors that they will be able to get their money out. It may also impose fiscal discipline, which is badly needed in some countries.

For these reasons, Chile's approach may be too cautious. In particular, saturation of the domestic market would come sooner in smaller countries, suggesting a need to relax investment rules at a much earlier stage and to a much larger extent. The scheme being considered in Argentina would permit investments of up to 10 percent in foreign securities from the start. One proposal for Bolivia would feature complete international diversification (Kotlikoff 1994).

Regulating Fees and Commissions

In principle, competition among plan administrators should make regulation of fees and commissions unnecessary. In practice, agency and information problems can lead to distortions in the structure of fees and commissions. Because mandatory saving schemes are by definition compulsory and economies of scale in the pension industry may result in concentration, investment companies may end up charging more than they would in a purely voluntary competitive system.

Chile regulates the types of fees that AFPs can levy but not the level of fees or the structure of commissions paid to agents. Authorized fees include a fixed fee per contribution, a prorated fee on wages subject to pension contributions, fees for opening new accounts, fees per pension payment, and fees for voluntary savings accounts. No AFP has imposed the last two fees, and only one has levied a fee on new accounts. Fees may not be assessed for closing an account—to prevent AFPs from discouraging account transfers. Nor may fees be charged as a percentage of assets—to avoid depleting the reserves of inactive accounts.

The flat fee per contribution is probably the most controversial. This fee would seem to be regressive, but it may simply reflect—or even understate—the real costs of managing an account. The fee was high in the early years of the program, leading to lower net rates of return to low-income workers, but competition combined with negative publicity has led most AFPs to abolish or greatly diminish it. A prorated fee of about 1.5 percent on wages subject to contributions is currently the major fee, and net returns have been roughly equalized across income groups (Acuña and Iglesias 1992).

Keeping a Lid on Operating Costs

Decentralized systems that allow workers to choose management companies and transfer accounts tend to incur higher operating costs than efficiently run centralized plans. Decentralized systems cannot achieve the same economies of scale. They incur high marketing and transaction (switching) costs. And they perform such added functions as investment research and processing (which may, however, result in higher rates of return). At the same time, decentralized plans have more incentive to operate efficiently than centralized plans that have a monopoly in a compulsory system. These diverse factors help explain why, in 1990, operating costs were 1.5 percent of covered wages and 2.3 percent of total assets in Chile, compared with 0.2 percent and 0.1 percent in Singapore and 0.4 percent and 0.2 percent in Malaysia, while the costs of Zambia's centralized system were twenty-five times higher than Singapore's and ate up half of all contributions (table 6.4 and issue brief 5).

The higher expense ratio in Chile as compared with Singapore and Malaysia may be an intrinsic cost of a decentralized system that has also produced a higher rate of return. It may nevertheless be possible to take steps to keep these costs down. Marketing costs are a particularly sore point. Where investors are relatively uneducated and uninformed about financial matters, they are susceptible to intensive marketing campaigns, which increase costs. Promotional expenses are estimated to account for as much as 30 percent of operating costs for Chile's AFPs. Paying salespeople by commission leads to high turnover of accounts and correspondingly high transaction costs. These costs are eventually passed on to consumers in the form of high fees. Advertising campaigns also emphasize short-term performance.

Table 6.4 Operating Costs and Investment Returns

Costs or returns	Chile, 1990	Malaysia, 1989	Singapore, 1990	Zambia, 1988–89
Operating costs as percentage of:				
Annual contributions	15.40	1.99	0.53	51.70
Average total assets	2.30	0.18	0.10	6.80
Covered annual wages	1.54	0.40	0.21	5.17
Affiliates times per capita income	2.31	0.54	0.16	4.48
Real investment returns on individual accounts (during 1980s)	7.5–10.5	4.82	2.86	-55.00

Source: Zambian National Provident Fund (1989); Asher (1992a, 1992b); Vittas (1992).

Requiring companies to provide data on fees and commissions as well as investment performance over longer periods (three, five, and ten years) would provide a more accurate picture of relative returns and might also help to keep operating costs down. Marketing costs and account turnover would decline if transfers, which workers might choose during an open enrollment period, were limited to one per year. Marketing costs might also fall if AFPs were allowed to pass along the savings to long-term affiliates in the form of a bonus on their rate of return or a reduction in their required fee. The entry of new AFPs in a competitive market may eventually lead to lower costs and fees. Economies of scale and learning by doing as the system grows will undoubtedly enhance efficiency. Indeed, costs fell dramatically through the 1980s, are continuing to fall, and are lowest for the largest AFPs (figure 6.1 and issue brief figure 5.2).

Figure 6.1 Relationship of Annual Administrative Expenditures to Total Assets, Chile, 1982–92

Administrative expenditures as a percentage of total assets

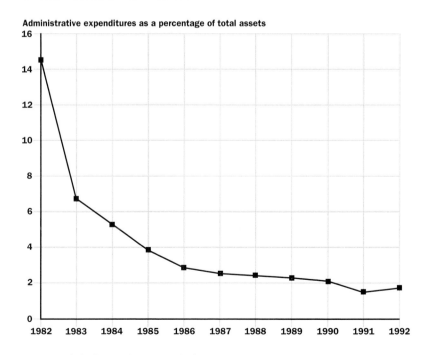

Administrative costs have fallen over time thanks to economies of scale, learning by doing, and competition.

Source: Abuhadba (1994); Acuña and Iglesias (1992); Valdes-Prieto (1993); Provida (1993).

Regulating Annuities

Although most provident funds simply pay lump sums upon retirement, there has been a move toward phased withdrawals or annuities—to prevent overly rapid consumption of savings. In Singapore, since 1987, retiring workers have been required to purchase a minimum pension. In Chile, workers are given a choice between purchasing an annuity or taking phased withdrawals over their expected lifetimes. Annuities must be indexed to the cost of living, and insurance companies meet this requirement by investing heavily in indexed public and private securities. These requirements give rise to a host of potential problems in the insurance market.

In Chile, annuity salespersons receive large commissions up front, giving them an incentive to withhold information or to shade the truth to gain a customer. Since the purchase of an annuity is an irreversible act, a wrong decision by an ill-informed retiree may have disastrous consequences that cannot be readily corrected. Chile is considering various measures to control commissions and inform workers about their options. One proposal would limit annuity products to two or three standard options, such as partially indexed life annuities for the retiree, combined with survivors' benefits for a ten- or twenty-year period, or joint annuities that cover the entire lifetime of the retiree plus a designated beneficiary. That would simplify comparison shopping for annuities offered by different companies. Broad disclosure on premiums and commissions would also be required. Other proposals call for independent professional advisers to assist retirees in evaluating annuity choices and for the establishment of an ombudsman to investigate complaints and arbitrate disputes. These proposals, focusing on better information flows, should help the market work better. But some believe that increased competition will eventually lead insurance companies to move toward direct sales of annuities, which would reduce the price by cutting out the commission.

Another problem concerns the worker's exposure to the risk of a sharp decline in the market at the time of retirement. This risk could be reduced by requiring workers to purchase small annuity contracts periodically once they reach a predetermined age, such as 50. By reducing the lumpiness of the purchase, this method would diversify the interest rate risk. In effect, it would convert a defined contribution program into a defined benefit program, partly protecting workers from investment risk after age 50. But it would, at the same time, raise the risk premium charged by the insurance company and increase workers' exposure to the risk of insurance company insolvency, making regulation of fiduciary standards all the more important.

The timing problem could be mitigated more effectively by developing variable annuities, whose value would rise and fall with the market rather than being fixed at the retirement date. This would reduce the exposure of the worker to market conditions at retirement time but would continue the investment risk throughout retirement. Such variable annuities are used in South Africa and the United States. Caps on annual movements in value of variable annuities might make this risk more acceptable to retirees (issue brief 10 provides a more general discussion of annuity market problems and possible solutions).

Monitoring Compliance by Investment Companies

Close monitoring of investment company behavior is essential to ensure compliance. Supervision in Chile's AFP system includes daily reports on investment transactions and monthly reports on each company's financial position and performance. Compliance with investment limits is monitored continuously. On-site inspections are undertaken periodically to ensure the accuracy of submitted returns.

Chile's system is supervised and controlled by the Superintendency of AFPs, an autonomous agency linked to the Ministry of Labor and Social Security. The superintendency, which enjoys considerable independence and authority, has the right to authorize and revoke the license of AFPs, to issue detailed regulations for the smooth functioning of the system, and to promote changes in the law. With more than 100 lawyers, financial auditors, examiners, and other employees, it supervises the investments of AFPs, the operation of profitability reserves, the crediting of member contributions, and the payment of pensions.

An ever-present danger in regulatory systems is that the regulated will "capture" the regulators and prevent them from operating effectively. Although this does not seem to have happened in Chile, countries with a weaker regulatory capacity might have a more difficult time monitoring decentralized firms. Countries should assess their institutional and human capital capacities for regulating effectively before undertaking a decentralized mandatory saving plan.

Guaranteeing Pensions and Pension Returns

Various types of government guarantees are designed to ensure at least some pension coverage for everyone. In countries with a mandatory saving scheme, social assistance is often provided to people who are not covered, and a minimum pension may be guaranteed to those who are covered.

Singapore provides modest benefits (12 percent of the average wage) to poor old people, widows, and orphans through a social assistance program financed from general revenues, and it sets the rate of return to its provident fund. But it does not provide a guaranteed minimum pension. Chile's system includes four types of state guarantees. First, the government pays a social assistance benefit of about 12 percent of the average wage to old people not covered by the mandatory saving plan. Second, for workers who have contributed to the mandatory saving plan for at least twenty years, the state guarantees a minimum pension of about 22 to 25 percent of the average wage. Third, a minimum profitability rate is guaranteed for each pension fund relative to the average for the country. Any shortfall in rate of return is covered first through the profitability reserve, then through the investment reserves of the AFP, and finally by the state. Fourth, the government guarantees annuity payments for old age pensions and disability and survivorship benefits in case the insurance company fails. The guarantee covers 100 percent of the minimum pension and 75 percent of the rest of the benefit involved up to a specified limit. These guarantees are financed out of general revenues and constitute the public pay-as-you-go plan in Chile's old age security system.

What are the likely costs of such guarantees? As long as the rate of return remains at least 2 percentage points above the growth rate of wages, most people who work full-time during their active years (about forty years) will receive a pension far above the minimum without any public transfers (table 6.1). But a problem arises if low-income workers will contribute just long enough to qualify for the subsidized minimum pension (twenty years) and then escape to the informal sector to avoid making further payments. As many as 30 to 40 percent of covered workers in Chile may fall below the minimum if strategic evasion is common or if fund performance falls drastically. But even then the government has to make up only the shortfall between the minimum pension and the benefit payable by the pension fund.

Simulations indicate that these guarantees will cost less than 1 percent of GDP, easily absorbed in a country such as Chile that has only a small budget deficit (Gillion and Bonilla 1992; Diamond and Valdes-Prieto 1994; Wagner 1991). But the cost of a minimum pension ought to be carefully calculated in advance to ensure that the state is not taking on a large unfunded liability that it will be unable to meet. If the cost is expected to be high, the minimum guarantee should be lowered or the required contribution rate raised, unless the government wishes to use general revenue finance as a redistributive instrument.

A contrasting problem is that a minimum pension of 22 to 25 percent of the average wage is well below the poverty line in most countries, and the social assistance of 12 percent is below subsistence. One way to attack both the evasion and the poverty problems is to guarantee a higher minimum pension to workers who have contributed for more years. For example, the guarantee could be set equal to 12 percent of the average economy-wide wage (the employment-related or means-tested floor for everyone over age 65) plus 0.5 percent for every year of contributing employment. A worker with twenty years of service would then be guaranteed 22 percent of the average wage, and one with forty-five years' service would be guaranteed 35 percent. Given the 10 percent contribution rate and the link to years of employment, which deters evasion, this scheme would not cost the government much more than the current one in Chile—and might even cost less.

Conclusion

MANDATORY PERSONAL SAVING SCHEMES REQUIRE WORKERS to accumulate a pool of long-term savings for consumption in old age. Since they are not tied to place of employment, they are more portable and diversify risk more than occupational plans. They are also likely to be more concentrated and therefore benefit more from economies of scale than occupational plans. Since they make benefits directly contingent on contributions, they are less likely than public plans to induce evasion and shifts of labor to the informal sector. Political pressures for poor design features—such as early retirement, nonsustainable pension levels, and hidden redistribution to influential groups—are avoided because each person's contribution determines the benefits that person ultimately gets. If evasion or early retirement does take place, the costs are borne by the individual worker, not by others in the plan.

Mandatory saving schemes have the potential to stimulate capital accumulation and the development of modern financial instruments and institutions. But if governments are given exclusive or favored access to the funds, many of these potential advantages are lost. When the pension funds are publicly managed, they are invariably required to be invested in government debt as a source of general revenue in return for low nominal rates of interest that become negative during inflationary periods. Often the government has used the funds for consumption rather than productive investments, canceling out the positive effect of these plans on long-term saving.

In principle, centralized national provident funds could become competitive by turning them over to one or more private managers on the basis of competitive bidding and with the authority to invest in private sector securities. This procedure, which has been considered in Malaysia, would enable the fund to minimize marketing costs, reap economies of scale, and possibly earn a higher rate of return. But the potential for corruption and cronyism in the bidding process would outweigh this advantage in many countries. Another option would retain centralized control but passively index the fund to the domestic and international stock markets, a procedure that is followed in the voluntary occupational plan for federal government employees in the United States. But many developing countries lack the necessary securities market for indexation. In any event, most governments have demonstrated that they do not want to relinquish privileged access to national provident funds.

Empirical experience indicates that decentralized mandatory saving schemes are likely to achieve higher returns and allocate capital more efficiently than centralized schemes. Political interference over investments is always a possibility, but decentralization makes this explicit and sets up a constituency against it—private pension funds and their worker affiliates. The danger is that workers' choices of investment might be ill informed, eventually leaving many people without adequate pensions. Regulation must walk a fine line between adequately protecting workers and giving funds enough latitude that competition and investment choice are not stamped out. To minimize risk:

- Only prudent companies, including joint ventures with experienced foreign firms, should be allowed to manage pension funds.
- Information disclosure should be emphasized.
- Investments should be diversified and subject to ceilings, not floors.
- There should be no requirement to invest funds in public securities.
- The range of funds, marketing expenses, and annuity products could be limited in the early years of the system and then gradually expanded.
- Investment in overseas securities should be encouraged in order to reduce exposure to country-specific risk.

Decentralized mandatory saving schemes will function best in middle- or high-income countries with a population well enough informed to make intelligent investment decisions, with financial markets that offer (or could be prompted to offer) a variety of debt and equity instruments, and with effective regulatory institutions or the capacity to develop these institutions quickly. Because financial market development and a regulatory apparatus are necessary for continued economic growth of all countries, funded pension plans are more viable as countries develop and can also speed up the development process.

Mandatory saving plans can provide an adequate pension for middle- and high-income workers, but they fail to protect workers with low wages as they grow old or to insure against sharp dips in investment performance. To alleviate long-term poverty and to help diversify risks, these plans must be accompanied by a minimum pension guarantee or other publicly financed redistributive benefits, thereby ensuring old age security for all.

CHAPTER 7

Putting the Pillars Together

HOW SHOULD A COUNTRY CHOOSE AMONG these alternative financing and managerial arrangements and develop a coherent strategy for providing old age security? Any strategy should have the basic goals of helping the old and helping the broader economy. That is, old age programs should be both a social safety net and an instrument for growth. Chapter 3 argued that they should help the old by:

- Facilitating people's efforts to shift some of their income from their active working years to old age (the saving or wage replacement function)
- Providing a basic income floor that protects those with low lifetime income (the redistributive or poverty alleviation function)
- Insuring against the many risks the old are especially vulnerable to, including disability, longevity, inflation, political, and investment risk (the insurance function).

And they should help the economy by:

- Minimizing hidden costs that impede growth—such as reduced employment, reduced saving, misallocated capital and labor, heavy fiscal burdens, high administrative expenses, and evasion
- Being sustainable—based on long-term planning that takes account of expected changes in economic and demographic conditions
- Being transparent to enable workers, citizens, and policymakers to make informed choices, and being insulated from political manipulations that lead to poor economic outcomes.

Since each of the three arrangements has different advantages, a combination, or multipillar system, is the best way to satisfy multiple goals.

Many countries with low incomes and young populations lack the governmental or private capacity to start a multipillar system immediately or in the near future. These countries should move slowly; doing nothing is better than doing wrong. Chapter 8 discusses the best strategy for these countries. This chapter outlines the multipillar system that is most appropriate for older middle- and high-income countries. Even if the time path is slow, all countries should have a sense of where they are headed in the long run—to prevent them from making wrong choices at the beginning that keep them from getting to the right point later on.

The Reasons for a Multipillar System

A CENTRAL POLICY ISSUE IN SYSTEM DESIGN IS THE BALANCE among the redistributive, saving, and insurance functions of old age security programs and the role of government in carrying out these functions. This study has argued that a country's old age security policies should encompass all three functions. But a different government role is appropriate for each.

Problems with a Dominant Public Pillar

Most countries—including almost all developing countries and some industrial countries—combine all three functions in a dominant public pillar—a publicly managed scheme that pays an earnings-related defined benefit and is financed out of payroll taxes on a pay-as-you-go basis. People with high incomes contribute more and get more, but some of their contributions are supposedly transferred to people with lower incomes. This combination of functions has been defended on the grounds that it keeps administrative costs low through economies of scale and scope and that it builds political support for the plan. The savings component encourages high-income earners to participate, while the redistributive component lets them express their solidarity with those less well-off.

But, as the evidence in chapter 4 suggested, public schemes that combine these functions are problematic—for both efficiency and distributional reasons. Some of these problems—such as high tax rates and large informal sectors—are readily observable. Others—such as reduced employment and growth—are more insidious because countries may be unaware of them until the damage has already been done.

Any scheme that redistributes to low-income workers while also providing adequate wage replacement to high-income workers will require a high contribution rate once populations age and systems mature. But defined benefit formulas do not make benefits actuarially contingent on these high contributions. In particular, contributions made when very young or after eligibility for the maximum pension has been established will have a below-market payoff. The high contribution rate is therefore likely to be perceived as a tax by workers, not as a price for services received. High tax rates lead to evasion—thereby defeating the purpose of a mandatory scheme. They also lead to strategic manipulation that enables workers to escape much of the tax but still qualify for benefits—thereby causing financial difficulties for the system. And they reallocate labor to the informal sector—causing difficulties for the broader economy. Employers who cannot pass payroll taxes on to workers cut back on employment, reducing national output. Older workers who are eligible for large pensions retire early, reducing the supply of experienced labor.

Such outcomes, of course, vary from country to country but are especially prevalent in developing economies, which have limited tax enforcement capacities, imperfect labor markets, and large informal sectors. In addition to these domestic effects, in an open global economy, payroll tax rates and defined benefit formulas that vary across countries can influence international labor and capital flows in inefficient ways. And they often imply capricious redistributions (for example, from workers with flat age-earnings profiles to those with steep profiles) that many societies would not regard as fair if they were carefully scrutinized.

The pay-as-you-go method of finance in the public pillar further separates benefits from contributions for the cohort as a whole. It inevitably produces low costs and large positive transfers to the first covered generations. It also inevitably produces negative transfers for later cohorts because of system maturation and population aging, increasing the labor market distortions and incentives to evade. In some cases, countries may wish to make this transfer across generations. More often, the transfer has not been foreseen or intentional. Ironically, the largest transfers seem to go to high-income groups in earlier cohorts, while middle- and sometimes even lower-income groups in later cohorts get negative transfers. The larger and more earnings-related the benefits in the public pillar, the greater are these perverse transfers.

A dominant pay-as-you-go public pillar also misses an opportunity for capital market development. When the first old generations get pensions that exceed their savings, national consumption may rise and savings may decline. The next few cohorts pay their social security tax instead of saving for their own old age (since they now expect to get a pension from the government), so this loss in savings may never be made up. In contrast, the alternative, a mandatory funded plan, could increase capital accumulation—an important advantage in capital scarce countries. A mandatory saving plan that increases long-term saving and requires it to flow through financial institutions stimulates a demand for (and eventually supply of) long-term financial instruments—a boon to development. These missed opportunities in a pay-as-you-go public pillar become lost income for future generations—and another source of intergenerational transfer.

Additionally, large pay-as-you-go public pillars often induce expenditures that exceed expectations—because of population aging, system maturation, and poor design features such as early retirement and high benefit rates. The costs of the system—whether covered by higher contribution rates or subsidies from the general treasury—make it difficult for the government to finance important public goods—another efficiency-inhibiting consequence.

But ultimately the costs (higher taxes and their distortionary effects on growth) have become too large to bear in many countries. When the public pillar fails to deliver on its promises, old people who depended on it exclusively have nowhere else to turn. Thus a dominant public pillar increases risk for the old. The most common failure occurs when inflation develops because demands on the national pie exceed its size and pensions, which are not fully indexed, lose much of their value.

For all these reasons, systems that have tried to do it all have all too often produced costly labor and capital market distortions, perverse redistributions to the rich, and insecurity for the old—outcomes that are not efficient or equitable or sustainable.

Some of the problems—such as the inevitability of intergenerational transfers and low rates of return to later cohorts—are inherent in pay-as-you-go systems. Some of the other problems do not seem to be inherent. Instead, they seem to result from poor design features—such as overly generous benefit formulas that place too much weight on final year salary, early retirement provisions that induce low labor force participation among experienced workers, and low ceilings on taxable earnings.

These design features can and should be fixed. But their commonality suggests that strong political factors are at work and may lead them to endure. Given their separation of benefits from contributions, their low initial costs that rise thereafter, and their complexity and nontransparency, large earnings-related pay-as-you-go public pillars are prone to political pressure from influential groups. These groups want provisions that will benefit them, they want others to finance these benefits, and pay-as-you-go defined benefit schemes make it easy for them to introduce poor design features that accomplish this goal in the early years of the plan. In this political sense, the design features may be inherent— not incidental—and they come back to haunt the country in later years. (For fuller discussion see chapter 4.)

Problems with Other Single Pillar Systems

Other single pillar systems, too, are problematic. Publicly managed mandatory saving plans (provident funds) have a record of misuse. Usually they are required to invest solely in public securities, and their availability at low interest rates may lead governments to borrow and spend more than they would have otherwise, in unproductive ways, yielding low or even negative returns for the pension funds. They are, essentially, a hidden tax on labor, subject to misuse precisely because it is hidden. By giving governments control over a major share of the financial assets in a country, they deprive the private sector of access to these funds and thereby inhibit growth. They contain no provisions for redistributing to low-income workers, and, in fact, they often include nontransparent redistributions to high-income workers—until finally the fund is depleted and can't pay much to anyone.

Privately managed occupational or personal saving plans would also fail as single pillar systems. (No country has ever tried to use them as such.) Occupational plans have better capital market effects than publicly managed plans but may impede the smooth functioning of labor markets. They redistribute in accordance with employer rather than social objectives. They do not protect those with limited labor market experience. And they are subject to employer or insurance company default. Personal saving accounts are beneficial for both capital and labor markets and are relatively immune from political manipulation by governments or strategic manipulation by workers, but they, too, do not address the problem of poverty among those with low lifetime incomes whose earning capacity is further diminished by old age. Nor do they insure against the risk of low investment returns or high longevity, in the absence of annuities markets. (See chapters 5 and 6 for fuller discussion.)

The Solution: A Multipillar System

To avoid these problems, which are inherent in single pillar schemes, this study recommends separating the saving function from the redistributive function and placing them under different financing and managerial arrangements in two different mandatory pillars—one publicly managed and tax-financed, the other privately managed and fully funded—supplemented by a voluntary pillar for those who want more (figure 3).

- The public pillar would then have the limited object of reducing old age poverty and coinsuring against a multitude of risks. Backed by the government's power of taxation, this pillar has the unique capacity to pay benefits to people growing old shortly after the plan is introduced, to redistribute income toward the poor, and to coinsure against long spells of low investment returns, recession, and private market failures. Having an unambiguous and limited objective for the public pillar should reduce the required tax rate substantially—and therefore evasion and misallocated labor—as well as pressures for overspending and perverse intra- and intergenerational transfers.

- The second mandatory pillar could be personal saving accounts or, in some cases, occupational plans. The important point is that it should be fully funded and privately managed, but publicly regulated, and it should link benefits closely to costs, because it carries out the income-smoothing or saving function. These characteristics should enable it to avoid some of the distortions and manipulations to which the public pillar is prone, should boost capital accumulation and financial market development, and should reduce political pressures to expand the public pillar. The economic growth this induces should make it easier to finance the public pillar.

- Voluntary occupational or personal saving plans would be the third pillar, providing additional protection for people who want more.

This multipillar system should have better-targeted redistributions, more productive savings, and lower social cost. In addition, it best achieves the third goal of old age security programs—insurance—since it reduces the exposure of workers to political, investment, and country-specific risks. In a single pillar system, by contrast, workers are putting all their eggs in one basket. And they will be in serious trouble if that basket—public or private—breaks. Because some of the risks of the next sixty years are not even dreamed of today, broad diversification across differing financial and managerial sources is the best way to insure in an uncertain world.

Choosing the Public Pillar—to Alleviate Poverty

I N A MULTIPILLAR SYSTEM, THE PUBLIC PILLAR SHOULD BE CHOSEN to achieve the redistributive and reinsurance goal at the lowest cost. Four options, each with different costs and benefits, meet this criterion. The first two are universal. The second two are tied to years of employment and exclude people (such as women) with little or no labor force participation. They would have to be supplemented by other arrangements (social assistance, survivors' insurance, or joint contributions between spouses) to reach these groups.

The Benefit Formula

A means-tested plan that pays benefits to people with low income and few assets is a relatively cheap way to alleviate poverty. If the public pillar for old age security takes the form of a means test it should be harmonized (and possibly administered jointly) with other social assistance programs—although eligibility criteria should take into account the low capacity of the old to work productively and benefit levels might vary by age, according to estimated consumption needs.

But means testing incurs administrative costs plus stigma and take-up problems. Ideally, lifetime income would be used as the means test, but this is especially difficult to track. If current income and assets are used, this sets up perverse incentives for people not to save when young or work when old and to spend down or give away their assets to qualify for benefits. The high marginal tax rate at the threshold creates a poverty trap. Middle-income households that are not near the threshold receive no insurance. For these reasons means-tested plans might become politically unpopular and vulnerable in times of budgetary stringency. The danger of the plan falling under the budgetary knife can be mitigated by using a broad definition of need rather than a narrow one. Australia uses a broad-based means-tested public pillar with an income and asset test for eligibility, financed from general revenues. It pays full or partial benefits (similar to the social assistance benefits paid to younger people who are unable to work) to about 70 percent of the old population.

The universal flat benefit is given to everyone of pensionable age, regardless of income, wealth, or employment history, as in New Zealand and the basic pensions paid by the Nordic countries. Administratively, this is the simplest structure, with the lowest transaction costs, for the public pillar—an important advantage in developing countries with limited institutional capacities and incomplete record-keeping systems. It avoids the disincentive to work and save inherent in means-tested plans. Its universal coverage helps ensure that the poverty reduction objectives are met, provides a basic income for all old people (coinsuring against low investment returns or high longevity), and might receive broad political support. It also facilitates the transition to a multipillar system, since the flat benefit paid to everyone pays off a large part of the social security debt.

The disadvantages are the incentive to evade contributions and the possibility that evaders will nonetheless collect benefits, which are not contingent on contributions or number of working years. In very low-income countries, the transaction costs of paying small pensions to every old person might be high relative to benefits. Total program costs are greater than for the other alternatives, because it is universal. In countries with very unequal income distributions, much of these benefits will go to the rich, who live longer but have ample support of their own; however, targeting public transfers to the poor is particularly important in these countries. Part of this cost might be "clawed back" by subjecting benefits to income taxes—which in a progressive system would charge higher tax rates for upper-income groups. Income clawed back from the rich could finance benefits for the poor. But this would not work effectively in developing countries that have little capacity to collect income taxes.

If used, the flat benefit might be set at around 20 percent of the average wage in the economy, when it is combined with a mandatory second pillar. This will only require a payroll tax of 2 percent in countries with young populations (that is, with one old person for every ten workers). But once the demographic transition has occurred, it will require a payroll tax rate of 8 to 10 percent or an equivalent amount from general revenues—much more than a means-tested scheme would cost.

An employment-related flat benefit overcomes some of the disadvantages of the universal flat. Coverage is limited to those in the formal labor force, and employees of small firms are often excluded, reducing transaction costs. But keeping track of employment histories adds to transactions costs; good employment records simply do not exist in many developing and transitional economies. If this method is used, a flat benefit of 20 to 30 percent might be paid to everyone who has worked and contributed a specified number of years, such as twenty or thirty, as in Argentina's new multipillar system. This, however, would exclude short-service workers such as women with interrupted labor force participation and would discourage contributions after eligibility is established. A better method would pay a flat benefit per year of contributing service, as in Switzerland and the United Kingdom. With a benefit per year of, say, 0.75 percent of the average wage in the economy, twenty years of work would earn a pension equal to 15 percent of the average wage, and forty years, 30 percent. This benefit formula deters evasion more than a universal flat, but it is also much less effective at eliminating poverty because some groups get very little. To become more inclusive, contributions—with corresponding credits—might be accepted or required from people who are not engaged in market work, such as housewives. This system is used in Japan, but it would be difficult to implement in developing countries.

A top-up scheme or minimum pension guarantee is the cheapest way to eliminate old age poverty, when coupled with another mandatory pillar to handle the saving function. If pension income from the other pillar is below some specified level—such as the poverty line, as it might be for low-income workers or because of low investment returns—the government tops it up to bring retirement income above the poverty line. In effect, a top-up scheme is an automatic means test in which the only means tested is other pension income. The big advantage over a broader means-tested scheme is that it eliminates transaction cost, stigma, and take-up problems, because it is automatic and based on records maintained by the "savings" pillar. It also eliminates some of the negative effects on work and saving, since saving is mandatory and an earnings test is not involved, and it encourages compliance with the mandatory saving plan by providing a bonus, in the form of a guarantee, to those who participate.

One disadvantage is that in an uncertain world it provides less insurance against income fluctuation to people who are above the minimum pension level than a flat public pillar would. Another disadvantage is that it leaves opportunities for strategic manipulation by low-income workers who are close to the poverty line—as soon as they qualify for the top-up, they might try to evade further contributions to their mandatory pension accounts. Both problems might be mitigated by letting the guaranteed minimum pension rise with years of contributing service. For example, the guaranteed minimum might be 1 percent for every year of service. Twenty years of work would then guarantee a pension at least 20 percent of the economy-wide average wage, and forty years, 40 percent. With a suitably high mandatory savings rate (of about 15 percent), this top-up could be financed by a payroll tax rate of 2 to 4 percent or a lower general revenue tax rate (see issue brief 11). The minimum guarantee could be higher than the flat or means-tested options yet cost less and have fewer distortionary effects, since it is built on the worker's own pension or savings in the funded mandatory pillar (see simulations below). These characteristics make it a very attractive option.

Other Design Features

Whatever the nature of the benefit, other design features—such as average replacement rate, retirement age, and indexation method—should be chosen carefully. The average replacement rate financed through the public pillar should be modest, in keeping with its poverty alleviation goal. And the age at which the pension is paid should be high, high enough so that it is a good proxy for the inability to work for the majority of people. A retirement age that implies a 1:3 passivity ratio (ratio of expected retirement to working years) makes the system much more affordable than a 1:2 passivity ratio. This also requires periodically raising the retirement age as life expectancy increases. People who want to retire earlier can finance this option through the voluntary pillar.

To encourage labor force participation from experienced workers—who will become an increasingly large share of the labor force as the population ages—an earnings test for receipt of pensions should be avoided. Benefits should be paid once a specified age is reached—or if payment is postponed, benefit increases should be actuarially fair. Disability and term life insurance should be included prior to retirement, and survivors' rights after retirement, to protect workers and their dependents in case of death or invalidity. Contribution credits might be split between spouses to further protect dependents. Pensions should be indexed to prices to maintain their real value or to a fifty-fifty combination of prices and disposable wages to give pensioners a stake in economic growth and a share in the risk of economic decline.

Choice of Tax Base

Policymakers must also decide how to finance the public pillar. Heavy reliance on a broad tax base, such as an income or consumption tax instead of a payroll tax, is most efficient in the long run, since it reduces the tax rate needed to finance benefits. It is also most consistent with the redistributive function of the public pillar, particularly when coverage is broad. General revenue finance has the added advantage that it does not pit workers against retirees. Instead, it taxes all generations according to their income or consumption.

Many developing countries, however, lack the administrative capacity to collect broadly based taxes, and those taxes that they collect (such as excise taxes) are often distortionary and regressive. In addition, when the public pillar gets started it usually covers only a small part of the population—those in the urban formal sector in which middle- and upper-income groups predominate. It would be inequitable to make transfers to these groups from general revenue.

For these reasons, the public pillar should initially be financed from payroll taxes levied on covered groups. The worker (rather than the employer) should pay much of this tax to make people politically aware of program costs and to reduce effects on labor demand in the presence of wage rigidities. To redistribute, the taxable wage might have a floor, but to keep tax rates low it might have no ceiling or a very high ceiling. Young or low-income workers might be exempt from the tax, and older workers might be exempt once they have reached retirement age or have contributed for a specified period, such as forty years. These are the groups where the potential negative effects on labor supply and demand are greatest. As coverage expands, benefits become more universal, and the government's tax collection capacity increases, greater responsibility should be shifted to a broader, more progressive tax based on income or consumption (see World Bank 1991b for a general discussion of tax policies).

Choosing the Mandatory Funded Pillar— for Efficiency and Growth

U NLIKE THE PUBLIC PILLAR—WHICH IS REDISTRIBUTIVE, centrally controlled, and tax-financed—the second mandatory pillar should emphasize saving. It should therefore be nonredistributive and fully funded, with decentralized control over the accumulated pension and saving reserves. It could be based on occupational schemes, personal accounts, or a combination of the two. The choice should depend on efficiency. Which type of pillar maximizes the return for a given risk in the capital market without creating new distortions in the labor market? Although private competitive management provides incentives for good performance, extensive government regulation is also important to compensate for market failures such as lack of information by workers and socially inefficient restrictions imposed by employers.

Mandatory Saving Schemes

The advantages of a mandatory (defined contribution) saving scheme—which requires people to save when they are young so that they will have adequate income when they are old—are that coverage can be broad and benefits are fully portable. Having a rudimentary banking system is a precondition, but a mandatory saving scheme can be part of a national policy to develop new financial institutions, deepen capital markets, mobilize saving, and allocate it to the most productive uses, including uses in the private sector. It also allows workers to increase their returns and insure against political or other country-specific risks through international diversification of investments.

The disadvantage is that governments may be tempted to manage these schemes themselves, as in national provident funds. Such management often preempts the funds for public sector uses only, in very non-transparent ways, earns low rates of return, and misallocates capital. Private competitive management is thus needed to secure the capital market benefits of mandatory saving schemes.

But some low-income countries lack the expertise and private financial infrastructure needed to get these schemes off the ground. And workers may lack the education and experience necessary to choose effective investments and investment managers. So, extensive regulatory capacity is needed to keep the investment companies financially sound and the workers' exposure to investment risk within reasonable bounds—capacity that many governments lack. (Chile currently uses a decentralized mandatory saving scheme, and Argentina, Colombia, and Peru are introducing this pillar in their new systems.)

Occupational Plans

Mandatory occupational pension plans are an alternative to mandatory saving plans. Occupational plans have the seeming advantage that they can start up on a voluntary basis before the market has the capacity to run—or the government to regulate—a mandatory plan. They can be implemented through payroll deductions with low record-keeping and marketing costs. They use the financial expertise of employers and pre-arranged groups of workers to overcome insurance market problems. The disadvantages are that these voluntary plans are likely to be spotty in coverage, to be offered mainly to middle- and upper-income workers, to involve large regressive tax expenditures, to be underfunded and therefore default-prone, and to restrict vesting and portability of benefits, impeding labor mobility and economic restructuring.

These problems can be avoided, in part, through regulation—requirements for broad information disclosure, full funding, backup insurance, nondiscriminatory benefits, and portability. Such regulations are important once occupational plans become widespread—and essential once they become mandatory. But setting up these rules is not easy, and the rules are never fully effective—in part because it is very difficult to define full funding in a defined benefit plan. It could take many years for plans that have sprung up under looser conditions to adjust to tighter controls. In the meantime, their pension promises will be problematic—so the right ground rules must be established from the start. Thus, one of the seeming advantages of occupational plans—regulatory simplicity—vanishes.

Voluntary plans also vanish to a large extent, since the regulations will discourage employers from establishing these schemes on their own. The regulations are also likely to lead employers to set up defined contribution plans—which avoid some of the problems inherent in defined benefit plans but create new conflict-of-interest problems as employers choose the investment managers while workers bear the investment risk. It does not appear to be efficient for workers to face different restrictions on their choice of investment manager, depending on their place of employment.

Occupational defined benefit plans may impede labor markets' efficiency. Occupational defined contribution plans avoid this problem but may pose agency problems. Neither allows the economies of scale that are likely in a mandatory saving plan, in which pension funds tend to be highly concentrated. Overall, personal saving schemes would seem to have the edge for the privately managed mandatory pillar, except in countries that already have substantial occupational coverage on which to build. (Australia and Switzerland, for example, had widespread coverage as a result of collective bargaining or employer discretion before their plans became mandatory.) So, the mandatory occupational route does not seem like a good way to go in most developing and transitional economies, though it may be a more desirable path for industrial countries.

Giving Workers the Choice between Occupational and Personal Saving Plans

A third option would give workers a choice between the first two options—that is, between occupational and personal saving plans. This choice would mitigate the job mobility risk in occupational defined benefit plans and the agency problem in defined contribution plans. Many workers would presumably choose personal saving plans, over which they have more control. Occupational plans that survive over the long run would do so because of genuine economies of scale and information. From this point of view, giving workers a choice may be the best alternative.

Choice, however, inevitably adds to the government's administrative and regulatory burden, since it requires monitoring multiple systems, keeping track of shifting affiliations, and making sure that options are fairly and accurately presented to workers. These problems are still being worked out in the United Kingdom, where employers can contract out of the public earnings-related scheme by offering an occupational plan and workers can opt out of the employer's plan and into their own personal plan. For most developing and transitional economies, giving workers a choice between a mandatory saving or an occupational scheme would probably not be the best option in view of their weak institutional and regulatory capacities. But it is a strong option for industrial countries.

The Voluntary (Personal or Occupational) Pillar

THE TWO MANDATORY PILLARS TOGETHER MIGHT AIM TO replace about 50 percent of gross average lifetime wage (revalued upward for inflation) or 40 percent of gross final year wage for workers who have contributed throughout their adult lives—with a floor to keep low-income households above the poverty line. But some households will want additional retirement income, and they can achieve this through voluntary arrangements. In Switzerland, where occupational plans have been mandatory for the last decade, many employers provide benefits beyond the required floor. In most countries people save on a voluntary basis. But the existence of a second mandatory pillar will reduce or crowd out some of this voluntary action, particularly for low-income workers for whom the mandatory amount is likely to exceed what they would have saved voluntarily.

If governments wish to increase capital accumulation, they can encourage voluntary occupational plans and long-term saving accounts in several ways: by creating a stable noninflationary economic environment, by setting up a regulatory framework that gives people confidence in financial institutions, by educating citizens about the high saving rate needed to ensure a comfortable retirement, and possibly by giving tax incentives. The first three policies are undeniably good for growth and efficiency in any event. The fourth policy needs to be applied cautiously, because it has a large cost in terms of forgone revenues to the government, most of the benefits will go to high-income groups that would have saved anyway, and the tax incentives may simply shift their saving into tax-advantaged instruments rather than increasing the total. One approach would index the initial investment for inflation and tax real returns only for long-term saving. Any tax incentives for voluntary arrangements should be equivalent for occupational plans and personal accounts.

Putting the Pillars Together

FOUR ALTERNATIVE COMBINATIONS ARE RECOMMENDED FOR a multipillar system (table 7.1):

- A mandatory personal saving plan with a flat benefit public scheme
- A mandatory personal saving plan with a minimum pension guarantee in the public scheme
- A mandatory occupational plan with a flat benefit public scheme
- A mandatory occupational plan with a means-tested public scheme.

Each of these mandatory combinations would be accompanied by public policies that facilitate voluntary saving and pension plans.

Empirical Evidence with Multiple Pillars

The first combination is now being implemented in Argentina. The second has been working in Chile since 1981. Variations on the third are found in the Netherlands (where occupational plans are quasi-mandatory through collective bargaining) and Switzerland (where the

Table 7.1 Recommended Multipillar Combinations

Alternative forms for the funded, privately managed pillar	Alternative forms for the tax-financed public pillar		
Mandatory savings	Flat	or	Minimum guarantee/top-up
Mandatory occupational	Flat	or	Means-tested

public pension includes an employment-related flat benefit). Australia has just introduced the fourth arrangement, by adding a mandatory occupational scheme to its existing means-tested public plan. (The minimum pension guarantee probably would not coordinate well with occupational plans in the second pillar because of variations among employer plans and moral hazard problems that would discourage firms from offering good benefits to low-income workers.) The United Kingdom has a multipillar system that is probably too complicated for most developing countries: the employment-related flat benefit in the public pillar is compulsory, but employers can contract out of the earnings-related tier and workers can opt out of the employer's plan.

Most OECD countries do not have well-developed multipillar systems, since, until recently, only the public pillar has been mandatory. But voluntary occupational and personal saving plans have developed on an uneven basis. Although the relative sizes of the mandatory and voluntary pillars—as measured by their relative shares of old people's income—differ widely, public pay-as-you-go plans have the lion's share of responsibility for providing old age security (figure 7.1).

Simulations of Multiple Pillars

Empirical experience with two mandatory pillars is too limited to allow for detailed comparisons of how they accomplish their dual goals of poverty reduction versus saving or wage replacement above the basic floor, and of their relative costs of doing so. But simulations show the effects of combining a fully funded defined contribution pillar (whether occupational or personal) with a flat, means-tested, or minimum pension guarantee financed on a pay-as-you-go basis in the public pillar (issue brief 11).

■ The flat benefit alone, if fixed at the poverty line or above, eliminates poverty—but it may require a high contribution rate to do so. It generates large intergenerational transfers, some of them perverse. It yields negative rates of return to later groups of retirees, even for low-income retirees, and thus is a poor savings vehicle for them. And it fails to provide adequate wage replacement for middle- and upper-income groups in all generations.

■ The defined contribution plan alone is an effective saving or wage replacement mechanism, but it leaves large pockets of people poor

249

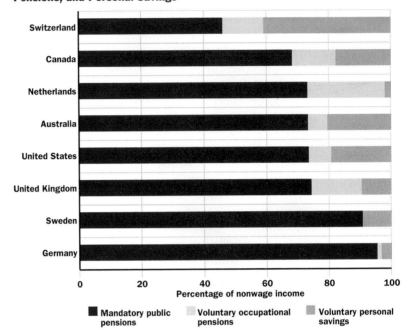

Figure 7.1 The Multipillar System in OECD Countries, Mid-1980s: Percentage of Nonwage Income from Public Pensions, Occupational Pensions, and Personal Savings

Most OECD countries have weak multipillar systems—the public pillar dominates, but other pillars are growing.

Note: Occupational plans became mandatory in Switzerland and Australia in 1985 and 1993, respectively.
Source: Luxembourg Income Study as presented in D. Mitchell (1993).

in their old age, unless the interest rate is very high. (If the contribution rate is high enough to alleviate poverty among all retirees, it creates poverty among low-income workers, who may be left with less disposable income when young than when old.)

■ Given that future interest and wage growth are uncertain, only the mixed systems can be counted on to achieve both the poverty reduction and saving or wage replacement goals. Over the long run, the minimum guarantee, combined with a defined contribution plan, achieves both objectives most effectively or at least cost.

■ Although the simulations do not capture effects on efficiency, saving, and growth, these are likely to be more positive for defined contribution schemes than for pay-as-you-go defined benefit plans, for all the reasons given above. This reinforces the argument for using a funded defined contribution scheme to accomplish the saving goal, while a tax-financed defined benefit plan concentrates on redistribution and poverty alleviation.

- Countries with older populations should expect to spend about 20 percent of their current wage bill on old age security arrangements. The split of the 20 percent between the public and private pillars should be about 10–10 if the public pillar is flat, 4–16 if a minimum pension guarantee is used, and somewhere in between with a means-tested public plan, depending on whether the means test is broad-based or narrow. Given the transaction costs and the possibility that small mandatory saving requirements will simply crowd out voluntary saving, the funded pillar should absorb at least 10 percent of wages when mature. But it might start at a smaller level and gradually increase with the growing capacity of the country's financial markets.

- Mixed schemes also reduce the exposure of pensioners to unexpected failure in the public or private sectors—for example, to fiscal mismanagement that forces the government to cut back on public defined benefits, or to bad investments that lead to low accumulations in the private defined contribution plan.

The different pattern of transfers means that different income and gender groups will have different preferences among these multipillar combinations. In general, poverty is eliminated most completely with the minimum pension guarantee, which might be preferred by the poor. Middle-income workers are ambivalent. If interest rates are expected to be low, they fare best under the flat benefit combination, but under high interest rates they might prefer a larger defined contribution allocation, as under the top-up scheme. High-income workers get a lower expected replacement rate and rate of return under the multipillar system with a flat benefit. Those who are very risk-averse might nonetheless prefer this because in exchange they get more diversification and income protection against investment risk before they fall below the poverty line. High-income workers who are not very risk-averse would prefer the combination with the minimum pension guarantee. Women fare better with a combination that includes a public pillar in which benefits are not tied to prior years of employment or earnings (box 7.1).

Box 7.1 How Do Men and Women Fare under Alternative Old Age Schemes?

BECAUSE OF THEIR DIFFERENT EMPLOYMENT histories, men and women are affected differently by each pillar and by their design features. Many women have not had a continuous employment history and have not earned as much as men while working. As a result, women benefit more from universal public schemes that offer flat or means-tested benefits, while men benefit more from employment- or earnings-related schemes. Extending benefits to survivors reduces poverty among women, who tend to outlive their spouses. But in most cases only half the marriage pension goes to survivors. This is generally inadequate for a single person, given economies of scale in housing and other household expenses.

Women are much less likely than men to receive occupational pensions, and they receive smaller pensions when they do. In defined contribution schemes, men fare better than women because of their higher earnings and contributions. Pooling the contributions of husbands and wives and dividing the proceeds between them equally tends to help women. When annuities are purchased, an important issue is whether gender-based life expectancy tables are allowed or whether pooled tables are required. If pooled tables are required, as in occupational schemes in the United States, women benefit because they tend to live longer. (But women lose if pooled tables are required for life insurance, which may also be provided by employers.)

Evidence from Microsimulations

The microsimulation of work and retirement behavior in the United Kingdom by Falkingham and Johnson (1993) allows us to examine the differential treatment of men and women under alternative pension plans. Based on their own lifetime earnings, women are concentrated in the bottom half of the population wage distribution, while men are concentrated in the upper half. Therefore, women are more than twice as likely as men to get positive lifetime transfers from the universal flat system both because they earn (and so contribute) less and because they live longer than men. These effects are sharply reduced if eligibility conditions based on years and amount of contributions are imposed. Under the defined contribution plan, which is not redistributive, most older women live in poverty. Not surprisingly, women benefit more than men from a plan that combines defined contributions with a minimum pension guarantee—almost 90 percent of the top-up goes to women, virtually eliminating old age poverty.

Some of the transfer goes to women who have worked but earned low incomes. But some of it goes to women who have not worked and are married to men with high incomes—it is not clear that society wishes to transfer income to this group. Other instruments are available to reduce their poverty at lower social cost. For example, the disparity between men and women can be substantially reduced by policies that require joint treatment of married couples, as recommended within the European Union and as required in many states of the United States. If employment credit and contributions of both partners are split evenly between them, poverty is eliminated for most women. And the cost of the top-up scheme falls, because most women receive adequate pensions that are financed by their husbands' contributions (box table 7.1). In effect, joint contributions and income pooling within the household provide informal insurance, although more limited than that provided by extended families. There is less disparity in wage and pension income among households than among individuals, and it is easier to alleviate poverty. But a formalization of this informal arrangement is needed for divorced or widowed women, who constitute the largest group among old people in poverty.

What Should Be Done?

Several approaches can be used, separately or in tandem, to improve old age security among women:

- A universal flat, means-tested, or minimum pension scheme that gets everyone above the poverty line, regardless of employment history
- Joint treatment of the employment credits and contributions of husbands and wives
- Mandatory survivor benefits that exceed 50 percent of the joint marriage benefit
- Special benefits for the very old, who have run out of their own resources (and are more likely to be women).

But the best way to improve the income security of old women is to raise the income of young women by eliminating gender-based wage and employment inequality—a strategy that has the added benefit of improving overall equity and economic growth.

Box Table 7.1 Simulated Poverty Rates among Men and Women

	40 percent flat	Employment-related flat	15 percent defined contribution	10 percent defined contribution plus 20 percent flat	10 percent defined contribution plus means test	15 percent defined contribution plus top-up
Own contributions						
Men	0	3	21	5	5	0
Women	0	35	67	52	52	0
Joint contributions						
Men	0	3	34	5	5	0
Women	0	8	36	18	18	0

Note: Poverty is defined as 40 percent of average economy-wide wage for each individual.

Source: Adapted from microsimulations based on demographic and earnings data for the United Kingdom in 1985 by Falkingham and Johnson (1993).

Conclusion

A MANDATORY MULTIPILLAR ARRANGEMENT FOR OLD AGE
security forces countries to:

- Make clear decisions about which groups should gain and which should lose through transfers in the mandatory public pillar, both within and across generations. This should reduce perverse or capricious redistributions—as well as poverty.
- Achieve a close relationship between incremental contributions and benefits in the mandatory private pillar. This should reduce effective tax rates, evasion, and labor market distortions.
- Use full funding and decentralized control in the second pillar. This should increase long-term saving, capital market deepening, and growth.
- Diversify risk to the fullest because of the mix of public and private management, political and market determination of benefits, the use of wage growth and capital income as the basis for finance, and the ability to invest in a wide variety of securities—both public and private, equity and debt, domestic and foreign.

The broader economy, including both old and young, should be better off as a result.

The right mix of pillars is not the same at all times and places. It depends on a country's objectives, history, and current circumstances, particularly its emphasis on poverty reduction versus saving, its financial markets, and its taxing and regulatory capacity. Middle- and high-income countries should move in this direction quickly, whereas low-income countries should see it as a long-term goal.

CHAPTER 8

Transitions

THE COSTS OF A TRANSITION FROM ONE SYSTEM OF old age security to another are large, and resistance is likely to be strong. A country intent on reform needs a clear vision of where it is starting from and where it wants to be well into the future to guide the steps it takes today (box 8.1). This chapter sketches out such a path for several sets of countries: countries with young populations, low incomes, and only rudimentary formal old age security systems; young but rapidly aging and rapidly growing countries with immature public pillars; and older middle- and high-income countries with large public pillars that need to be reformed gradually or, in some cases, urgently.

Laying the Groundwork: Countries with Young Populations

Consider first a country with a young population, low per capita income, and only a small public pillar or provident fund covering primarily public sector employees. Many countries in Africa and South Asia are at this stage. Weakening informal systems of old age support and an absence of reliable financial instruments are prompting calls for an expanded public pillar. These countries may not have the financial markets or regulatory capacity necessary to establish a decentralized funded pillar. But they should be preparing the environment for voluntary—and later mandatory—saving and pension plans by:

- Keeping inflation down.

Box 8.1 Taking Stock

ANY PLANS TO ESTABLISH OR REFORM A COUNTRY's old age security system should be preceded by a stock taking that considers the contributions of the extended family, financial institutions, occupational pension plans, and government programs to the welfare of the old. A checklist of questions for such a survey should include the following:

- How much poverty is there among the old? Where are the pockets of old age poverty (widows, the very old, urban or rural areas)? What government programs exist to alleviate pockets of poverty among the old, and what programs might be added to target these groups?
- How effective is the informal system of old age support? Where does it break down? What government programs can retard this process?
- What percentage of GDP is spent on pensions? What proportion of public spending is spent on pensions? How does this share compare with other countries at the same stage of economic and demographic development?
- What proportions of workers and old people are covered by formal pension plans? How does coverage vary by occupation, income, and gender? What are the plans for coverage expansion in the years ahead?
- What is the dependency ratio in the public pillar? How does it compare with the demographic dependency ratio? How will this relationship be affected by design features, system maturation, and demographic change in the future?

- Are contributions high enough to cover expected payouts in the near and distant future? How does this affect employers and employment?
- How large is the informal labor sector and what impact does (or will) the old age security system have on its size?
- What is the estimated evasion rate? What aspects of the public pillar invite evasion?
- Are there active, reliable financial institutions such as banks, insurance companies, and stock markets? What steps should be taken to strengthen them?
- What instruments are there for voluntary saving and annuities? How can these be expanded? What are the impediments to expansion?
- How do tax policies on saving and consumption differ? Should more tax incentives be introduced to encourage long-term saving? Where does retirement saving fit into this picture?
- How prevalent are occupational pension schemes? How well do they work? What regulations and tax privileges apply and should these be changed?
- What are the restrictions on international capital flows? At what pace should they be relaxed?
- What is the regulatory capacity of government? What is the level of financial training in the population?
- How do the very old fare? How do women fare? Do the public and private sectors have the ability to run complex long-term programs?

- Avoiding interest rate and exchange controls.
- Establishing reliable savings institutions accessible to people in rural as well as urban areas (the postal savings system in Japan and other East Asian countries might be a model).
- Developing a regulatory framework that gives people confidence in banks, insurance companies, and other financial institutions.

- Instituting an effective tax policy and tax administration.
- Building the human capital that is essential for the effective management of financial and regulatory systems.

These basic conditions are important for the old age system and, more broadly, for continued economic growth.

These countries should also be introducing measures more directly related to old age security that will eventually fit into a multipillar system. The noes—using methods that avoid the problems to which large pay-as-you-go plans are prone—are as important as the yeses. This means that countries should:

- Keep the existing contributory public pillar small, flat, and limited to urban areas and large enterprises in which transaction costs are relatively small, fraud is easiest to detect, and the informal system breaks down first.
- Provide social assistance to the poorest groups in society, including the old poor who are not covered by contributory plans, taking into account their vulnerability stemming from their diminished ability to work.
- Carry out simulations of the long-run impact of alternative public plans (coverage, benefit level, retirement age) on taxes and the distribution of transfers across and within generations. This requires making assumptions about wage growth, interest rates, labor force participation, unemployment, and evasion—and recognizing that the choice of system will affect these parameters (box 8.2).
- Phase out (or convert to voluntary status) centrally managed provident funds, which are often misused.
- Set up the legal and institutional framework for personal saving and occupational pension plans, requiring full funding, portability of benefits, and disclosure of information for the latter.
- Give equivalent tax treatment to occupational and personal retirement plans that meet prudent standards.
- Avoid crowding out informal support systems and offer incentives to families to continue taking care of their older relatives.
- Avoid the pitfalls—overgenerous pensions, early retirement, benefit contribution structures that encourage evasion or discourage saving, and perverse redistributions to high-income groups in public plans; and unregulated, unfunded, nonportable occupational

Box 8.2 Design Choices for the Public Pillar

- Coverage and eligibility period for benefits: Should the plan cover government employees and urban workers only? Employees of small firms? Agricultural workers? The self-employed?
- Average wage replacement rate: What level will be sustainable in the long run on the basis of a tax rate that is low enough to avoid evasion and labor market distortions?
- Retirement age: What should it be, and should it rise automatically with life expectancy? How can it be structured to avoid rewards for early retirement and penalties for late retirement?
- Benefit structure: Should it be universal or employment-related flat, means-tested, or minimum guarantee? How will these options affect different income and gender groups?
- Earnings-related formula: If one is used, how compressed and how long should the averaging period be?
- Treatment of married couples and single wage earners: Should contributions by spouses be joint? Should cross-subsidization between married and single wage earners be included or avoided?
- Size of survivors' benefits: What level will prevent poverty among widows?
- Provisions for disability benefits: How can both poverty and moral hazard be avoided?
- Indexation: Should it be by wages or prices?
- Source of finance: Should it be by payroll taxes or general revenues?
- Contribution rate: How low a rate will avoid harmful effects on labor allocation and employment?
- Floor on taxable earnings: Should young or low-income workers face a lower tax rate?
- Ceiling on taxable earnings: Should there be a high ceiling or no ceiling for a broad tax base?
- Tax incentives: Should benefits or contributions be tax-exempt?
- Investment strategy for reserves: Should they be publicly or privately managed, or should reserves be eliminated?

plans—that are so tempting, especially in young countries with immature schemes and limited regulatory capability (box 8.3).

Young but Rapidly Aging Countries

THE NEXT SET COMPRISES COUNTRIES, ALSO WITH YOUNG populations, that are aging and often growing rapidly—since rapid economic growth is associated with falling fertility rates and rising longevity. Many East Asian countries are at this stage. In addition to accelerating all the actions just mentioned, these countries should:

- Begin designing and introducing a mandatory decentralized funded pillar (box 8.4). For countries that do not already have

Box 8.3 Pillars and Pitfalls

POLICYMAKERS NEED TO BE AWARE OF THE HAZARDS TO SIDE-
step as well as the features to strive for in designing an old age security
system. Besides avoiding fiscal instability, which spells trouble for any
program of old age security, countries need to watch out for several
common pitfalls:

- *In public pension plans:* granting large windfall benefits to high-
  income workers, who are likely to be the first group covered,
  and establishing overly generous benefit levels and early retirement opportunities that cannot be sustained in the long run.
  Avoidance strategy: Start with modest flat or means-tested benefits, a high retirement age, and actuarially fair penalties for
  workers who retire early.
- *In personal saving plans:* making the plan mandatory before the
  preconditions and regulatory structure are in place (see text),
  which dooms the scheme to failure. *Avoidance strategy:* Begin by
  establishing a stable financial, legal, and regulatory structure,
  and phase the program in.
- *In occupational plans:* allowing such plans to get started with tax
  advantages, but without adequate funding, vesting, and portability provisions—it is difficult to correct for this later on.
  Avoidance strategy: Introducing the requirements up front,
  which makes occupational schemes more credible, less distortionary, and more compatible with an eventual multipillar system, and providing equal tax treatment for all long-term saving,
  whether in personal or occupational plans.

widespread occupational plans, the second pillar is likely to consist
of mandatory personal saving accounts. Preconditions for this pillar are government regulatory capability, a banking system, a secondary government bond market, and an emerging stock
market—or the ability to develop these institutions quickly in response to demand from new pension funds. Income per capita or
average wage per worker is another important criterion. If wages
are low, transaction costs could wipe out much of the contributions to a decentralized pillar. So the covered wage should be high
enough to get transaction costs down to a reasonable rate, and the
mandatory second pillar should be confined to countries or subgroups that meet this criterion.

Box 8.4 Design and Regulatory Issues for the Mandatory Saving Pillar

- Coverage: Should employees of small firms and self-employed workers be covered?
- Contribution rate: Is it high enough to produce a minimally adequate replacement rate under expected wage growth and interest rate conditions?
- Tax incentives: Should contributions and investment income be tax-exempt?
- Fiduciary standards for fund managers: Should they be vetted and required to post bond?
- Investment restrictions: Do they give investment managers considerable discretion but emphasize prudent decisions and diversification?
- Information disclosure: Does it enable informed choice of investment companies by workers?
- Penalties for poor performance: Do managers have incentives for maximizing yield subject to risk?
- Restrictions on fees: Should the market set prices?

- Conditions for withdrawing funds: Should withdrawals be lump sum or annuities? Should withdrawals be permitted for housing, education, or medical expenses?
- Survivors' and disability insurance: Should purchase through insurance companies be required?
- Joint contributions and benefits for spouses: Should these be required to avoid poverty among widows or divorced women?
- Government guarantees: Should they be included?
- International diversification: At what pace should this be introduced, and should it be limited or unlimited?
- Estimated administrative costs: How can marketing costs be contained?
- Foreign investment managers: How can they be encouraged to provide much-needed expertise?
- Monitoring and enforcement mechanisms: How can regulators learn how to do their job?

- Start by setting up a strong regulatory framework, and determining the required contribution rate and the target wage replacement rate. Establishing this structure and phasing in the second pillar could take several years. Countries should not rush ahead too fast, beyond their institutional capabilities. But if they do not move ahead fast enough strong political pressures will otherwise develop, from middle- and high-income workers, for a dominant earnings-related public pillar—and all its associated problems.
- Gradually expand coverage for the public pillar, keeping it modest and redistributive, while satisfying workers' saving or income-smoothing needs through the mandatory private pillar. Benefit promises should be based on long-term projections and simulations. Otherwise these countries will face the much more difficult task of restructuring later.
- If (as in China) the public pillar is already in trouble, one of the first steps should be to reform it by emphasizing poverty reduction and coinsurance.

- Initially use a payroll tax for the public pillar to avoid inefficiencies from excise taxes and transfers from uncovered to covered groups, but shift greater responsibility to a broader tax base as coverage becomes universal, the government's ability to collect general income and consumption taxes increases, and the redistributive function can be emphasized.

Gradual Transitions in Middle Age

COUNTRIES IN THIS GROUP ARE ALREADY MIDDLE-AGED AND rapidly growing older. The costs of their widespread public pension programs will soar over the next three decades, along with dependency ratios. Although the degree of urgency varies, all these countries face imminent problems with their old age systems. Rather than relying on an ever more costly public pillar to do it all and at high tax rates that inhibit growth and bring low rates of return to workers, the time is ripe for these countries to make the transition to a mandatory multipillar system.

- The first step is to reform the public pillar by raising the retirement age, eliminating rewards for early retirement and penalties for late retirement, downsizing benefit levels (in the frequent cases in which they are overgenerous to begin with), and making the benefit structure flatter (to emphasize the poverty reduction function), the tax rate lower, and the tax base broader.
- The second step is to launch the private pillar by setting up the appropriate contribution and regulatory structure. The transition can be accomplished by:
  1. Downsizing the public pillar gradually while reallocating contributions to a second mandatory pillar or
  2. Holding the public benefit relatively constant (in cases in which it is low to begin with) but raising contribution rates and assigning them to the second pillar or
  3. Recognizing accrued entitlements under the old system and agreeing to pay them off while starting a completely new system right away.

The first two "gradual" transitions are discussed here; the third, or "radical," alternative is discussed in the next section. A gradual transition may be appropriate for countries whose payroll tax and benefit levels are still "moderate" but will not remain so for long unless reforms are undertaken. Several OECD countries are in this category.

The simplest gradual transition transforms the public pension into a modest, flatter benefit. The average pension might be downsized by indexing benefits to prices rather than to wages, thereby holding them constant in absolute but not relative terms. Or the average benefit could be held constant while the benefit structure is flattened by indexing lower-level pensions fully to wages while higher-level pensions are indexed to prices and only partially. Both strategies reduce the average wage replacement rate, requiring a lower contribution rate.

If the population remained stable and productivity grew at 2 percent a year, it would take about thirty-six years for real wages to double. By that time, if real benefits were held constant, the average wage replacement rate would be half its original rate and half of total contributions would be released to be reallocated to the second "saving" pillar. If the break-even contribution rate is 10 percent at the beginning of the period, in thirty-six years the public pillar would require just a 5 percent contribution rate and the remaining 5 percent could go into workers' funded plans. But thirty-six years is a long time for a transition; and in any event populations will age over this period, swallowing up much of the projected 5 percentage point savings in the contribution rate and leaving young workers with meager retirement income. So cutting wage replacement rates gradually will not finance the transition by itself, although the principle of allocating productivity growth to the new pillar is useful.

Another way to reduce benefits—and to make a direct positive impact on GDP—is to raise the retirement age. Raising the retirement age enough each year to hold the dependency rate constant—two to three months a year in many countries—would permit the full savings from the lower wage replacement rate to be allocated to the second pillar. However, even with a rapid rise in retirement age, this alternative still leaves only a 5 percent contribution to the second pillar, not enough to provide most older workers with an adequate pension. So this alternative, too, will not suffice.

Finally, in countries that have small public pillars and low contribution rates from the start, the funded pillar can be started up gradually by raising taxes. The cost of the public pillar could be shifted to general tax finance, while the payroll tax is allocated to the private pillar, where it is directly linked to benefits and has smaller distortionary effects.

In countries where occupational pension plans are already wide-spread, the mandatory private pillar is likely to involve these plans, as in Australia and Switzerland, or a choice between occupational pension and personal saving plans, as in the United Kingdom. Australia has just made the occupational pillar mandatory. Mandatory contributions start at 3 percent of wages and will rise to 12 percent by 2002, absorbing most of the productivity growth over this period. Australia has the advantage that its public pillar, a modest, broad-based income- and asset-tested plan financed from general revenues, needs supplementation and fine-tuning, not a major overhaul. Thus the transition in Australia consists of adding a second "savings" pillar to a redistributive public pillar—a move that will head off pressures that might otherwise have developed for an enlarged public pillar. Most other OECD countries will have to go through the more painful process of separating the saving and redistributive functions and of reshaping and downsizing their public plans to avoid massive distortionary and evasionary effects as dependency rates and system costs rise. That will mean disappointing some groups, who will not get what they had been led to expect.

Middle-Aged Countries in Trouble— Considering Radical Reform

FINALLY, CONSIDER THE COUNTRIES THAT HAVE LARGE, EXPENsive public pension programs in urgent need of reform. The payroll tax rate is 25 percent or higher in some countries, and still they cannot meet their obligations because of poor system design and widespread evasion. Many countries in Latin America and Eastern Europe are in this situation and some OECD countries are approaching it. They need to lower the tax rate, not raise it, and to put their old age systems on sound financial footing at the same time. To accomplish these divergent goals, several countries are considering radical reform of their systems—paying off the old social security debt to existing workers and pensioners and starting afresh with a new system. This involves designing the new system, calculating the benefits implicitly owed under the old system, and figuring out how to finance it all in a way that is both politically and economically acceptable.

Reforming the Old Public Pillar and Calculating the Social Security Debt

A strong recommendation of this report is that the old public plan must be reformed simultaneously with or just before the transition. Reform of the public plan is important because it improves economic efficiency and equity. It also redefines the claims that workers and pensioners have on the system and therefore reduces the taxes or government borrowing needed to pay off the social security debt. Finally, since workers are often given a choice, it increases the incentive to switch to the new system.

To illustrate the complexities involved in reforming the public plan and calculating the social security debt, consider the choice of benefit rate. The statutory wage replacement rate is high in many countries with bankrupt plans, but the plans will never be able to pay out these high benefits. Many Latin American and Eastern European countries have cut benefits covertly by failing to index them for inflation, a politically expedient strategy. The public plan should be reformed by setting a new statutory rate that is more realistic, and this modest rate should be indexed for future inflation. Once this change has been introduced, which value should be used to determine the amount society "owes" pensioners—the old statutory value, the postinflation de facto value, or the new statutory indexed value? What about cases in which workers have contributed little but lay claim to large benefits? Should they be paid an amount based on a "reasonable" rate of return or the immoderate rate of return allowed by a flawed system?

The choice of retirement age involves similar complexities. One reason many plans are in trouble today is that they have granted early retirement too liberally. Raising the retirement age will increase the productive capacity of the nation and reduce the social security debt, but it will face opposition from workers who feel they have been promised an early retirement age. Chile raised the retirement age two years before the new system was implemented; Argentina and Colombia did so when they introduced their reforms. The retirement age should be raised as rapidly as is politically feasible, and the new higher retirement age should be used to calculate the social security debt.

More generally, should payoffs be designed to meet expectations or to be more equitable and realistic from a long-run point of view? As in the renegotiation of any failing debt, the answer involves complex political considerations about what is feasible, fair, and acceptable to all parties concerned. Several principles might guide these negotiations:

- The groundwork must be laid by an extensive public information campaign to bring expectations into line with the reality that the old promises are bad for the economy and impossible to keep. Making sure that workers understand the full cost of the current program, including employer contributions, should be part of this campaign.

- Retirees and workers approaching retirement at the time of the transition should receive a pension from the reformed public pillar that keeps them out of poverty. They have few alternative means of support and little time to adapt to the new ground rules.

- The valuation of accrued entitlements for younger workers might be based on a lower, more realistic benefit rate. As a quid pro quo, these workers get indexation of benefits, in some cases pay lower payroll taxes than they would have otherwise, and will have ample opportunity to increase their pensions and diversify their risks through a mandatory saving or occupational scheme.

- New entrants to the labor force and newly covered groups should immediately be brought into the reformed system, instead of adding to the debt of the old system.

- Since length of retirement has increased rapidly over the past half century along with life expectancy—a trend likely to accelerate during the next half century—the fairest and most tolerable way to reduce benefits often will be to raise the retirement age.

- Once the old public plan has been reformed, a new multipillar system should be established as an alternative. The new system would include a still smaller public pillar supplemented by a second mandatory pillar that is funded and decentralized. For example, if the old statutory benefit rate was 50 to 60 percent of wages, the reformed public benefit might be 40 percent, and the multipillar system might consist of a smaller public pillar that pays 20 percent plus a 10 percent defined contribution. Countries must decide whether to give workers a choice between the old reformed public plan and the new multipillar system. Argentina, Chile, Colombia, and Peru have all given current workers that choice. In Chile, most people under the age of forty chose the new system; the results are yet to be determined in the other Latin American countries.

Financing the Social Security Debt

The social security debt is the value of expected benefit rights that workers and pensioners have accrued under the old system. The debt arises because the first generations of beneficiaries received more than they paid and the workers who financed these payouts expect to be compensated with generous defined benefits later on. Although difficult to estimate, the total implicit debt is probably as much as 100 to 250 percent of GDP for OECD and Eastern European countries, 30 to 50 percent of GDP in middle-income countries with younger populations and lower coverage, and less than 20 percent in the poorest countries (chapter 4). As contributions are diverted to the new system, some other means must be found to finance this debt.

First and most important, efficiency gains should help to pay off the debt. Under some circumstances the shift of labor from the informal to the formal labor market could boost productivity and growth substantially (Corsetti and Schmidt-Hebbel 1994). Raising the effective retirement age would increase the labor force and GDP by 10 to 30 percent in some cases (Cavalcanti 1993; Rashid 1993), resulting in an efficiency gain as long as the value of the increased output is greater than the value of leisure time lost. More output gains are achieved if the new system increases saving, international competitiveness, and inflow of foreign capital—although that is likely to be a very long-run effect. These efficiency gains together with the reduction in evasion generate increased tax revenues that can be used to pay off part of the debt. Since the reason for the transition is to reap these efficiency gains, in principle it should be possible to make everyone better off. But in practice this is difficult, especially for generations nearing retirement at the time of the transition.

Additional debt reduction comes from reform of the public pillar. If the public pillar in the new multipillar system takes the form of a modest flat benefit, say at a third of the previous average level, this is roughly a 33 percent payoff of the debt. If the new public pillar pays a means-tested benefit or minimum pension guarantee, that is less easily viewed as a payoff of the old debt. It is, however, likely to cost less and to free up resources that could be directly tapped to pay for the social security debt.

What remains of the debt can be financed by issuing government bonds, cutting other government expenditures, selling public assets, or raising tax rates. The methods chosen will determine savings, growth, and the generational distribution of the benefits and costs of the transition (Arrau and Schmidt-Hebbel 1993; Valdes-Prieto 1994; Arrau, Valdes-Prieto, and Schmidt-Hebbel 1993). As part of their general fiscal planning, countries should estimate in advance the mix of tax and bond finance or reduced government spending required at each point in time. The experience of Chile offers several guidelines (box 8.5).

Debt finance simply exchanges the old implicit debt and interest payments for new explicit debt and interest payments. Property rights in the debt are solidified, and market interest rates must be paid. This method of handling the debt does not require current generations to reduce their

---

Box 8.5 How Did Chile Pay Off Its Social Security Debt?

SO FAR, CHILE IS THE MAIN COUNTRY THAT HAS turned its implicit social security debt into an explicit debt, although other Latin American countries are now going through this same process. How did Chile calculate and finance this debt? The social security debt included (1) pensions for those who had already retired when the new system was introduced, (2) future pension payments for workers who had not yet retired but who decided to stay with the old—but recently reformed—system, and (3) accumulated entitlements under the old system for workers who decided to switch to the new system. The first two groups were paid off in the form of pensions, which were financed by the general treasury. For the third group, the accumulated entitlements were paid off by an immediate issue of "recognition bonds" that were nontransferable, earned 4 percent real interest, and were redeemable for lump sum payments into their mandatory saving accounts upon retirement.

The recognition bonds were supposed to equal the expected present value of the benefits these workers had thus far earned. Their value had been reduced by the reform of the old system in the late 1970s, especially by the rationalization of indexing, the elimination of special regimes, and the raising of the retirement age. Calculating the social security entitlement is difficult in developing countries, where employment records are incomplete. Chile

solved its calculation problem by estimating the number of months for which workers appeared to have made contributions, using their taxable income over that period to establish past earnings, applying actuarial factors to approximate expected lifetimes by gender and age, and assuming the same wage growth for everyone.

How large was Chile's implicit pay-as-you-go debt? One way to measure it is to calculate the present value of actual pension system deficits (postreform) during 1981–92, add in forecasted amounts for 1993–2025, and discount appropriately. The annual deficit starts at 0.6 percent of GDP in 1981, rises gradually to 4.8 percent in 1991, and begins to decline thereafter, as older retirees die. The pension debt will gradually diminish until the last covered retiree dies and the last worker with a recognition bond retires, around 2025. Estimates of the present value of these flows as of 1981, when the new system was introduced, vary from 38 to 128 percent of GDP, depending on the discount rate used (the high rate of return paid by the new pension funds or the lower GDP growth rate). The most relevant discount rate, the actual and projected interest rate paid on government debt, which measures the actual cost to the government, yields a present value of 80 percent of GDP (Arrau 1992). This is smaller than the debt in Eastern European countries, which have older populations

(Box continues on the following page.)

Box 8.5 *(continued)*

and more extensive coverage, but larger than the debt in younger countries, such as Mexico or China.

Under the old system, the implicit debt was financed by contributions coming into the system. Under the new, most contributions were going into the mandatory saving scheme, so other ways had to be found to finance the debt. To prepare for the pension transition, the Chilean government built up a budget surplus in the mid-1970s and continued this practice for most of the 1980s, offsetting much of the pension deficit. In effect, the pension deficit was used to absorb a budget surplus, preempting any move to cut taxes or increase government spending (box table 8.5) and in this sense keeping national saving above what it might have been otherwise. Proceeds from the sale of public enterprises during the 1980s facilitated this process. Most other countries that do not have budget surpluses or marketable public enterprises would have a more difficult time. Workers

who switched to the new system carried part of the debt until they retired, since the recognition bonds were not transferable or redeemable before then. Beyond that, the government has issued bonds and incurred a fiscal deficit during the transition. Most of the bonds were held by the new pension funds, which were rapidly accumulating financial assets that had to be invested somewhere.

Swapping the old implicit social security debt for new explicit government debt did not cause interest rates to rise. Rates fell throughout most of the 1980s, possibly because of the increased saving that was taking place. Chile shows that a country with a reasonably competitive banking system, a well-functioning debt market, and a fair degree of macroeconomic stability can finance large transition deficits without large interest rate repercussions. The government bonds can be paid off at the desired rate over the long run by levying taxes.

Box Table 8.5 Public Sector Deficits and National Savings under Chile's Pension Reform, 1979–92

	1979–81	*1982–85*	*1986–89*	*1990–92*
Fiscal balance and national saving (percentage of GDP)				
Overall public sector deficit	-3.5	14.0	-1.3	-1.8
Pension debt	0.6	3.6	3.9	4.7
Public sector deficit excluding				
pension debt	-4.1	10.4	-5.2	-6.5
Explicit public domestic debt[a]	2.3	42.7	33.1	40.8
National saving	11.5	3.7	13.5	18.5
Public saving	10.5	-3.8	4.7	5.1
Private saving	1.0	7.5	8.8	13.4
Gross domestic investment	20.5	12.1	17.2	19.7
Real interest rates				
Bank deposits (90–365 days)	12.0	9.1	4.9	6.7
Public debt yields	—	8.9[b]	5.7	7.7
Pension funds	—	16.7	7.8	22.7

— Not available.

a. End-of-period stock of public domestic debt as a share of previous year's GDP.

b. 1983–85 data.

Source: Central Bank of Chile (various issues); Arrau (1992); Chilean National Institute of Statistics (various issues); Chilean Ministry of Finance data.

lifetime consumption, but neither does it boost future saving and growth, so future generations derive no benefit. Much of the demand for the new bond issue will come from the new pension funds, which are rapidly accumulating savings that have to be invested somewhere. But a new bond issue may be politically difficult in countries that already have a large deficit. People would suddenly become aware of how enormous the social security debt is. The transition would treble the size of the explicit debt in most high-income and many older middle-income countries. Although the change from implicit to explicit debt should have no macroeconomic impact in a country with fully informed citizens, it might change government budgetary behavior in the more realistic case in which the change provides new information to policymakers and citizens.

Tax finance lays the burden of paying off the debt on the taxed generations (usually the working age generation). Their reduced consumption increases national saving, which may increase economic growth and benefit future generations. The key is to spread the tax burden out in an economically and politically acceptable way. Lower-income groups should be protected from the additional cost. Taxes could be imposed after a rapid growth spurt in the economy. While these taxes last, they are distortionary—but eventually they come to an end. General revenue rather than payroll taxes should be used as a more efficient and progressive form of taxation.

Cutting other government expenditures is another course of action. Budget cuts hurt groups that would otherwise have benefited from the programs that are cut—current cohorts if current spending is cut and future cohorts if government investments are cut. Since total spending is reduced, national saving increases.

Governments that are running a surplus can use it to finance the transition. Because the surplus could also be used to reduce taxes or increase other government spending, this alternative has economic effects similar to those already discussed—although its political effects may be different. Chile was running a surplus when it introduced its new system, which facilitated the transition for Chileans, but few countries are in that position today.

Finally, the proceeds from selling the assets of state-owned enterprises that are being privatized can be used to pay off part of the debt, an option in Latin America and the transitional economies (box 8.6).

The discussion below assumes that a combination of debt and other methods of finance is used. Bonds are issued to finance the transition initially and are gradually retired through reduced government spending and

Box 8.6 Using Privatized Public Assets to Pay Off the Social Security Debt in the Transitional Economies

THE PRESENT VALUE OF PENSION OBLIGATIONS in the formerly socialist countries of Eastern Europe has been roughly estimated at about one and a half to three times GDP (Holzmann 1994). One tempting proposal is to transfer state-owned assets, valued at around 2.5 times GDP, to pension funds to pay off obligations and create the basis for a new, funded system. Is that suggestion feasible?

How many assets are really available? At least 20 percent of the assets are in public infrastructure, which will not be privatized. Another 30 to 40 percent are in housing and agricultural land, which in most Eastern European countries are being turned over to former owners or tenants. Still another 20 percent are in commercial real estate belonging to the municipalities—and not available to the federal government. That leaves the state enterprise sector, with roughly 50 to 75 percent of GDP, clearly not big enough to pay off the social security debt (Holzmann 1994). Even this may be an overestimate of the value of privatizable assets, as market prices have been disappointing.

What are the assets really worth and who would buy them? The prices fetched in the sale of privatizable assets have been disappointing. Overstaffed, poorly managed, undercapitalized, and indebted state enterprises are not easy to sell under any circumstance. The domestic private sector has little cash with which to buy these assets, a weak domestic banking sector is in no position to provide the necessary liquidity, and most countries are not willing to transfer large chunks of the state enterprise sector to foreign hands. If the state were to sell the assets to domestic investors over a reasonable period of, say, three to five years, the sales would amount to giveaways to the few people who have cash or access to credit—generally, people who prospered under the former system. Most countries have concluded that the political consequences of selling the assets outweigh the potential revenue gains and have chosen to distribute them to the entire population, in the form of vouchers, or to encourage employee buyouts.

Why not put the vouchers directly into pension funds to pay off retirees? The equities are not likely to pay high dividends or to be very liquid for the first ten years, so state transfers would still be needed to pay pensions over that period.

taxes imposed on a stream of generations that ultimately bear the cost of reduced consumption. The burden is spread out according to the time schedule society prefers, but the gain is realized at a correspondingly slower rate. Chile scheduled retirement of its social security debt over a period of about fifty years, but money is fungible, so no one will know whether general debt finance has been used to postpone further the day of reckoning.

The Politics of Transition

THE ONLY WAY TO WIN BROAD SUPPORT FOR PENSION REform is to structure the new program so that there are more influential winners than losers. The gains need to be allocated in

Would pension funds be good enterprise monitors? Eastern European countries at the forefront of the transition have felt that the only way to end the fiscal bailout of former state enterprises is to get real private owners to work actively with companies to restructure or liquidate. There is little confidence that pension funds under state sponsorship, or with a state guarantee, could provide the firm hand necessary to enforce critical changes quickly and forcefully. Clearly, the funds would have to be independent if they were to exercise proper corporate governance. The higher the share of these state enterprise equities in the portfolio of pension funds and the more regulated the funds, the greater the danger that they will perpetuate the status quo rather than take the risks necessary to push the restructuring forward.

Who will regulate these funds? Although the work forces in the transitional economies are highly educated compared with those in other countries at comparable income levels, financial skills—not much in demand under socialist systems—are in short supply. To do their job, pension fund regulators normally rely on another set of regulators who rate the investments of pension fund managers— bank regulators, bond market regulators, stock market regulators, real estate regulators. This first tier of regulators is just emerging in most countries. If funds are built up slowly, regulatory capability could catch up. But if funds were suddenly infused with assets worth 50 percent of GDP, the regulatory challenge will be immense.

What about a more modest approach? Public assets could be used to pay off a portion of the social security debt. Workers in midcareer whose retirement age has been abruptly raised might be partially compensated by receiving vouchers for their pension accounts. Active workers might be permitted to place their vouchers in pension funds, in lieu of mandatory payroll contributions. Alternatively, the pension funds could gradually buy up some of the vouchers, increasing their liquidity. Pension fund managers could thus become active investors in a few companies. This solution would allow pension funds to play a role in the privatization process without becoming the main owners of the industrial sector.

ways that are fair and that make the reform politically popular. Both young and old need to be convinced that the new system will make them better off. If there are efficiency gains, a surplus is available to make most people better off, but this requires careful planning.

Winners and Losers across Generations

Winners and losers across generations are determined by the way the social security debt is measured and financed. If the calculation of the implicit debt is generous, pensioners and older workers gain, because they continue to receive benefits that the state might have defaulted on otherwise. If the calculation is stricter, older generations lose—or believe that they have lost—because they receive less than they would have gotten under the old formula. Pensioners are a very risk-averse lot. When they are also well organized, they have considerable political influence. It is essential to come up with a new valuation of pensions that the old as well as the young regard as fair. At the same time, the payoff to these groups cannot be too generous, and the reform generally requires downsizing the new public pillar. The old will buy this contraction only if they are convinced that the existing benefit level cannot feasibly be maintained. In Chile, top government officials conducted an intensive media campaign to convince people of the bankruptcy of the old system.

If the transition is fully financed through higher taxes, taxpayers in the current generation lose. They will have to pay higher taxes to cover the debt while also saving for their own retirement. Countries that already have very high tax rates will have to rely on reduced benefits, reduced government spending, and partial debt finance in the short run, with somewhat different distributional effects. The biggest winners are likely to be the generations following the transition, who will reap the economic gains of increased efficiency and growth. Is this transfer from present to future generations fair and socially desirable? This, of course, involves a value judgment about which people may disagree. But policymakers who take the long-run perspective face a formidable political obstacle: the current generation is alive and making itself heard at the time pension reforms are being debated, while future generations of pensioners are just children or not yet born.

The Chilean government convinced the current generation of workers that reform was good for them by slashing contribution rates from 22 percent to about 13 percent for those who opted for the new system. The lower cost reflected the expected savings from reduced evasion, distortions, and inequities. Workers were required to pay the entire contribution themselves, rather than sharing it with their employers, to make them more cost-conscious, but those who switched received a one-time wage increase that put them ahead in terms of take-home pay. The debt payoff was financed more ambiguously out of general revenues, including a budgetary surplus that the government had accumulated in advance.

Winners and Losers in the Same Generation

The transition also involves redistribution within the same generation. Who wins and who loses depends on whether the old pay-as-you-go system was progressive or regressive and on whether the reform package includes measures for the poor. Since many current systems are not redistributive toward the poor in practice, whatever their intentions, low-income groups may well be the winners from the transition and high-income groups the losers. Workers as a group gain if productivity rises with the reduction in labor market distortions and the increase in capital accumulation that accompany reform—an effect that can improve the welfare of low-income groups in the future. Private entrepreneurs gain as a new supply of funds for corporate equities and bonds flows into the market.

Institutional Winners and Losers

With the pension transition, managers of social security institutions lose some of the power that comes with wielding monopolistic control over large flows of money, and workers in these institutions may lose their jobs. The social security bureaucrats may try to mobilize political parties and pressure groups to oppose the transition. Severance pay may help to defray their opposition. Private financial institutions gain, especially those that reap the large profits available to early entrants into the market, so they can be expected to lobby in favor of a decentralized funded pension system. In many Latin American countries, unions may expect to lose and may oppose the transition if they were previously the sole representatives of the workers in the social security program. Unions may be won over by letting them establish new pension funds, as in Chile and Argentina.

Countries in Transition

OVER THE PAST THREE YEARS, MANY COUNTRIES HAVE MADE major changes in their old age security systems. Australia added a mandatory funded occupational pillar to its means-tested public pillar. Several Latin American countries are following the Chilean model of mandatory personal savings accounts, with the public pillar offering a flat benefit or a minimum pension guarantee. Other countries with problem-plagued public plans are at a crossroads and are trying to decide which way to move. China and the transitional socialist economies are the most notable examples, but a number of OECD countries are also in this group. Countries in Africa and South Asia, where informal systems are gradually breaking down, are just beginning to build up their public plans—and watching other countries move in the opposite direction. Observing older countries in transition should be a cautionary experience for younger countries, spurring them to evaluate carefully where they want to be thirty years from now and how best to get there.

Australia's Mandatory Occupational Pillar

Australia has long relied on an income- and asset-tested public pension financed from general revenues. By the standards of most OECD countries, its public pillar was fiscally modest and redistributive, costing about 4 percent of GDP (appendix table A.5). A second pillar, a mandatory funded employer-based retirement scheme, was added in 1991. This scheme had its origins in a political agreement between the government and the unions in 1986 that set the national umbrella compensation increase at the inflation rate, with half the increase in the form of a retirement fund contribution. This arrangement solved several important political economy problems. It enabled unions to claim a large compensation increase without creating new inflationary pressures. It addressed the retirement concerns of an aging population without adding to the government's fiscal burden. And it was seen as a way to increase national saving and growth. In 1986 only 40 percent of Australian workers were covered by occupational schemes. In 1991 occupational schemes became mandatory for all employees. Simultaneously, the retirement age at which the funds could be tapped was raised (Bateman and Piggott 1993).[1]

This superannuation scheme is scheduled to be phased in over ten years. Starting with a 3 percent requirement in 1992, the employer's contribution rises to 9 percent by 2002. Toward the end of the period, a 3 percent employee contribution will be added, bringing the total contribution rate to 12 percent. This higher contribution rate is expected to be financed by holding the line on wage hikes as productivity grows. For example, a 1 percent annual increase in productivity would cover superannuation costs while holding real take-home pay roughly constant.

Contributions to the retirement fund must be fully vested, portable, and funded. Most plans are defined contribution, which facilitates compliance with these regulations. The funds are supervised by boards of trustees that include an equal number of employer and worker representatives—another reason for union support of the second pillar. Disclosure requirements and tight prudential standards are specified by legislation. All workers in a firm must be in the same fund, with a single investment strategy, a feature that could cause conflicts between young and old workers or risk-averse and risk-prone workers.

The tax treatment is complex: contributions, earnings, and benefits are partially taxed and partially deductible, the result of a pragmatic attempt to reduce tax expenditures, especially those benefiting higher-income individuals, while encouraging compliance. Employer contributions are tax deductible up to specified limits that increase with the worker's age. Fund earnings are taxed but at a low flat rate. Benefits beyond a specified floor are taxed but at a lower rate if the benefit is taken as an annuity rather than a lump sum.

Once the plan is phased in, it will increase annual private saving by an estimated 0.8 percent of GDP. Public saving may increase in the long run (as spending on the means-tested pension declines) but decrease in the first few years (because of tax exemptions for contributions and interest). Overall, the plan will more than offset the savings decline expected as the population ages. Estimates of the positive impact on national saving range from 0.5 to 1.3 percent of GDP, in either case a substantial increment to the current net national saving rate of 5 percent of GDP.

Australia, like Chile, mandates a funded decentrally controlled pillar as an important part of its old age security system. Both decentralized schemes include a detailed regulatory structure. To facilitate regulation, there are no provisions for splitting a worker's pension accumulation between two or more funds. Thus risk cannot be reduced through diversification. This limitation should be reevaluated because it is a large social cost of the regulatory system. Australia permits retirees to take their pension accumulation as a lump sum rather than as an annuity or in phased withdrawals, as required in Chile. If the lump sum is dissipated too soon, the result could be low incomes and poverty among the very old. Costs, especially marketing costs, might be lower in the Australian scheme, where employers choose the pension fund on a relatively long-term basis. But since most plans are defined contribution—workers bear the risk while employers choose the investment manager—the incentives for high returns might be lower in Australia than in Chile. Data on costs and returns are not yet available for Australia, so these hypotheses cannot be tested.

The public pillars in Australia and Chile are redistributive and financed out of general revenues. Australia's public pillar, which pays a universal income- and asset-tested benefit to about 70 percent of the retired population, is much more generous and expensive than the minimum pension guarantee scheme that constitutes Chile's public pillar. As a result, Australia's scheme has a greater impact on poverty and a higher expected wage replacement rate for a typical worker—but it also will cost more.

Denmark and Switzerland have also adopted mandatory occupational pillars in recent years, and this trend will probably spread to other OECD countries as they struggle to cope with aging populations in a time of slow economic growth and fiscal stringency.

Latin America's New Privatized Pension Plans

Nowhere has the influence of the Chilean experiment been felt more strongly than in Latin America. During the debt and fiscal crises of the 1980s, Latin America's pension schemes became seriously underfunded. By the end of the decade falling real pensions, increasing evasion, large social security deficits, and depleted reserves had irreparably damaged the credibility of traditional pension schemes. The pension crises coincided with a generalized debate over the role of government, a push toward privatization, and a strong desire to build up domestic capital markets. As the region entered the 1990s, the movement to privatize pensions gained momentum, urged on by the success in Chile.

In 1992 governments in Argentina and Peru proposed fundamental changes that effectively privatized a large share of pension programs. Peru implemented a new pension law in 1993, and Argentina's pension reform, which squeaked by in 1993 with a one-vote majority, is scheduled to begin in 1994. Both countries were running enormous pension deficits before making the transition, with implicit social security debts estimated at about two-thirds of GDP. Colombia, too, is about to introduce a new privatized pension system, though its immature scheme has no current pension deficit and has a much smaller social security debt because of lower coverage. All three countries have set up schemes similar to Chile's and have largely adopted Chile's regulatory structure. Some of Chile's pension companies (AFPs) are moving into these new markets. Mexico has also instituted a small compulsory mandatory saving scheme, and Bolivia is on the verge of adopting a Chilean-type reform (table 8.1).

Table 8.1 Pension Reforms in Latin America

	Chile	*Peru*	*Argentina*	*Colombia*
Year implemented	*1981*	*1993*	*1994*	*1994*
Transition arrangements				
What happens to old system?	Phased out	Continues with changes	Continues with changes	Continues with changes
Is current labor force allowed to remain in old scheme ?	Yes	Yes[a]	Yes	Yes
Is new system mandatory for new labor force entrants?	Yes	No	No	No
Can workers switch back to public system after entering AFP?	No	Yes, for two years	No	Yes, every three years.
Recognition bonds	Yes	Yes	Yes[b]	Yes[c]
Profile of new pension scheme				
What role for public pillar?	Minimum pension guarantee Social assistance	Social assistance	Flat and minimum pension	Minimum pension guarantee Social assistance
Total contribution rate for new system				
available for old age annuity	10	10	8	10
disability/survivors/administrative	3	2.3	3	3.5
public pillar and social assistance	General revenues	1	16[d]	1
Total contribution rate: before reform	19	9	27	8
after reform	13	13.3	27	13.5–14.5[e]
Maximum percentage of portfolio allowed in				
Domestic equities	30	to be decided	50	to be decided
Foreign equities	10	to be decided	10	to be decided
Government bonds in 1994	45	to be decided	50	50

a. Workers must decide by 1998.

b. "Compensatory pension" is paid upon retirement, not as a bond. The value is based on years of contribution and last ten years' earnings.

c. Workers with fewer than 150 weeks of contributions are not eligible for a recognition bond.

d. This is paid by the employer.

e. The rate shown is for 1996 and following years. The contribution rate will increase gradually between 1994 and 1996.

Source: Rofman (1994); Vittas (1994a); Colombia (1993); World Bank internal documents.

The transition in these countries has key features in common with that in Chile. For example, Argentina, Colombia, and Peru give workers a choice between remaining in the old social security system and transferring to the new privatized system. If most workers under the age of 40 transfer, the assets of the new private pension companies are projected to grow to 10 to 20 percent of GDP over the next decade. Workers who switch will receive recognition bonds or pensions based on years of service under the old system as a payoff of the social security debt.

All three countries reformed their public pension plans before introducing the new structure. Argentina raised retirement age by five years and eligibility from fifteen to thirty years of service and lowered the pensionable wage base. Colombia increased the eligibility period and the contribution rate for workers who remained in the old system. That encouraged workers to choose the privatized pillar and reduced the social security debt owed to those who switched.

The new schemes also differ from Chile's in certain important respects, a consequence of their unique political climates and institutions. Argentina includes both a flat benefit and a higher minimum pension guarantee as part of its new system. All eligible workers receive a flat benefit from the public pillar equal to about 25 percent of the average covered wage besides their pension from the second funded pillar. Additionally, the state guarantees workers at least 40 percent of the average covered wage under the combined pillars. So long as underreporting does not cut the average covered wage, this guarantee is much larger than Chile's. But the thirty-year eligibility period excludes many workers, including most women. The flat pension in the public pillar plus the payoff of the old social security debt will be financed by a 16 percent payroll tax paid by employers. Workers pay another 11 percent into the new second pillar. The total contribution rate is the same as it was under the old system (Vittas 1994a; Rofman 1994).

Colombia, like Chile, offers a minimum pension guarantee to redistribute to the lifetime poor and insure workers against severe investment failure. Peru's new system has no public pillar; the only backup is social assistance. Many workers may be reluctant to assume the full investment risk of the new system; but they will have to compare this risk with the political risk of the old system, which is also substantial.

Proponents of reform in Mexico found it difficult to challenge the fifty-year tradition of a dominant public pillar. Mexico compromised by leaving the public system intact and adding a small mandatory savings scheme in 1991 that placed 2 percent of wages in individual capitalization accounts. This is unlikely to be an equilibrium solution for an aging population. High transaction costs per account are another drawback. Probably in the long run contributions to the funded pillar will grow— or it will be phased out.

While the new Latin American schemes are welcomed reforms, design and planning flaws may create problems for them in the medium term. First are the difficulties in calculating the value of the old social security entitlement. In Peru the absence of reliable records forced officials to accept the sworn statement of workers to establish their past contributions—a method obviously subject to abuse. Colombia's formula for calculating the recognition bond is so complex that it may be impossible to implement uniformly. In Argentina the index that will be used to revalue past earnings and contributions has not yet been specified. Calculations of old entitlements may be subject to political pressures that increase the fiscal costs of the transition substantially or, conversely, that leave retirees with lower pensions than they thought they would be getting.

A second set of problems concerns the indefinite continuation of the old system, albeit with reforms. In Chile, new entrants to the labor force have to join the privatized pension scheme. The other reformers in Latin America allow new entrants to choose between the new and the old systems. In Colombia and Peru, they can even switch back and forth. This freedom introduces incentive problems, uncertainty, and higher administrative costs for the old age system as a whole. Colombia will offer an inflation-indexed replacement rate of 85 percent of final wages in the old system after only twenty-three years of contributions. Workers will probably choose to remain with that system if they believe this promise.

In Argentina, workers can choose to put their 11 percent contribution into the new privatized pillar or the reformed publicly managed system. The public system pays a defined benefit equal to 25.5 percent of the final ten years' average wage for a worker with thirty years of service. (This is in addition to the flat benefit of 25 percent of the average covered wage that everyone gets, financed by the employer's contribution.) In the privatized pillar, less than 8 of the 11 percent worker contribution gets invested; the rest goes to cover plan expenses and disability and life insurance. Except for very young and short-term workers, the public system may be preferred because it promises higher expected benefits than the new private option. A 7 to 8 percent contribution rate will not yield an adequate pension in a defined contribution plan unless the interest rate is very high. But simulations indicate that the public defined benefit system may not break even once the population ages, unless wage growth in the country is very high. These old systems may become bankrupt in the future, just as they did in the past.

Also questionable is whether the government's regulatory capacity and domestic capital markets are up to the job of running a mandatory saving plan. In Chile the planning process took several years. An elaborate system of government regulations and guarantees was constructed and a legal framework was developed that permitted a full range of indexed bonds and other indexed financial instruments to be traded. For the first few years, most pension funds were invested in bank and government debt as financial regulations were modernized, although new investments are much more diversified. In contrast, Peru has few people trained to be potential pension regulators or administrators. The short supply of government bonds and the absence of a secondary market for public debt raise questions about where the new pension funds can be invested. Colombia's new legislation does not specify investment restrictions. In Argentina, stock market capitalization is low, so the entry of large new funds may bid up prices sharply until new stock issues enter the market. Imperfections in domestic capital markets can be avoided through international diversification, but all these countries, including Chile, limit that option. If the new private pension companies do not operate in a reasonably prudent manner and earn good returns during their first few years, the new system may be irrevocably discredited.

Bolivia, Brazil, Costa Rica, Uruguay, and Venezuela are contemplating the future of their pension systems. Bolivia has tied pension reform to state enterprise reform. Shares of privatized enterprises are slated to be transferred to the population at large in the form of assets for the new privatized pension funds. Economies of scale in pension provision pose a problem for decentralized systems in this small country, especially for accounts of low-income workers and peasants. In Venezuela tensions among unions, business interests, and government are stalling reform.

The general distrust of government institutions and the more specific distrust of social security arrangements make it likely that an increasing number of workers will trade in public promises for AFP accounts in Latin America. Whether these new systems will ultimately prove successful depends on a host of design and implementation details, and early indications are that these will differ from one country to another.

China at the Pension Reform Crossroads

The rapid aging of China's population, accelerated by the one-child policy and impressive improvements in health care, will severely strain both formal and informal old age support systems in the next few decades. By 2030 nearly 22 percent of China's one billion people will be over age 60 and the number of workers per old person will fall from 6 to 2.3, giving China an age profile similar to that of the oldest OECD country today. Pension reforms are necessary if China is to restructure its economy and care for its old.

Informal systems of caring for the old still predominate in rural China, where more than 80 percent of the old live with children or other family members. Most old people in rural areas continue to work, and only one person in twenty receives a formal pension (Cangping 1991). In contrast, most urban workers are covered by a complex network of formal retirement schemes administered, until recently, on a pay-as-you-go basis by the state enterprises for which they work. This system has become a major impediment to economic reform.

It is impossible to shut down inefficient enterprises without eliminating the mini-welfare state each represents. Potentially profitable enterprises, especially those with a high proportion of aging workers, are burdened by the costs of administering benefits for thousands of pensioners. The government has been under pressure to bail out companies that can no longer keep their pension promises. Ignoring the cost of mounting pension liabilities, enterprises have been encouraged to shed surplus workers by offering early retirement or disability pensions—but this ultimately adds to total costs.

In addition, worker mobility has been discouraged by the system's fragmentation. Wage replacement rates are high—over 75 percent of the average urban wage—but usually pensions are not indexed. This has reduced real pensions as inflation pressures have grown. Lax enforcement and benefit formulas that tie pensions to final year wages have induced workers and employers to evade and manipulate the system. And the cost of the scheme is soaring. Between 1978 and 1988 pension expenditures per covered worker doubled in real terms, and total pension expenditures as a share of GDP almost doubled, from 1.4 to 2.7 percent (ILO data). Without significant reform, these expenditures will skyrocket over the next few decades. (For further discussion of problems with the current system, see Friedman 1994.)

Because the coming demographic shift is so dramatic, China will soon face a turning point in its old age security system. It will need to decide whether to centralize the old age system nationally, allow provinces or localities to handle it on a coordinated basis, or let the old enterprise-based system remain. Maintaining the status quo is clearly not a reasonable option in view of the impediments this presents for labor mobility and enterprise restructuring. In more than 2,100 cities and counties around China, pension pooling arrangements among enterprises have already been established, and local governments have begun to assume the management of these pooled schemes. But differences in contribution rates and benefit formulas have created inequities and portability problems. China must decide whether to centralize further to the provincial or national level or to allow local differences to prevail.

One advantage of local or provincial control is greater adaptability to the vast differences in income and labor market conditions, differences that will likely widen over the next decade. Another advantage is that it allows room for experimentation, which might be useful in a country that has not yet reached consensus on a single best policy. Indeed, several localities are already experimenting with a variety of schemes—sometimes without careful preparation. A compromise would allow local or provincial plans to operate subject to national guidelines on prudent investment, portability, actuarial, and disclosure requirements.

China also needs to decide whether to retain a dominant pay-as-you-go system or move to a multipillar system with a large funded component. A pay-as-you-go system would be particularly sensitive to the upcoming demographic transition, so China would be unwise to put all its eggs in that basket.

China is fortunate to be experiencing an unprecedentedly high growth rate: over 10 percent a year for the last decade, with high growth expected to continue for the next decade (IMF IFS 1993). Diverting part of the fruits of its productivity increases to a funded pension pillar would enable China to build up the capital stock to maintain its growth and support its aging population. China is well placed to do that, since it starts out with a relatively small pay-as-you-go system, a flat wage and benefit structure, and a retirement age with lots of headroom. Transition costs are low now, compared with what they might be in another ten years if the pay-as-you-go system expands. The current generation of old people could be protected by the public pillar, which would continue to provide a safety net, while younger workers, who will have much higher lifetime incomes, could finance much of their own retirement savings as well as pay off the social security debt through taxes.

If China goes the multipillar route, including a funded defined contribution pillar, should it follow the Chilean model (decentralized fund management) or the Singaporean model (centralized), and what regulatory apparatus should it install? The preconditions for running a privately managed funded system are present in China—to a greater extent than in most countries at its stage of development. Though capital markets and financial regulation are still rudimentary, stock markets are beginning to develop—and banks must undergo a major restructuring in any event. Many foreign financial institutions would willingly jump into the enormous Chinese market if given a chance, including those in Hong Kong, which is about to become part of China. Indeed, overseas Chinese have already invested heavily in China. Pension funds could encourage the development of capital markets and facilitate privatization, as in Chile.

However, the government may be reluctant to relinquish control over these potentially large funds and may therefore prefer the Singaporean model. Policymakers may be tempted to use the pension funds to subsidize failing enterprises or to finance expenditures on housing and infrastructure, both of which are in short supply in China. The cost of this approach would be the scarcity of investable funds for profitable private sector growth.

New occupational schemes that are likely to be offered by multinationals and large domestic firms to attract personnel present another set of concerns. Basing the second mandatory pillar on these occupational schemes seems a poor idea, since that would perpetuate many of the problems of the enterprise-based schemes. Yet voluntary employer-sponsored plans seem inevitable. To avoid big problems down the road, China needs to think through a careful regulatory framework for new occupational schemes from the beginning. Adequate funding must be required to ensure that firms are able to honor their pension promises when they come due. And vesting arrangements must be worked out to make sure that these plans do not get in the way of the labor flexibility needed for continued economic growth.

China also needs to decide on a tax framework for these plans and for voluntary personal retirement saving schemes. This framework should balance the usefulness of incentives for voluntary pensions and savings, the equity implications of these incentives, and the government's need for tax revenues. Private voluntary saving could be expanded by introducing appropriate tax policies, reforming the banking system, avoiding inflationary policies, and establishing reliable savings institutions, preferably with indexed financial instruments.

Recently the government has begun a small contributory pension program for rural workers. But the formal pension system will not reach most rural areas for many years, and voluntary saving is unlikely to suffice. The informal system in these areas could be bolstered by government subsidies (housing and medical allowances) to children or other relatives who care for aging family members. One promising avenue is expansion of the Wu Bao program, which provides food, shelter, clothing, medical care, and other support to the needy old as well as to orphans and the disabled. This effort could be financed out of general revenues, both local and national. In 1985 Wu Bao provided help to about 2.4 million old people, about 5 percent of the old in rural areas (World Bank 1990). But even as far-reaching pension reforms are introduced into the formal contributory system, the country's limited resources, large number of old people, and growing income inequality mean that the informal system combined with social assistance programs will continue to play an important role in China's old age support system.

Eastern Europe—Magnified Problems and Difficult Solutions

Countries in Eastern Europe and the former Soviet Union face the typical problems of middle-income countries with publicly managed pay-as-you-go systems: high and rising dependency ratios, overly generous wage replacement rates (with little or no indexation), liberal early retirement and disability provisions, soaring fiscal costs, bloated contribution rates, and negative returns on pension reserves (see box 4.7 for details). But the problems are magnified in the transitional economies because they have the aging demographic profiles, widespread coverage, system maturity, and aspirations of high-income countries but the resources, tax systems, and government capacities of middle- and low-income countries. Old age security programs are much larger in Eastern Europe and the former Soviet Union than in Latin America. They are an enormous fiscal drain in these countries and a major drag on labor demand in the formal market. Solutions will be more difficult as well in countries reeling from declining GDP, economic and political turmoil, and widespread institutional change.

Like China, these countries need to decide whether to maintain a dominant public pension plan with an earnings-related benefit formula or to adopt a multipillar system. If they shift to a multipillar system they must decide whether the public component should be flat, means-tested, or a minimum pension guarantee and whether to phase in the second pillar gradually, by cutting benefits or increasing contributions, or to make a radical break and start up a new system at once. If they choose the radical route, they will have to figure out how to pay off an implicit social security debt that is much larger than that in Latin America because their populations are older and coverage is broader.

Reforming public pension plans. Whatever else they decide, the first step is to reform public pension plans. Although essential reforms vary by country, the most common include reducing and flattening benefits, indexing for inflation, raising the retirement age, changing the tax base, separating the accounts of different social insurance plans, and eliminating reserves, which (where they exist) earn a low or negative rate of return. Quickly lowering the average wage replacement rate (from 50 to 70 percent, where it now is in many countries) to 35 to 40 percent would bring replacement rates in line with those in many OECD countries, cut the contribution rate substantially, and lower the social security debt. The quid pro quo for reducing benefits should be to replace the current erratic indexation with automatic indexation under clearly stated rules. If a multipillar system is phased in, the wage replacement rate in the new public pillar could be gradually reduced to 20 percent by using an indexation method in which pensions rise more slowly than wages or by switching to a minimum guarantee.

Reducing average benefits makes it all the more important that the public pillar concentrate on poverty elimination. Conditions in transitional economies—no employment records, high rates of labor force participation in the old command economy, relatively flat wage structures, and little or no personal savings—make a universal flat pension the best way to go in the short run—maybe the only feasible way. Flat benefits provide basic insurance to all, are administratively simple, and constitute a partial payoff of the social security debt. The shift to a flat benefit structure ought to be easy since the effective rate is already nearly flat, thanks to relatively undifferentiated wages and inflation-eroded benefits that have placed many retirees at the minimum pension.

The two most important reforms are to raise the retirement age for women to that for men and to eliminate special early retirement job categories, bringing the average effective retirement age up from 55, where it is now in most of these countries, to 60. This step could be achieved in two to five years. After that, the normal retirement age could be raised more gradually to 65 (and beyond, as longevity rises). Simulations for the countries of the former Soviet Union show that pushing up the normal retirement age six months each year for ten years would cut the required contribution rate by 30 percent (Cavalcanti 1993). Poland could save roughly 3 percent of GDP annually by 2010 by cutting the number of early retirees in half (Rashid 1993). Romania could cut projected system dependency ratios and costs by 25 percent by equalizing the normal retirement age at 65 for men and women and at 60 for most early retirees (Romanian government projections). These savings could become the major source of funds for starting up the second pillar.

The public pillar should also shift to a broader tax base in the long run, for efficiency and distributional bases. But until these countries establish a personal income tax and value added tax, the payroll tax is likely to be the only game in town. Workers should bear at least half the total tax responsibility—the employer pays it all now—as a deduction from take-home pay. (A one-time increase in wage scales, as in Chile, may be needed to hold disposable income constant.) Nothing creates a constituency for change as quickly as seeing how expensive the current system really is.

Establishing a mandatory saving pillar. The downsizing of the public pillar and the introduction of a decentralized second pillar would have special political and psychological benefits in transitional economies. These choices would signal the government's intention to transfer responsibility to individuals for their own well-being, backed up by a public social safety net, and establish a constituency for macroeconomic stability, financial sector reform, and enterprise privatization and restructuring. Pension fund assets could help to stimulate foreign direct investment through joint ventures with large foreign investment firms.

Since payroll tax rates need to be lowered, not raised, to stimulate private enterprise and trade, how can this transformation be accomplished? The reform of public pension plans just outlined provides a clue about how to reduce taxes and phase in a second pillar simultaneously. Increasing the average retirement age from 55 to 60 and lowering the average replacement rate from 50 to 40 percent by the year 2000 would allow a typical older Eastern European country to cut payroll taxes from 30 to 18 percent, freeing up 12 percent to be split between the second pillar and tax cuts. If 10 percent of payroll went to the funded pillar this would produce assets equal to about 3 percent of GDP per year—small enough for the financial systems of most of these countries to handle and large enough to help the economy. Indexing public pensions half to wages and half to prices would allow productivity increases to cover the cost of rising dependency rates and further cut the contribution rate over a period of years. Simulations of a possible transition path for Eastern Europe are outlined in issue brief 12.

Paying off the social security debt: Equity among age groups. If all goes well, young workers (under age 35) and their children are likely to be the big winners, gaining from higher wages thanks to productivity growth, the accumulated capital in their pension accounts, and the added insurance that comes from risk diversification. Reform will not get off the ground, however, unless it deals with obligations to people who have worked all their lives with the expectation that they would be taken care of when they grew old.

Taking care of older groups implies shifting some income from younger to older generations to pay off the social security debt. Estimating this debt is more complicated for the transitional economies than for Argentina or Chile because the complete change of economic and political systems demands a renegotiation of the implicit contract between workers and the state. That contract never envisioned conditions in which per capita income falls abruptly, broad wage differentials suddenly appear, taxes cannot be collected, and monthly inflation reaches double digits. A further complication is the absence of employment records. What can be done under these circumstances?

Older cohorts already retired have nowhere else to turn for old age security but the public pension plans on which they have counted all their lives. This group had little opportunity or incentive to save, since most of their income was earned during the era of central planning, when salaries were low and pensions were guaranteed. Households that did accumulate some savings before the transition lost it in the ensuing inflationary economic upheaval. This group does not have enough productive years left to accumulate pension capital in the private funded pillar. Renegotiation of the debt owed to this group should recognize that their income cannot fall much farther. In the transition just outlined, this group would be taken care of through a continuation of the public pillar but with a flatter structure of benefits that maintains its real value through time and keeps all retirees above the poverty line. Low-income pensioners would fare about as well as they would have under the old system. High-income retirees would get somewhat less, but in compensation they get automatic indexation plus the right to reenter the formal labor force without losing their pensions.

Workers 35 to 55 years old, especially those who were previously eligible for early retirement, bear the brunt of the costs of the proposed reform: their retirement age is raised while their public pensions are substantially lowered. But this group is partially compensated by the higher wages and lower payroll taxes brought about by the reform and by the capital they manage to accumulate in the funded pillar. The younger the worker and the more profitable the funds' investments, the greater is this compensation. This group also benefits from improved insurance against inflation, from productivity growth that occurs after their retirement, since pensions are indexed partially to real wages, and from protection against political and investment risks through diversification.

This group could be compensated further by depositing some of the assets of state enterprises in their pension accounts. Several caveats are in order: The assets of state enterprises could pay off only a small part of the social security debt. Workers and pension funds would have to receive a diverse set of assets, not those of a single privatized company, because some companies will turn out to be profitable and others worthless. Fund managers would need to have full autonomy to manage their investments, and governments or unions would have to refrain from exerting pressures to prevent the restructuring or liquidation of state enterprises (box 8.6).

Finally, this group might be further compensated through recognition bonds that could be cashed in for higher pensions at retirement—financed from the economic growth that has taken place in the meantime.

Regulating the occupational pillar. Voluntary occupational and other private schemes are already springing up in Bulgaria, the Czech Republic, Estonia, Hungary, and Russia, and have been proposed in Poland and Romania, a response to the lack of confidence in the public schemes. Countries suffering from administrative overload and a shortage of financial experts may be tempted to allow these plans to develop on their own, with minimal government intervention. That would be a costly mistake over the long run.

Unregulated occupational plans are, for the most part, underfunded, promising more than they can deliver. Companies that are here today may be gone tomorrow, leaving workers and governments in the lurch. Without regulation, occupational plans would impose vesting and portability restrictions that would impede enterprise restructuring and the movement of workers from the public to the private sector. Uninformed workers might make employment decisions that are not in their own best interest. Governments should move quickly to regulate defined benefit schemes by requiring funding, vesting, portability, and equitable coverage. These regulations will probably retard the growth of occupational plans, especially defined benefit plans, but the plans that survive will at least have a fighting chance of being financially sound. Later, when the second pillar is made mandatory, workers and policymakers may choose whether to include regulated occupational schemes as an alternative to regulated personal saving schemes.

Obstacles to reform. Most Eastern European economies have introduced piecemeal reforms but have not yet attempted an overall restructuring of their old age security systems (box 8.7). Why has reform stalled in the transitional economies, while moving full steam ahead in Latin American countries facing similar problems? Countries in Latin America had the advantage that voters and policymakers knew full well the weaknesses of the old system after years of high taxes and failed benefit promises; that market mechanisms, banks, and private investments were familiar institutions; and that a few politicians were ready to advocate sweeping change, supported by a cadre of well-trained, experienced technocrats. In Eastern Europe and the former Soviet Union such preconditions for a second pillar as well-functioning financial and legal systems are absent, civil servants and politicians are suffering from reform overload, and citizens at large are bewildered by a suddenly unpredictable world, while having almost no notion of how dismally the public pillar has performed or how much it has hurt the economy. Nor do they appreciate that the large public pillars of some of their Western neighbors are likely to be in serious trouble five to ten years from now. Several of the following preconditions to reform are absent in many transitional economies:

- A legislative framework clearly spelling out property and contract rights, and a judicial system for enforcing them
- Well-functioning financial institutions and instruments, such as solvent banks, insurance companies, and stocks and bonds
- Prudential regulations for financial markets
- People trained in financial and regulatory affairs or institutes to provide this training
- Modern accounting and auditing standards

289

Box 8.7 What Reforms Have Eastern European Economies Introduced So Far?

MOST TRANSITIONAL ECONOMIES HAVE INTRODUCED SOME pension reforms, though not in any systematic way that provides a long-term solution to their problems. Among them are the following:

- *Poland* introduced a new benefit formula in 1991 that abolished differences in benefit levels by occupation, increased the number of working years used in calculating the earnings base, lowered the maximum pension, and indexed pensions to the average wage.
- *Romania* raised contribution rates in 1992 for those employed in occupations with early retirement provisions and raised benefits in the funded scheme. Multiple pension schemes are gradually being unified.
- *Bulgaria* raised contribution rates in 1991 for employees eligible for early retirement. In 1992 it raised the minimum retirement age, reduced the number of workers eligible for early retirement, and added incentives for those above retirement age to keep working.
- *Hungary* placed a ceiling on contributions in 1992, increased the minimum number of contribution years, slightly revised the benefit formula and pension indexation, and created an independent social insurance fund, which separates contributions by use.
- *Albania* established an independent social insurance agency in 1992, with an independent budget and financing. The pension fund was separated in 1993. Major reform legislation was passed in 1993, covering a gradual increase in the minimum contribution period for full pensions, ceilings on pensions and contributions, employee contributions, and a flat contribution for the self-employed. The benefit formula was restructured and is now based on years of contributions and indexed annually.

- Market-determined prices to signal real costs and benefits
- Macroeconomic stability, which lessens the threat of high inflation
- Tax administration capability.

A few countries, such as the Czech Republic, Hungary, and Poland, have already established many of these preconditions and could soon begin to build a multipillar system. Several other countries should be in a position to do so within three to five years. The large demand for financial security will prevent the government from scaling back the public pillar, so the high payroll tax, distorted labor markets, and scarcity of capital will continue to paralyze these economies until a viable alternative is offered. Once one country in the region introduces a successful multipillar system, others are likely to follow suit quickly. But it is not clear whether any country will make the first move, because the most essential ingredients—citizens who believe the old system is unsustainable, technocrats and civil servants ready and able to implement a new system, and policymakers committed to change—may be lacking.

Concluding Thoughts

AROUND THE WORLD, COUNTRIES ARE REEVALUATING their arrangements for providing income security for the old. As their populations age and their old age security systems consume an ever-increasing share of national resources, it becomes more and more important to get these arrangements right. Policymakers and citizens are finding that the old systems did not always deliver what they promised. Although each country has its own story, the problems of pension systems are surprisingly universal, rooted in demography and political economy. New options are available that promise to be better.

In evaluating these options, a few basic principles should be kept in mind. The system should:

- Provide a safety net for older people who can no longer work to support themselves or easily adapt to unexpected circumstances— or turn back the clock to undo earlier mistakes
- Provide incentives and requirements for work and saving behavior that foster economic growth
- Minimize opportunities for individuals and governments to manipulate the system for private benefit at public expense
- Take the very long-run perspective—planning for old age covers sixty years or more for individuals and spouses, and another thirty to forty years for one's children.

The experience of many countries with failed systems and a smaller number of countries with successful systems suggests that the best way for most countries to meet constructively the challenge of an aging world is through a multipillar system featuring:

- A mandatory tax-financed public pillar designed to alleviate poverty
- A mandatory funded, privately managed pillar (based on personal accounts or occupational plans) to handle people's savings
- A supplementary voluntary pillar (again based on personal saving or occupational plans) for people who want more protection.

Together, the three pillars coinsure against life's risks and uncertainties. Although the pace of reform must be guided by individual country circumstances, all countries should begin planning now.

Note

1. The section on Australia draws heavily from the work of Bateman and Piggott and other articles in the Superannuation Economics Research Group Research Paper Series, University of New South Wales, Australia.

Issue Briefs

Issue Brief 1 How Much Should a Pension Pay Out? The Target Wage Replacement Rate

PENSIONS ARE DESIGNED TO REPLACE WAGES when a person is too old to work productively. But how high a wage replacement rate should the household aim for? And how much of that target should government mandate? If the household's targeted rate is too low, a retiree may become a burden on society. If the government's mandatory rate is too high, heavy contributions will be required to finance it, and welfare losses will be accompanied by fiscal and labor market problems. But how low is "too low," and how high is "too high"?

Many different bases can be used to calculate the wage replacement rate. The targeted rate is usually expressed as a percentage of a worker's final year salary or average salary over several years, such as the average annual lifetime salary. Sometimes it is expressed as a proportion of the average wage in the economy. Pensions can be calculated as a percentage of gross earnings before pension contributions or of net earnings after contributions. Many households might wish to replace about 75 percent of their gross average lifetime salary, but the government-mandated replacement rate should probably be only about half of the gross average lifetime salary for the average worker, with a floor at the poverty line for low-income workers.

Household Wage Replacement Targets

According to the life cycle theory of consumption, people want to smooth their consumption over their lifetime. In a simplified version of the theory, people want to consume the same amount each year, whether they are young or old, so they set aside income in their high-earning years to allow themselves to consume more in their low-earning years. In this case, workers try to acquire a pension that will pay 100 percent of their real net average lifetime wage.

A more realistic version of the theory assumes that people will want to consume different amounts at different periods in their life. Many want to consume more when they are young, raising children, and forced by job considerations to live in high-cost areas. Others, who have large medical bills or more leisure time or who have grown accustomed to a comfortable lifestyle may want to consume more as they age. In addition, if per capita income in the economy is growing, people will have to consume more as they age to maintain their relative standing. Uncertainty about health and cost of living further complicates the picture. Some people will therefore be willing to pay for pensions that exceed 100 percent of their net average lifetime wage, while others will take less.

The appropriate replacement rate also depends on the wage base. For workers in a growing economy or those with special skills, earnings rise with age, so their final year salary will be much higher than their average. For them, a pension that pays 100 percent of their average lifetime wage will be a much smaller percentage of their final year wage. For example, if wages rise 2 percent a year for 40 years, the final year wage is nearly 50 percent greater than the average lifetime wage. This means that a pension offering 100 percent of a net average lifetime wage would pay only 70 percent of the net final year wage (issue brief table 1.1, column 1).

The distinction between net and gross earnings introduces another complication. Because people need to put aside some part of their earnings in savings or payroll taxes for their old age, gross earnings exceed net. If the saving or contribution rate is 22.5 percent, for example, a pension that is 100 percent of the net average lifetime wage would constitute 77.5 percent of the gross average lifetime wage.

Three conclusions emerge from an examination of these relationships:

- The "right" target replacement rate varies greatly, depending on the circumstances and preferences of each household and the rate of economic growth.
- Depending on the wage base, the same pension yields different wage replacement rates.
- The replacement rates suggested in issue brief table 1.1 are probably reasonable targets for many households: about 75 percent of gross average lifetime salary or half of gross final year salary. This pension target would allow a comfortable standard of living for a high-wage household but would be near subsistence for a low-wage household.

Issue Brief Table 1.1 Target Wage Replacement Rates

Pension as percentage of	Household target	Mandatory target		
		Low-income	Middle-income	High-income
Net average lifetime wage	100	81	78	78
Gross average lifetime wage	78	63	60	60
Net final year wage	70	55	53	53
Gross final year wage	54	44	42	42
Gross economy-wide wage	n.a.	33	42	42

n.a. Not applicable.

Note: The table is based on the following assumptions:
• The household target pension is 100 percent of the net average lifetime wage.
• The mandatory target pension is 60 percent of gross average lifetime earnings, with a floor at 33 percent of the economy-wide wage. The floor takes hold for low-income groups.
 • Everyone begins work at age 20, retires at 60, dies at 80, and there are equal numbers of poor, middle-income, and rich workers.
 • Starting wage is 33 percent higher for middle class and 67 percent higher for rich than for poor.
 • Annual wage growth is 2 percent.
 • A saving or contribution rate of 22.5 percent is assumed in net-to-gross calculations.
 • In economy-wide average calculations, the population is split between low-, middle-, and high-income groups in the ratio 3:2:1.
Source: World Bank calculations.

Mandatory Wage Replacement Targets

The government should not necessarily mandate the full pension that might be desirable for individual households. Because people have different preferences about relative consumption in youth and old age, a government can actually reduce some people's welfare by setting mandatory saving or contribution rates higher than they desire. Some analysts argue that the government should mandate pensions only to meet basic needs so that individuals with a low propensity to save do not become a burden on society. Setting a low mandatory pension allows people who want more to supplement it voluntarily—and minimizes evasion as well as capital and labor market distortions caused by mandatory pension programs. Other analysts argue that the mandatory level should exceed basic needs, to remedy insurance market failures by requiring everyone to participate in the annuity pool.

For example, the government might require saving or contributions that would replace about 60 percent of the worker's gross average lifetime wage, with a floor at about a third of the gross economy-wide average wage (issue brief table 1.1, columns 2–4). Some OECD countries have wage replacement rates of this magnitude. The mandatory plans could be publicly or privately managed, although the floor might require public transfers. The floor alone would come close to the household replacement target for many low-income workers. The mandatory pension could be supplemented by voluntary arrangements for many middle- and high-income workers who have higher household targets.

Issue Brief 2 Pay-as-You-Go or Fully Funded—Which Costs Less?

A SENSE OF THE RELATIVE COST OF PAY-AS-you-go and fully funded financing of defined benefit systems can be obtained by considering the hypothetical case of a system that aims to provide retired workers with 40 percent of their final year's gross salary. Pensions are assumed to be indexed to wages, rising automatically with the average wage in the economy. This discussion ignores the feedback effects on wage growth of pay-as-you-go compared with full funding. Wages are assumed to be unaffected by the choice of pension financing methods.

The Pay-as-You-Go Contribution Rate

The following equation shows the case of the hypothetical pension under pay-as-you-go financing, when pensions are indexed to wages and financed by a payroll tax:

$$(2.1) \qquad C = BD$$

where B is the target benefit rate, fixed as a percentage of the average wage; D is the system dependency rate (the ratio of beneficiaries to contributing workers); and C is the contribution rate, as a percentage of wages necessary to cover BD.

The Fully Funded Contribution Rate

Relationships are more complex with fully funded plans. Workers must accumulate enough capital during their working years to pay the targeted flow of pensions during their retirement years. Thus a worker contributes CW in the initial year, where W is the starting wage. But in subsequent years wages and contributions grow at the rate of $1+ g$ each year, and the capital accumulated in prior years grows at the rate of $1+ r$ each year, where g is the growth rate of wages and r is the interest rate. By the year of retirement the capital accumulation for an average worker is:

$$(2.2) \qquad CW[(1 + r)^n + (1 + g)(1 + r)^{n-1} + \dots (1 + g)^{n-1}(1 + r)].$$

If pensions are indexed to wages at a benefit rate of B, the present value of pension payouts over m retirement years, discounted back to the beginning of the year of retirement, is:

$$(2.3) \qquad BW(1 + g)^n[1 + (1 + g)/(1 + r) + \dots (1 + g)^{m-1}/(1 + r)^{m-1}]$$

where n is the number of working years and m/n is the passivity ratio; g, r, n, and m are assumed to be constant over time.

If the interest rate, r, equals the growth rate of wages, g, expressions 2.2 and 2.3 can be simplified to expressions 2.4 and 2.5, respectively:

$$(2.4) \qquad CW(1 + g)^n n$$

and

$$(2.5) \qquad BW(1 + g)^n m.$$

Under fully funded plans, capital accumulation at retirement must equal the present value of the stream of pension payments after retirement. So, expression 2.2 must equal expression 2.3, and if the interest rate equals the rate of wage growth, expression 2.4 must equal expression 2.5. The required contribution rate is then:

$$(2.6) \qquad C = B(m/n).$$

If the interest rate is lower than the rate of wage growth $(r<g)$, the required contribution rate is higher than $B(m/n)$, and vice versa.

Comparing Contribution Rates

When *B* is fixed at 40 percent and pensions are indexed to wages, the required contribution rate depends on assumptions about the dependency ratio, the passivity ratio, the interest rate, and the rate of wage growth (see table 1). The required contribution rate under pay-as-you-go financing depends only on the old age dependency ratio. The higher the dependency ratio, the more retirees there are relative to workers and the higher the contribution rate required to support them.

Example: A dependency ratio of one retiree for every two workers requires a payroll tax rate of 20

percent. Dropping this ratio to one for three reduces the tax rate to 13.3 percent. As real wages rise, so does the real pension, but the ratio between the two remains constant, so the contribution rate is unchanged (issue brief table 2.1, columns 1 and 2).

Under full funding the required contribution rate depends on two other factors: the passivity ratio and the difference between the real interest rate and the growth rate of real wages. A lower passivity ratio means that workers spend a smaller proportion of their adult lives in retirement, which reduces the required contribution rate. The contribution rate also drops if the interest rate exceeds the rate of wage

Issue Brief Table 2.1 Contribution Rate Needed to Pay a Pension Equal to 40 Percent of Final Year Salary
(indexed to wages)

	Pay-as-you-go (dependency rate)		Fully funded (passivity rate)					
	1/2	1/3	1/2			1/3		
Real wage growth	—	—	0	2	5	0	2	5
Real interest rate								
0	20	13	20	35	77	13	23	49
2	20	13	11	20	46	7	13	30
5	20	13	4	8	20	3	5	13
Real pension rate at death[a]	—	—	40	60	106	40	54	83
Relative pension rate at death[b]	40	40	40	40	40	40	40	40

—Not available.

Note: Real wage growth is assumed to apply equally to each cohort, and the average wage for the retiring cohort is the same as the average wage for the economy as a whole. Under pay-as-you-go numbers apply to the average wage worker, whose pension upon retirement is 40 percent of his final wage. Under fully funded each worker gets 40 percent of his own final salary at the start. Plan expenses and disability and survivors' benefits are not included. These would raise the required contribution rate about 3 to 5 percentage points in a well-run mature system. Costs due to unemployment and evasion are also not included. The one-half passivity rate stems from an assumption of forty working years and twenty years of retirement; the one-third passivity rate implies forty-five working years and fifteen years of retirement.

a. Real pension in year of death as proportion of final year's salary. For pay-as-you-go, it depends on wage growth in the economy.

b. Pension relative to average wage in the economy in year of death.

Source: Schwarz (1992a); Vittas (1993b).

growth. But if wages grow faster than interest rates, the required contribution rate rises. Accumulated pension assets are not increasing as fast as earnings, thus forcing workers to save more to meet the 40 percent benefit rate.

Example: If the real interest rate equals the rate of wage growth and the passivity ratio is one to two, the required contribution rate is 20 percent; lowering the passivity ratio to one to three reduces the rate to 13.3 percent (issue brief table 2.1, columns 3 through 8).

Several conclusions follow:

- When the dependency ratio equals the passivity ratio and the interest rate equals the rate of wage growth, pay-as-you-go and fully funded schemes require the same contribution rate.
- When the interest rate exceeds the rate of wage growth, fully funded plans have a cost advantage over pay-as-you-go plans, which do not benefit from the high interest rate. The opposite is true when the rate of wage growth exceeds the interest rate.
- When the dependency ratio is smaller than the passivity ratio, pay-as-you-go plans require a lower contribution rate than fully funded plans (and vice versa) if interest and wage growth rates are equal. In general, if the population covered by the system is growing, there are more people for each "young" age group than for each "old" age group, so the dependency ratio is smaller than the passivity ratio.

Under a set of simplifying assumptions, such as zero transaction costs and zero feedback effects on wage growth, these comparisons may be summed up as follows:

- Full funding costs less than pay-as-you-go (or yields a higher rate of return) if the interest rate is higher than the rate of wage growth plus the rate of population growth. If the interest rate is lower than wage growth plus population growth, the cost advantage lies with pay-as-you-go.

Which Set of Conditions Is More Likely?

If an economy is dynamically efficient, the interest rate should be at least as high as the rate of growth of GDP or total earnings (which include growth in wages per worker and growth in the labor force). Full funding in this case would be at least as cost-effective as pay-as-you-go—and possibly more. Real world data confirm this expectation of the cost advantage of full funding over long periods for several countries.

Earnings growth and the interest rate. Although the relation between earnings growth and the interest rate varies over time and by country, the rate of return to long-term capital, especially equity capital, has been considerably higher than the rate of wage growth over the last three decades—indeed over the last 100 years (Maddison 1987; Siegel 1992). While the variation among countries is wide, the unweighted average growth rate of wages for all countries between 1962 and 1990 was less than 2 percent. In some African and Latin American countries the rate was negative for much of this period. Real wages in most OECD countries rose 3 to 4 percent a year during the 1960s but slowed to about 1 percent during the 1980s. In all these regions the rate of return to investment, proxied by the return to human capital, was much higher (issue brief table 2.2).

In OECD countries the real interest rate on government bonds was slightly below the growth rate of wages during 1971–90 (the exact relationship varies by country). But a portfolio with half stocks and half bonds would have yielded a rate of return ranging

Issue Brief Table 2.2 Real Earnings Growth versus Returns to Human Capital

	Real earnings growth[a]	*Social returns to education investment*		*Private returns to education investment*		*Rate of return per year of education*
		Secondary	*Higher*	*Secondary*	*Higher*	
Sub-Saharan Africa	-1.4	18.2	11.2	26.6	27.8	13.4
Asia	2.4	13.3	11.7	18.9	19.9	9.6
Eastern Europe, North Africa, and the Middle East	2.6	11.2	10.6	15.9	21.7	8.2
Latin America and the Caribbean	-1.1	12.8	12.3	16.8	19.7	12.4
OECD	2.5	10.2	8.7	12.4	12.3	6.8
World	1.5	13.1	10.9	18.1	20.3	10.1

a. Compound real growth in wages for countries with data for at least ten years.
Source: Earnings growth rates calculated using UNIDO data base; data for Latin America and Sub-Saharan Africa come from Mazumdar (1994). Returns to investment in education from Psacharopoulos and others (1993); average of real earnings growth for OECD includes all the countries except Belgium, France, Germany, Greece, Iceland, the Netherlands, and Switzerland. For Asia it includes Bangladesh, Fiji, the Republic of Korea, Malaysia, Nepal, Pakistan, the Philippines, Singapore, Sri Lanka, and Thailand. For Eastern Europe, North Africa, and the Middle East it includes Afghanistan, Algeria, Cyprus, the Czech Republic, Egypt, Hungary, Iran, Iraq, Israel, Jordan, Kuwait, Lybia, Malta, Morocco, Tunisia, and the Federal Republic of Yugoslavia. Latin America includes Argentina, Chile, Colombia, Costa Rica, the Dominican Republic, El Salvador, Guatemala, Honduras, Mexico, Panama, and Peru. Sub-Saharan Africa includes Botswana, Burundi, Egypt, The Gambia, Ghana, Kenya, Malawi, Mauritius, Sierra Leone, Swaziland, and Zimbabwe.

from 3 to 6 percent, about 3 percentage points higher than wage growth (issue brief table 2.3). From the very long-term (100-year) perspective most relevant to pension plans, labor productivity in the United Kingdom and the United States appears to have grown about 2 to 3 percent a year. Again, this was about the same as the real interest rate on bonds but much less than a portfolio equally divided between stocks and bonds (Maddison 1987; Siegel 1992). Data for selected developing countries (those with emerging stock markets during the 1970s and 1980s) show that rates of return to equities and education—which ranged from 6 to 42 percent—were much higher than the growth rate in earnings, which ranged from -4 to 8 percent (issue brief table 2.4). The high returns to capital reflect its scarcity and risk and the selectivity of the sample; it is likely

that stock markets will emerge in countries with favorable investment prospects. (For further data on wage growth over time see appendix table A.3.)

The fact that capital has become far more mobile than labor (except where there are government restrictions) further boosts the expected returns to capital and the potential cost advantage of fully funded pension plans. Full funding permits international diversification of investments, which allows pensioners in slow-growth countries to benefit from the higher yields in high-growth countries. This comparison suggests that full funding has a strong cost advantage over pay-as-you-go.

The dependency ratio and the passivity ratio. In previous decades, the potential cost advantage of full funding was offset by the fact that the world's population was growing so rapidly that the dependency

Issue Brief Table 2.3 Real Wage Growth Contrasted with Real Returns on Capital, Selected OECD Countries, 1971–90

(percent)

Country	Real wage growth	Real average annual return on equities	Real average annual return on government bonds	Real average annual return on balanced portfolio[a]	Returns on 50–50 portfolio minus real wage growth
Canada	1.1	5.0	1.1	3.1	2.0
Denmark	2.5	9.4	4.5	7.0	4.5
France	4.0	9.6	1.3	5.5	1.5
Germany	3.6	9.3	2.6	6.0	2.4
Japan	3.0	11.2	0.0	5.6	2.6
Netherlands	1.4	8.6	1.8	5.2	3.8
Switzerland	1.8	4.7	-1.7	1.5	-0.3
United Kingdom	2.4	10.8	1.6	6.2	3.8
United States	0.1	5.9	1.2	3.6	3.5

Note: The numbers shown are simple annual averages.

a. Balanced portfolio consists of 50 percent government bonds and 50 percent equities.

Source: Real earnings growth in France from IMF *International Financial Statistics* (various years), other data from Davis (1993).

Issue Brief Table 2.4 Rates of Return to Labor, Human, and Nonhuman Capital

Economy	Real return to equities [a]	Rates of return per year of education	Real wage growth[b]
Argentina	20.5 (1975–92)	10.3	1.9 (1963–88)
Chile	26.4 (1975–92)	12.0	6.6 (1963–88)
Colombia	41.5 (1984–92)	14.0	1.0 (1963–88)
India	11.5 (1975–92)	4.9	3.0 (1980–89)
Korea, Rep. of	11.2 (1975–92)	10.6	7.8 (1966–88)
Malaysia	6.7 (1984–92)	9.4	2.5 (1968–88)
Mexico	14.5 (1975–92)	14.1	–3.9 (1980–89)
Pakistan	16.4 (1984–92)	9.7	3.8 (1963–86)
Philippines	40.6 (1984–92)	8.0	0.4 (1963–88)
Taiwan (China)	17.9 (1984–92)	6.0	—
Thailand	14.1 (1975–92)	10.4	3.4 (1970–86)
Venezuela	18.5 (1984–92)	8.4	–0.8 (1963–88)
Unweighted average	**20.0**	**9.8**	**2.3**

— Not available.

a. Total returns are given in real U.S. dollars. Years are given in parentheses.

b. Geometric mean.

Source: Stock market data from IFC files, based on returns for years since 1975. Rates of return per year of education, or Mincerian rates of return, from Psacharopolous (1993). Real wage growth from UNIDO data base and World Bank (1992d).

ratio was likely to be smaller than the passivity ratio in many countries. Dubbed the "biological rate of interest," population growth was used in the 1950s to justify the expansion of pay-as-you-go systems in industrial countries. An implicit assumption was that rapid population growth and pay-as-you-go would not depress earnings. Yet, as noted above, wage growth slowed precipitously in OECD countries throughout the 1970s and 1980s, as the baby boom generation entered the labor force. In Africa, where population was growing most rapidly, wage growth turned negative.

In recent years demographic conditions have become less favorable to pay-as-you-go. Today OECD countries barely attain the population replacement rate, and East Asia, Eastern Europe, and parts of Latin America are moving rapidly in the same direction. The demographic dependency ratio is fast approaching the passivity ratio. In addition, because pay-as-you-go plans break the link between benefits and contributions, they may induce evasion, early retirement, or other types of strategic manipulation—problems that push the system dependency ratio above the demographic dependency ratio in many countries (see chapter 4). It is quite likely, therefore, that in middle- and high-income countries the system dependency ratio will be at least as great as the

passivity ratio in coming decades. Thus, the influence of the higher return to capital, reflecting its productivity, should dominate.

And the Winner Is...

It is possible, of course, that falling birthrates could mean scarcer labor and higher wages. It is also possible that if many countries adopted funded pension plans, savings would increase and interest rates would fall. Both developments would be favorable to pay-as-you-go financing. But in a world of international flows of capital and goods, this outcome is unlikely to occur before most countries have stable populations and funded pension plans—and even then these price changes are far from certain.

In sum, any cost advantage that pay-as-you-go plans might have had in the past was the result of demographic factors that no longer hold in many countries. In the future, if interest rates and earnings growth maintain their relative positions, and especially if pension funds are able to benefit from equity investments, capital mobility, and international diversification, a fully funded system will require lower contribution rates than a pay-as-you-go system to achieve the same pension benefits.

Issue Brief 3 Pay-as-You-Go under the Demographic Transition

AS INCOME RISES, FAMILIES TEND TO HAVE fewer children and people tend to live longer. Together, these forces have raised the old age dependency ratio in many countries. This demographic transition is already well under way in OECD countries, and support ratios—the inverse of the dependency ratio—are expected to plummet in much of Latin America, Central Asia, Eastern Europe, and China over the next two decades. By the year 2050 only Africa will still be "young."

As the resources of fewer workers are stretched to support a larger old population, pay-as-you-go schemes will inevitably yield rapidly diminishing payoffs to future generations, unless productivity rises fast enough to offset the effects of demography. Projected demographic profiles for Argentina, China, Hungary, Japan, and Kenya illustrate the increasing costs and decreasing returns to younger cohorts under pay-as-you-go pension plans, with populations aging between now and 2075 (issue brief table 3.1).

Japan's population is younger than those in most OECD countries today, but it will age rapidly. Although its population is still growing slightly, growth will turn negative after 2005. Hungary, a typical Eastern European country, has a population that is already old and shrinking, though the decline will be more gradual than in Japan. The number of people in Argentina, as in many other Latin American countries, is expected to increase for the next century, though at a declining rate. Argentina's old age dependency rate will thus increase less dramatically than Hungary's or Japan's. China now has a younger population than the others, but the old age dependency ratio will increase precipitously when the large working age population retires and is replaced by much smaller cohorts of younger workers. Kenya starts out young, with a rapidly growing population, and remains young until after 2030, when today's children will be bearing children and when its demographic transition is projected to begin.

For each country the projections show the contribution rate required to finance a 40 percent average benefit rate (that is, the average benefit divided by the average wage) and the lifetime transfer that this type of pension system implies for a program begin-

Issue Brief Table 3.1 Simulated Pension Schemes under Different Demographic Scenarios

Year	Argentina	China	Hungary	Japan	Kenya
	Old age dependency rate				
1995	0.27	0.16	0.37	0.36	0.12
2025	0.29	0.34	0.53	0.68	0.10
2050	0.43	0.53	0.61	0.79	0.21
2075	0.48	0.60	0.61	0.68	0.44
	Income transfers resulting from pension system				
1995	13.5	13.5	13.5	13.5	13.5
2005	10.9	11.8	9.8	9.7	12.4
2015	8.3	9.7	5.6	4.5	11.5
2025	5.5	7.0	0.4	-2.0	10.6
2035	2.6	3.1	-5.0	-9.0	9.5
2045	1.7	0.3	-6.9	-12.6	9.1
2055	0.1	-2.9	-8.7	-15.1	8.0
2065	-1.5	-5.7	-9.6	-16.2	6.2
2075	-3.2	-7.6	-10.4	-16.4	3.6

Note: This table is based on the following assumptions:
• Pension system begins in 1995 and coverage is 100 percent immediately. Individuals all begin work at age 20 and retire at age 60.
• Age-earnings growth of 1 percent is assumed over the career of each worker.
• Economy-wide real wage growth of 1 percent per year.
• The discount rate for calculating present value is assumed to be a real 2 percent.
• Evasion, unemployment, early retirement, and administrative expenses are assumed to be zero.
Source: Schwarz (1994).

ning in 1995. Everyone is assumed to start work at age 20 and retire at age 60. Everyone over 60 receives the same pension—including, at the beginning, those who never contributed. The real average wage in the economy is assumed to rise 1 percent each year, and wages also grow 1 percent for every year of experience. Pensions are indexed to the economy-wide average wage.

In all five countries the dependency ratio rises throughout the life span of the individuals born in 1995, when the plan is implemented. This effect is greatest in China, where the old age dependency rate nearly quadruples. In all five countries the result is a sharp rise in contribution rates of later generations, if

the benefit rate is held constant at 40 percent (issue brief figure 3.1). To maintain a constant 40 percent benefit rate over this period, the contribution rate would have to double in most countries and more than triple in China. If evasion, administrative expenses, unemployment, disability, survivors' benefits, and early retirement are also taken into account, the required contribution rate would exceed 35 percent when today's children have retired. This high contribution rate, in addition to the income tax rate, increases the probability that people will evade and retire early, making the situation worse.

The first few generations—the grandparents and parents in 1995—experience large and positive gains

Issue Brief Figure 3.1 Contribution Rates Required to Maintain Pension System Solvency for a 40 Percent Average Benefit Rate

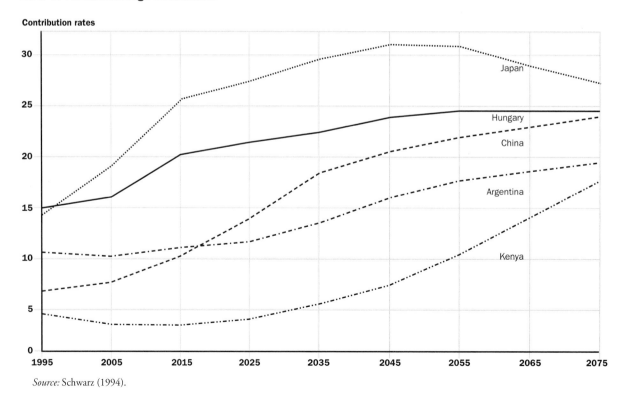

Source: Schwarz (1994).

(net present value of pension benefits received by each generation minus the net present value of its contribution stream divided by the net present value of its lifetime earnings, assuming a 2 percent discount rate). This happens because older cohorts contributed for only part of their working lives but receive full pensions, and because they have many young workers to support them. But in Hungary and Japan the net gain turns negative for cohorts who retire in 2035 and 2025, respectively. In China, children who are born in 1995, the year the program is put in place, and retire in 2055 lose lifetime income. If the discount rate is higher than 2 percent—which seems plausible—the negative transfer would be greater and would start sooner. These cohorts will never recoup in pensions the present value of the taxes they paid to support the pensions of their parents and grandparents. Evidence from OECD coun-

tries, where populations are already aging, is consistent with this pattern of rising tax rates, lower benefit rates, and intergenerational redistributions. Since their systems began many years ago, they are already well along in this process of high tax rates and low returns.

While variables such as retirement age, contribution rate, and expected longevity can change, the underlying pattern remains. When less predictable perturbations—natural disasters, famines, epidemics, immigration, and wars—are superimposed on this pattern, some cohorts fare better and others fare worse than the projections here show. But the trend toward higher old age dependency rates is inevitable, as are higher required contribution rates or lower pension rates and the redistribution from younger to older cohorts for the next fifty years or more, under pay-as-you-go.

Issue Brief 4 Impact of Pension Financing on Saving

THE IMPACT OF PENSION FINANCING—PAY-as-you-go or full funding—on saving has been a subject of considerable controversy on both theoretical and empirical grounds. Most analyses start with the life cycle theory: people want to maintain a roughly constant level of consumption throughout their lives. To achieve that, they save part of their income during their working years—to spend (dissave) when they are too old to work. This motive is considered to be a major source of long-term saving in the economy.

Introducing Pay-as-You-Go Funding

Now suppose the government introduces a mandatory pay-as-you-go old age security plan that requires young people to contribute payroll taxes (equivalent to their previous saving) to the plan and pays them a pension (equivalent to their previous dissaving) later on. Introducing the system reduces national saving initially, because the first group to benefit from the program—generally those who were 50 to 65 years old when the plan was introduced—receives a windfall gain. Those who qualify get a pension for which they had neither planned nor paid. The pension is financed by the reduced saving of the younger generation, who now pay the payroll tax instead of saving. Because the increased consumption by the first generation of pensioners is not offset by reduced consumption of the younger generation, fewer resources are left to be saved and invested during the initial period, permanently reducing capital stock and national income.

This effect is even worse if the younger generations of workers—30 to 50 years old when the new pension is introduced—receive pensions that exceed their contributions, as has occurred in many coun-

tries. If they anticipate this transfer, they might try to borrow against their future pensions to consume more when they are young, further reducing national saving. If the country has deliberately chosen to improve the income of these groups, national welfare improves, but the price is lower saving and growth for future generations.

Despite the logic of this argument, numerous empirical investigations (most of them based on U.S. data) have been unable to prove conclusively that saving did, indeed, drop once pay-as-you-go programs were established. Part of the ambiguity results from the inability to estimate accurately what people would have saved if social security had not been introduced. After all, many other things were changing at the same time. Using the same data, some studies of the U.S. situation conclude that social security substantially reduced private saving, whereas others find no significant impact. Analyses of saving rates in other countries yield similar conflicting results. Studies of the saving impact of old age security programs in Canada, France, the Federal Republic of Germany, Japan, Sweden, and the United Kingdom found no significant impact, except for a slightly positive aggregate effect in Sweden, where the pension program is heavily funded. Why don't the facts seem to fit the theory? Several possibilities:

- Some young people may be shortsighted or may not have had access to reliable savings instruments, and therefore may not have been saving adequately for their old age before the pay-as-you-go program was introduced. If the payroll tax exceeds their previous saving, young people have to cut their current consumption to pay the tax, which mitigates the program's negative effect on saving—and implies that a pay-as-you-go scheme permanently shifts people's consumption from youth to old age.

- Even if young people were not saving, they might have accumulated some assets that they could dissave, or they might borrow against their future pension income. This would cause the negative saving effect to reappear. But imperfect capital markets, including restrictions on consumer credit, make this response difficult or impossible in many places, especially in developing countries. The intertemporal shift in consumption and the attenuation of the negative effect on saving thus remain.

- The first cohorts of pensioners may not be able to adjust their spending habits fast enough, or they may not want to—so they may save part of their windfall gain, perhaps to leave larger bequests to their children. The bequest motive may increase if people foresee the higher taxes that their children eventually must pay to finance the new pension plan.

- Children may cut down on private transfers to their parents, who would now receive an unexpected public pension. If private intergenerational transfers adjust to offset the public transfers, the program will have no impact on saving. But it will also have no impact on the consumption or welfare of the old or the young, making the program superfluous.

- People may have little faith in the new pension scheme or its ability to keep up with inflation, so they may continue to save for retirement just as they did before. This response may be particularly evident among upper-income workers (who do most of the saving), especially if they expect the system to pay pensions mainly to the poor.

- Design features of old age security programs could lead workers to retire earlier than they

would otherwise (considerable empirical evidence supports this view). They might then boost their saving rate to finance a longer expected retirement, offsetting any decline in saving.

All these forces reduce the negative effect on saving of pay-as-you-go old age security plans. The net impact is understandably difficult to detect in empirical studies.

Introducing Full or Partial Funding

Suppose, instead, that the government introduces a fully funded scheme that requires people to save a specified amount. If people were previously saving this amount voluntarily, they would simply substitute the compulsory pension saving for their voluntary saving, and net national saving would remain unchanged. (This also means that the pension plan has not achieved its objective of increasing income and consumption in old age.) *But the same forces that reduced the negative effect of pay-as-you-go financing on saving intensify the positive effect of full funding.*

- If people are shortsighted, they probably were not saving much before, and if financial instruments were lacking, people have no accumulated assets to dissave. So some of the required pension saving must come from reduced consumption, particularly by young people and poor people. Shortsighted people may be tempted to borrow against their future funded pensions, but limited access to credit markets reduces this possibility, especially in developing countries.

- Raised awareness of the importance of saving, decisions to retire early, and the lack of credibility of pension schemes all lead people to continue to save in addition to their mandatory pension saving, increasing overall national saving. This saving is committed for the long term—potentially the most productive kind of saving.

If many of these forces apply, full funding increases saving. If they are absent, pay-as-you-go will decrease saving. This means that *although a mandatory pay-as-you-go pension scheme may have an ambiguous effect on saving (relative to the voluntary situation), its effect should clearly be negative compared with a mandatory fully funded scheme.* The higher the contribution rate, the greater the positive effect on saving of a fully funded scheme.

Few empirical studies have measured the impact of fully funded pension schemes on saving—and even fewer have tested the effect of a switch from pay-as-you-go to fully funded, because until 1994 only Chile had made that switch. For funded occupational plans in the United States only 60 percent of pension saving is offset by reductions in household saving, so the net effect is positive (Munnell and Yohn 1992; Pesando 1991). In Australia a 50 percent crowd-out effect is expected under the new funded mandatory occupational scheme. Private saving would then rise by 0.8 percent of GDP a year, once it has been phased in, while the public pension scheme is expected to decrease saving 0.5 percent of GDP over the same period (Bateman and Piggott 1992b, 1993). Malaysia and Singapore, which have large mandatory retirement saving programs, have high national saving rates. When Chile switched its mandatory plan from pay-as-you-go to fully funded, private saving rose substantially, by much more than the government dissaving needed to pay off the old social security debt. But numerous other forces were also at work in this period of rapid economic growth.

Many analysts argue that saving is below optimum in most countries and, probably, worldwide, because capital is mobile. Having a favorable effect on capital accumulation would thus be an attractive feature of fully funded schemes. But if the policy goal is to increase saving, pension policy needs to be accompanied by other measures—for example, keeping inflation under control, increasing the availability of safe instruments for saving, discouraging consumer borrowing, and possibly providing tax incentives to long-term savings, such as taxing real rather than nominal returns.

Impact on Public Saving and Capital Allocation

Old age security schemes may have their strongest impact by changing the spending and saving behavior of governments. For example, the negative effect of pay-as-you-go schemes on saving could be offset if governments increased public saving by running budget surpluses. But the opposite has occurred more often, especially in developing countries: governments have run deficits to meet generous pension benefit promises. That causes national saving to fall, even if household saving is unchanged.

Also troublesome are the partially or fully funded plans controlled by governments. Typically, the law requires these funds to be invested in public bonds, which yield low or even negative real returns (see box 4.3). If access to these funds increases public consumption and deficits, this can more than offset any increased household saving, causing national saving to fall. Even privately managed pension reserves can be regulated in ways that give government privileged access and thus run the danger of increasing government spending and dissaving.

The policy conclusion: *Funded plans have the potential to increase household saving and productive capital formation, whereas pay-as-you-go plans do not. But this potential may not be realized unless pension funds are insulated from government control and their resources are channeled through the capital market, on a competitive basis, with incentives for productive investment.*

For more information on the impact of pensions on saving and capital markets, see the For Further Reading section.

Issue Brief 5 Comparing Administrative Expenses of Alternative Pension Schemes

THE EFFICACY OF A PENSION SCHEME DE-pends greatly on its administrative costs. Other things constant, high costs mean lower benefits in retirement or higher contributions during working years. This is true for any pension scheme, whether managed publicly or privately, and whether funded or pay-as-you-go. But some managerial and financing arrangements may incur higher costs than others.

Publicly Managed or Privately Managed

It is not always easy to measure administrative costs. Privately managed companies have an incentive to keep track of costs. But publicly managed programs may omit some inputs and may receive others at below-market rates. The pension agency may not pay rent for its premises and may purchase its mail and telephone services at subsidized rates. Depreciation and fringe benefits often do not appear on the agency's budget. The costs of collecting the payroll tax may be passed on to another agency. Private pension plans charge a risk premium for the longevity, inflation, and interest rate risk they assume. Public pension plans do not charge this risk premium explicitly but instead pass it along to the rest of society, implicitly. For all these reasons, publicly managed old age programs may appear much cheaper than they are, relative to privately managed plans.

Most private schemes accumulate pension reserves that they invest, usually in a combination of public and private, debt and equity securities—a process that raises their administrative costs. Most public plans do not have large pension reserves, and even if they do they do not carry out the same function of evaluating alternative investments, because they invest primarily in government bonds. Further-more, to attract savings, the private sector incurs marketing costs. But balanced against these higher costs is the incentive of private pension funds to behave efficiently, and to perform a capital allocation function that would otherwise have to be performed elsewhere in the economy. For all these reasons, it is difficult to compare the costs of publicly and privately managed pension plans, and few such studies have been conducted.

Comparing Publicly Managed Plans

It is somewhat easier, but still problematic, to compare the costs of different publicly managed pay-as-you-go plans. Two frequently cited measures are biased against developing countries with immature systems. The first is the ratio of administrative costs to benefit expenditures in a given year, a measure extremely sensitive to the maturity of the scheme and to demographic changes. In Belize, a young country with an immature pension scheme, the ratio of costs to benefit expenditures in the late 1980s was more than 50 percent, because few workers had been in the system long enough to qualify for pensions.

The second indicator used is the ratio of administrative costs to contributions. One obvious problem with this indicator is that contribution revenues will be higher, making the expense ratio appear lower, in countries with higher contribution rates. Because these countries typically have more mature schemes and older populations, this measure is also biased against pension schemes in developing countries.

A better way to compare administrative costs across publicly managed pay-as-you-go plans is to calculate the cost per participant (worker plus pensioner) in the program. The most important functions for these plans are collecting contributions and paying benefits, so the number of participants should determine efficient costs.

Administrative Costs Normalized by Per Capita Income

For some purposes it is useful to normalize the administrative cost by the average wage or income per capita—that is, to examine the ratio of administrative cost per participant to income per capita across countries. The average wage or income per capita indicates the capacity of the country to pay for old age pensions and their administrative costs, once the dependency rate is given. The higher the administrative cost per participant, the less funds will be available to pay the beneficiaries. If unskilled labor is the predominant administrative input into pension plans, one might expect this ratio (of administrative cost per participant to income per capita) to be negatively related to per capita income, because poor countries have plentiful unskilled labor and low wages. But if skilled labor and capital inputs predominate, one would expect this ratio to be positively related to per capita income.

Examination of the data show the latter to be the case (issue brief figure 5.1). Apparently, educated labor, computers, communications infrastructure, and other capital intensive inputs are important elements in the pension production function, so the administrative cost per participant relative to per capita income is much higher in low-income countries, where these inputs are scarce and expensive. This number is sixty-five times higher in Zambia than in the United States; it is eighty-four times higher in Burundi than in Switzerland. Further analysis indicates that administrative costs fall as the

Issue Brief Figure 5.1 Administrative Costs of Publicly Managed Pension Plans in Selected Countries

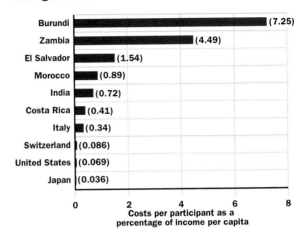

Note: Data are for years ranging from 1988 to 1992.
Source: James and Palacios (1994a).

number of participants increase, for both public and private plans, suggesting significant economies of scale (issue brief figure 5.2).

If this is the case, low-income countries, especially small ones, should think twice before they establish complex formal systems of old age security. Industrial countries started their present systems at much higher levels of per capita income, education, and infrastructure than many developing countries today. If low-income countries initiate formal old age systems, they should keep the record-keeping and other administrative demands simple and should concentrate them in urban areas and in large firms, where transaction costs will be low.

For further reading see Valdes-Prieto (1993); Sünden and Mitchell (1994); James and Palacios (1994a).

Issue Brief Figure 5.2 Administrative Costs as a Percentage of Assets, Private Plans in the United States and Chile

Administrative costs as a percentage of total assets

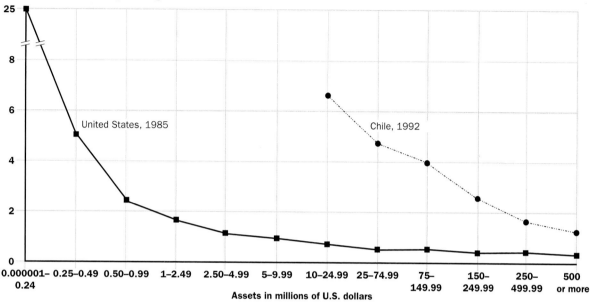

Note: This figure refers to occupational plans in the United States and AFPs in Chile.
Source: Turner and Beller (1989); Acuña and Iglesias (1992); Abuhadba (1994); Provida (1993).

Issue Brief 6   The Life Cycle of Pay-as-You-Go Public Pension Schemes

PAY-AS-YOU-GO SCHEMES HAVE A TYPICAL life cycle—with its stages defined by the old age dependency ratio and the system dependency ratio. These ratios, in turn, strongly influence the required contribution rate, pension expenditures, and the current surplus or deficit. The life cycle may be divided into three stages—the young, the expanding, and the mature. Issue brief table 6.1 provides fundamental data averaged across countries that fall into each of these categories.

Stage 1: Youth, Accumulation, Windfall Benefits, and Low Contribution Rates

The youngest countries are in stage 1 of the life cycle. These countries have more than fifteen people of working age for every old person, and their public pillars have an even higher ratio of contributors to pension recipients (system support ratio). Their schemes are immature (the coverage rate among old people is much less than the coverage rate among workers), and labor force coverage is sparse. Less than 1 percent of GDP is spent on pensions. Although contribution rates are low, the schemes run current surpluses that are large relative to their revenues.

Because the population is young and growing and the ratio of old people to workers is low, the government can make transfers to old people who have paid very little into the system. Rates of return to pensioners are far higher than rates they could receive for investments in the private market. These generous pension promises are easy to keep when few people qualify for benefits.

With low coverage rates and a low share of labor in GDP, the implicit social security debt is negligible. The high ratio of contributors to beneficiaries enables stage 1 schemes to accumulate large current surpluses to fund this debt. But these surpluses are usually invested in government bonds, which become a cheap source of public sector credit and are often decapitalized during inflationary periods. That happened in Germany in the 1920s and in Argentina, Brazil, Paraguay, and Uruguay in the 1950s.

Almost all countries in stage 1 today are in Africa, Latin America, and the Middle East.

Stage 2: Coverage Expansion and Rising Contribution Rates

The population is somewhat older at stage 2, but the ratio of workers to pensioners remains relatively

Issue Brief Table 6.1   The Life Cycle of Pay-as-You-Go

Stage	Support ratio	Pension expenditures/ GDP	Payroll tax rate	Labor force coverage	Surplus as share of revenues	Simulated social security debt/GDP [a]
1	17.5	0.6	8.0	15.7	47.1	5
2	11.8	3.3	13.7	45.4	34.9	40
3	5.3	8.5	24.6	89.4	−19.6	150

a. This is based on a simulation; the other numbers are actual averages.

high—eight to fourteen people of working age for every old person. The schemes are somewhat older, too, and cover more than one-third of the labor force. About 2 to 5 percent of GDP goes to pensions.

The first cohorts of workers from the "founding generation"—30 to 50 years old when the scheme was established—begin to collect pensions. Their rates of return are high, and the positive transfers they receive are larger than those of the first windfall generation, because they often qualify for full benefits but have not contributed for their full working lives. Though contribution rates rise and surpluses shrink or disappear, the schemes are extremely popular, because most members of the founding generation are big winners. Political pressure from older, influential citizens keeps benefits high and retirement ages low, threatening the long-run financial stability of the schemes.

This stage is often extended by expanding coverage to new groups of young workers, usually from lower-income groups. The expanded coverage improves the system's old age support ratio and keeps the promised benefits flowing. Newly covered workers are not resentful because they expect generous pensions themselves. But they may be disappointed. The growing social security debt—ranging from about a quarter to half of GDP—is a harbinger of the difficult times ahead.

Brazil and Turkey illustrate problems at this stage. Their schemes have high evasion rates because as tax rates rise many workers escape to the informal sector as soon as they qualify for benefits. The result is a ratio of contributors to pensioners far lower than would be expected for the age structure of the population—and a serious threat of bankruptcy.

Stage 3: System Maturity and the Collapse of the Pyramid Scheme

By this stage the old age security system has matured and is over 40 years old. Most workers are covered and eligible for full benefits. The population has aged—there are fewer than six people of working age for every old person, and the support ratio continues to fall. Many countries with mature schemes have experienced a leveling of growth—brought on, in part, by high payroll taxes and inadequate saving. Contribution rates average more than 20 percent, and pensions consume more than 8 percent of GDP. Most schemes run large current deficits. The accumulated social security liability, now 100 to 200 percent of GDP, signals that higher taxes and deficits are to come.

Some OECD and formerly socialist countries, such as the Netherlands and Romania, have loosened their eligibility criteria to absorb increasing numbers of unemployed workers. Increasing evasion in some countries means that there are fewer contributors for each of these new pensioners. Workers begin to suspect that they will not receive the high returns of previous generations.

Governments dip into general revenues to cover pension obligations, reducing spending on other public programs, such as education, that benefit the younger generation. Although at the beginning of stage 3 many countries still allow early retirement and easy eligibility conditions, in the end the share of GDP spent on pensions reaches double digits, benefits are cut, and eligibility conditions are tightened. Because many young people now become losers—getting much less from the system than they put in—political pressure builds for a major structural change. Change is resisted, however, by old and middle-aged people, who have built up substantial entitlements in the old system. Finding ways to pay off this debt, while shifting to a more decentralized funded pension scheme, becomes the challenge at the end of stage 3.

Issue brief figure 6.1 illustrates a typical life cycle of a public pay-as-you-go scheme, as it evolved in

Issue Brief Figure 6.1 Life Cycle of a Publicly Managed Pension Scheme, Chile, 1945–71

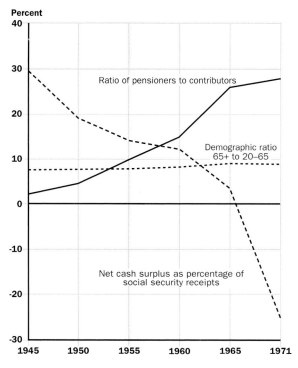

Source: Wallich (1982).

Chile, from stage 1 in the 1940s, stage 2 in the 1950s, and stage 3 in the 1960s—until the system collapsed in the 1970s. In 1981, Chile introduced a new mandatory funded privately managed pension plan, supplemented by a much smaller tax-financed public pillar.

What Young Countries Can Learn from Old Countries

More than half the world's people live in countries with young population profiles. Many of them, from China and India to the young republics of the former Soviet Union, to Africa and Central America, are considering major reforms of their pension systems. Knowing the hazards, young countries still have time to choose whether to follow in the footsteps of countries that long ago adopted defined benefit pay-as-you-go schemes. The experiences of the older countries suggest the following cautions:

- Pay-as-you-go schemes can obscure the real state of public finance when short-term surpluses provide a false sense of confidence and long-term pension liabilities are not explicitly recognized.
- The financial condition of a pay-as-you-go scheme always deteriorates as a country moves through the demographic transition and as the system matures—a point that will be reached much faster in developing countries than it was in OECD countries.
- Starting with limited coverage and gradually expanding it delay the reckoning, but this solution is regressive under a pay-as-you-go scheme, because the first workers covered tend to be higher-income workers whose generous returns are paid for by lower-income workers who enter late.
- The increased consumption afforded early generations of retirees may come at the expense of national saving and growth.
- Labor market distortions and incentives to evade increase as contribution rates rise in later stages.
- The demographic transition and system maturation make intergenerational transfers inevitable in a pay-as-you-go scheme.
- Pay-as-you-go schemes are easy to put together but difficult to take apart.

Issue Brief 7 Evasion

W HEN BENEFITS ARE NOT CLOSELY linked to contributions, people are likely to evade paying into mandatory pension schemes.

- Workers may be dissatisfied because their pensions will not increase commensurately with their contributions.
- They may value present consumption more than future pensions.
- They may believe they can get a better rate of return elsewhere.
- They may expect to die relatively early.

The incentives to evade are greater when the social security tax adds to an already burdensome tax and regulatory structure, when penalties or the probability of being penalized are low, and when there is a large informal sector where workers can disappear.

Escape to the Informal Sector

The informal sector is a refuge from the taxes and regulations of the formal economy—workers and entrepreneurs in the informal sector simply do not register in the formal system. The informal sector accounts for more than half the labor force in many developing countries (figure 4.4). The large size of the informal sector in developing countries makes evasion easier, which stimulates the sector's further growth.

In Caracas, Venezuela, social security payroll taxes represented more than one-third of the costs of becoming formal. Hernando de Soto's well-known study of the informal sector in Peru, *El Otro Sendero*, shows that entrepreneurs can be very sensitive to these costs. In Brazil, escape to the informal sector

and other forms of evasion increased as payroll tax rates rose during the economic downturn of the 1980s. A World Bank study (World Bank 1994a) found that because of the increased evasion, a 1 percentage point rise in the contribution rate led to a 2 percentage point drop in total receipts. Under Uruguay's mandatory pension scheme, labor force coverage fell 13 percent during the 1980s, as social security payroll taxes rose. Business managers in Uruguay cited social security taxes as a major impediment to expansion in the formal sector (World Bank 1994b).

Other Ways to Evade

Moving to the informal sector is not the only way to evade social security taxes. *Underreporting* earnings is another. Estimates for Uruguay in 1988 put unreported working hours at more than 30 percent of the total, and estimates put revenue losses at 3 percent of GDP. Managerial personnel in Brazil shift much of their compensation into *fringe benefits,* such as free housing and company cars, not counted by the social security system. Self-employed workers— doctors, lawyers, even taxi drivers—keep much of their earnings hidden from the authorities while contributing just enough to qualify for large pension benefits.

Simply *refusing to comply* is an approach used frequently in countries with low penalties and lax enforcement. In Brazil more than 50,000 registered firms have refused to pay into the pension scheme in recent years—cumulatively the equivalent of 5 percent of GDP or an entire year's worth of contributions. *Delaying contribution payments* can reduce the real value of the tax in an inflationary environment. In Venezuela the late payment penalty of 1 percent a month was lower than the inflation rate, running 5 percent a month at times during the 1980s. Brazilian employers also benefited from payment delays during periods of high inflation, because penalties were not fully indexed. The biggest arrears are due from the central government and other public agencies in many countries—including Brazil, Ecuador, and Venezuela. It is difficult to bring moral suasion to bear on the private sector when the government is defaulting on its social security contributions.

During the 1980s, rates of evasion and delayed payments soared to 60 percent in Brazil, 44 percent in Barbados and Jamaica, 35 percent in Venezuela, and 33 percent in Peru (Schulz 1992). High evasion rates are not unique to Latin America. Of a registered membership of 12.9 million in the Philippines's system in 1990, only 2.8 million workers were contributing to the national social insurance scheme. In Rwanda in the late 1980s, 15 percent of expected contributions were in arrears. Tunisia's main public pension scheme received only two-thirds of expected contributions in 1990 (Vittas 1993a). In Turkey only 1 percent of registered members contribute regularly to the Bag-Kur pension scheme for the self-employed (World Bank 1993d).

The transitional economies of Eastern Europe are also beginning to feel the impact of tax evasion on their social insurance schemes. When enterprises are financially pressed, they allow payroll tax arrears to mount, knowing that public tax administration has not kept pace with the growing private sector. Arrears in Estonia in 1992 were 29 percent of total social insurance revenues, and arrears in Hungary were more than 20 percent (Cavalcanti 1993; World Bank data).

What Evasion Does

When contribution rates prompt greater evasion, labor allocation decisions are distorted by workers moving to the informal sector or to other jobs to avoid paying social security taxes. Labor productivity suffers. Evasion also defeats the purpose of mandatory pension plans—to make sure that people have some source of support in their old age. When workers evade contributions but still qualify for benefits, the pension system runs into serious financial difficulties. Evasion rates as high as 50 percent in Argentina have driven the old age pension scheme deeply into deficit, adding to the burden on the general government budget and eventually leading to the adoption of a new system.

In the worst case, evasion can lead to the near collapse of the pension scheme. As confidence in the plan evaporates, more people try to evade contributions, increasing the financial strain. Drastic reforms may be required just to achieve a merely minimal level of credibility. Countries such as Argentina, Brazil, and Turkey now face this crisis of confidence, and the same vicious circle of loss of confidence and of increasing evasion is beginning to cripple pension finance in Eastern Europe.

What to Do

When escape to the large informal sector and other means of evasion are easy, it is more important than ever to keep payroll taxes low and link benefits closely to these taxes. One way to do that is to keep redistributive public pension programs modest, while supplementing them with large, mandatory retirement saving plans that directly link workers' contributions to their benefits.

Issue Brief 8 Public Pensions and Retirement

ONCE PEOPLE ARE COVERED BY A FORMAL pension scheme, public policies directly influence their decisions about retirement. The legal retirement age in poor countries is much lower than that in rich countries, varying from an average of 64 for men in OECD countries to less than 57 in Sub-Saharan Africa. Women are often allowed to retire earlier even though they generally live longer than men.

In terms of general health and expected longevity, a worker in, say, Burundi is older at age 60 than one in Switzerland. This explains, in part, the lower retirement age in Burundi. Nevertheless, life expectancy at the legal retirement age is greater in low-income countries than it is in high-income countries (figure 4.5). The expected retirement period is probably even longer than the estimates in figure 4.5 show, since the life expectancy of covered workers is greater than the national average and many workers retire before they reach the legal retirement age.

Early Retirement

A number of countries have liberal early retirement provisions that put the average effective retirement age far below the normal legal retirement age. The average retirement age is 53 in Albania and Poland, for example. Pensions for early retirees are frequently reduced far less than the actuarially fair amount, which means that people who continue to work are penalized.

Some countries allow early retirement under special circumstances, such as extended unemployment or disability, loosely defined. In the Netherlands one in five pensioners retires early as "disabled." For people doing "arduous work," Brazil permits retire-

ment at age 50, Burundi at 45, China at 55 for men and 45 for women, and Romania at 50 for men and 45 for women. In Romania and Tunisia a mother with three children can retire early. Morocco, Pakistan, Peru, and Portugal permit early retirement for miners, while teachers can retire early in Brazil, Bulgaria, Nicaragua, Poland, and Uruguay. Most countries in francophone Africa allow the "prematurely aged" to retire at 50 or 55. Brazil allows some categories of workers to retire after thirty years of service, regardless of age. Early retirement has been used as an alternative to unemployment and an aid to enterprise restructuring in China, Eastern Europe, and OECD countries (box 4.4).

Promises of early retirement are cheap. Politicians can easily promise generous benefits today, knowing that it will be years before anyone tries to collect on those promises. But when that day comes—as it already has in many parts of the world—system dependency ratios will shoot above demographic dependency ratios and pension schemes will run into financial difficulty.

Older Workers Are Dropping Out of the Work Force Earlier

In Austria, France, Germany, Italy, and Spain, fewer than one person in ten over the age of 60 is still in the work force. In Argentina, Trinidad and Tobago, Uruguay, much of Eastern Europe, and most of the remaining OECD countries, four out of every five persons over the age of 60 have retired. Between 1960 and 1990 the labor force participation rate for workers over the age of 65 fell from 33 to 11 percent in high-income countries and from 56 to 33 percent in low-income countries (issue brief table 8.1). The old age activity rate is higher in de-

Issue Brief Table 8.1 Changes in Labor Force Participation of Older Men in Selected Countries, Early 1960s–Late 1980s

	Age 65-plus			Age 55 to 64		
	1960–66	*1986–90*	*Change*	*1960–66*	*1986–90*	*Change*
OECD countries						
Australia	24.9	9.2	-15.7	86.1	63.3	-22.8
Austria	15.1	2.2	-12.9	77.5	38.9	-38.6
Canada	28.5	11.4	-17.1	81.9	64.9	-17.0
Denmark[a]	34.5	13.4	-21.1	91.4	67.8	-23.6
Finland	39.7	6.8	-32.9	85.5	45.4	-40.1
France	27.8	3.5	-24.3	78.7	45.8	-32.9
Germany	22.8	6.3	-16.5	81.5	78.4	-3.1
Greece	43.7	13.6	-30.1	81.5	65.7	-15.8
Ireland	48.4	16.8	-31.6	90.0	91.0	1.0
Italy	23.6	8.1	-15.5	70.4	52.6	-17.8
Japan	54.3	39.2	-15.1	87.8	86.5	-1.3
Luxembourg	15.6	2.5	-13.1	66.4	34.1	-32.3
Netherlands	19.9	3.9	-16.0	87.7	45.7	-42.0
New Zealand	23.6	11.2	-12.4	83.4	56.8	-26.6
Portugal	62.6	20.0	-42.6	86.1	66.9	-19.2
Spain	55.5	3.7	-51.8	91.9	61.7	-30.2
Sweden	23.9	10.7	-13.2	87.5	75.4	-12.1
Switzerland[a]	41.9	15.1	-26.8	92.7	88.7	-4.0
United Kingdom	23.4	8.6	-14.8	91.3	67.9	-23.4
United States	29.7	15.5	-14.2	83.6	67.1	-16.5
Average	**33.0**	**11.1**	**21.9**	**84.2**	**63.2**	**-20.9**
Non-OECD countries						
Argentina	38.3	23.5	-14.8	65.3	68.4	3.1
Chile	51.4	30.3	-21.1	80.6	71.8	-8.8
Ecuador	85.3	64.3	-21.0	96.5	88.5	-8.0
El Salvador	79.2	47.2	-32.0	94.6	85.4	-9.2
Guatemala	74.4	62.9	-11.5	92.9	92.5	-0.4
Hong Kong[b]	39.8	20.8	-19.0	84.2	68.2	-16.0
Hungary	57.0	1.2	-55.8	82.9	33.2	-49.7
Korea, Rep. of	29.1	40.9	11.8	74.5	78.2	3.7
Mauritius	31.9	14.8	-17.1	75.9	61.4	-14.5
Mexico	91.7	45.9	-45.8	96.2	74.1	-22.1
Nigeria	90.2	50.0	-40.2	96.6	89.0	-7.6
Peru	68.7	32.0	-36.7	94.2	72.2	-22.0
Poland	55.5	32.5	-23.0	87.4	63.7	-23.7
Romania	39.3	13.8	-25.5	79.7	38.0	-41.7
Trinidad and Tobago[c]	29.7	18.2	-11.5	79.7	62.3	-17.4
Uruguay	22.5	16.2	-6.3	63.6	64.8	1.2
Venezuela[d]	70.1	49.1	-21.0	91.6	82.9	-8.7
Average	**56.1**	**33.2**	**-23.0**	**84.5**	**70.3**	**-14.2**

Note: Averages are unweighted. The ranges of years for some countries are the following: (a) 1960–80, (b) 1971–91, (c) 1970–90, (d) 1961–81.

Source: ILO. Data on activity rate over 65 for 1986–90 for Uruguay are from the U.S. Bureau of the Census, Center for International Research, International Data Base on Aging. Eekelaar and Pearl (1989).

veloping countries, in spite of liberal early retire-ment provisions, perhaps because most people are not covered by pension schemes and many workers continue working in the informal sector even after they have officially retired.

Many forces account for the declining labor force participation rate among older workers—including early retirement provisions in private pension schemes and rising real incomes, which some people choose to spend on increased leisure. Although it is difficult to determine exactly how much public pension plans have contributed to this decline, there is little doubt that they have influenced people's re-tirement decisions. The windfall transfer to older workers (when pension schemes are introduced) in-creases their income late in life, and earlier retire-ment is one of the few ways they can "spend" this added income. Younger workers may also retire ear-lier because public pension programs have forced them to "contribute" for their retirement more than they would have otherwise. A high payroll tax that is not linked to future benefits may have a negative effect on the labor supply of older workers. Most countries require people to stop working as a condi-tion for receiving pensions. In some OECD countries benefits are reduced for workers who continue to work past the normal retirement age, and these ben-efits are never recouped.

As evidence of the responsiveness to these finan-cial incentives: In China, most workers in rural areas are excluded from the formal public sector scheme, whereas urban retirees receive generous pensions. Not surprisingly, 85 percent of the urban old, but less than half of the rural old, are retired. The Republic of Korea, where less than 5 percent of the old are eligible for public pensions, has a high and unchanging activity rate. In Sweden, which provides generous partial retirement benefits to workers who continue working part-time, labor

force participation rates for older workers have fallen less than they have in other OECD countries.

Consequences of Early Retirement

If the labor force participation rate for people 55 to 64 years old was the same in 1990 as it was in 1960, the labor force would have been 1 to 2 percent larger in developing countries and 3 to 6 percent larger in Eastern European and OECD countries. As populations age over the next three decades, this employment loss will grow. The loss in national output as a consequence of early retire-ment is approximately 1 percent of GDP for devel-oping countries and 2 to 4 percent of GDP for OECD countries, assuming that older workers are at least as productive as younger workers. This loss of output is inefficient if its value exceeds the value of the extra leisure that retired people receive. If re-captured, this lost GDP would cover more than half of total pension spending in many countries.

Early retirement also has undesirable conse-quences for the distribution of GDP, because the main beneficiaries are civil servants and other priv-ileged groups. Added to the fact that upper-income workers live longer than lower-income workers, the result is that better-off workers collect pensions for many more years than their poorer compatriots.

Policy Implications

The retirement conditions established for public pension plans have important consequences for the financial health and distributive impact of these schemes and for the economy as a whole. Several principles should guide policy on this issue:

■ Avoid excessively long retirement periods.

- Don't penalize people who work beyond the normal retirement age.
- Reduce pension levels on an actuarially fair basis for people who retire early, except for those who are truly disabled.
- Set the same retirement ages for men and women.

- Eliminate special regimes that grant early retirement for privileged groups.
- Don't use retirement as a remedy for unemployment.
- Raise the retirement age regularly as life expectancy increases.

Issue Brief 9 Redistribution between Generations

PUBLIC OLD AGE SECURITY PROGRAMS ARE often justified on equity grounds. They redistribute income across generations to help cohorts whose ability to support themselves in old age has been weakened by factors beyond their control: war, inflation, recession. The net effect of these plans is difficult to determine, because they may crowd out private saving and transfers to some extent (see issue brief 4). But in most OECD countries they seem to have improved the income position of the group currently old, whose poverty rate decreased faster than that of any other population group over the past thirty years. But these public pension plans will reduce the lifetime incomes of many people working today.

This gain in real income by one generation at the expense of a permanent loss to another generation is the intergenerational transfer. (See box 4.5 for a discussion of same-generation transfers.) It is an inevitable outcome of pay-as-you-go pension systems. Every empirical analysis conducted so far has found that the transfers from one generation to another, specifically from future generations to generations that were working when the scheme was created, are far larger than any transfers within generations.

Who Gains and How Much?

Intergenerational transfers always occur in pay-as-you-go schemes, because the first generations of pensioners receive benefits that exceed the value of their contributions over their relatively short periods of covered employment. Supporters of pay-as-you-go schemes view this ability to help the old immediately as an advantage over funded schemes.

This windfall gain from system immaturity can be compressed or stretched out over several cohorts of workers, according to the eligibility conditions set. When the Netherlands adopted its current scheme in 1957, it provided generous pensions immediately to people who had already retired and to those who retired soon after. The windfall gain was highly concentrated in these cohorts. More often, eligibility restrictions keep transfers small for people who are old when the scheme is introduced, stretching the windfall out over several cohorts of workers. In the United States fewer than one in ten old people was receiving benefits ten years after the first social security contributions were collected. Switzerland applied a means test to the old in the first windfall generation. Most Koreans who were old when their system was established in 1988 will have died by the time the system pays out its first full benefits. In such cases the scheme accumulates a partial reserve in its early years, with the largest benefits likely to be received by people who are 30 to 50 years old when the scheme is introduced—the founding generations. They pay contributions for only part of their working lives but collect generous pensions for many years.

Changes in the old age dependency rate (the ratio of retirees to workers), and in productivity or real wage growth, also contribute to the tendency of pay-as-you-go schemes to redistribute income across generations. Succeeding generations of workers get back in benefits more than they have contributed if the system support ratio (ratio of contributors to pensioners) is rising and if wage growth exceeds the interest rate. But under the opposite conditions they lose part of their lifetime income. For the past half century the first set of conditions held. In the next half century the second set will likely dominate because of the combined impact of the demographic transition and slow productivity growth. Early generations will have been made better off by pay-as-you-go schemes, but later generations will be made worse off. Lifetime income is being transferred from later to earlier generations (see chapter 3 and issue brief 3).

Studies of the U.S. social security system find that, thanks to windfall startup gains and expanding coverage and population, members of the founding generations received three to four times more than they had contributed during their working lives. Real rates of return were more than 15 percent for workers retiring in the 1950s and 1960s and close to 8 percent for workers retiring at the end of the 1970s—much higher than these workers could have earned in some other investment, such as the stock or bond market (issue brief figure 9.1). Higher-income workers received the largest transfers because of their greater earnings, pensions, and longevity. Many of today's young workers, however (including low- and middle-income workers), can expect to earn negative trans-

Issue Brief Figure 9.1 Real Rates of Return on U.S. Social Security (OASI) Contributions versus Stocks and Bonds for Generations Retiring between 1942 and 2027

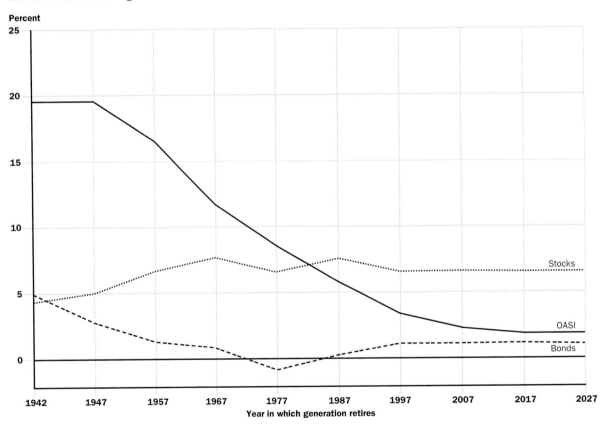

Note: OASI (Old-Age and Survivor's Insurance) rates of return are based on Moffitt (1984) and Boskin and others (1987); stock returns (based on Standard and Poor's index) and bond returns (based on long-term government bond yields) are from Ibbotson and Sinquefield (1989); after 1997, average return for 1925–87 is applied.

fers, because they are required to contribute more than they will ever receive back in pensions. If, in addition, benefits to these younger workers are cut because of fiscal pressures and if real wages fall because of reduced saving and growth, the loss in lifetime income will be even greater (Steurle and Bakija 1994; Moffitt 1984; Boskin and others 1987).

Germany, the Netherlands, and Sweden have had similar experiences (Dinkel 1986; Nelissen 1987; Stahlberg 1989). In Sweden the present value of lifetime benefits for people born between 1904 and 1914 was 3.75 times higher than the present value of contributions, using a 3 percent discount rate. For people born between 1940 and 1944, estimated future lifetime benefits are only 0.6 times the value of contributions. Workers who retire in the future would probably be better off if they were allowed to save their contributions and invest them in a mixed portfolio of stocks and bonds or in the education of their children.

Empirical evidence on intergenerational transfers in developing countries is more difficult to come by. Most of the schemes are immature, so the first windfall generation is still benefiting. Furthermore, coverage rates are low, so the financial base can be strengthened for some time simply by expanding coverage to new groups of young workers. This pattern of gradual expansion is usually regressive because higher-income workers are brought into the program first, and they receive the highest rate of return, while the last groups to join are lower-income workers. Without dramatic changes in productivity, today's young workers will receive low pensions and negative rates of return on their contributions under pay-as-you-go systems (see issue brief 3).

What Should Be Done?

Before adopting or expanding their old age security systems, countries should carefully evaluate the intergenerational transfers that are likely over the long run. They should establish a system of generational accounting that traces the projected flows to and from different generations, as well as the distribution of these flows within each generation (Auerbach and Kotlikoff 1987). They may find that the transfers implied by large pay-as-you-go schemes—as a result of system maturation, increasing coverage, and changing patterns of population and productivity growth—are not at all what they intended. Danger points to be avoided are large positive transfers to higher-income groups in the first few generations of retirees and negative transfers to low-income groups among the later retirees. In general, transfers can be made more equitable by using a very progressive benefit and tax formula in public pension plans, imposing a floor but no ceiling on taxable earnings, switching to general revenue finance once coverage is widespread, and using privately managed funded plans that make benefits contingent on contributions, to provide higher pensions to higher-income groups.

Issue Brief 10 Annuity Market Problems and How to Resolve Them

AN ANNUITY IS A SERIES OF PAYMENTS IN return for a lump sum paid up front. In a typical situation the payments are made for the remaining lifetime of the annuitant or the annuitant plus survivors (such as a husband and wife). Sometimes the payment is guaranteed for a specified period, such as ten years. If the annuitant dies, payments are continued to a designated beneficiary until the end of the period. Often annuities receive favorable tax treatments. One reason frequently given for public provision of pension benefits is that private annuities markets are beset by problems. How could these problems be resolved to enable the provision of pension benefits by a decentralized mandatory saving scheme?

Annuities markets may suffer from *adverse selection*, leading to the nonavailability of annuities at an actuarially fair price to "good risks," in this case to people who expect to die young. Empirical evidence from the United States indicates that these markets do not completely disappear but that people who buy annuities tend to have above-average longevity, requiring a commensurately high price that discourages such purchases from those with below-average longevity (Friedman and Warshavsky 1990). This may result from adverse selection or from the fact that annuities are considered a luxury good, purchased primarily by high-income people (whose expected longevity happens to be high). Insurance companies can handle adverse selection, in part, by offering different types of annuity contracts that separate people with high and low expected longevity (see below). Or governments can solve this problem by making the purchase of annuities mandatory, at least up to a limit. Once annuities are mandatory, everyone must buy them. The price then reflects average, rather than above-average, risk, making them more affordable.

If annuities are mandatory, an important public policy issue concerns *which risk categories* insurance companies will be permitted to use, for differentiating premiums or benefits. In a competitive market, each company has an incentive to offer better rates to people who fall into better risk categories. For example, low-income people, whose expected longevity is lower, might be offered a lower annuities price than high-income people, and men may be offered a better price than women. Which income, gender, racial, and other characteristics should be permitted for rate setting in mandatory annuities markets? In the United States, for example, race and gender are not permissible categories for employment-related pensions or life insurance. Differentiated annuities prices might become divisive. But uniform prices imply ex ante transfers, from low-risk groups to high-risk groups. (In a public scheme, in which everyone is placed in the same annuity pool, such ex ante transfers are implicit.) In particular, low-income workers are penalized if differentiated prices are not permitted for annuities. This effect might be mitigated by offering a variety of contracts for participants to choose from. People who expect to have low longevity would self-select contracts that provide a death benefit for survivors or that have a guaranteed payout period for retirees and their beneficiaries. If each type of contract is priced to be self-supporting, this helps to mitigate the adverse selection problem (see above) and the problem of undesired ex ante redistribution among groups.

Once permissible risk categories are set, *annuity companies may try to "cream" the best risks* in each category—that is, to sell annuities to those people with lower-than-average expected longevity in each group to maximize their profits. While adverse selection stems from circumstances in which the insurance company does not have information about the individual's risk category, creaming occurs when the company does have this information. Consider the case where, by law, everyone of a given age must be charged the same price. Then, cigarette smokers, sky divers, miners, and people with poor medical histories would become desirable targets, sought after by annuity companies, while other consumers would be less desirable. Those who are way above average in risk might even be rejected as consumers, if this is permitted. So, a policy that makes annuities mandatory must either prohibit insurance companies from excluding consumers or must set up a special fund that covers "bad risks" (such as healthy people). If exclusion and price differentiation are not permitted, some insurance companies (those located in "healthy" areas, for example) may end up with a disproportionate share of bad risks and may then go broke. If a special "bad risk" pool is used, a large proportion of the population may end up in the special pool, which requires subsidies from the association of companies or from the state. (Exclusion is generally ruled out for a mandatory public scheme.)

A mandatory scheme with a deadline (such as date of retirement) for the purchase of an annuity creates a *high investment risk for workers*, because of the possibility that the market value of their accumulated assets, or the interest rate on which annuity prices depend, may be abnormally low on that date. One possible solution is to encourage the development of *variable or participating annuities* in which people purchase annuity units whose prices fluctuate as market conditions change, similar to adjustable rate mortgages. This has the advantage of mitigating the risk associated with requiring a purchase on a specified date. But it has the disadvantage that the retiree must bear the risk of a fluctuating pension amount for the rest of his or her life. Another solution would spread out the purchase of annuities—

that is, require a smaller purchase of *deferred annuities* each year, from the time the worker reaches a given age such as 50. Still another solution would allow workers to take gradual withdrawals from their retirement accounts, such as 5 percent of the assets each year after age 65, in lieu of purchasing annuities. But this voluntary choice between phased withdrawals and annuities brings back the adverse selection problem discussed above and may leave some very old people without adequate financial resources. (A public defined benefit scheme ordinarily does not involve investment risk. Nevertheless, different cohorts may be treated differently depending on political risk.)

It is often claimed that private companies cannot credibly *insure against inflation,* especially high unanticipated inflation. (But many public programs also do not protect against inflation.) As one possible solution, insurance companies could be required to index their benefits and encouraged to hold indexed securities, real assets whose value is likely to increase with inflation, or foreign investments that are immune to country-specific inflation. In Chile annuities are indexed and backed by such assets. Indexed benefits imply a cost for the worker—for any given premium, a lower pension will be paid in the early years to cover the probability that a higher pension must be paid later on. So, it is not clear that workers are better off if full indexation is required.

Longevity, even the longevity of the cohort as a whole, is difficult to predict. In recent years, people have been living longer than expected, and some demographers believe this disparity in longevity will increase in the years ahead. People who purchase annuities, particularly large annuities, may have longer life expectancy than the rest of the population (adverse selection). This poses a great longevity risk for private insurance companies, which will therefore charge a high-risk premium. Even with a high premium, some insurance companies might go bankrupt and be unable to pay pensioners if they underestimate the growth in longevity. A capital reserve fund may be important for this reason. Another solution to this problem is for companies to match life insurance and annuity exposures. Still another approach is to use private annuities only for a limited period, such as the first twenty years of retirement, and resort to a larger public benefit for the very old. (A public pay-as-you-go scheme implicitly passes the costs of higher longevity on to the next generation and can do so through its power of taxation.)

Because annuity purchases are lumpy and irreversible, *high commissions* are often paid to salespersons who complete a deal. This in turn gives salespersons an incentive to engage in high-pressure techniques that raise costs and lead uninformed consumers to wrong choices. Possible solutions here include regulations that limit these commissions, requirements that salespersons be salaried rather than commissioned, the use of standard form contracts that facilitate price comparisons, the imposition of a trial period (such as three months) during which the workers can reverse their decisions, and the availability of public consumer counselors who help inform workers about choices.

Clearly, private annuities markets must be heavily regulated, particularly if annuities become mandatory. At the very least, permissible risk categories must be defined, pools for bad risks created, survivors' benefits required, standard contract forms used, consumer information provided by some impartial organization, variable annuities offered, and a reserve fund created or reinsurance purchased by insurance companies to ensure that they will be able to meet their obligations. Reliable mortality tables must be constructed—these are lacking in most developing countries and should probably be a government responsibility because they are public goods. And joint ventures should be encouraged in developing countries that lack the technical expertise for running insurance companies and other modern financial institutions.

The complexity of these problems probably limits the degree to which annuities should be mandatory. In a mandatory saving scheme workers should not be required to purchase annuities with their entire retirement savings. Other reasons for limiting the required annuity purchase are that people's consumption needs in old age may be lumpy (they may have large medical expenses at some point) and they may wish to leave part of their estates as bequests for their children. In Singapore only the purchase of a "minimum pension" is required, and in Chile a regimen of scheduled withdrawals is permitted as an alternative to annuities. In this type of system accumulated savings are spread over the worker's expected lifetime, though little may be left by the end for workers who live longer than average. Voluntary retirement saving plans in Canada and the United States give retirees a choice between phased withdrawals and annuities.

Public pension schemes also face many of these problems, including the difficulty in insuring against higher than expected inflation or longevity and the likelihood that ex ante transfers will be involved, albeit in a somewhat different, less transparent way. The risks in private plans become greater for very long-term commitments. Using private insurers to carry part of the burden brings to bear risk diversification and the accumulation of a large pool of capital for investment and backup reserves. The best solution may be a combination of public pensions and private annuities, with the former assuming a larger role for the very old, and with retirees given a choice between annuities and other withdrawal arrangements beyond a specified minimum.

Issue Brief 11 Simulations of Alternative Multipillar Systems

THIS ISSUE BRIEF SUMMARIZES A SERIES OF simulations to show the distributional effects within and across generations of different pillars and their combinations.

Simulations Based on Demographic Change

The first set of simulations is conducted for two scenarios—moderate growth, moderate aging (2 percent interest rate, 1 percent economy-wide real wage growth plus 1 percent age-earnings wage growth) and fast growth, fast aging (5 percent interest rate, 3 percent real wage growth plus 1 percent age-earnings wage growth) (Schwarz 1994). In each case it is assumed that the country introduces a new pension system in 1995 and that the first pensioners covered under the new system retire in 2005. The population

is divided into poor (50 percent), middle class (33 percent), and rich (17 percent). Their relative wage rates are 1:2:4. All pensions are assumed to be indexed to wages. The simulations investigate the success of alternative schemes in alleviating poverty, replacing wages, and providing a reasonable rate of return on saving to deter evasion. Results are presented for 2065, when the system is mature, population growth is very low, and the grandchildren of the first retirees retire (issue brief tables 11.1 and 11.2).

Moderate Growth, Moderate Aging. The first simulation is of a universal flat benefit financed on a pay-as-you-go basis set to provide 40 percent of the economy-wide wage, which was defined as the poverty line. In 2065 this would require a 19 percent tax rate to break even. Four alternative systems were then simulated, holding the 19 percent contribution

Issue Brief Table 11.1 Alternative Pillars and Their Combinations: Moderate Aging, Moderate Growth, 2065

	Flat 40 percent of average wage	19 percent defined contribution	10 percent defined contribution and 20 percent flat	13 percent defined contribution and means tested pension	16 percent defined contribution and minimum guaranteed
Contribution rate	19	19	19	19	19
Poverty elimination	*			*	*
Lifetime transfer					
Poor	+	0	+	+	+
Middle	–	0	0	–	–
Rich	–	0	–	–	–
Wage replacement rate of final wage					
Poor	67	51	60	68	67
Middle	34	45	41	39	38
Rich	17	41	30	28	34

Note: The assumptions and definitions for this table begin on p. 336. * denotes that poverty has been eliminated. Poverty line is assumed to be 40 percent of economy-wide average wage. Plus and minus denote positive and negative transfer, respectively. A zero denotes transfer of less than 0.5 percent of lifetime wages.

Source: Schwarz (1994).

Issue Brief Table 11.2 Alternative Pillars and Their Combinations: Rapid Aging, Rapid Growth, 2065

	Flat 40 percent of average wage	19 percent defined contribution	10 percent defined contribution and 20 percent flat	13 percent defined contribution and means tested pension	16 percent defined contribution and minimum guaranteed
Contribution rate	23	19	21	20	18
Poverty elimination	*	*	*	*	*
Lifetime transfer					
Poor	0	0	0	+	0
Middle	–	0	–	–	–
Rich	–	0	–	–	–
Wage replacement rate of final wage					
Poor	81	82	84	97	81
Middle	43	76	61	62	64
Rich	22	72	49	49	60

Note: The assumptions and definitions for this table begin on p. 336. * denotes that poverty has been eliminated. Poverty line is assumed to be 40 percent of economy-wide average wage. Plus and minus denote positive and negative transfers, respectively. A zero denotes transfer of less than 0.5 percent of lifetime wages.

Source: Schwarz (1994).

rate constant: a funded 19 percent defined contribution pillar, a 10 percent defined contribution plan combined with a 10 percent flat benefit, a means-tested benefit, and a minimum pension guarantee set to bring everyone to the poverty line or above. The simulations assume that costs of administration, evasion, labor and capital market distortions, unemployment, disability benefits, and life insurance are zero, but more qualitative analysis takes some of these effects into account.

The flat pay-as-you-go benefit eliminates poverty but is ineffective as a savings instrument, since it yields returns far below the market interest rate and very low wage replacement rates to the middle and upper classes. It generates large intergenerational transfers; everyone, including the rich, gets large positive transfers at the beginning, while the middle and upper classes both get negative transfers at the end. This is perverse because the rich in the early co-

horts have higher wages than the middle class in the last few cohorts, yet the latter redistributes to the former. It is also perverse because the 19 percent payroll tax leaves the poor better off in their retirement years than in their early working years; that is, their pension when old exceeds their net wage when young. (Since the gross starting wage of the poor is 43 percent of the economy-wide average, a 19 percent tax rate leaves them with a net wage of 35 percent, which is below the poverty line, when they enter the labor force.)

The 19 percent defined contribution plan is more effective as a saving mechanism, since it avoids negative transfers, and it provides the highest replacement rate for the top half of the population—but it leaves the bottom half below the poverty line. Among the mixed schemes, both the minimum guarantee and the means-tested scheme eliminate poverty; the minimum guarantee does so with the best wage replacement for the rich and the lowest distortionary effect (see below). But the middle class fares better with the combination of 10 percent defined contribution plus 10 percent defined benefit.

Rapid Growth, Rapid Aging. The same defined benefit, defined contribution combinations were simulated for the rapid growth, rapid aging case. Rapid aging raises the costs of the 40 percent flat benefit, which is pay-as-you-go financed, and makes it practically impossible to transfer lifetime income to the poor. The larger gap between interest rates and wage growth raises the replacement rate yielded by the defined contribution plan. As a result, all the plans eliminate poverty in this case. But the flat benefit requires a higher contribution rate than before—23 percent—and produces larger intergenerational transfers, while the minimum pension guarantee eliminates poverty with the lowest required contribution rate and the highest replacement rates for the middle and upper classes, among the multipillar schemes.

Uncertainty. The "best" system therefore depends on economic and demographic conditions, as well as on social objectives. Population aging, which is predictable, makes it very costly to reduce poverty and replace wages through a single pillar that is pay-as-you-go-financed. If one knew for sure that the interest rate would be relatively high, a strong case could be made for a pure defined contribution plan. But in a context of uncertainty, this could leave large pockets of poverty. Among the various multipillar alternatives simulated, the poor get a larger transfer from the means-tested scheme, the rich would prefer the minimum pension guarantee, and the position of the middle class is ambiguous, in a certain world. Nevertheless, once uncertainty is taken into account, this strengthens the preference of the risk-averse poor for the guarantee—which is sure to eliminate

poverty—and increases the preference of the middle class for the 20 percent flat plus 10 percent defined contribution—which insures them against income loss from interest rate declines, before they reach the poverty line.

If a high value is placed on eliminating old age poverty, the minimum guarantee scheme will achieve this with the greatest degree of certainty, at the lowest cost, and has the added advantage of achieving better wage replacement for upper income groups at the same time. But a word of caution: the high tax rate required for any of these systems leaves low-income groups in greater poverty when they are young, unless a floor is set on taxable earnings.

How Do Administrative Costs, Evasion, and Efficiency Affect These Results?

These results are strengthened once transaction costs, evasion, and labor and capital market distortions are taken into account. Although it is difficult to predict these effects with precision, the following seem indicated:

- Administrative costs are probably higher for the defined contribution scheme (which incurs investment costs) than for the universal flat and are probably highest for the defined contribution scheme combined with the means-tested public pillar.
- Costs of evasion and labor market distortions are probably lowest for the pure defined contribution plan, where there are no transfers, and for the defined contribution plus minimum pension guarantee (top-up), where tax rates for the public pillar are only 2 to 3 percent and negative transfers are small; they will be highest for the flat benefit where large negative transfers are involved.

- The privately managed defined contribution scheme may enhance capital accumulation and capital and labor market efficiency; this will increase productivity but will not reduce old age costs if pensions are indexed to wages. It will reduce absolute poverty but not relative poverty—that is, poverty relative to the economy-wide wage, so a multipillar system continues to be necessary for this purpose.

- Once costs of administration, evasion, and economic distortions are taken into account, this raises the required contribution rate far higher than 19 percent in all multipillar scenarios, but least of all in the top-up scheme.

- The defined contribution plan with the minimum pension guarantee remains the least costly way to accomplish the dual goals of poverty elimination and saving or wage replacement.

Taking Behavioral Differences among People into Account

The simulations just discussed assume that everyone behaves the same—entering and leaving the labor force at the same time and being fully employed in between. In reality, of course, people have very different patterns of labor force behavior, and some people never enter the labor force or contribute to the pension system. Analyzing these effects requires detailed information about individual behavior that is rarely available.

Nevertheless, one analysis of alternative old age schemes for the United Kingdom has simulated many of these differences among individuals (Falkingham and Johnson 1993). The analysis uses a dynamic cohort microsimulation model (LIFEMOD) that simulates the life histories of 2,000 men and 2,000 women, who are representative of the popula-

tion in the United Kingdom in 1985. The study assumes a mature pension system and zero population growth (so intergenerational transfers are not investigated), average annual wage growth of 1.5 percent, and a net annual interest rate of 2.5 percent.

This study, too, finds that poverty among the old can be completely eliminated through a universal flat benefit, but such a system provides very low wage replacement rates for upper-income groups. Making the scheme employment-related—based on years of contributions—rather than universal substantially lowers the number of people covered and the effectiveness of the flat pension at alleviating poverty. A funded defined contribution scheme is effective for replacing wages, but does not eliminate poverty—old people in the bottom half of the income distribution get a pension that puts them below the poverty line. The mixed schemes do better but some poverty remains, except with the top-up scheme, which eliminates poverty and also achieves a reasonable wage replacement rate for all groups. The universal top-up scheme helps women in particular, who are disadvantaged in any old age security arrangement based on earnings and employment (box 7.1).

Assumptions and Definitions for the Tables

The following assumptions and definitions are used for issue brief tables 11.1 and 11.2:

- Column 1: the public pillar is a pay-as-you-go flat defined benefit pegged at 40 percent of the economy-wide average wage; this is defined as the poverty line.
- Column 2 is a fully funded 19 percent defined contribution plan.
- Column 3 is a combination of a 10 percent defined contribution plan plus a 20 percent flat benefit.

- Column 4 is a combination of a 13 percent defined contribution plan plus a means-tested benefit that pays 20 percent of the economy-wide average wage for the poor and 10 percent for the middle class.

- Column 5 is a 16 percent defined contribution plan plus a top-up scheme (minimum pension guarantee), financed on a pay-as-you-go basis, that brings everyone up to the poverty line.

- The population is divided into the poor, the middle class, and the rich in the ratio 3:2:1. The wages of the middle class are double that of the poor, and the rich are twice as well off as the middle class. These numbers yield an aggregate income distribution similar to that of many developing and transitional countries.

- Workers enter the labor force at age 20, retire at age 60, and die at ages 78, 82, and 84, respectively, for each income group. Average age at death is 80. The assumed mortality differential is consistent with empirical evidence from many countries. In the defined contribution plan, each income group is in its own annuity pool, so there are no redistributions stemming from mortality differentials.

- In the moderate growth case real wage growth is 1 percent per year for the economy as a whole plus a 1 percent annual return to worker experience, and the real interest rate is 2 percent per year.

- In the rapid growth case, wage growth is 3 percent for the economy, 1 percent for experience, and the interest rate is 5 percent.

- The demography of the moderate aging case is similar to that of Argentina; the rapid aging is similar to that of China.

- All pensions are indexed to economy-wide wages.

- Since pensions are indexed to wages, their value relative to final salary grows during the retirement period. The value given is the average ratio over this period. Their value relative to the economy-wide wage is constant over the retirement period.

- Lifetime transfers are the present value of benefits minus lifetime contributions, discounted at the prevailing interest rate (2 and 5 percent for slow- and fast-growth scenarios, respectively).

- The contribution rate is that paid by workers in 2065. Under pay-as-you-go it rises each year because of system maturation and demographic change, but it remains constant under the defined contribution funded scheme.

- Revenue losses and expenditures stemming from evasion, strategic manipulation, withdrawal from the labor force, unemployment, survivors' and disability insurance, and administrative expenses are ignored. In reality this would raise total system costs by varying amounts ranging upward from 30 percent.

- Distortionary effects on the labor and capital markets are also ignored, as are effects stemming from risk and uncertainty. Thus, these simulations ignore efficiency effects and focus on distributional effects.

- The pension system is introduced in the year 1995 with a ten-year eligibility period. The first pensioners retire in 2005. Their grandchildren are born in 2005 and retire in 2065; this is the cohort considered in these simulations.

Issue Brief 12 Simulation of an Eastern European Transition

CONSIDER A STYLIZED TRANSITION FROM A single pillar to a multipillar system in a typical Eastern European economy. The demography of Hungary is used for this example. For the initial situation in 1995 it is assumed that all people begin working at age 20 and retire at age 55. (Although the statutory retirement age is higher, early retirement, disability, and other special provisions have brought the effective retirement age down to 55 in most Eastern European countries.) The dominant public pillar offers an average benefit rate of 50 percent of the gross economy-wide average wage. A 15 percent overhead charge for administrative costs and evasion is added to system costs both in the initial situation and after the reform. The initial break-even contribution rate is 30 percent.

Reform of the public pillar begins in 1995. It has three components:

1. The effective retirement age is raised one year per year until it reaches 60 in the year 2000. Thereafter, it is raised six months per year until it reaches age 65 in 2010. This means that no retirement takes place after 1995 until 2002, when all new retirees are 61. (Effectively, this could be achieved by eliminating special early retirement regimes.)
2. Replacement rates in the public pillar are cut to 40 percent of the gross economy-wide average wage in 2000.
3. After 2000, the real value of the pension is augmented by half the rate of real wage growth annually—that is, indexation is 50 percent to prices and 50 percent to wages. So, if growth occurs, the real value of the pension rises, but not by as much as the average wage, requiring

a declining contribution rate to finance the public pillar.

This "shock treatment" generates resources to reduce the tax rate and finance the second pillar. The rise in retirement age increases GDP, the total wage bill, and the tax base. In 2000 the reformed public pillar will require a contribution rate of only 17.5 percent, instead of 30 percent. At that point, a mandatory saving pillar is introduced, with a 10 percent contribution rate. The simulations show the benefits derived from and contribution rates required by this multipillar system, between the years 2000 and 2065, under two alternative scenarios— slow growth (1 percent annual wage growth, 2 percent real interest) and fast growth (3 percent annual wage growth, 5 percent real interest). The first pension from the mandatory saving pillar is received in 2010 and it is assumed to be wage indexed. The last year shown is 2065, the year of retirement for children born in the first year of the reform (issue brief table 12.1).

The major results:

1. The current benefit rate is not sustainable with a 30 percent contribution rate, as the population ages. By 2015 the required rate is 40 percent, and by 2035 it is 45 percent—on top of taxes for health and other purposes. The implied total tax rate could easily exceed 80 percent—a political and economic impossibility. Thus, benefits will inevitably decline—the only questions are how and when?
2. As a result of the reform, the dependency rate and required contribution rate drop sharply by 2000 and continue to drop thereafter. Even after a 10 percent contribution is allocated to

Issue Brief Table 12.1 Simulated Pension Reform in a Transitional Socialist Economy *(percent)*

	Dependency rate		Contribution rate [b]			Benefits			
Year	Old dependency rate	Reformed dependency rate	Payroll tax for old public pillar	Payroll tax for reformed public pillar	Contribution for new mandatory savings pillar	Reformed public pillar pension/ average wage [c]	New mandatory savings pension/ average wage [d]	New combined pension/ average wage	Combined new pension/ 1995 pension [e]
	*Slow growth scenario* [a]
1995	53	53	30	30	10	50	0	50	100
2000	55	38	31	18	10	40	0	40	86
2010	68	28	38	12	10	37	8	45	110
2020	73	36	41	14	10	35	16	51	150
2030	78	38	44	14	10	34	23	57	172
2040	81	41	45	14	10	32	31	63	208
2050	83	44	46	14	10	30	35	65	238
2065	83	44	47	13	10	28	35	63	267
	*Rapid growth scenario* [a]
1995	53	53	30	30	10	50	0	50	100
2000	55	38	31	17	10	40	0	40	95
2010	68	28	38	11	10	34	8	42	135
2020	73	36	41	12	10	29	16	45	198
2030	78	38	44	10	10	25	25	50	297
2040	81	41	45	10	10	22	35	57	452
2050	83	44	46	9	10	19	40	59	631
2065	83	44	47	7	10	15	40	55	923

Note: Dependency rates based on demographic trends in Hungary as projected by the World Bank population data base. The old dependency rate is based on a retirement age of 55. The new dependency rate is based on a retirement age of 60 in 2000 and 65 thereafter. Labor force participation is assumed to begin at age 20. Under the old system, the ratio of average benefits to the average wage is 50 percent. As discussed in the text, these benefits would not have been sustainable. Under the reformed public pillar, benefits will drop to 40 percent in 2000; after that they are indexed 50 percent to wages and 50 percent to prices.

a. The slow growth scenario assumes 1 percent real wage growth, a 1 percent age-earnings profile, and a 2 percent real interest rate. The rapid growth scenario assumes 3 percent real wage growth, a 1 percent age-earnings profile, and a 5 percent real interest rate.

b. These simulations assume no unemployment, evasion, or administrative costs other than a 15 percent overhead added to the public pillar.

c. This is the flat benefit received by everyone, relative to the economy-wide wage, in the given year.

d. This is the average benefit rate from the mandatory saving pension, relative to the economy-wide wage received by the cohort retiring in a given year. Wage indexation is assumed, so this benefit rate remains constant for each cohort.

e. This is the average benefit rate from both pillars received by the cohort retiring in a given year, relative to the average pension in 1995.
Source: World Bank projections.

the second pillar, the total contribution rate is almost cut in half by 2010. Most of the initial decrease is caused by the raise in retirement age. Subsequent decreases are due to the change in method of indexation.

3. The actual reduction in contribution rate may be greater for three reasons: The 10 percent contribution to the defined contribution pillar may be considered as saving, not a tax, so evasion may decrease. For the same reason, labor

market distortions may decrease, causing productivity and real wages to rise. And the accumulation of capital in the second pillar further increases productivity. These productivity gains may help the economy shift from a "no-growth" to a "fast-growth" scenario. This is the major reason for making the transition.

4. The public pension also drops relative to the economy-wide average wage. But when the benefit from the mandatory saving pillar is added back in, the combined replacement rate climbs above 40 percent for cohorts retiring in 2010 and above 50 percent for cohorts retiring in 2020 (slow growth) and 2030 (fast growth). The combined pension rises above its 1995 real value even sooner. The tax rate is thus much lower, and by the time middle-aged workers retire, benefits are higher under the new system than they would have been under the old system.

5. The determination of winners and losers depends on how the rise in retirement age is valued, whether the new system has induced growth, and for how long the old system would have been sustainable. Workers who retire after 2020 or 2030 (who are under 30 or 40 in 1995) are clear winners because they pay lower taxes and receive higher benefits than they would have under the old system. Workers and retirees who are aged 53 or older in 1995 would seem to be clear losers, since their retirement age is raised, their pension rate is cut, and they do not benefit from lower taxes or from a buildup of savings in the second pillar. Workers aged 35 to 52 in 1995 are in an ambiguous category. If the new system enables the economy to move from a no-growth to a fast-growth scenario, these workers receive higher monetary benefits and pay lower taxes.

But offset against this is the loss of leisure time as a result of their delayed retirement. The older members of this group are likely to feel they are losers, while the younger members may feel they have come out ahead. The group of winners increases dramatically if people realize that the old system was not sustainable and that inflation is likely to erode real benefits sooner rather than later.

6. The implicit social security debt to these people could be paid off by recapturing part of the tax cut and using it to finance higher pensions temporarily. For example, a payroll tax of 2 to 4 percent between 2000 and 2020 would bring the wage replacement rate to more than 50 percent while keeping the total tax rate below 30 percent. Additionally, older workers could be paid off by receiving a larger claim on the assets of privatized state enterprises.

The Bottom Line

After a relatively short period of loss, pensioners get more for less—and the higher the wage growth and investment return, the more they receive. If early retirement was not valued highly, or if the reform produces productivity gains, it should be possible to make everyone better off. The shift to a market economy has lowered the relative value of nonmarket time and thereby reduced the value of early retirement. So, productivity gains and their distribution should dominate. Policymakers should focus on two crucial questions: Will the multipillar system help shift the economy from no growth or slow growth to fast growth? And how can the current group of old people, particularly its lowest-income members, be protected from short-term loss from which later retirees are likely to benefit?

Appendix

Table A.1 Demographic Indicators, 1990

Economy	Population over 60 years old	Population over 65 years old	Population over 75 years old	Population over 65/ population 15–64	Population over 60/ population 20–59	Women over 60/ Men over 60
	Percentage					*Ratio*
OECD[a]						
Australia	15.0	10.7	4.1	16.0	27.3	1.2
Austria	20.2	15.0	7.0	22.3	36.4	1.7
Belgium	20.7	15.0	6.7	22.4	37.8	1.4
Canada	15.6	11.3	4.5	16.7	27.6	1.3
Denmark	20.2	15.4	6.7	22.7	36.2	1.3
Finland	18.4	13.3	5.6	19.8	32.8	1.6
France	18.9	13.8	6.5	20.8	35.3	1.4
Germany	20.3	14.9	7.2	21.7	35.2	1.7
Greece	20.2	14.2	6.4	21.2	37.4	1.3
Iceland	14.5	10.6	3.9	16.4	27.6	1.2
Ireland	15.2	11.4	4.6	18.4	31.4	1.2
Italy	20.6	14.8	6.5	21.6	37.2	1.4
Japan	17.3	11.9	4.7	17.1	30.9	1.3
Luxembourg	19.3	13.8	6.1	19.9	33.5	1.4
Netherlands	17.8	13.2	5.6	19.1	31.3	1.3
New Zealand	15.2	11.1	4.4	16.7	28.6	1.2
Norway	21.2	16.4	6.9	25.4	40.0	1.3
Portugal	18.0	13.0	5.2	19.5	34.5	1.4
Spain	18.5	13.2	5.4	19.8	34.8	1.3
Sweden	22.9	18.0	8.1	27.8	43.5	1.2
Switzerland	19.9	14.9	6.8	21.8	34.5	1.4
United Kingdom	20.8	15.7	6.8	24.0	38.8	1.4
United States	16.6	12.3	5.0	18.7	30.3	1.4
Simple average	**18.6**	**13.6**	**5.9**	**20.4**	**34.0**	**1.4**
Weighted average	**18.2**	**13.2**	**5.6**	**19.6**	**32.9**	—

(Table continues on the following page.)

Table A.1 *(continued)*

Economy	Population over 60 years old	Population over 65 years old	Population over 75 years old	Population over 65/ population 15–64	Population over 60/ population 20–59	Women over 60/ Men over 60
	Percentage					*Ratio*
Latin America and Caribbean						
Antigua and Barbuda	7.6	5.1	1.3	8.9	18.2	2.0
Argentina	13.1	9.0	3.2	14.8	26.9	1.3
Bahamas	6.7	4.3	0.8	6.7	13.6	1.1
Barbados	14.8	11.3	5.1	17.3	28.6	1.4
Belize	6.4	4.3	1.1	8.0	16.7	1.0
Bolivia	5.4	3.4	0.9	6.3	13.1	1.2
Brazil	6.7	4.4	1.3	7.2	14.1	1.1
Chile	8.7	5.9	2.1	9.3	17.0	1.4
Colombia	6.0	4.0	1.2	6.6	12.5	1.2
Costa Rica	6.4	4.2	1.4	7.1	13.3	1.1
Cuba	11.8	8.4	3.4	12.1	21.4	1.0
Dominica	11.1	8.3	2.8	15.0	28.6	1.0
Dominican Rep.	5.5	3.4	1.0	5.7	11.9	1.0
Ecuador	5.5	3.6	1.1	6.4	12.5	1.1
El Salvador	5.6	3.6	1.0	6.8	14.5	1.3
Grenada	9.9	6.6	2.2	11.1	20.9	1.3
Guadeloupe	11.1	7.8	2.8	12.0	21.3	1.4
Guatemala	4.9	3.0	0.8	5.9	12.6	1.1
Guyana	6.4	4.1	1.3	6.7	13.5	1.1
Haiti	6.2	4.1	1.2	7.3	14.4	1.2
Honduras	4.8	3.1	0.9	6.0	12.4	1.1
Jamaica	8.9	6.5	2.8	11.0	19.7	1.2
Martinique	13.3	9.7	3.6	14.7	24.6	1.4
Mexico	5.7	3.7	1.2	6.3	12.6	1.2
Nicaragua	4.2	2.6	0.7	5.1	10.8	1.2
Panama	6.7	4.5	1.4	7.5	14.3	1.0
Paraguay	5.2	3.4	1.0	6.2	12.0	1.2
Peru	5.8	3.7	1.1	6.3	12.7	1.2
St. Kitts and Nevis	20.0	15.0	5.0	26.1	50.0	1.0
St. Lucia	8.7	6.0	2.0	10.6	22.2	1.6
Suriname	6.7	4.3	1.3	7.0	14.3	1.3
Trinidad and Tobago	8.3	5.7	2.0	9.3	16.9	1.2
Uruguay	16.4	11.4	4.4	18.2	33.3	1.3
Venezuela	5.6	3.6	1.1	6.1	12.2	1.2
Simple average	8.2	5.6	1.9	9.5	18.0	1.2
Weighted average	6.9	4.6	1.5	7.6	14.9	—

Economy	Population over 60 years old	Population over 65 years old	Population over 75 years old	Population over 65/ population 15–64	Population over 60/ population 20–59	Women over 60/ Men over 60
	Percentage					Ratio
Eastern Europe and former Soviet Union						
Albania	8.1	5.3	1.9	8.7	16.7	1.2
Armenia	11.0	6.9	2.0	10.9	21.7	1.4
Azerbaijan	9.0	5.5	1.7	9.0	18.5	1.5
Belarus	17.6	11.9	4.0	18.4	33.3	1.9
Bulgaria	19.7	13.4	5.0	20.2	37.2	1.2
Croatia	17.8	12.1	4.6	17.9	32.3	1.5
Czech Rep.	16.9	11.8	5.0	18.2	32.3	1.5
Estonia	17.2	11.9	4.3	18.2	32.3	1.8
Georgia	15.9	10.8	3.5	16.5	30.3	1.6
Hungary	19.3	13.5	5.5	20.2	35.9	1.4
Kazakhstan	9.5	6.4	2.0	10.4	19.2	1.8
Kyrgyz Rep.	8.5	5.6	1.7	10.0	19.6	1.6
Latvia	17.9	12.4	4.4	18.9	33.3	1.9
Lithuania	16.2	11.1	3.9	16.8	30.3	1.7
Moldova	12.5	8.5	2.5	14.3	26.3	1.4
Poland	14.8	10.0	4.0	15.4	27.8	1.5
Romania	15.6	10.3	4.0	15.9	29.4	1.3
Russia	16.5	11.4	3.9	17.5	31.3	2.0
Slovenia	16.2	11.1	4.3	16.4	29.4	1.6
Tajikistan	6.2	4.0	1.2	7.7	15.9	1.3
Turkmenistan	6.3	4.0	1.2	7.4	14.7	1.5
Ukraine	18.7	13.5	4.6	20.7	35.7	1.9
Uzbekistan	6.5	4.2	1.3	7.7	15.4	1.5
Yugoslavia, Fed. Rep. of	13.6	8.5	3.4	12.5	25.0	1.3
Simple average	**13.8**	**9.3**	**3.3**	**14.6**	**26.8**	**1.6**
Weighted average	**15.3**	**10.5**	**3.7**	**16.4**	**29.7**	—
Middle East and North Africa						
Algeria	5.4	3.7	1.3	7.0	13.7	1.2
Bahrain	4.4	2.8	0.8	4.5	8.3	1.0
Cyprus	14.5	10.8	4.7	16.8	27.2	1.2
Egypt	6.4	4.1	1.2	7.3	14.4	1.2
Iran, Islamic Rep. of	4.7	3.1	0.9	5.8	11.6	1.0
Iraq	4.4	2.7	0.7	5.4	11.3	1.1
Israel	12.1	8.9	3.7	14.9	25.6	1.2
Jordan	4.2	2.6	0.8	4.9	10.6	1.0

(Table continues on the following page.)

Table A.1 *(continued)*

Economy	Population over 60 years old	Population over 65 years old	Population over 75 years old	Population over 65/ population 15–64	Population over 60/ population 20–59	Women over 60/ Men over 60
	Percentage					*Ratio*
Middle East and North Africa (cont.)						
Kuwait	2.7	1.4	0.4	2.3	5.0	0.7
Lebanon	8.9	5.7	2.1	9.8	20.7	1.1
Libya	4.0	2.4	0.6	4.6	10.1	0.9
Malta	14.1	9.9	3.7	14.6	25.4	1.4
Morocco	5.8	3.6	1.2	6.4	13.7	1.1
Oman	4.1	2.4	0.6	4.8	10.0	1.1
Qatar	3.4	1.6	0.5	2.5	6.3	0.4
Saudi Arabia	4.2	2.6	0.7	5.1	10.2	1.0
Syrian Arab Rep.	4.4	2.8	0.9	5.7	11.9	1.1
Tunisia	6.5	4.1	1.2	7.0	14.3	0.9
Turkey	7.1	4.3	1.5	7.0	14.9	1.1
United Arab Emirates	3.0	1.6	0.4	2.3	5.1	0.5
Yemen, Rep. of	4.9	3.0	0.8	6.3	13.9	1.1
Simple average	**6.2**	**4.0**	**1.4**	**6.9**	**13.5**	**1.0**
Weighted average	**5.7**	**3.6**	**1.2**	**5.7**	**13.4**	**—**
Average[b]	**7.0**	**4.7**	**1.6**	**10.0**	**20.0**	**1.1**
Sub-Saharan Africa						
Angola	5.0	3.1	0.8	5.9	12.5	1.2
Benin	4.4	2.7	0.7	5.5	11.7	1.2
Botswana	5.2	3.5	1.2	7.2	14.0	1.2
Burkina Faso	5.0	3.1	0.8	6.0	12.7	1.0
Burundi	4.6	3.0	0.9	5.9	11.6	1.5
Cameroon	5.8	3.8	1.1	7.6	15.1	1.2
Cape Verde	6.7	4.3	1.9	8.4	17.6	1.3
Central African Rep.	5.5	3.0	0.6	5.5	13.4	1.1
Chad	5.8	3.6	0.9	6.6	13.7	1.2
Comoros	4.2	2.5	0.8	5.1	11.2	1.2
Congo	6.1	3.9	1.0	7.7	16.0	1.4
Côte d'Ivoire	4.2	2.5	0.6	5.0	10.8	1.0
Djibouti	4.4	2.6	0.5	4.8	10.5	1.1
Equatorial Guinea	6.5	4.1	1.2	7.5	15.2	1.3
Ethiopia	4.5	2.8	0.7	5.6	11.7	1.4
Gabon	7.5	4.9	1.5	8.8	16.9	1.2
Gambia, The	4.5	2.6	0.5	4.9	10.5	1.1
Ghana	4.5	2.9	0.8	5.7	11.9	1.2
Guinea	4.3	2.6	0.6	5.2	11.1	1.2
Guinea-Bissau	5.5	3.4	0.8	6.3	13.5	1.2
Kenya	4.3	2.8	0.9	6.0	12.4	1.1
Lesotho	5.7	3.6	1.0	6.8	13.8	1.3
Liberia	4.9	3.1	1.0	6.0	12.2	1.1

Economy	Population over 60 years old	Population over 65 years old	Population over 75 years old	Population over 65/ population 15–64	Population over 60/ population 20–59	Women over 60/ Men over 60
	Percentage					Ratio
Sub-Saharan Africa (cont.)						
Madagascar	4.8	3.0	0.8	5.8	12.0	1.2
Malawi	4.2	2.6	0.6	5.0	10.8	1.2
Mali	4.9	3.1	0.9	6.3	13.1	1.0
Mauritania	5.4	3.3	0.8	6.3	13.6	1.2
Mauritius	8.3	5.4	1.6	8.2	15.5	1.2
Mozambique	5.1	3.1	0.8	6.0	12.5	1.2
Namibia	5.1	3.1	0.9	6.2	13.0	1.2
Niger	4.2	2.6	0.6	5.1	10.9	1.2
Nigeria	3.8	2.3	0.5	4.4	9.8	1.3
Rwanda	4.0	2.5	0.6	5.0	10.8	1.2
São Tomé and Principe	8.5	5.1	1.7	8.8	19.2	1.0
Senegal	4.3	2.6	0.6	5.2	11.2	1.2
Seychelles	10.3	7.4	2.9	12.2	22.7	1.3
Sierra Leone	5.1	3.1	0.7	5.8	12.3	1.2
Somalia	4.8	2.9	0.8	5.8	12.0	1.1
South Africa	6.2	4.0	1.2	6.9	13.5	1.3
Sudan	4.6	2.9	0.8	5.5	11.6	1.1
Swaziland	4.1	2.4	0.6	4.9	11.1	1.1
Tanzania	4.7	2.9	0.9	5.8	12.3	1.1
Togo	4.8	3.0	0.8	6.2	12.8	0.9
Uganda	4.5	2.8	0.8	5.8	12.8	1.1
Zaire	4.2	2.6	0.7	5.1	10.6	1.3
Zambia	3.6	2.3	0.6	4.7	10.0	1.0
Zimbabwe	3.9	2.5	0.8	4.7	9.9	1.1
Simple average	**5.2**	**3.2**	**0.9**	**5.9**	**12.5**	**1.2**
Weighted average	**4.6**	**2.8**	**0.8**	**5.6**	**11.7**	—
Asia						
Afghanistan	3.9	2.3	0.5	4.5	9.8	1.0
Bangladesh	4.9	3.1	1.0	5.8	12.0	0.9
Bhutan	5.6	3.4	0.8	6.0	12.7	1.1
Brunei	5.9	3.5	0.8	5.6	11.5	0.7
Cambodia	5.0	2.9	0.7	4.7	9.7	1.3
China	8.9	5.8	1.8	8.7	16.6	1.1
Fiji	5.2	3.2	0.9	5.4	11.0	1.0
Hong Kong	13.0	8.9	3.0	12.7	22.4	1.1
India	6.9	4.4	1.2	7.4	15.0	1.0
Indonesia	6.4	3.9	1.1	6.5	13.9	1.1
Korea, Dem. People's Rep. of	6.5	4.2	1.3	6.1	12.2	1.9
Korea, Rep. of	7.7	4.9	1.5	7.1	13.7	1.4

(Table continues on the following page.)

Table A.1 *(continued)*

Economy	Population over 60 years old	Population over 65 years old	Population over 75 years old	Population over 65/ population 15–64	Population over 60/ population 20–59	Women over 60/ Men over 60
	Percentage					*Ratio*
Asia (cont.)						
Lao People's Dem. Rep.	4.9	3.0	0.7	5.6	11.9	1.1
Macao	11.1	7.4	2.4	10.8	19.2	1.1
Malaysia	5.7	3.6	1.1	6.3	12.5	1.1
Maldives	4.7	2.3	0.5	4.3	11.5	0.4
Micronesia, Fed. States of	5.8	3.9	1.0	7.1	14.7	2.0
Mongolia	5.5	3.4	0.9	6.2	12.7	1.1
Myanmar	6.5	4.1	1.2	7.0	14.3	1.1
Pakistan	4.6	2.8	0.7	5.3	11.2	0.9
Papua New Guinea	4.9	2.7	0.4	4.7	11.4	1.0
Philippines	5.3	3.4	1.0	5.9	11.9	1.1
Singapore	8.5	5.6	1.9	7.8	14.3	1.1
Solomon Islands	4.7	2.8	0.6	5.6	12.7	0.9
Sri Lanka	7.8	5.0	1.5	7.9	15.4	1.0
Taiwan (China)	9.7	6.1	1.7	9.3	18.2	0.8
Thailand	6.0	3.8	1.1	6.0	12.2	1.2
Vanuatu	4.6	2.6	0.7	4.8	11.1	0.4
Viet Nam	6.7	4.5	1.4	8.1	15.6	1.4
Simple average	**6.4**	**4.1**	**1.2**	**6.7**	**13.5**	**1.1**
Weighted average	**7.4**	**4.8**	**1.4**	**7.7**	**15.3**	**—**

— Not available.

a. Turkey is included in the Middle East and North Africa.

b. This total excludes Bahrain, Kuwait, Qatar, Saudi Arabia, and the United Arab Emirates.

Source: World Bank staff estimates.

Table A.2 Percentage of Population over Sixty Years Old, 1990–2150

Economy	1990	2000	2010	2020	2030	2050	2075	2100	2125	2150
OECD[a]										
Australia	15.0	15.3	18.1	22.8	27.7	30.4	30.0	30.4	30.8	30.9
Austria	20.2	21.5	24.9	28.9	34.5	33.9	30.6	30.4	30.7	30.9
Belgium	20.7	22.5	24.8	28.7	32.2	31.2	30.1	30.4	30.8	31.0
Canada	15.6	16.8	20.4	25.9	30.2	30.6	30.2	30.5	30.8	31.0
Denmark	20.2	20.4	24.8	28.4	32.1	30.9	29.9	30.2	30.7	30.9
Finland	18.4	19.8	24.4	28.7	30.9	29.9	29.8	30.3	30.7	30.9
France	18.9	20.2	23.1	26.8	30.1	31.2	30.3	30.5	30.8	31.0
Germany	20.3	23.7	26.5	30.3	35.3	32.5	30.4	30.5	30.8	31.0
Greece	20.2	24.2	26.5	29.1	32.5	34.4	30.7	30.5	30.8	31.0
Iceland	14.5	14.9	17.3	21.4	26.0	29.0	29.9	30.2	30.6	30.7
Ireland	15.2	15.7	17.8	20.1	22.9	28.2	29.4	30.1	30.6	30.9
Italy	20.6	24.2	27.4	30.6	35.9	36.5	30.9	30.5	30.8	31.0
Japan	17.3	22.7	29.0	31.4	33.0	34.4	31.0	30.7	30.9	31.0
Luxembourg	19.3	21.2	25.3	29.5	33.0	30.1	30.2	30.1	30.4	30.5
Netherlands	17.8	19.0	23.4	28.4	33.4	31.7	30.2	30.4	30.8	31.0
New Zealand	15.2	15.9	18.9	22.7	26.8	29.0	29.6	30.2	30.7	30.9
Norway	21.2	20.2	22.4	26.0	29.6	30.2	30.1	30.4	30.8	30.9
Portugal	18.0	19.8	21.4	24.6	29.7	33.0	30.2	30.3	30.7	30.9
Spain	18.5	20.6	22.4	25.6	30.9	34.2	30.3	30.3	30.7	30.9
Sweden	22.9	21.9	25.4	27.8	30.0	28.7	29.9	30.5	30.8	31.0
Switzerland	19.9	21.9	26.6	30.5	34.0	31.6	30.4	30.6	30.9	31.0
United Kingdom	20.8	20.7	23.0	25.5	29.6	29.5	29.7	30.3	30.7	30.9
United States	16.6	16.5	19.2	24.5	28.2	28.9	29.7	30.3	30.7	30.9
Simple average	**18.6**	**20.0**	**23.2**	**26.9**	**30.8**	**31.3**	**30.2**	**30.4**	**30.7**	**30.9**
Weighted average	**18.2**	**19.9**	**23.1**	**27.0**	**30.7**	**31.2**	**30.1**	**30.4**	**30.8**	**31.0**
Latin America and Caribbean										
Antigua and Barbuda	7.6	11.1	10.6	12.3	16.9	29.0	29.3	30.5	31.0	30.8
Argentina	13.1	13.7	15.1	17.2	19.3	25.9	28.6	29.7	30.4	30.8
Bahamas	6.7	7.6	10.1	12.9	18.7	25.7	28.3	29.6	30.2	30.5
Barbados	14.8	13.3	14.9	21.9	28.3	30.3	29.7	30.2	30.9	31.2
Belize	6.4	6.5	6.3	6.2	10.6	18.8	27.7	29.5	30.3	30.6
Bolivia	5.4	5.7	6.4	7.9	10.0	17.6	26.0	28.1	29.6	30.3
Brazil	6.7	7.7	9.7	13.1	16.9	24.2	27.7	29.3	30.2	30.6
Chile	8.7	9.8	12.2	16.1	20.8	26.4	28.7	29.8	30.4	30.8
Colombia	6.0	6.7	8.7	12.6	18.0	25.5	28.0	29.4	30.2	30.6
Costa Rica	6.4	7.8	10.0	14.3	19.2	26.4	29.2	30.1	30.6	30.9
Cuba	11.8	13.5	17.0	20.2	27.2	29.8	29.9	30.3	30.7	30.9
Dominica	11.1	11.4	9.9	9.8	14.2	26.0	30.1	30.7	31.9	31.7
Dominican Rep.	5.5	6.7	8.6	11.7	16.3	24.3	27.8	29.3	30.2	30.6
Ecuador	5.5	6.0	7.4	10.1	13.7	22.4	27.3	29.0	30.0	30.5
El Salvador	5.6	6.1	6.6	7.5	10.2	20.3	27.3	29.0	30.0	30.5
Grenada	9.9	10.8	5.7	10.0	16.5	25.2	28.3	29.6	30.5	31.5

(Table continues on the following page.)

349

Table A.2 *(continued)*

Economy	1990	2000	2010	2020	2030	2050	2075	2100	2125	2150
Latin America and Caribbean (cont.)										
Guadeloupe	11.1	12.2	14.8	17.7	24.0	27.9	29.2	30.3	30.8	31.0
Guatemala	4.9	5.1	5.4	6.6	8.8	16.2	26.4	28.7	29.9	30.4
Guyana	6.4	7.3	8.7	11.7	16.6	24.1	27.2	28.9	29.9	30.6
Haiti	6.2	6.0	5.9	6.7	8.2	13.1	22.1	26.9	29.0	29.9
Honduras	4.8	4.8	5.4	6.7	9.3	17.2	26.7	28.9	30.0	30.5
Jamaica	8.9	9.3	10.4	13.3	19.1	26.7	29.0	30.0	30.6	30.8
Martinique	13.3	14.3	15.9	19.6	27.3	28.4	29.7	30.2	30.4	30.8
Mexico	5.7	6.6	8.3	11.2	15.7	24.6	28.3	29.6	30.3	30.7
Nicaragua	4.2	4.4	5.1	6.8	9.3	17.1	26.9	29.1	30.1	30.6
Panama	6.7	7.8	10.1	13.6	18.5	26.6	28.9	29.9	30.5	30.8
Paraguay	5.2	5.1	5.6	8.0	10.4	16.1	25.8	28.9	30.0	30.5
Peru	5.8	6.4	7.7	10.2	13.7	21.5	26.8	28.8	29.9	30.5
St. Kitts and Nevis	20.0	14.3	8.8	5.4	14.6	23.9	24.5	26.5	26.0	26.0
St. Lucia	8.7	9.1	8.9	7.9	13.0	24.7	28.8	29.8	30.8	30.9
Suriname	6.7	7.2	7.8	10.8	16.3	23.3	28.0	29.5	30.1	30.8
Trinidad and Tobago	8.3	9.0	11.2	14.9	19.1	25.6	28.6	29.7	30.5	30.7
Uruguay	16.4	17.8	18.7	20.3	22.5	27.8	29.3	30.1	30.5	30.9
Venezuela	5.6	6.4	8.5	11.7	15.5	23.6	28.1	29.5	30.3	30.7
Simple average	**8.2**	**8.8**	**9.6**	**12.0**	**16.4**	**23.7**	**27.9**	**29.4**	**30.2**	**30.6**
Weighted average	**6.9**	**7.7**	**9.3**	**12.2**	**16.0**	**23.5**	**27.7**	**29.3**	**30.2**	**30.6**
Eastern Europe and former Soviet Union										
Albania	8.1	9.7	11.4	14.9	19.1	25.9	28.8	29.8	30.5	30.8
Armenia	11.0	13.4	14.5	19.6	22.1	27.9	29.1	30.0	30.6	30.8
Azerbaijan	9.0	10.9	11.3	15.9	19.9	26.8	28.7	29.8	30.4	30.8
Belarus	17.6	19.4	20.5	24.1	25.3	27.8	29.2	30.1	30.6	30.8
Bulgaria	19.7	22.8	24.9	26.3	26.7	28.7	29.2	29.9	30.5	30.8
Croatia	17.8	21.2	23.9	26.9	28.7	30.0	29.7	30.1	30.6	30.9
Czech Rep.	16.9	16.9	19.2	22.6	24.0	27.5	28.8	29.7	30.4	30.7
Estonia	17.2	19.0	20.8	23.6	25.1	27.5	29.0	30.0	30.5	30.8
Georgia	15.9	18.2	18.9	22.3	24.4	27.6	29.1	30.0	30.5	30.8
Hungary	19.3	20.9	23.1	26.7	26.8	28.8	28.9	29.6	30.3	30.7
Kazakhstan	9.5	11.5	12.9	16.7	18.8	25.8	28.1	29.4	30.3	30.7
Kyrgyz Rep.	8.5	8.7	8.8	11.8	14.2	22.5	28.1	29.5	30.3	30.7
Latvia	17.9	20.0	21.2	24.2	25.9	27.7	29.0	29.9	30.5	30.8
Lithuania	16.2	18.2	19.7	23.5	26.3	28.3	29.3	30.0	30.6	30.8
Moldova	12.5	13.8	14.7	17.3	17.8	25.3	28.1	29.4	30.3	30.7
Poland	14.8	16.2	17.5	22.2	23.3	26.8	28.5	29.6	30.3	30.7
Romania	15.6	17.8	17.9	20.2	21.9	26.1	28.1	29.4	30.2	30.6
Russia	16.5	18.7	20.5	24.4	24.9	27.6	29.0	29.9	30.5	30.8
Slovenia	16.2	19.4	22.7	26.5	29.1	31.6	30.0	30.2	30.6	30.9
Tajikistan	6.2	6.2	6.0	8.2	10.8	19.3	28.0	29.5	30.3	30.7
Turkmenistan	6.3	6.5	7.0	10.2	13.1	21.8	27.4	29.0	30.1	30.5
Ukraine	18.7	21.3	22.1	24.5	25.5	27.5	29.1	30.0	30.5	30.8

Economy	1990	2000	2010	2020	2030	2050	2075	2100	2125	2150
Eastern Europe and former Soviet Union (cont.)										
Uzbekistan	6.5	6.7	7.0	10.2	13.2	22.1	28.1	29.5	30.3	30.7
Yugoslavia, Fed. Rep. of	13.6	17.3	18.8	22.2	24.9	27.5	28.9	29.9	30.5	30.8
Simple average	**13.8**	**15.6**	**16.9**	**20.2**	**22.2**	**26.6**	**28.8**	**29.8**	**30.4**	**30.8**
Weighted average	**15.3**	**17.0**	**18.2**	**21.5**	**22.7**	**26.5**	**28.7**	**29.8**	**30.4**	**30.8**
Middle East and North Africa										
Algeria	5.4	5.4	5.7	7.6	10.9	19.4	27.7	29.2	30.1	30.6
Bahrain	4.4	5.4	8.7	13.8	14.4	17.4	26.5	29.4	30.2	30.7
Cyprus	14.5	16.0	18.8	22.7	26.2	28.8	29.8	30.3	30.8	30.9
Egypt	6.4	7.0	7.9	10.6	12.9	20.2	26.0	28.2	29.6	30.3
Iran, Islamic Rep. of	4.7	4.6	5.0	5.8	6.6	9.1	16.2	25.6	29.4	30.3
Iraq	4.4	4.5	5.0	6.0	7.6	14.1	25.3	28.7	29.9	30.4
Israel	12.1	10.2	12.1	16.4	21.3	27.0	29.5	30.3	30.8	30.9
Jordan	4.2	4.6	5.2	6.7	10.3	17.1	27.0	29.2	30.1	30.6
Kuwait	2.7	5.6	10.8	17.6	20.4	27.3	29.2	30.1	30.7	30.9
Lebanon	8.9	9.0	7.9	8.5	11.9	20.4	26.9	28.8	29.9	30.5
Libya	4.0	4.4	5.0	5.5	6.1	9.9	18.9	28.0	29.9	30.5
Malta	14.1	16.4	20.6	24.3	25.6	27.8	29.0	29.7	30.3	30.6
Morocco	5.8	5.9	6.1	8.4	11.3	18.7	26.4	28.4	29.7	30.4
Oman	4.1	4.4	5.4	6.4	7.1	11.8	23.0	29.2	30.2	30.6
Qatar	3.4	5.7	10.0	14.0	14.3	17.3	26.4	29.3	30.2	30.6
Saudi Arabia	4.2	4.3	5.1	6.4	7.0	11.6	22.6	28.8	30.0	30.5
Syrian Arab Rep.	4.4	4.3	4.2	5.2	7.0	13.0	24.5	29.0	30.1	30.6
Tunisia	6.5	7.3	7.4	10.5	14.9	23.1	27.7	29.3	30.2	30.6
Turkey	7.1	8.3	9.5	12.1	16.0	23.0	27.6	29.3	30.2	30.6
United Arab Emirates	3.0	5.8	12.7	21.0	20.1	21.5	28.6	29.8	30.4	30.8
Yemen, Rep. of	4.9	4.2	3.4	2.8	3.5	6.1	14.0	23.7	27.3	29.0
Simple average	**6.2**	**6.8**	**8.4**	**11.1**	**13.1**	**18.3**	**25.4**	**28.8**	**30.0**	**30.5**
Weighted average	**5.7**	**6.0**	**6.5**	**8.0**	**9.8**	**14.5**	**21.6**	**27.3**	**29.5**	**30.3**
Average[b]	**7.0**	**7.3**	**8.1**	**10.0**	**12.4**	**18.1**	**25.0**	**28.6**	**29.9**	**30.5**
Sub-Saharan Africa										
Angola	5.0	4.9	4.7	4.8	5.3	8.1	16.9	25.3	27.7	29.1
Benin	4.4	4.2	4.1	4.6	5.7	11.2	20.9	25.8	28.2	29.4
Botswana	5.2	4.8	5.4	7.3	10.3	20.9	27.7	29.2	30.2	30.6
Burkina Faso	5.0	4.6	4.3	4.1	5.1	8.5	17.6	24.9	27.5	29.0
Burundi	4.6	3.6	3.2	4.0	4.7	7.4	16.7	25.3	27.7	29.1
Cameroon	5.8	5.2	5.0	5.5	6.5	12.0	22.3	27.1	29.1	30.0
Cape Verde	6.7	5.4	3.7	4.6	8.6	15.2	26.6	29.0	30.2	30.6
Central African Rep.	5.5	6.1	5.6	5.2	6.1	10.7	20.3	25.6	28.1	29.4
Chad	5.8	5.8	5.8	6.0	6.5	9.5	18.7	25.3	27.8	29.2
Comoros	4.2	3.9	4.2	4.6	5.7	11.0	21.7	27.0	29.1	30.0
Congo	6.1	5.1	4.2	4.4	5.6	9.3	19.1	26.8	28.9	29.8

(Table continues on the following page.)

Table A.2 *(continued)*

Economy	1990	2000	2010	2020	2030	2050	2075	2100	2125	2150
Sub-Saharan Africa (cont.)										
Côte d'Ivoire	4.2	4.2	4.2	4.7	5.7	10.5	20.9	27.2	29.1	30.0
Djibouti	4.4	4.5	5.2	5.9	6.5	10.4	19.7	25.7	28.2	29.4
Equitorial Guinea	6.5	6.7	6.6	7.0	7.7	10.9	20.2	25.1	27.8	29.2
Ethiopia	4.5	4.1	3.9	3.9	4.2	6.8	15.1	25.0	27.8	29.2
Gabon	7.5	7.1	6.5	6.5	6.7	9.2	18.9	26.4	28.7	29.7
Gambia, The	4.5	4.8	4.9	5.2	5.3	7.7	15.8	24.1	26.9	28.6
Ghana	4.5	4.5	4.7	5.4	6.8	12.3	22.1	26.5	28.7	29.8
Guinea	4.3	4.2	4.0	4.3	4.9	7.6	15.8	24.0	26.8	28.6
Guinea-Bissau	5.5	4.9	4.3	4.1	4.9	8.0	16.0	22.0	25.2	27.6
Kenya	4.3	3.9	3.6	4.4	5.9	11.7	22.6	27.8	29.5	30.2
Lesotho	5.7	5.7	6.1	6.8	8.2	14.4	24.0	27.2	29.1	30.0
Liberia	4.9	5.0	5.4	6.0	7.5	13.1	22.7	27.1	29.1	30.0
Madagascar	4.8	4.6	4.7	5.4	6.7	11.9	21.3	25.7	28.1	29.4
Malawi	4.2	3.9	3.8	3.8	4.3	6.8	15.0	24.8	27.6	29.1
Mali	4.9	4.5	4.3	3.9	4.5	7.8	16.1	24.6	27.5	29.0
Mauritania	5.4	5.1	4.6	4.1	4.6	6.9	14.9	24.2	27.1	28.8
Mauritius	8.3	9.4	11.7	17.3	23.4	28.8	29.1	29.8	30.4	30.7
Mozambique	5.1	4.6	4.2	4.2	4.8	7.5	16.6	25.3	27.7	29.1
Namibia	5.1	5.0	5.2	6.0	7.6	14.1	24.3	27.9	29.5	30.2
Niger	4.2	4.1	3.9	3.9	4.1	5.9	13.2	23.3	27.0	28.8
Nigeria	3.8	4.0	4.4	5.1	6.5	11.7	20.6	25.7	28.1	29.3
Rwanda	4.0	3.7	3.4	3.3	3.8	6.0	14.3	24.3	27.9	29.3
São Tomé and Principe	8.5	7.3	8.1	9.1	10.8	18.8	26.9	28.6	30.1	30.7
Senegal	4.3	3.7	3.5	3.7	4.3	7.6	17.2	25.1	27.7	29.1
Seychelles	10.3	10.7	10.8	12.0	17.6	24.6	27.7	28.7	28.5	29.0
Sierra Leone	5.1	5.2	5.0	5.0	5.2	7.7	15.6	23.7	26.4	28.3
Somalia	4.8	4.7	4.6	4.8	5.4	8.4	17.1	25.0	27.6	29.0
South Africa	6.2	6.7	7.8	9.8	12.4	18.9	26.7	28.7	29.9	30.5
Sudan	4.6	4.7	5.0	5.6	6.6	11.2	20.6	25.8	28.2	29.4
Swaziland	4.1	3.9	4.2	4.9	6.1	11.7	22.0	27.0	29.1	30.0
Tanzania	4.7	4.2	4.0	3.9	4.5	7.6	16.7	24.9	27.5	29.0
Togo	4.8	4.5	4.4	4.7	5.8	10.9	21.0	26.3	28.6	29.7
Uganda	4.5	3.8	3.1	3.1	4.1	7.8	17.0	24.8	27.5	29.0
Zaire	4.2	4.3	4.4	5.0	6.1	10.7	20.7	26.4	28.7	29.7
Zambia	3.6	3.2	3.0	3.4	4.4	8.9	19.5	26.7	28.9	29.8
Zimbabwe	3.9	4.2	4.9	6.8	9.6	18.3	26.0	28.9	30.0	30.5
Simple average	**5.2**	**5.0**	**4.9**	**5.5**	**6.8**	**11.2**	**20.0**	**26.1**	**28.3**	**29.5**
Weighted average	**4.6**	**4.4**	**4.5**	**4.9**	**5.9**	**9.9**	**18.8**	**27.7**	**28.1**	**29.4**
Asia										
Afghanistan	3.9	3.9	3.9	4.2	4.7	7.0	14.2	22.5	25.6	27.8
Bangladesh	4.9	5.4	6.0	7.6	10.1	17.4	22.6	26.2	28.4	29.5
Bhutan	5.6	5.5	5.7	6.3	7.3	11.0	20.1	25.2	27.8	29.1
Brunei	5.9	7.1	9.6	14.6	18.6	23.9	29.2	30.1	30.6	30.8
Cambodia	5.0	5.6	7.2	10.1	13.0	16.9	23.3	26.6	28.7	29.8

Economy	1990	2000	2010	2020	2030	2050	2075	2100	2125	2150
Asia (cont.)										
China	8.9	10.2	12.0	16.0	21.9	26.1	28.3	29.6	30.4	30.7
Fiji	5.2	6.8	9.3	12.6	15.6	23.5	27.2	28.9	29.9	30.4
Hong Kong	13.0	15.6	18.8	27.3	33.9	35.2	30.9	30.6	30.8	31.0
India	6.9	7.5	8.3	10.3	13.1	20.4	25.7	27.9	29.5	30.2
Indonesia	6.4	7.3	8.3	10.9	14.1	21.7	25.5	27.8	29.3	30.1
Kiribati	4.3	8.3	8.2	7.3	10.7	16.7	23.8	27.5	29.7	30.3
Korea, Dem. People's Rep. of	6.5	8.2	10.5	14.9	21.9	26.5	28.8	29.9	30.5	30.8
Korea, Rep. of	7.7	10.7	13.9	19.5	25.5	29.8	29.1	29.8	30.4	30.7
Lao People's Dem. Rep.	4.9	4.8	4.9	5.2	5.8	9.4	19.3	25.8	28.1	29.4
Macao	11.1	11.4	14.4	22.2	27.9	28.2	29.0	30.1	30.8	30.8
Malaysia	5.7	6.5	8.0	11.0	14.5	22.1	28.3	29.6	30.4	30.7
Maldives	4.7	5.7	5.4	5.5	7.0	13.0	23.6	27.9	29.8	30.3
Micronesia, Fed. States of	5.8	6.1	5.5	8.2	10.8	19.8	27.9	29.4	30.3	30.8
Mongolia	5.5	5.9	6.9	8.3	11.1	18.4	26.9	28.8	29.9	30.5
Myanmar	6.5	7.2	7.7	9.9	13.4	20.9	26.5	28.5	29.8	30.4
Nepal	5.2	5.7	6.4	7.3	8.5	14.2	22.8	26.3	28.5	29.6
Pakistan	4.6	4.7	4.9	6.3	8.4	14.2	22.8	26.7	28.8	29.8
Papua New Guinea	4.9	5.1	5.7	6.5	8.5	15.0	23.9	26.8	28.8	29.8
Philippines	5.3	5.9	7.3	10.1	13.5	22.3	27.0	28.8	29.9	30.5
Singapore	8.5	10.9	15.6	23.9	29.4	29.8	29.6	30.1	30.6	30.9
Solomon Islands	4.7	4.9	5.4	6.6	8.7	16.3	26.4	28.9	29.8	30.4
Sri Lanka	7.8	9.2	12.0	16.2	20.6	27.0	28.7	29.8	30.4	30.8
Taiwan (China)	9.7	12.0	14.1	20.6	26.1	30.8	29.8	30.1	30.6	30.8
Thailand	6.0	7.4	9.1	12.8	18.0	25.3	27.8	29.2	30.1	30.6
Vanuatu	4.6	4.9	5.3	6.9	9.1	15.7	25.2	28.8	30.0	30.4
Viet Nam	6.7	6.6	6.6	9.2	13.7	22.2	27.4	29.2	30.1	30.6
Simple average	**6.3**	**7.3**	**8.6**	**11.6**	**15.0**	**20.7**	**25.9**	**28.3**	**29.6**	**30.3**
Weighted average	**7.4**	**8.3**	**9.5**	**12.3**	**16.3**	**22.1**	**26.2**	**28.3**	**29.6**	**30.3**

— Not available.

a. Turkey is included in the Middle East and North Africa.

b. This total excludes Bahrain, Kuwait, Qatar, Saudi Arabia, and the United Arab Emirates.

Source: World Bank staff estimates.

Table A.3 Average Annual Compound Real Growth Rate of Wages, Selected Periods

Country	(1) 1970–88	(2) 1980–88	(3) Longest period available	Years for column 3
Low-income economies				
Afghanistan	—	–1.0	–1.0	(1980–88)
Bangladesh	–1.9	–1.5	–1.9	(1970–88)
Burkina Faso	—	—	6.0	(1974–83)
Burundi	—	—	–4.9	(1971–83)
Ethiopia	—	0.3	0.3	(1980–88)
Haiti	0.6	5.8	0.6	(1970–88)
Kenya	—	1.0	1.0	(1980–88)
Nepal	—	—	0.6	(1977–87)
Somalia	—	—	–9.3	(1967–86)
Sri Lanka	—	—	1.7	(1966–81)
Togo	—	—	–0.2	(1974–84)
Simple average	**–0.7**	**0.9**		
Lower middle-income economies				
Argentina	0.1	–0.3	1.9	(1963–88)
Bolivia	–4.5	–9.3	–4.5	(1970–88)
Cameroon	—	—	3.6	(1970–84)
Chile	5.4	0.5	6.6	(1963–88)
Colombia	0.6	1.6	1.0	(1963–88)
Congo	—	—	4.7	(1968–85)
Ecuador	2.7	–0.7	2.4	(1963–88)
Guatemala	—	–1.5	–1.5	(1980–88)
Malaysia	2.7	3.8	2.7	(1970–88)
Nicaragua	—	—	–5.7	(1972–85)
Philippines	0.3	6.4	0.4	(1963–88)
Turkey	0.8	–2.8	2.3	(1963–88)
Zimbabwe	0.9	–0.4	0.9	(1970–88)
Simple average	**1.0**	**–0.3**		

Country	(1) 1970–88	(2) 1980–88	(3) Longest period available	Years for column 3
Upper-middle-income economies				
Barbados	—	—	4.2	(1976–87)
Cyprus	5.2	4.5	4.7	(1963–88)
Czech Rep.	1.5	0.7	1.5	(1970–88)
Hungary	—	2.9	2.9	(1980–88)
Korea, Rep. of	7.1	5.3	7.1	(1970–88)
Malta[a]	5.8	1.4	5.6	(1963–88)
South Africa	—	0.5	0.5	(1980–88)
Uruguay	—	2.2	2.2	(1980–88)
Yugoslavia, Fed. Rep. of	-0.2	-1.4	-0.2	(1970–88)
Simple average	**3.9**	**2.0**		
High-income economies				
Australia	1.6	0.3	2.1	(1963–88)
Austria	2.9	2.0	3.3	(1963–88)
Canada	1.0	0.1	1.5	(1963–88)
Denmark	1.6	0.6	2.2	(1963–88)
Finland	2.7	2.6	3.0	(1963–88)
Ireland	3.4	2.6	3.5	(1963–88)
Israel	3.4	-4.2	3.9	(1963–88)
Italy	2.7	1.2	2.7	(1970–88)
Japan	2.8	1.8	4.3	(1963–88)
Luxembourg	1.9	0.9	2.9	(1963–88)
Norway	1.8	1.2	2.1	(1963–88)
Portugal	2.0	1.2	2.9	(1963–88)
Singapore	4.0	5.1	3.6	(1963–88)
Spain	2.6	0.5	3.7	(1963–88)
Sweden	0.3	0.4	1.1	(1963–88)
United Kingdom	2.4	2.9	2.6	(1963–88)
United States	0.4	0.7	0.5	(1963–88)
Simple average	**2.2**	**1.2**		
Simple world average	**1.9**	**0.8**		

— Not available.

a. Data through 1987.

Sources: UNIDO data base, World Bank (1992); World Bank staff estimates.

Table A.4 Public Pension Scheme Coverage, Selected Countries

Country	Year for column 1	(1) Contributors/ labor force[a]	(2) Pensioners/ persons over 60	(3) Pensioners/ contributors	(4) Covered wage bill GDP[b]
		Percentage			
Sub-Saharan Africa					
Burundi	1989	4.7	4.7	17.5	5.4
Cameroon	1989	13.7	—	—	6.9
Chad	1989	1.1	—	—	—
Côte d'Ivoire	1989	9.3	5.7	12.3	—
Ghana	1989	13.2	—	—	15.7
Madagascar	1989	8.2	4.1	8.0	—
Mali	1989	2.5	—	—	—
Mauritius[c]	1987	—	100.0	—	12.5
Niger	1990	2.8	—	—	4.4
Rwanda	1989	9.3	5.6	4.9	10.7
Tanzania	1990	5.1	—	—	6.3
Zambia	1989	13.8	—	—	7.9
Unweighted average	—	**6.4**	**24.0**	**8.5**	**8.7**
Asia					
Bangladesh	1985	3.5	—	—	—
China	1989	23.7	22.5	13.9	—
Hong Kong[c]	1990	—	50.0	—	—
India	1990	10.5	—	—	3.4
Indonesia	1991	12.4	9.8	—	1.7
Malaysia	1991	44.6	—	—	20.6
Pakistan	1989	3.8	—	7.7	1.2
Philippines	1990	19.1	7.0	12.5	8.3
Singapore	1990	75.8	—	—	35.3
Sri Lanka	1990	18.4	—	—	11.4
Unweighted average	—	**23.5**	**22.3**	**11.4**	**11.7**
Latin America and Caribbean					
Argentina	1989	53.2	72.4	66.7	—
Bolivia	1985	16.9	17.8	32.3	4.4
Brazil	1989	50.3	47.1	40.0	—
Chile	1992	62.2	—	—	—
Colombia	1989	24.5	10.0	9.3	9.5
Costa Rica	1989	54.2	36.4	11.8	23.6
Ecuador	1989	37.8	21.5	8.8	8.6
El Salvador	1989	12.4	4.3	6.9	9.7
Guatemala	1986	27.0	13.0	6.0	6.6
Honduras	1990	18.7	—	—	9.4
Jamaica	1991	40.1	27.0	13.2	8.1
Mexico	1988	40.2	—	—	10.0

Country	Year for column 1	(1) Contributors/ labor force[a]	(2) Pensioners/ persons over 60	(3) Pensioners/ contributors	(4) Covered wage bill GDP[b]
		Percentage			
Latin America and Caribbean (cont.)					
Nicaragua	1989	22.7	19.9	11.9	—
Panama	1990	39.5	31.9	13.0	35.8
Peru	1992	25.7	17.6	—	9.7
Trinidad and Tobago	1989	60.7	—	9.4	—
Uruguay	1989	68.8	81.7	47.6	22.8
Venezuela	1990	34.3	30.0	10.9	8.9
Unweighted average	—	**38.3**	**30.8**	**21.0**	**12.9**
OECD [d]					
Australia[c]	1990	—	74.3	—	—
Austria	1990	—	—	58.8	33.5
Canada[c]	1989	—	75.2	—	30.0
Denmark[c]	1990	—	87.5	—	—
Finland[c]	1990	—	96.9	—	—
Germany	1990	93.6	88.0	—	36.3
Iceland[c]	1990	—	75.7	—	26.7
Japan	1990	94.5	68.5	21.7	21.4
Netherlands	1990	93.6	80.7	—	49.3
New Zealand[c]	1990	—	100.0	—	—
Norway[c]	1990	—	81.1	—	—
Spain	1992	85.3	80.0	45.5	29.4
Sweden	1990	—	88.4	37.0	—
Switzerland	1990	99.4	98.0	41.7	60.0
United Kingdom	1990	94.2	83.6	—	—
United States	1989	96.7	82.9	30.3	38.5
Unweighted average	—	**93.9**	**84.1**	**39.2**	**36.1**
Middle East and North Africa					
Egypt	1989	62.2	—	—	—
Israel	1985	—	91.0	—	37.5
Morocco	1989	17.4	20.0	22.2	5.6
Tunisia	1990	50.9	42.1	14.9	16.7
Turkey	1990	34.6	76.9	45.5	3.8
Unweighted average	—	**41.3**	**57.5**	**27.5**	**15.9**

— Not available.

a. Workers contributing during the past year.

b. This usually refers only to the main public pension scheme.

c. The main benefit is a universal flat or means-tested pension financed by general revenues.

d. Turkey is included in the Middle East and North Africa.

Source: Palacios (1994a, b).

Table A.5 Public Pension Spending Indicators *(percentages)*

Country	Public pension spending /GDP	Public pension spending /GOV[a]	Pension spending for public employees/ total public pension spending	Earmarked payroll tax minus benefit spending/ benefit spending
OECD[b]				
Australia	3.9	16.0	—	n.a.
Austria	14.8	37.9	29.9	-18.0
Belgium	11.0	17.6	30.6	-17.0
Canada	4.2	19.1	5.8	n.a.
Denmark	9.9	24.8	11.8	n.a.
Finland	10.3	34.3	—	n.a.
France	11.8	25.8	20.5	-32.0
Germany	10.8	34.4	17.7	-18.0
Greece	12.3	30.6	18.8	-80.0
Iceland	4.8	—	—	n.a.
Ireland	6.1	15.7	—	—
Italy	14.4	37.0	15.6	-39.0
Japan	5.0	—	2.5	-32.0
Luxembourg	12.0	25.4	30.1	-26.0
Netherlands	9.8	17.9	22.0	-28.0
New Zealand	7.5	15.6	—	n.a.
Norway	10.1	22.3	—	n.a.
Portugal	7.7	18.9	—	—
Spain	7.5	23.2	—	—
Sweden	11.6	28.1	—	-32.0
Switzerland	9.9	—	—	-29.0
United Kingdom	9.5	24.1	—	—
United States	6.5	24.5	25.9	-3.0
Average	**9.2**	**24.7**	**19.3**	**-29.5**
Latin America and Caribbean				
Argentina	4.6	—	—	-17.0
Belize	1.1	—	92.2	1,028.0
Bolivia	1.5	1.1	—	22.0
Brazil	2.9	10.6	—	—
Chile	5.7	27.5	—	-56.0
Colombia	0.8	5.9	39.3	23.0
Costa Rica	3.7	12.0	49.5	91.0
Dominica	—	—	—	277.0
Dominican Rep.	0.1	—	—	228.0
Ecuador	1.1	5.7	6.8	56.0
El Salvador	0.4	3.4	22.5	13.0
Grenada	1.5	—	92.9	125.0
Guatemala	0.4	2.0	—	54.0
Guyana	1.4	—	—	37.0
Honduras	0.2	0.7	42.4	324.0
Jamaica	0.7	—	—	—
Mexico	1.0	1.5	35.6	117.0
Nicaragua	0.8	2.8	—	—

Country	Public pension spending /GDP	Public pension spending /GOV[a]	Pension spending for public employees/ total public pension spending	Earmarked payroll tax minus benefit spending/ benefit spending
Latin America and Caribbean (cont.)				
Panama	5.1	19.7	10.8	-9.0
Paraguay	0.4	3.7	—	—
Peru	0.7	4.1	—	32.0
Trinidad and Tobago	3.4	9.6	—	—
Uruguay	8.8	33.4	—	-18.0
Venezuela	0.5	1.5	—	8.0
Average	**2.0**	**8.5**	**43.6**	**122.9**
Eastern Europe and former Soviet Union				
Albania	7.9	13.4	—	—
Armenia	3.6	—	—	—
Azerbaijan	5.6	18.3	—	—
Belarus	7.3	14.8	—	—
Bulgaria	7.9	21.5	—	—
Czech Rep.	8.2	—	—	-50.0
Estonia	6.9	—	—	—
Georgia	11.0	31.0	—	—
Hungary	9.7	18.6	—	-7.0
Kazakhstan	4.7	10.3	—	—
Kyrgyz Rep.	6.1	—	—	—
Latvia	6.7	—	—	—
Lithuania	6.6	—	—	—
Poland	12.4	24.8	—	-50.0
Romania	6.9	—	—	—
Russia	7.1	—	—	—
Slovenia	9.3	—	—	—
Ukraine	13.0	—	—	—
Uzbekistan	10.3	—	—	—
Average	**8.0**	**19.1**	**—**	**-35.7**
Middle East and North Africa				
Bahrain	0.4	0.9	41.6	—
Cyprus	4.0	13.7	—	—
Egypt	3.0	5.8	40.0	93.0
Israel	4.3	8.9	22.3	-41.0
Jordan	0.3	0.8	—	528.0
Kuwait	3.1	5.3	—	—
Malta	9.5	23.8	—	—
Morocco	1.2	—	72.9	-30.0
Syrian Arab Rep.	0.3	0.8	—	—
Tunisia	2.5	—	39.7	6.0
Turkey	2.4	11.3	34.4	-21.0
Average	**2.8**	**7.9**	**41.8**	**89.2**

(Table continues on the following page.)

Table A.5 *(continued)*

Country	Public pension spending /GDP	Public pension spending /GOV[a]	Pension spending for public employees/ total public pension spending	Earmarked payroll tax minus benefit spending/ benefit spending
Sub-Saharan Africa				
Benin	0.3	—	64.9	13.0
Burkina Faso	0.7	5.8	68.7	133.0
Burundi	0.3	0.9	38.1	163.0
Cameroon	0.2	—	68.5	668.0
Central African Rep.	0.3	—	—	28.0
Chad	0.0	0.2	—	977.0
Ethiopia	1.1	2.9	100.0	36.0
Gabon	0.7	1.7	30.0	36.0
Guinea	0.0	—	—	13.0
Kenya	0.5	2.1	—	243.0
Malawi	0.4	1.3	—	—
Mali	0.7	2.5	71.1	-5.0
Mauritania	1.4	—	84.0	—
Mauritius	2.6	—	—	n.a.
Mozambique	0.0	—	100.0	-43.0
Niger	0.2	—	71.0	55.0
Nigeria	—	—	—	485.0
Rwanda	0.3	—	—	263.0
Senegal	0.9	—	—	79.0
Sudan	0.0	—	—	354.0
Swaziland	0.3	1.3	41.5	294.0
Tanzania	0.2	1.4	—	237.0
Togo	0.4	1.0	—	—
Uganda	0.0	0.0	—	—
Zaire	—	—	—	274.0
Zambia	0.3	1.1	—	—
Average	**0.5**	**1.8**	**67.1**	**204.9**
Asia				
Bangladesh	0.0	0.1	84.9	159.0
China	2.6	10.7	—	—
Fiji	8.5	14.7	—	81.0
India	0.6	8.3	75.5	—
Indonesia	0.1	—	—	856.0
Malaysia	1.6	5.8	57.3	192.0
Pakistan	0.6	2.3	95.5	—
Philippines	0.6	3.2	—	—
Singapore	2.2	34.6	4.0	25.0
Sri Lanka	2.2	6.9	89.3	19.0
Average	**1.9**	**9.6**	**67.7**	**222.0**

— Not available.

a. GOV denotes government spending for the same year.

Source: See Palacios (1994a, b) for further description of data and sources.

Note: This table refers to pension spending for years ranging from 1985 to 1992.

b. Turkey is included in the Middle East and North Africa.

Table A.6 Publicly Managed Pension Scheme Financing, Selected Countries, 1986

Country	Receipts as a percentage of GDP	Share of receipts from		
		Payroll taxes	Investment income	General revenues
OECD				
Australia[a]	4.7	0.0	2.0	98.0
Austria	16.1	79.0	0.2	20.0
Belgium	10.3	76.0	2.1	21.0
Canada[a]	6.3	30.0	27.6	42.0
Denmark[a]	9.6	17.0	7.9	76.0
Finland	7.4	84.0	16.0	0.0
France	9.3	86.0	4.0	10.0
Germany[b]	11.4	74.1	0.6	25.0
Iceland[a]	2.7	20.0	0.0	80.0
Italy[c]	7.4	73.0	0.4	26.0
Japan	7.6	46.0	20.2	33.0
Luxembourg	14.3	60.0	6.4	33.0
Netherlands	14.8	70.0	28.3	2.0
New Zealand[a]	—	—	—	100.0
Sweden	14.7	57.0	23.4	19.0
Turkey	2.3	63.0	23.3	13.0
Switzerland[b]	8.0	72.7	5.9	21.4
United States	8.4	68.0	19.4	12.0
Average	**9.1**	**57.4**	**11.0**	**35.1**
Latin America and Caribbean				
Argentina	5.1	74.0	0.0	26.0
Bahamas[b]	—	59.6	37.3	3.2
Belize[c]	1.4	63.0	36.6	0.0
Bolivia	1.7	49.0	14.1	36.0
Colombia	1.5	66.0	10.1	23.0
Costa Rica	4.7	64.0	21.6	14.0
Dominica	2.3	72.0	27.0	0.9
Dominican Rep.	0.0	77.0	1.4	21.2
Ecuador	3.0	58.0	15.4	26.0
El Salvador	0.7	55.8	44.2	0.0
Guatemala	0.5	66.0	0.0	33.9
Guyana	6.1	38.0	62.0	0.0
Honduras	1.5	52.0	45.5	2.0
Jamaica[b]	1.4	44.0	50.8	5.2
Mexico	1.3	72.0	3.7	24.3
Panama	5.2	68.0	27.2	4.6
Peru	0.0	100.0	0.0	0.0
Uruguay	6.4	92.0	1.1	6.9
Venezuela	1.0	42.0	39.0	20.0
Average	**2.4**	**63.8**	**23.0**	**13.0**

(Table continues on the following page.)

Table A.6 *(continued)*

Country	Receipts as a percentage of GDP	Share of receipts from		
		Payroll taxes	*Investment income*	*General revenues*
Eastern Europe and former Soviet Union				
Albania[d]	—	50.0	0.0	50.0
Bulgaria[e]	6.3	75.0	0.0	25.0
Czech Rep.	7.9	—	—	—
Hungary[d]	10.4	9.3	0.1	1.0
Poland	8.5	85.0	1.0	13.7
Romania[e]	6.2	96.0	0.0	4.0
Yugoslavia, Fed. Rep. of	8.0	96.0	0.0	4.0
Average	**7.9**	**68.6**	**0.2**	**16.3**
Middle East and North Africa				
Bahrain	2.6	64.0	36.7	0.0
Egypt	8.1	63.0	14.0	22.9
Israel	4.6	69.0	10.5	21.0
Jordan	2.4	83.0	16.7	0.0
Kuwait	7.5	18.0	21.1	61.0
Morocco	1.5	59.0	14.5	26.1
Tunisia	3.8	86.0	8.9	5.1
Average	**4.4**	**63.1**	**17.5**	**19.4**
Sub-Saharan Africa				
Benin	0.4	95.6	4.4	0.0
Burkina Faso	0.8	60.0	39.2	0.6
Burundi	0.4	70.0	30.8	0.0
Cameroon[c]	0.7	66.0	33.8	0.0
Cape Verde	1.1	100.0	0.0	0.0
Central African Rep.	0.3	100.0	0.0	0.0
Côte d'Ivoire	0.7	65.0	35.5	0.0
Ethiopia	1.5	96.0	4.2	0.0
Gabon[c]	0.9	100.0	0.0	0.0
Guinea	—	90.7	9.3	0.0
Kenya	—	32.2	66.5	1.3

Country	Receipts as a percentage of GDP	Share of receipts from		
		Payroll taxes	Investment income	General revenues
Sub-Saharan Africa (cont.)				
Mali	0.8	94.0	0.0	0.0
Madagascar	0.2	99.5	0.5	0.0
Nigeria	0.1	42.0	57.2	0.0
Rwanda	0.9	66.0	33.2	0.0
Senegal	1.0	86.4	13.6	0.0
Swaziland[c]	1.1	62.0	36.7	0.0
Tanzania	0.8	61.0	20.6	17.8
Togo	0.8	80.0	19.6	0.0
Zaire[c]	0.4	90.0	0.0	10.0
Average	**0.7**	**77.8**	**20.3**	**1.5**
Asia				
Bangladesh	0.0	78.0	20.5	2.0
China	2.2	99.0	0.7	0.4
Fiji	8.2	48.0	42.6	9.2
Indonesia[c]	0.1	68.0	30.7	0.5
Malaysia	7.4	63.0	35.6	0.0
Pakistan	0.7	8.1	8.9	83.0
Singapore	17.2	74.0	25.3	0.0
Solomon Islands	5.4	69.0	30.4	0.0
Sri Lanka	5.8	45.0	22.7	32.0
Average	**5.2**	**61.3**	**24.2**	**14.1**

— Not available.

a. More than 50 percent of total pension spending is on universal flat or means-tested pensions.

b. Year referred to is 1989.

c. This refers to the main scheme only.

d. Year referred to is 1992.

e. Year referred to is 1990.

Source: Most data are from ILO (1992a and forthcoming); see Palacios (1994b) for other sources and explanation of data.

Table A.7 Main Publicly Mandated Pension Scheme Design Features, 1991

Economy	Normal retirement age		Covered years required for full pension	Payroll tax for pensions			Pension payroll tax/total labor cost[a]	Automatic indexa-tion of pensions in progress	Benefit type
	Women	Men		Worker	Employer	Combined			
Sub-Saharan Africa									
Benin	55	55	20	3.6	5.4	9	8.5	Prices	CR
Burkina Faso	55	55	15	4.5	4.5	9	8.6	Prices	CR
Burundi	55	55	15	4	4.5	8.5	8.1	None	CR
Cameroon	60	60	15	2.8	4.2	7	6.7	None	CR
Cape Verde	60	65	3	4	3	7	6.8	None	CR
Central African Rep.	50	55	20	2	3	5	4.9	None	CR
Congo	55	55	20	2.4	3.6	6	5.8	Prices	CR
Côte d'Ivoire	55	55	10	1.6	2.4	4	3.9	None	CR
Chad	55	55	15	2	4	6	5.8	None	CR
Equatorial Guinea	60	60	10	4.5	21.5	26	21.4	None	CR
Ethiopia	55	55	10	4	6	10	9.4	None	CR
Gabon	55	20	—	2.5	4.5	7	6.7	None	CR
Gambia, The	55	55	—	5	10	15	13.6	n.a.	PR
Ghana	60	60	20	5	12.5	17.5	15.6	None	CR
Guinea	55	55	15	1.6	2.4	4	3.9	None	CR
Kenya	55	55	—	5	5	10	9.5	n.a.	PR
Liberia	60	60	8.3	3	3	6	5.8	None	CR
Madagascar	55	60	15	1	3.5	4.5	4.3	Wages	CR
Mali	55	55	10	3.6	5	9	8.6	Prices	CR
Mauritania	55	60	20	1	2	3	2.9	None	CR
Mauritius	60	60	—	3	6	9	8.5	n.a.	UF-CR
Niger	60	60	20	1.6	2.4	4	3.9	None	CR
Nigeria	55	55	—	6	6	12	11.3	n.a.	PR
Rwanda	55	55	20	3	3	6	5.8	Prices	CR
São Tomé Principe	60	65	25	4	6	10	9.4	Wages	CR
Senegal	55	55	1	3.5	5.3	8.8	8.4	None	CR
Seychelles	63	63	—	5	10	15	13.6	n.a.	PR
South Africa	60	65	0	0	0	0	0.0	n.a.	CR
Sudan	55	60	12	5	9	14	12.8	None	CR
Swaziland	45	50	—	5	5	10	9.5	n.a.	PR
Tanzania	55	55	—	10	10	20	18.2	n.a.	PR
Togo	55	55	20	2.4	3.6	6	5.8	None	CR
Uganda	55	55	—	5	10	15	13.6	n.a.	PR
Zaire	60	62	5	3	3.5	6.5	6.3	None	CR
Zambia	50	50	—	5	5	10	9.5	n.a.	PR
Average	**56.0**	**56.2**	**13.8**	**3.6**	**5.6**	**9.1**	**8.5**		
Asia									
China	55	60	10	0	18	18	15.3	None	CR
Fiji	55	55	—	7	7	14	13.1	n.a.	PR

Economy	Normal retirement age		Covered years required for full pension	Payroll tax for pensions			Pension payroll tax/total labor cost[a]	Automatic indexation of pensions in progress	Benefit type
	Women	Men		Worker	Employer	Combined			
Asia (cont.)									
Hong Kong	65	65	0	0	0	0	0.0	n.a.	UF-MT
India	55	55	—	10	10	20	18.2	n.a.	PR
Indonesia	55	55	—	1	2	3	2.9	n.a.	PR
Kiribati	50	50	—	5	5	10	9.5	n.a.	PR
Korea, Rep. of	60	60	20	1.5	1.5	3	3.0	None	CR
Malaysia	55	55	—	9	11	20	18.0	n.a.	PR
Marshall Islands	60	60	6	5	5	10	9.5	None	CR
Micronesia, Fed. States of	60	60	6	4	4	8	7.7	None	CR
Nepal	—	—	—	10	10	20	18.2	n.a.	PR
Pakistan	55	60	15	0	5	5	4.8	None	CR
Palau	60	60	6	3	3	6	5.8	None	CR
New Guinea	55	55	—	5	7	12	11.2	n.a.	PR
Philippines	60	60	10	3.3	4.7	8	7.6	None	CR
Singapore	55	55	—	10	25	35	28.0	n.a.	PR
Solomon Islands	50	50	—	5	7.5	12.5	11.6	n.a.	PR
Sri Lanka	50	55	—	8	12	20	17.9	n.a.	PR
Taiwan (China)	55	60	15	1.4	5.6	7[b]	0.0	n.a.	CR
Western Samoa	55	55	—	5	5	10	9.5	None	PR
Average[c]	**55.6**	**56.5**	**10.4**	**5.1**	**7.9**	**13.0**	**10.6**		
Middle East and North Africa									
Afghanistan	55	60	25	3	0	3	3.0	None	CR
Algeria	55	60	15	3.5	3.5	7	6.8	None	CR
Bahrain	55	60	15	5	7	12	11.2	None	CR
Cyprus	63	65	3	6	6	12	11.3	Wages	CR
Egypt	60	60	10	14	26	40	31.7	None	CR
Iran	55	60	10	7	20	27[b]	0.0	None	CR
Iraq	55	60	20	5	12	17	15.2	None	CR
Israel	60	65	12	2.7	1.2	3.9	3.9	Wages	CR
Jordan	55	60	10	5	8	13	12.0	None	CR
Kuwait	50	50	15	5	10	15	13.6	None	CR
Lebanon	55	60	20	0	8.5	8.5	7.8	None	CR
Libya	65	65	20	2.1	3	5.1	5.0	None	CR
Malta	60	61	3	8.3	8.3	16.6[b]	0.0	None	CR
Morocco	60	60	8.9	1.7	3.4	5.1	4.9	None	CR

CR: contribution-related benefit.
DC: defined contribution.
MT: means-tested benefit.
PR: provident fund.
UF: universal flat.

(Table continues on the following page.)

Table A.7 *(continued)*

Economy	Normal retirement age		Covered years required for full pension	Payroll tax for pensions			Pension payroll tax/total labor cost[a]	Automatic indexation of pensions in progress	Benefit type
	Women	Men		Worker	Employer	Combined			
Middle East and North Africa (cont.)									
Saudi Arabia	60	60	10	5	8	13	12.0	None	CR
Syria	60	60	15	7	14	21	18.4	None	CR
Tunisia	60	60	10	1.3	2.5	3.8	3.7	None	CR
Average	**57.8**	**60.4**	**13.1**	**4.8**	**8.3**	**10.6**	**9.4**		
Eastern Europe and former Soviet Union									
Albania	—	—	—	—	—	25	25.0	None	CR
Bulgaria	55	60	25	0	30	30	23.1	None	CR
Czech Rep.	55	60	25	0	25	25	20.0	None	CR
Hungary	55	60	20	6	24.5	30.5	24.5	Net wages	CR
Poland	60	65	25	0	30	30	23.1	Prices	CR
Romania	55	60	30	—	—	21.2	21.2	None	CR
Former U.S.S.R.	—	—	—	—	—	30	30.0	None	CR
Armenia	—	—	—	—	—	—	0.0	n.a.	CR
Azerbaijan	55	60	—	—	—	14	14.0	None	CR
Belarus	55	60	—	—	—	42	42.0	None	CR
Estonia	55	60	—	—	—	20	20.0	Prices	CR
Georgia	55	60	—	—	—	38[b]	0.0	None	CR
Kazakhstan	55	60	—	—	—	22	22.0	None	CR
Kyrgyz Rep.	55	60	—	—	—	31.8	31.8	None	CR
Latvia	55	60	—	—	—	23.4	23.4	Prices	CR
Lithuania	55	60	—	—	—	—	0.0	n.a.	CR
Moldova	—	—	—	—	—	—	0.0	n.a.	CR
Russia	55	60	—	—	—	26.6	26.6	None	CR
Tajikistan	—	—	—	—	—	—	—	n.a.	CR
Turkmenistan	—	—	—	—	—	—	0.0	n.a.	CR
Ukraine	55	60	—	—	—	31.1	31.1	n.a.	CR
Uzbekistan	55	60	—	—	—	33	33.0	None	CR
Average	**55.3**	**60.3**	**25.0**	**0.0**	**28.3**	**25.5**	**18.0**		
Latin America and Caribbean									
Antigua and Barbuda	60	60	9.6	3	5	8	7.6	None	CR
Argentina	55	60	15	10	11	21	18.9	Partial	CR
Bahamas, The	65	65	14.4	3.4	7.1	10.5	9.8	None	CR
Barbados	65	65	9.6	5.5	5.8	11.3	10.7	None	CR
Bermuda	65	65	4.8	—	—	—	0.0	None	CR
Bolivia	50	55	15	5	2.5	7.5	7.3	Wages	CR
Brazil	60	65	5	8	21.5	29.5	24.3	None	CR
Colombia	55	60	9.6	2.2	4.3	6.5	6.2	Wages	CR
Costa Rica	59	61	3.5	2.5	4.8	7.3	7.0	None	CR-MT
Chile	60	65	20	13.3	0	13.3	13.3	n.a.	DC
Cuba	55	60	25	0	10	10[b]	0.0	n.a.	CR

Economy	Normal retirement age Women	Normal retirement age Men	Covered years required for full pension	Payroll tax for pensions Worker	Payroll tax for pensions Employer	Payroll tax for pensions Combined	Pension payroll tax/total labor cost[a]	Automatic indexation of pensions in progress	Benefit type
Latin America and Caribbean (cont.)									
Dominica	60	60	5.7	3	6.8	9.8	9.2	None	CR
Dominican Rep.	60	60	15.4	2.5	7	9.5[b]	0.0	None	CR
Ecuador	55	55	30	9.4	10.9	20.3[b]	0.0	None	CR
El Salvador	55	60	14.4	1	2	3	2.9	Prices	CR
Grenada	60	60	9.6	4	4	8	7.7	None	CR
Guatemala	60	60	15	1.5	3	4.5	4.4	None	CR
Guyana	60	60	14.4	4.4	6.6	11[b]	0.0	None	CR
Haiti	55	55	20	2	2	4	3.9	None	CR
Honduras	60	65	15	1	2	3	2.9	None	CR
Jamaica	60	65	3	2.5	2.5	5[b]	0.0	None	CR
Mexico	65	65	9.6	1	4.9	5.9	5.6	None	CR
Nicaragua	60	60	14.4	2	6.5	8.5	8.0	None	CR
Panama	55	60	15	6.3	2.8	9.1	8.9	None	CR
Paraguay	60	60	15	9.5	13	22.5[b]	0.0	None	CR
Peru	55	60	15	3	6	9	8.5	None	CR
Trinidad and Tobago	60	60	14.4	2.8	5.6	8.4	8.0	n.a.	MT-CR
Uruguay	55	60	30	13	16.5	29.5	25.3	Wages	CR
Venezuela	55	60	14.4	—	—	6.75	6.8	None	CR
Average	**58.7**	**60.8**	**13.9**			**10.5**	**7.1**		
OECD									
Australia	60	65	0	—	—	—	—	Prices	MT
Austria	60	65	15	10.3	12.6	22.9	20.3	Wages	CR
Belgium	65	65	45	7.5	8.9	16.4	15.1	Prices	CR
Canada	65	65	1	2.3	2.3	4.6	4.5	Prices	UF-MT-CR
Denmark	67	67	0	—	—	—	0.0	Prices	UF-MT-CR
Finland	65	65	40	0	16.8	16.8	14.4	Prices	CR-UF
France[d]	60	60	37.5	10	9.8	19.8	18.0	Wages	CR
Germany	65	65	5	8.9	8.9	17.8	16.3	Net wages	CR
Greece	60	65	11.1	5.3	10.5	15.7	14.2	Prices	CR
Iceland	67	67	0	0	2	2	2.0	Wages	UF-MT-CR
Ireland	65	65	3	5.5	12.2	17.7	15.8	n.a.	CR-MT

CR: contribution-related benefit.
DC: defined contribution.
MT: means-tested benefit.
PR: provident fund.
UF: universal flat.

(Table continues on the following page.)

Table A.7 *(continued)*

Economy	Normal retirement age		Covered years required for full pension	Payroll tax for pensions			Pension payroll tax/total labor cost[a]	Automatic indexation of pensions in progress	Benefit type
	Women	Men		Worker	Employer	Combined			
OECD (cont.)									
Italy	55	60	15	7.3	18.9	26.2	22.0	Prices and wages	CR
Japan	65	65	25	14.6	2.3	16.9	16.5	Prices	CR
Luxembourg	65	65	10	8	8	16	14.8	Prices and wages	CR
Netherlands	65	65	49	15.2	0	15.2	15.2	Wages	CR
New Zealand	60	60	0	—	—	—	0.0	Prices	UF
Norway	67	67	40	7.8	16.7	24.5[b]	0.0	Prices	UF-MT-CR
Portugal	62	65	10	11	24.5	35.5[b]	0.0	Prices	CR
Spain	65	65	15	2.8	13.9	16.7	14.7	Prices and wages	CR
Sweden	65	65	3	8	13	21	18.6	Prices	CR-UF
Switzerland[d]	62	65	40	11.7	11.7	23.4	20.9	Prices and wages	CR
Turkey	55	60	25	9	11	20	18.0	Prices and wages	CR
United Kingdom	60	65	40	8.3	10.5	18.8	17.0	Prices	CR
United States	65	65	10	6.2	6.2	12.4	11.7	Prices	CR
Average[c]	**62.9**	**64.4**	**18.3**	**7.4**	**11.0**	**16.3**	**12.6**		

CR: contribution-related benefit.
DC: defined contribution.
MT: means-tested benefit.
PR: provident fund.
UF: universal flat.
— Not available.
Note: The contribution structures in many countries are very complex, distinguishing among different groups of workers. This table reports the number thought to apply to the largest proportion of workers. It includes payments to mandatory occupational plans (France or Switzerland) or mandatory saving plans (Chile).
a. Total labor cost is defined as wages plus employer share of payroll tax.
b. This includes contributions for programs other than old age.
c. Except for the retirement age, averages do not include countries that rely primarily on universal flat or means-tested pensions.
d. The payroll tax pension for France and Switzerland includes mandatory occupational schemes.
Source: U.S. Social Security Administration (1993).

Table A.8 Percentage of Recent Average Earnings Paid as a Pension after Thirty Years of Covered Employment, Selected Countries, 1991

Latin America and Caribbean		Sub-Saharan Africa	
Argentina	70	Benin	60
Ecuador	75	Burkina Faso	40
Guatemala	70	Burundi	50
Honduras	65	Cameroon	45
Mexico	60	Central African Rep.	45
Panama	88	Chad	48
Paraguay	67	Congo	50
Peru	80[a]	Gabon	45
St. Lucia	60	Liberia	51
Uruguay	60[a]	Mauritania	40
		Niger	40
		Rwanda	45
Middle East and North Africa		Sudan	50
Algeria	75	Togo	40
Bahrain	50		
Egypt	67	*Europe*	
Iran	87	Austria	57
Iraq	75	Czech Rep.	55
Jordan	60	Portugal	66
Kuwait	95	Spain	90
Libya	75	Turkey	70
Saudi Arabia	60	Fed. Rep. of Yugoslavia	65[a]
Syria	66		
Tunisia	80	*South Asia*	
Yemen	75	Pakistan	60

a. This indicates the percentage paid for a male.

Source: U.S. Social Security Administration (1993).

Table A.9 Comparison of Administrative Costs of Publicly Mandated Pension Schemes

Country	Year	Per member administrative cost/income per capita (percent)	Per member administrative cost in U.S. dollars[a]	Country	Year	Per member administrative cost/income per capita (percent)	Per member administrative cost in U.S. dollars[a]
Belgium	1986	0.18	20.6	Luxembourg	1986	0.28	38.1
Burundi	1989	7.25	14.9	Malaysia	1986	0.54	9.2
Canada	1989	0.05	10.0	Mauritius	1986	0.05	0.7
Chile (new)	1991	2.30	50.2	Mexico	1986	0.89	14.4
China	1989	0.20	0.5	Morocco	1989	0.89	8.1
Costa Rica	1992	0.36	7.5	Netherlands	1989	0.13	20.1
Czech Rep.	1989	0.07	2.2	Nigeria	1986	0.89	3.8
Denmark	1989	0.02	3.9	Pakistan	1989	0.86	3.0
El Salvador	1986	1.54	12.3	Paraguay	1987	0.59	6.9
Finland	1989	0.26	63.7	Philippines	1990	1.01	7.3
Germany	1989	0.18	35.9	Rwanda	1989	3.58	11.2
Ghana	1989	3.86	5.0	Singapore	1986	0.16	10.8
Guatemala	1986	0.39	4.0	Spain	1989	0.11	10.4
Honduras	1990	0.59	7.3	Sweden	1988	0.07	15.5
India	1989	0.72	2.4	Switzerland	1991	0.09	28.9
Israel	1989	0.10	9.5	Tanzania	1990	7.96	7.9
Italy	1986	0.34	35.6	Tunisia	1986	1.03	12.1
Jamaica	1989	0.34	5.5	Turkey	1986	0.41	4.6
Japan	1989	0.04	8.3	United States	1989	0.05	11.3
Kenya	1989	0.80	1.8	Zambia	1988	4.49	16.3

a. This uses the average exchange rate during each year.

Source: Data from various sources. See James and Palacios (1994) for methodology and description of data.

Table A.10 Expected Duration of Retirement at Official Retirement Age, by Income Level, Selected Countries

Country	Retirement Age Male	Retirement Age Female	Expected duration of retirement Male	Expected duration of retirement Female	Year
Countries with GDP per capita greater than $8,000					
Australia	65	60	18.0	23.0	1989
Austria	65	60	14.5	22.0	1989
Belgium	65	65	13.0	16.9	1982
Canada	65	65	14.9	19.2	1985–87
France	60	60	18.7	23.9	1988
Germany	65	65	13.8	17.6	1987
Hong Kong	65	65	15.1	18.8	1990
Israel	65	60	15.1	20.7	1988
Italy	60	55	17.4	26.3	1985
Netherlands	65	65	14.4	19.0	1989
Spain	65	65	14.8	17.9	1982
Sweden	65	65	15.0	18.7	1988
Switzerland	65	62	15.3	—	1989
United Kingdom	65	60	13.6	21.3	1989
United States	65	65	14.9	18.6	1988
Average	**64.3**	**62.5**	**15.2**	**18.6**	
Countries with GDP per capita between $4,000 and $8,000					
Algeria	60	55	15.9	21.0	1983
Argentina	60	55	15.6	24.1	1980–81
Bulgaria	60	55	15.9	23.3	1987–89
Colombia	60	55	17.3	19.3	1980–85
Greece	65	60	14.6	20.6	1980
Hungary	60	55	14.8	23.1	1989

(Table continues on the following page.)

Table A.10 *(continued)*

Country	Retirement Age		Expected duration of retirement		Year
	Male	Female	Male	Female	
Countries with GDP per capita between $4,000 and $8,000 (cont.)					
Malaysia	55	55	19.5	22.1	1988
Panama	60	55	18.8	24.9	1985–89
Poland	65	60	12.5	20.1	1988
Romania	60	55	16.1	22.8	1989
Uruguay	60	55	16.7	25.0	1984–86
Venezuela	60	55	17.3	24.2	1985
Yugoslavia, Fed. Rep. of	60	55	16.3	23.7	1990
Average	**60.4**	**56.0**	**16.8**	**23.0**	
Countries with GDP per capita less than $4,000					
China	60	55	15.7	22.2	1981
Czech Rep.	60	55	14.9	23.3	1988
Ecuador	55	55	21.4	23.4	1985
Guatemala	60	60	16.6	17.5	1980
India	55	55	17.1	19.3	1976–80
Peru	60	55	15.4	21.1	1980–83
Philippines	60	60	15.4	17.2	1989
Rwanda	55	53	16.7	18.2	1978
Sri Lanka	55	50	21.5	23.7	1981
Trinidad and Tobago	60	60	15.8	18.4	1980–85
Former U.S.S.R.	60	55	15.4	24.0	1990
Zambia	50	50	21.3	22.2	1980
Average	**57.5**	**55.3**	**17.3**	**20.9**	

— Not available.

Note: Income per capita is calculated in 1990 U.S. dollars as defined in the United Nations International Comparison Program.

Source: United Nations (1992b); U.S. Social Security Administration (1993); World Bank (1992d), table 30; World Bank (1990); Australian Social Security Institute (1989).

Table A.11 Public Pension Schemes in Transitional Economies, Post-1990 *(percentages)*

Country	System dependency ratio[a]	Old age dependency ratio in 1990	Pension expenditure/ GDP	Gross pension/ gross wage[b]	Pension payroll tax	Overall payroll tax
Eastern Europe						
Albania	37[c]	17	12.4[d]	55	25	26
Bulgaria	77[c]	37	9.5[c]	37[c]	26.7–38	35–50
Croatia	59[c]	32	—	—	22	—
Czech Rep.	—	32[e]	10.0[d]	49[d]	30	50
Hungary	66[e]	36	10.3[e]	38[e]	30.5	62
Poland	49[c]	28	12.4[c]	57[c]	30	48
Romania	63[c]	30	6.9[d]	43[c]	16.5–25.9	31–41
Slovak Rep.	42	—	9.9	—	26.5	50
Slovenia	50[d]	29	11.3[d]	—	30	41
Former Soviet Union						
Armenia	—	22	4.9[d]	—	—	—
Azerbaijan	—	18	5.6[d]	—	14	40
Belarus	49[d]	34	7.3[d]	42[c]	—	42
Estonia	52[e]	32	6.9	33[c]	20	20
Georgia	45[d]	30	11.0[d]	70[c]	—	41
Kazakhstan	40[c]	19	4.7[d]	—	22	41
Kyrgyz Rep.	34[d]	20	6.1[d]	34[c]	34	39
Latvia	51[d]	33	6.7[c]	33[e]	23	38
Lithuania	53[d]	30	6.6[d]	41[c]	—	31
Russia	48[c]	—	7.1[c]	34[c]	32.6	40
Ukraine	50[c]	35	13.0[c]	39[c]	31	37
Uzbekistan	34[d]	15	10.3[c]	—	33	40

— Not available.

a. System dependency ratios are not adjusted for old age pensioner equivalents. The ratio for Estonia is for the first quarter of 1993.

b. Replacement rates refer to the average of old age, survivors', and invalidity pensions. Old age replacement rates are higher. For Romania, this refers to nonagricultural workers only. Ukrainian data are for the first quarter of 1992.

c. 1992.

d. 1991.

e. 1993.

Source: Holzmann (1992, 1994); Cavalcanti (1993); Rashid (1994); World Bank data; appendix table A.1. See Palacios (1994) for further details.

Table A.12 Portfolio Distribution of Pension Funds in Eight OECD Countries *(percentage of assets)*

Country	Equities	Private bonds	Public bonds	Loans	Other	Share of portfolio invested abroad
Canada						
1970	22	15	38	11	14	—
1990	29	8	39	4	20	6
Denmark						
1970	0	61	11	7	21	—
1990	7	56	11	7	19	—
Germany						
1970	4	10	9	50	27	—
1990	18	8	17	45	12	1
Japan						
1970	6	——12[a]——		52	30	—
1990	27	——47——		14	12	7
Netherlands						
1970	11	3	12	54	20	7
1990	20	4	19	43	14	15
Switzerland						
1970	3	——25[a]——		48	24	—
1990	16	——29——		22	33	—
United Kingdom						
1970	49	14	18	—	19	2
1990	63	3	11	—	23	18
United States						
1970	45	38	7	6	4	—
1990	46	16	20	2	16	4

a. This denotes the sum of private and public bonds; data are not available separately.
Source: Davis (1993).

Bibliography

Aaron, H. J. 1966. "The Social Insurance Paradox." *Canadian Journal of Public Economics and Political Science* 32: 371–7.

———. 1977. *Demographic Effects on the Equity of Social Security Benefits.* Washington, D.C.: Brookings Institution.

———. 1982. *Economic Effects of Social Security.* Washington, D.C.: Brookings Institution.

Aaron, H. J., and G. Burtless. 1984. *Retirement and Economic Behavior: Studies in Social Economics Series.* Washington, D.C.: Brookings Institution.

Aaron, H. J., B. P. Bosworth, and G. T. Burtless. 1989. *Can America Afford to Grow Old?* Washington, D.C.: Brookings Institution.

Aaron, H. J, J. Pechman, and M. Taussig. 1968. *Social Security: Perspectives for Reform.* Washington, D.C.: Brookings Institution.

Abel, Andrew. 1987a. "Aggregate Savings in the Presence of Private and Social Insurance." In R. Dornbusch and J. Bossons, eds., *Macroeconomics and Finance: Essays in Honor of Franco Modigliani.* Cambridge: MIT Press.

———. 1987b. "Operative Gift and Bequest Motives." *American Economic Review* 77 (5): 1037–47.

Abuhadba, Mario. 1994. "Aspectos Organizacionales y Competencia en el Sistema Previsional." CIEPLAN (Corporacion de Investigaciones Economicas para Latino America). Santiago, Chile.

Acuña, R., and A. Iglesias. 1992. *Chile: Experienca con un Regimen de Capitalizacion 1981–1991.* Regional Project on Financial Policies. ECLAC-UNDP (Economic Conference for Latin America and the Caribbean-United Nations Development Program). Santiago, Chile.

Agarwal, Bina. 1989. *Social Security and the Family in Rural India: Coping with Seasonality and Calamity.* London: Development Economics Research Programme, STICERD (Suntory-Toyota International Centre for Economics and Related Disciplines).

Ahmad, Ehtisham, ed. 1991. *Social Security in Developing Countries.* Oxford: Oxford University Press.

Aldrich, Jonathan. 1982. "The Earnings Replacement Rate of Old Age Benefits in Twelve Countries, 1969–1980." *Social Security Bulletin* 45 (11): 3–11.

Allen, Steven G., Robert Clark, and Ann McDermed. 1988. "Job Mobility, Older Workers and the Role of Pensions." *Research on Aging* 10 (4): 459–71.

———. 1993. "Pensions, Bonding, and Lifetime Jobs." *Journal of Human Resources* 28 (3): 463–81.

Altekar, A. S. 1956. *The Position of Women in Hindu Civilization.* Delhi: Motilal Banarsidass.

Arellano, Jose-Pablo. 1985. "The Impact of Social Security on Savings and Development." In Mesa-Lago (1985).

Arnold, Fred, and others. 1975. *The Value of Children: A Cross-National Study*. Vol. 1. Honolulu: East-West Population Institute, East-West Center.

Arrau, Patricio. 1990. *Social Security Reform: The Capital Accumulation and Intergenerational Distribution Effect*. Washington, D.C.: World Bank.

———. 1992. "El Nuevo Regimen Previsional Chilena y su Financiemiento Durante la Transicion." *Coleccion Estudios CIEPLAN* 32: 5–44.

Arrau, Patricio, and Klaus Schmidt-Hebbel. 1993. *Macroeconomic and Intergenerational Welfare Effects of a Transition from Pay-as-You-Go to Fully Funded Pension Systems*. Policy Research Department, Macroeconomics and Growth Division, World Bank, Washington, D.C.

———. 1994. "Pension Systems and Reforms: Country Experiences and Research Issues." *Revista de Análisis Económico* 9 (1): 3–20.

Arrau, Patricio, S. Valdés-Prieto, and Klaus Schmidt-Hebbel. 1993. *Privately Managed Pension Systems: Design Issues and the Chilean Experience*. Policy Research Department, Macroeconomics and Growth Division, World Bank, Washington, D.C.

Asher, Mukul G. 1992a. "Income Security for Old Age: The Case of Malaysia." National University of Singapore, Department of Economics and Statistics.

———. 1992b. "The Singapore Central Provident Fund." National University of Singapore, Department of Economics and Statistics.

ASTEK (Indonesian Provident Fund). 1992. *Astek Annual Report*. Jakarta, Indonesia.

Atkinson, A. B. 1987. "Income Maintenance and Social Insurance." In A. J. Auerbach and M. Feldstein, eds., *Handbook of Public Economics*. Vol. 2. Amsterdam, North Holland.

———. 1989. *State Pensions, Taxation and Retirement Income, 1981–2031*. London: Simon and Schuster International.

———. 1991a. "The Development of State Pensions in the United Kingdom." In W. Schmähl, ed., *The Future of Basic and Supplementary Pension Schemes in the European Community: 1992 and Beyond*. Baden-Baden, Germany: Nomos Verlag.

———. 1991b. "A National Minimum? A History of Ambiguity in the Determination of Benefit Scales in Britain." In T. and D. Wilson, eds., *The State and Social Welfare*. London: Longman.

Atkinson, A. B., and R. Altmann. 1982. "State Pensions, Taxation and Retirement Income: 1981–2031." In M. Fogarty, ed., *Retirement Policy*. London: Heineman.

Auerbach, A. J. 1989. "The Economic Dynamics of Ageing Populations: The Case of Four OECD Economies." *OECD Economic Studies* (spring): 97–130.

Auerbach, A. J., and Laurence J. Kotlikoff. 1984. "Social Security and the Economics of the Demographic Transition." In Aaron and Burtless (1984).

———. 1987. *Dynamic Fiscal Policy*. Cambridge: Cambridge University Press.

———. 1990. "Demographics, Fiscal Policy and U.S. Saving in the 1980s and Beyond." In Lawrence H. Summers, ed., *Tax Policy and the Economy*. Vol. 4. Cambridge: MIT Press.

Auerbach, A. J., J. Ghokale, and L. J. Kotlikoff. 1994. "Generational Accounting: A Meaningful Way to Assess Generational Policy." *Journal of Economic Perspectives* 8 (1): 73–94.

Auerbach, A. J., L. J. Kotlikoff, and J. Skinner. 1983. "The Efficiency Gains from Dynamic Tax Reform." *International Economic Review* 24 (1): 81–100.

Banco de Prevision Social. 1991. *La Seguridad Social en el Uruguay.* Montevideo, Uruguay.

Barr, Nicholas. 1992. "Economic Theory and the Welfare State: A Survey and Interpretation." *Journal of Economic Literature* 30 (2): 741–803.

———, ed., 1994. *Labor Markets and Social Policy in Central and Eastern Europe: The Transition and Beyond.* New York: Oxford University Press.

Barro, R. J. 1974. "Are Government Bonds Net Wealth?" *Journal of Political Economy* 82 (6): 1095–117.

———. 1978. *The Impact of Social Security on Private Saving: Evidence from the U.S. Time Series.* Washington, D.C.: American Enterprise Institute.

Barro, R. J., and G. MacDonald. 1979. "Social Security and Consumer Spending in an International Cross Section." *Journal of Public Economics* 11 (5): 275–89.

Bartel, Ann, and George Borjas. 1977. "Middle Age Job Mobility: Its Determinants and Consequences." In Seymour Wolfbein, ed., *Men in Their Preretirement Years.* Philadelphia: Temple University Press.

Bateman, Hazel, and John Piggott. 1992a. "Australian Retirement Income Policy." *Australian Tax Forum* 9 (1): 1–26.

———. 1992b. "The Superannuation Guarantee Charge: What Do We Know about Its Aggregate Impact?" Superannuation Economics Research Group Research Paper Series 7. University of New South Wales, Australia.

———. 1993. "Australia's Mandated Private Retirement Income Scheme: An Economic Perspective." Superannuation Economics Research Group Research Paper Series 10. University of New South Wales, Australia.

Bateman, Hazel, Geoffrey Kingston, and John Piggott. 1993. "Notes on the Equity Implications of Mandated Funded Pension Schemes." Superannuation Econom-ics Research Group Research Paper Series 9. University of New South Wales, Australia.

Bateman, Hazel, Jack Frisch, Geoffrey Kingston, and John Piggott. 1991. "Demographics, Retirement Saving and Superannuation Policy: An Australian Perspective." Superannuation Economics Research Group Research Paper Series 1. University of New South Wales, Australia.

Bernheim, D. 1987. "Ricardian Equivalence: An Evaluation of Theory and Evidence." *NBER Macroeconomics Annual.*

Bernheim, D., and L. Levin. 1989. "Social Security and Personal Saving: An Analysis of Expectations." *American Economic Review Papers and Proceedings* (May): 97–106.

Bernheim, D., A. Schleifer, and L. Summers. 1985. "The Strategic Bequest Motive." *Journal of Political Economy* 93 (6): 1045–76.

Birdsall, Nancy, and Richard Sabot. 1994. *Virtuous Circles: Human Capital, Growth, and Equity in East Asia.* World Bank, Policy Research Department, Washington, D.C.

Blanchet, Didier, and Denis Kessler. 1991. "Optimal Pension Funding with Demographic Instability and Endogenous Returns on Investment." *Journal of Population Economics* 4 (2): 137–54.

Blinder, Alan S., Roger H. Gordon, and Donald E. Wise. 1980. "Reconsidering the Work Disincentive Effects of Social Security." *National Tax Journal* 33: 431–42.

———. 1983. "Social Security, Benefits and the Life-Cycle Theory of Saving: Cross-Sectional Tests." In Modigliani and Hemming (1983).

Bloom, David, and R. Freeman. 1992. "The Fall in Private Pension Fund Coverage in the US." *American Economic Review* 82 (2): 539–45.

Bodie, Zvi. 1990a. "Managing Pension and Retirement Assets: An International Perspective." *Journal of Fiscal Services Research* 4 (4): 419–60.

——. 1990b. "Pension Funds and Financial Innovation." *Financial Management* (autumn).

——. 1990c. "Pensions as Retirement Income Insurance." *Journal of Economic Literature* 28: 28–49.

Bodie, Zvi, and Alicia Munnell. 1992. *Pensions and the Economy: Sources, Uses, and Limitations of Data.* Philadelphia: University of Pennsylvania Press.

Bodie, Zvi, and John Shoven, eds. 1983. *Financial Aspects of the United States Pension System.* Chicago: University of Chicago Press/National Bureau of Economic Research.

Bodie, Zvi, A. Marcus, and R. Merton. 1988. *Defined Benefit versus Defined Contribution Pension Plans: What Are the Real Trade-offs?* Chicago: University of Chicago Press.

Bodie, Zvi, John Shoven, and David Wise. 1987. *Issues in Pension Economics.* Chicago: University of Chicago Press.

Bos, Dieter, and Sijbren Cnossen. 1992. *Fiscal Implications of an Aging Population.* Berlin: Springer-Verlag.

Boskin, M. J. 1977. "Social Security and Retirement Decisions." *Economic Inquiry* 15: 1–25.

Boskin, M. J., and M. D. Hurd. 1978. "The Effect of Social Security on Early Retirement." *Journal of Public Economics* 10: 361–77.

Boskin, M. J., L. J. Kotlikoff, and J. B. Shoven. 1988. "Personal Security Accounts: A Proposal for Fundamental Social Security Reform." In Wachter (1988).

Boskin, M. J., L. J. Kotlikoff, D. Puffert, and J. B. Shoven. 1987. "Social Security: A Financial Appraisal across and within Generations." *National Tax Journal* 40 (1): 19–34.

Bosworth, Barry, Rudiger Dornbusch, and Raul Laban, eds. 1994. *The Chilean Economy: Policy Lessons and Challenges.* Washington, D.C.: Brookings Institution.

Boyle, P., and J. Murray. 1979. "Social Security Wealth and Private Saving in Canada." *Canadian Journal of Economics* 12: 457–68.

Brancato, Carolyn K. 1994. "The Brancato Report on Institutional Investment." The Conference Board: Seminar on Trends in U.S. Institutional Investment and Implications for Corporate Governance. New York.

Breyer, Friedrich. 1989. "On the Intergenerational Pareto Efficiency of Pay-as-You-Go Financed Pension Systems." *Journal of Institutional and Theoretical Economics* 145 (4): 643–48.

Brittain, John. 1972. *The Payroll Tax for Social Security.* Washington, D.C.: Brookings Institution.

Browning, Edgar. 1975. "Why the Social Insurance Budget Is Too Large in a Democracy." *Economic Inquiry* 13: 373–88.

Brunner, Johann. 1990. "Optimum Social Security and Intragenerational Redistribution." Sozial Und Wirtsohaftswissenschaftliche Fakultat. Working Paper 9028 (October). Johannes Kepler Institute, Johannes Kepler University, Linz, Austria.

Brunner, Johann, and Bengt-Arne Wickstrom. 1991. "Politically Stable Pay-as-You-Go Pension System: Why the Social Insurance Budget Is Too Small in a Democracy." Sozial Und Wirtsohaftswissenschaftliche Fakultat. Working Paper 9115 (November). Johannes Kepler Institute, Johannes Kepler University, Linz, Austria.

Buchanan, J. 1968. "What Kind of Redistribution Do We Want?" *Economica* 35: 185–90.

Bulatao, Rodolfo. 1979. "On the Nature of the Transition in the Value of Children." East-West Center Population Institute Paper 60-A. East-West Center. Honolulu.

Bulatao, Rodolfo, and Eduard Bos. 1989. *Projecting Mortality for All Countries.* Washington, D.C.: World Bank.

Bulatao, Rodolfo, Eduard Bos, Patience Stephens, and My T. Vu. 1989. *Europe, Middle East, and Africa (EMN) Region Population Projections: 1989–1990 Edition.* Washington, D.C.: World Bank.

Bulow, Jeremy. 1981. "Early Retirement Pension Benefits." National Bureau of Economic Research Working Paper Series 654. Cambridge, Mass.

———. 1982. "What Are Corporate Pension Liabilities?" *Quarterly Journal of Economics* 97 (3): 435–52.

Burkhauser, R. 1980. "The Early Acceptance of Social Security: An Asset Maximization Approach." *Industrial and Labor Relations Review* 33: 484–92.

Burkhauser, R., and J. Warlick. 1981. "Disentangling the Annuity from the Redistributive Aspects of Social Security in the United States." *Review of Income and Wealth* 27 (4): 401–21.

Burkina Faso National Social Security Scheme. 1985. *Annuaire Statistique de la Sécurité Sociale.* Burkina Faso.

Burns, Eveline. 1944. "Social Security: Social Insurance in Evolution." *American Economic Review* 34: 199–211.

Burtless, Gary T., and Robert A. Moffitt. 1984. "The Effect of Social Security Benefits on the Labor Supply of the Aged." In Aaron and Burtless (1984).

Cain, Mead. 1981. "Risk and Insurance: Perspectives on Fertility and Agrarian Change in India and Bangladesh." *Population and Development Review* 7: 435–74.

———. 1983. "Fertility as an Adjustment to Risk." *Population and Development Review* 9 (4): 688–702.

Caja Costarricense de Seguro Social. 1992. *Anuario Estadistico.* Costa Rica.

Caja de Seguro Social Republica de Panama. 1990. *Memoria 1989–1990.* Panama.

Cangping, Wu. 1991. *The Aging of Population in China.* Malta: International Institute on Aging.

Carmichael, J. 1982. "On Barro's Theorem of Debt Neutrality: The Irrelevance of Net Wealth." *American Economic Review* 72 (1): 202–13.

Carmichael, J., and K. Hawtrey. 1981. "Social Security, Government Finance and Savings." *Economic Record* 57: 332–43.

Cartaya, V. 1992. "The Costs of Becoming Legal for an Informal Firm: The Case of Venezuela." In Victor Tokman, *Beyond Regulation: The Informal Economy in Latin America.* Boulder, Colo.: Rienner.

Cavalcanti, Carlos. 1993. "Bridging the Poverty Gap in the Former Soviet Union." World Bank, Europe and Central Asia Division, Country Department IV, Washington, D.C.

Central Bank of Chile. Various issues. *Annual Report.* Santiago, Chile.

Chang, Angela. 1991. *Explanations for the Trend Away from Defined-Benefit Pension Plans.* Washington, D.C.: Congressional Research Service.

Chilean National Institute of Statistics. Various issues. *Statistical Yearbook.* Santiago, Chile.

Clark, Robert L., and R. Anker. 1990. "Labour Force Participation Rates of Older Persons: An International Comparison." *International Labour Review* 129 (2): 255–71.

Cohen, Wilbur, and Milton Friedman. 1972. *Social Security: Universal or Selective.* Washington, D.C.: American Enterprise Institute.

Colombia, Government of. 1993. *Ley de la Reforma de Pensiones.* Bogotá, Colombia (December).

Corsetti, Giancarlo, and Klaus Schmidt-Hebbel. 1994. "An Endogenous Growth Model of Social Security and the Size of the Informal Sector." World Bank, Policy Research Department, Macroeconomic and Growth Division, Washington, D.C.

Cox, Donald, and Emmanuel Jimenez. 1992. "Social Security and Private Transfers in Developing Countries: The Case of Peru." *World Bank Economic Review* 6 (1): 155–70.

———. Forthcoming. "Private Transfers and the Effectiveness of Public Income Redistribution in the Philippines." In Dominique van de Walle and Kimberly Nead, eds., *Public Spending and the Poor: Theory and Evidence.* Washington, D.C.: World Bank.

Creedy, John. 1982. "The British State Pension: Contributions Benefits and Indexation." *Bulletin of Economics and Statistics* 44 (2): 97–112.

Creedy, John, and Richard Disney. 1989a. "Can We Afford to Grow Older? Population Aging and Social Security." *European Economic Review* 33 (2/3): 367–76.

———. 1989b. "The 'Twin Pillar' Approach to Social Insurance in the UK." *Scottish Journal of Political Economy* 36 (2): 113–24.

———. 1992. "Financing State Pensions in Alternative Pay-as-you-go Schemes." *Bulletin of Economic Research* 44 (1): 39–53.

Creedy, J., R. Disney, and E. Whitehouse. 1992. "The Earnings-Related State Pension, Indexation and Lifetime Redistribution in the UK." Institute for Fiscal Studies Working Paper W92/1. London.

Cremer, H., D. Kessler, and Pierre Pestieau. 1992. "Intergenerational Transfers within the Family." *European Economic Review* 36 (1): 1–16.

Cukierman, Alex, and Allan Meltzer. 1989. "A Political Theory of Government Debt and Deficits in the Neo-Ricardian Framework." *American Economic Review* 79 (4): 713–32.

Dailey, L. 1989. "Private Pension Statistics in Nine Countries." In Turner and Beller (1989).

Darby, Michael. 1979. *Effects of Social Security on Income and Capital Stock.* Washington, D.C.: American Enterprise Institute.

Davies, J., and Ian Wooton. 1989. "Payroll Taxes in Brazil: An Analysis of the Major Efficiency and Equity Issues."

Davis, E. P. 1993. "The Structure, Regulation, and Performance of Pension Funds in Nine Industrial Countries." Working Paper 1229 (December). World Bank, Policy Research Department, Washington, D.C.

———. 1994. *Pension Funds, Income Security, and the Development of Financial Systems: An International Perspective.* Oxford: Oxford University Press.

Daykin, C. D. 1990. "United Kingdom: Pension Statistics." Presented at the International Conference on Private Pension Policy and Statistical Analysis. Paris.

Deaton, Angus, and Christina H. Paxson. 1991. "Patterns of Aging in Thailand and Côte d'Ivoire." Living Standards Measurement Study Working Paper No. 81. World Bank, Poverty and Human Resources Division, Washington, D.C.

———. 1994. "Saving, Growth and Aging in Taiwan." In Wise, ed., (1985) *Studies in the Economics of Aging.* Chicago: University of Chicago Press.

Deaton, Richard Lee. 1989. *The Political Economy of Pensions.* Vancouver, Canada: University of British Columbia Press.

Deolalikar, Anil, and R. P. Singh. 1990. "The Impact of Bequests on Lifetime Wealth Accumulation: An Econometric Study of Two Generations of Rural Households in India." *Review of Income and Wealth* 36 (4): 353–64.

de Oliviera, Francisco B. 1993. "Seguridade Social Na America Latina: A Experiencia Da Argentina, Brasil, Chile e Venezuela." IPEA (Instituto de Pesquisa Economica Aplicada). Rio de Janeiro, Brazil.

de Soto, Hernando. 1986. *El Otro Sendero: La Revolucion Informal.* Lima, Peru: El Barranco.

De Vos, Susan. 1985. "An Old Age Security Incentive for Children in the Philippines and Taiwan." *Economic Development and Cultural Change* 33 (4): 794–813.

Diamond, Peter. 1977. "A Framework for Social Security Analysis." *Journal of Public Economics* 8: 275–98.

Diamond, Peter, and J. Hausman. 1984. "Individual Retirement and Savings Behavior." *Journal of Public Economics* 23: 81–114.

Diamond, Peter, and Salvador Valdés-Prieto. 1994. "Social Security Reform." In Bosworth, Dornbusch, and Laban, eds. (1994).

Dicks-Mireaux, L., and M. A. King. 1984. "Pension Wealth and Household Savings: Tests of Robustness." *Journal of Public Economics* 23 (1/2): 115–39.

Dilnot, Andrew. 1989. *The Economics of Social Security.* New York: Oxford University Press.

Dilnot, Andrew, Richard Disney, Paul Johnson, and Edward Whitehouse. 1994. *Pensions Policy in the UK: An Economic Analysis.* London: Institute for Fiscal Studies.

Dinkel, Reiner. 1986. "Social Security and Intergenerational Equity." In J. M. von der Schulenburg, ed., *Essays in Social Security Economics: Selected Papers of a Conference of the International Institute of Management.* Berlin: Springer-Verlag.

Disney, Richard, and Edward Whitehouse. 1990. "Do Wage Differentials Compensate for Occupational Pension Entitlements? A Preliminary Look at the Evidence." Institute for Fiscal Studies (September). Washington, D.C.

———. 1992. "Contracting-out and Lifetime Redistribution in the UK State Pension System." University of Kent, Working Paper Series (92/4), Canterbury, United Kingdom.

Dixon, John. 1989. "National Provident Funds: The Enfant Terrible of Social Security." International Fellowship for Social and Economic Development Inc.

Dobbin, Frank. 1992. "The Origins of Private Social Insurance: Public Policy and Fringe Benefits in America, 1920–1950." *American Journal of Sociology* 97 (5): 1416–50.

Dorsey, Stuart. 1987. "The Economic Functions of Private Pensions: An Empirical Analysis." *Journal of Labor Economics* 5 (4): 171–89.

Dreze, Jean. 1990. "Widows in Rural India." London School of Economics: Development Economics Research Programme DEP 26.

Eekelaar, John, and David Pearl, eds. 1989. *An Aging World: Dilemmas and Challenges for Law and Social Policy.* Oxford, United Kingdom: Clarendon Press.

Ekpenyong, S., O. Y. Oyeneye, and M. Piel. 1986. "Reports on Study of Elderly Nigerians." Birmingham, United Kingdom: University of Birmingham.

Entwistle, B., and C. R. Winegarden. 1984. "Fertility and Pension Programs in LDCs: A Model of Mutual Reinforcement." *Economic Development and Cultural Change* 32 (2): 332–53.

Esping-Andersen, Gosta. 1990. *The Three Worlds of Welfare Capitalism.* Cambridge, Mass.: Polity.

Eurostat. 1992. *Digest of Statistics on Social Protection in Europe.* Luxembourg: Eurostat. European Economic Community.

Euzeby, Chantal. 1989. "Non-contributory Old-Age Pensions: A Possible Solution in the OECD Countries." *International Labour Review* 128 (1): 11–28.

Even, William E., and David A. Macpherson. 1990. "Employer Size and Compensation: The Case of Pensions." August. Miami University, Oxford, Ohio.

Falkingham, Jane, and Paul Johnson. 1993. "Life-Cycle Distributional Consequences of Pay-as-You-Go and Funded Pension Systems." Policy Research Working Paper 1200. World Bank, Policy Research Department, Washington, D.C.

Fang, Yuan, Wang Chuanbin, and Song Yuhua. 1992. "Support for the Elderly in China." In Kendig, Hashimoto, and Coppard (1992).

Feldstein, Martin. 1974. "Social Security, Induced Retirement and Aggregate Capital Formation." *Journal of Political Economy* 82 (5): 905–26.

———. 1977. "Social Security and Private Savings: International Evidence in an Extended Life-cycle Model." In M. Feldstein and R. Inman, eds., *The Economics of Public Services.* London: Macmillan.

———. 1978. "Reply." In R. Barro, *The Impact of Social Security on Private Saving: Evidence from the U.S. Time Series.* Washington, D.C.: American Enterprise Institute.

———. 1980. "International Differences in Social Security and Saving." *Journal of Public Economics* 14: 225–44.

———. 1982. "Social Security and Private Saving: Reply." *Journal of Political Economy* 90 (3): 630–42.

———. 1983. "Social Security Benefits and the Accumulation of Pre-Retirement Wealth." In Modigliani and Hemming (1983).

Feldstein, Martin, and Anthony Pellechio. 1979. "Social Security and Household Wealth Accumulation: New Micro Econometric Evidence." *Review of Economic Statistics* 61: 361–68.

Feldstein, Martin, and Andrew Samwick. 1992. "Social Security and Marginal Tax Rates." *National Tax Journal* 45 (1): 1–22.

Fernandez Riva, Javier. 1992. "La Regresividad del Sistema Pensional." *Carta Financiera* (October): 29–39.

Ferrara, Peter. 1980. *Social Security: The Inherent Contradiction.* San Francisco: Cato Institute.

———. 1985. *Social Security: Prospects for Real Reform.* Washington, D.C.: Cato Institute.

FESCOL (Fundacion Friedrich Ebert de Colombia). 1991. "La Reforma del Regimen Pensional en Colombia." Working Paper. Colombia.

Fields, Gary S., and Olivia S. Mitchell. 1984a. "Economic Determinants of the Optimal Retirement Age: An Empirical Investigation." *Journal of Human Resources* 19 (winter): 245–62.

———. 1984b. "Effects of Social Security Reforms on Retirement Ages and Retirement Incomes." *Journal of Public Economics* 25: 143–59.

———. 1993. "Reforming Social Security and Social Safety Net Programs in Developing Countries." *Annual Report of the Joint Ministerial Committee.* Joint Ministerial Committee of the Boards of Governors of the World Bank and the International Monetary Fund, Washington, D.C.

Förster, Michael F. 1993. "Comparing Poverty in Thirteen OECD Countries—Traditional and Synthetic Approaches." Luxembourg Income Study Working Paper Series No. 100. Luxembourg. (August).

Fox, Louise. 1993. "Bulgaria: Social Insurance and Social Assistance." World Bank, Europe and Central Asia—Country Department I, Washington, D.C.

———. 1994. "Old Age Security in Transition Economies." Policy Research Working Paper 1257 (February). World Bank, Policy Research Division, Washington, D.C.

Friedlander, S., and M. Silver. 1967. "A Quantitative Study of the Determinants of Fertility Behavior." *Demography* 4 (1): 30–70.

Friedman, Barry, and Leonard J. Hausman. Forthcoming. "Social Protection and Economic Restructuring in China." Manuscript. Brandeis University, Department of Economics, Waltham, Mass.

Friedman, Benjamin, and Mark Warshawsky. 1988. "Annuity Prices and Saving Behavior in the United States." In Zvi Bodie and John Shoven, eds., *Pensions in the U.S. Economy.* Chicago: Univ. of Chicago Press.

——. 1990. "The Cost of Annuities: Implications for Saving Behavior and Bequests." *Quarterly Journal of Economics* 105 (1): 135–54.

Gaiha, Ragav, and Kazmi Gaiha. 1982. "Aspects of Poverty in Rural India." Delhi University, Faculty of Management Studies. Delhi, India.

Getubig, I. P., and S. Schmidt, eds. 1992. *Rethinking Social Security: Reaching Out to the Poor.* Malaysia: Asian and Pacific Development Center.

Gillion, Colin, and Alejandro Bonilla. 1992. "Analysis of a National Private Pension Scheme: The Case of Chile." *International Labour Review* 131 (2): 171–95.

Gokhale, J., L. J. Kotlikoff, and J. Sabelhaus. 1994. "Understanding the Postwar Decline in U.S. Saving." Boston University, Department of Economics, Boston.

Gordon, Margaret S. 1988. *Social Security Policies in Industrial Countries: A Comparative Analysis.* Cambridge: Cambridge University Press.

Graebner, William. 1980. *A History of Retirement: The Meaning and Function of an American Institution 1885–1978.* New Haven: Yale University Press.

Greene, Kenneth. 1974. "Toward a Positive Theory of Intergenerational Income Transfers." *Public Finance* 29 (3): 306–24.

Gruat, Jean Victor. 1990. "Social Security Schemes in Africa: Current Trends and Problems." *International Labour Review* 129 (4): 406–21.

Guillemard, Anne-Marie. 1991. "France: Massive Exit through Unemployment Compensation." In M. Kohli, M. Rein, A. Guillemard, and H. van Gunsteren, eds., *Time for Retirement.* Cambridge: Cambridge University Press.

Gustaffson, B. A., and N. Klevmarken. 1989. *The Political Economy of Social Security.* New York: Elsevier Science.

Gustman, Alan L., and Thomas L. Steinmeier. 1984. "Partial Retirement and the Analysis of Retirement Behavior." *Industrial and Labor Relations Review* 37 (3): 403–15.

——. 1987. "Pensions, Efficiency Wages, and Job Mobility." Dartmouth College, Department of Economics, Hanover, N.H.

——. 1989. "An Analysis of Pension Benefit Formulas, Pension Wealth, and Incentives from Pensions." In Ronald G. Ehrenberg, ed., *Research in Labor Economics.* Vol. 10. Greenwich, Conn.: Jai Press.

——. 1990. "Pension Portability and Labor Mobility: Evidence from the Survey of Income and Program Participation." *Journal of Public Economics* (March): 299–323.

——. 1992. "Stampede toward Defined-Contribution Pension Plans: Fact or Fiction?" *Industrial Relations* 31: 361–69.

Guyana, Government of, National Insurance Scheme. 1987. *Annual Report 1987.* Guyana.

Haaga, J., C. Peterson, J. DaVanzo, and S. M. Lee. 1993. "Health Status and Family Support of Older Malaysians." Population Working Paper Series 93–17. Rand Institute: DRU-378-NIA (June). Santa Monica, Calif.

383

Haanes-Olsen, Leif. 1990. "Investment of Social Security Reserves in Three Countries." *Social Security Bulletin* 53 (2): 2–8.

Hadden, W., G. Fischer, G. Pappas, and S. Queen. 1993. "The Increasing Disparity in Mortality between Socioeconomic Groups in the United States, 1960 and 1986." *Journal of the American Medical Association* 329 (2): 103–09.

Hagemann, Robert. 1989. "Aging Populations and the Pressure on Pensions." *OECD Observer* (October): 12–7.

Hagemann, Robert, and Giuseppe Nicoletti. 1989. "Population Ageing: Economic Effects and Some Policy Implications for Financing Public Pensions." *OECD Economic Studies* 0 (12): 51–96.

Halter, W., and R. Hemming. 1987. "The Impact of Demographic Change on Social Security Financing." *IMF Staff Papers* 34 (3): 471–502.

Hamermesh, D. 1984. "Life-Cycle Effects on Consumption and Retirement." *Journal of Labor Economics* 2: 353–70.

Hannah, Leslie. 1986. *Inventing Retirement: The Development of Occupational Pensions in Britain.* Cambridge: Cambridge University Press.

Hansson, I., and C. Stuart. 1989. "Social Security as Trade among Living Generations." *American Economic Review* 79 (5): 1182–95.

Hauser, Richard. 1987. "Comparing the Influence of Social Security Systems on the Relative Economic Positions of Selected Groups in Six Major Industrialized Countries; The Case of One-parent Families." *European Economic Review* 31 (1/2): 192–201.

——. 1988. "Problems of Comparative Social Policy Analysis: The Case of Pensions and Income Security for the Elderly." Luxembourg Income Study (May). Luxembourg.

Hauser, Richard, Peter Meyer, and Urs Ober Hansli. 1983. "Die Obligatorische Altersvorsorge in der Schweiz: Rentabilitätsüberlegungen und Einkommensverteilungsapekte." *Revue Suisse d'Economie Politique et de Statistique* (June): 139–61.

Heller, Peter, R. Hemming, and Peter Kohnert. 1986. *Aging and Social Expenditure in the Major Industrial Countries, 1980–2025.* Washington, D.C.: International Monetary Fund.

Hepp, Stefan. 1990. *The Swiss Pension Funds.* Zurich: Haupt.

Hill, Polly. 1972. *Rural Hausa: A Village and a Setting.* Cambridge: Cambridge University Press.

Hiriashi, N. 1987. *Social Security.* Tokyo: Japanese Institute of Labour.

Hoddinott, John. 1992. "Rotten Kids or Manipulative Parents: Are Children Old-Age Security in Western Kenya?" *Economic Development and Cultural Change* 40 (3): 545–66.

Holm, C. F. 1975. "Social Security and Fertility: An International Perspective." *Demography* 12: 629–44.

Holzmann, Robert. 1992. "Pensions in the Ex-Socialist Countries." World Bank, Washington, D.C.

——. 1994. "Funded and Private Pensions for Eastern European Countries in Transition." Austria: University of Saarland.

Homburg, Stefan. 1990. "The Efficiency of Unfunded Pension Schemes." *Journal of Institutional Theoretical Economics* 146 (4): 641–47.

Hong Kong, Government of. 1992. "A Community-wide Retirement Protection System." Education and Manpower Branch. Hong Kong.

Hu, S. C. 1982. "Social Security, Majority Voting in Equilibrium and Dynamic Efficiency." *International Economic Review* 23: 269–87.

Hurd, Michael, and John B. Shoven. 1982. "Real Income and Wealth of the Elderly." *American Economic Review* 72 (2): 314–25.

———. 1985. "The Distributional Impact of Social Security." In Wise (1985).

Ibbotson, R., and R. Sinquefield. 1989. "Stocks, Bonds, Bills, and Inflation: Historical Returns 1926–1987." Research Foundation of the Institute of Chartered Financial Analysts, Charlottesville, Va.

IDB (Inter-American Development Bank). 1993. "Sistemas de Seguridad Social en la Region: Problemas y Alternativas de Solucion: Argentina." Washington, D.C.

ILO (International Labour Office). Various years. *Yearbook of International Labour Statistics.* Geneva, Switzerland.

———. 1987. *L'investissement des Fonds de la Sécurité Sociale dans les Pays en Développément.* Geneva, Switzerland.

———. 1989. *From Pyramid to Pillar: Population Change and Social Security in Europe.* Geneva, Switzerland.

———. 1992a. *The Cost of Social Security.* Geneva, Switzerland.

———. 1992b. *Social Security and the Process of Economic Restructuring.* Geneva, Switzerland.

———. Forthcoming. *The Cost of Social Security.* Geneva, Switzerland.

IMF (International Monetary Fund). Various years. *International Financial Statistics.* Washington, D.C.

India Employees' Provident Fund. 1991. *Annual Report 37, 1989–90.* New Delhi, India: Employees' Provident Fund Organization.

Instituto Mexicano de Seguridad Social. 1993. *Anuario Estadistico.* Mexico City, Mexico.

Instituto Venezolano de Seguro Social. Various years. *Anuario Estadistico.* Caracas, Venezuela.

Ippolito, Richard A. 1986. *Pensions, Economics, and Public Policy.* Homewood, Ill.: Dow Jones-Irwin.

———. 1989. *The Economics of Pension Insurance.* Boston: IRWIN.

———. 1990. "Toward Explaining Earlier Retirement after 1970." *Industrial and Labor Relations Review* 43 (5): 556–69.

———. 1991. "Encouraging Long Term Tenure: Wage Tilt or Pensions?" *Industrial and Labor Relations Review* 44 (3): 520–35.

ISSA (International Social Security Association). 1987. *Conjugating Public and Private: The Case of Pensions.* Geneva, Switzerland: International Labour Office.

———. 1988. *Economic and Social Aspects of Social Security Financing.* Geneva, Switzerland.

———. 1990a. *Grupo de Trabajo Regional Americano Sobre Pensiones.* Buenos Aires, Argentina.

———. 1990b. "Reforma de la Pension de Vejez China: El Proceso Continua." *Revista Internacional de Seguridad Social* 43 (4): 447–60.

———. 1990c. "Report of the ISSA Regional Meeting of Asia and the Pacific on the Methods of Financing Social Security with Special Reference to Long-term Benefits." New Delhi, India.

———. 1993. *Responding to Changing Needs: Development and Trends in Social Security throughout the World, 1990–1992.* Acapulco, Mexico: International Labour Office.

Jamaica, Government of. 1993. *Economic and Social Statistics of Jamaica.* Jamaica.

James, Estelle. 1992. "Income Security for Old Age: Conceptual Background and Major Issues." World Bank,

Policy Research Department, Poverty and Human Resources Division, Washington, D.C.

James, Estelle, and Robert Palacios. 1994. "Comparing Administrative Costs of Pension Schemes." World Bank, Policy Research Department, Poverty and Human Resources Division, Washington, D.C.

Japanese Organization for International Cooperation in Family Planning. 1989. "Population Aging in Asia." Tokyo.

Jensen, Eric. 1990. "An Econometric Analysis of the Old Age Security Motive for Childbearing." *International Economic Review* 31 (4): 953–80.

Jensen, Michael. 1989. *Eclipse of the Public Corporation.* Cambridge: Cambridge University Press.

Johnson, P., C. Conrad, and D. Thomson, eds. 1989. *Workers versus Pensioners: Intergenerational Justice in an Ageing World.* Manchester, United Kingdom: Manchester University Press.

Johnson, Paul. 1985. "The Economics of Old Age in Britain: A Long-Run View 1881–1981." CEPR Discussion Paper Series (February).

———. 1987. "Savings Behavior, Fertility and Economic Development in Nineteenth Century Britain and America." CEPR Discussion Paper Series 203 (September).

Johnson, Paul, and Jane Falkingham. 1992. *Ageing and Economic Welfare.* London: Sage Publications.

Ju, Chen, and Gavin Jones. 1989. "Ageing in Asia: Its Socioeconomic Consequences." Singapore: Institute of South Asian Studies.

Kagitcibasi, C. 1982. "Old Age Security Value of Children: Cross-National Socioeconomic Evidence." *Journal of Cross-Cultural Psychology* 13: 29–42.

Keller, Jennifer. 1994. "Demographic Distribution of Poverty in Five Latin American Countries." In Palacios (1994b).

Kelley, Allen. 1973. "Population Growth, the Dependency Rate and the Pace of Economic Development." *Population Studies* 27 (3): 405–14.

———. 1988. "Australia: The Coming of Age." *The Australian Economic Review* 82: 27–44.

Kelly, W. R., P. Cutright, and D. Hittle. 1976. "Comment on Charles F. Hohm's Social Security and Fertility: An International Perspective." *Demography* 13: 581–86.

Kendig, H., Akiko Hashimoto, and Larry C. Coppard. 1992. *Family Support for the Elderly: The International Experience.* Oxford: Oxford University Press.

Kenney, Genevieve M. 1988. "The Security Demand for Children in Peninsular Malaysia." Urban Institute, Washington, D.C.

Kenyan National Provident Fund. 1989. Nairobi, Kenya.

Khan, James A. 1988. "Social Security, Liquidity, and Early Retirement." *Journal of Public Economics* 35: 97–117.

King, M. A., and L. Dicks-Mireaux. 1982. "Asset Holdings and the Life-Cycle." *Economic Journal* 92: 247–67.

Kinsella, Kevin. 1988. "Aging in the Third World." U.S. Dept. of Commerce, Bureau of the Census, International Population Reports Series P-95, No. 79. Washington, D.C.

Kinsella, Kevin, and Victoria A. Velkoff. 1993. "Aging in Eastern Europe and the Former Soviet Union." U.S. Department of Commerce, Washington, D.C.

Kitagawa, E., and P. Hauser. 1973. *Differential Mortality in the United States: A Study of Socioeconomic Epidemiology.* Cambridge: Harvard University Press. 1973.

Kling, Jeff, and Lant Pritchett. 1994. "Population Growth and Economic Growth: Is It Factor Accumulation or Productivity?" World Bank, Policy Research Department, Poverty and Human Resource Division, Washington, D.C.

Knodel, John, Aphichat Chamratrithirong, and Nibhon Debavalya. 1987. *Thailand's Reproductive Revolution, Rapid Fertility Decline in a Third World Setting.* Madison: University of Wisconsin Press.

Knodel, John, Napaporn Chayovan, and Siriwan Siriboon. 1992. "The Impact of Fertility Decline on Familial Support for the Elderly: An Illustration from Thailand." *Population and Development Review* 18: 79–103.

Knodel, John, Napaporn Havanon, and Anthony Pramualratana. 1984. "Family Transition in Thailand." *Population and Development Review* 10: 297–328.

Knodel, John, Chanpen Saengtienchai, and Werasit Sttitrai. 1992. "The Living Arrangements of Elderly in Thailand: Views of the Populace." Population Studies Center, Comparative Study of the Elderly in Asia, Research Report 92–20. University of Michigan, Ann Arbor.

Kohl, Jurgen. 1987. "The Politics of Old Age Security in Comparative Perspective." Luxembourg Income Study Working Paper Series. Luxembourg.

——. 1990. "Minimum Standards in Old Age Security and the Problem of Poverty in Old Age." Luxembourg Income Study. Luxembourg.

Kohler, Peter, and Hans Zacher. 1982. *The Evolution of Social Insurance 1881–1981.* New York: St. Martin's Press.

Kohli, Martin, Martin Rein, Anne-Marie Guillemard, and Herman van Gunsteren, eds. 1991. *Time for Retirement.* Cambridge: Cambridge University Press.

Koitz, David. 1988. "Social Security: Its Impact on the Federal Budget Deficit." Congressional Research Service, Washington, D.C.

Koitz, David, and G. Kollmann. 1988. "Social Security: Illustrations of Current Benefit Levels for Persons Born from 1895–1935." Congressional Research Service, Washington, D.C.

Kollmann, G. 1988. "Summary of Major Changes in Social Security Cash Benefits Program: 1935–1987." Congressional Research Service, Washington, D.C.

——. 1992. "How Long Does It Take to Recover the Value of Their Social Security Taxes?" Congressional Research Service, Washington, D.C.

Kopits, George. 1992. "Social Security." In Vito Tanzi, ed., *Fiscal Policies in Economies in Transition.* Washington, D.C.: International Monetary Fund.

Kopits, George, and P. Gotur. 1980. "The Influence of Social Security on Household Savings: A Cross-Country Investigation." *IMF Staff Papers* 27 (March): 161–90.

Koskela, Erkki, and Matti Viren. 1983. "Social Security and Household Saving in an International Cross Section." *American Economic Review* 73 (1): 212–17.

Kotlikoff, Laurence J. 1979. "Testing the Theory of Social Security and Life-cycle Accumulation." *American Economic Review* 69: 396–410.

——. 1987. "Justifying Public Provision of Social Security." *Journal of Policy Analysis and Management* 6 (4): 674–89.

——. 1989a. "An Examination of Empirical Tests of Social Security and Savings." In Kotlikoff (1989b).

——. 1989b. *What Determines Savings?* Cambridge: MIT Press.

——. 1994. "A Critical Review of the World Bank's Social Insurance Analysis." World Bank, Educational and Social Policy Department, Washington, D.C.

Kotlikoff, Laurence J., and David A. Wise. 1987a. "The Incentive Effects of Private Pension Plans." In Wise (1985).

——. 1987b. "Labor Compensation and the Structure of Private Pension Plans: Evidence for Contractual vs. Spot Labor Markets." In Wise (1987).

——. 1989. *The Wage Carrot and the Pension Stick.* Kalamazoo, Mich.: W. E. Upjohn Institute.

Kotlikoff, Laurence J., J. Shoven, and A. Spivak. 1989. "Annuity Insurance, Savings, and Inequality." In Kotlikoff (1989b).

Kotlikoff, Laurence J., A. Spivak, and L. H. Summers. 1982. "The Adequacy of Savings." *American Economic Review* 72: 1056–69.

Kuehlwein, Michael. 1993. "Life-Cycle and Altruistic Theories of Saving with Lifetime Uncertainty." *The Review of Economics and Statistics* 75 (1): 37–47.

Lakonishok, Josef, Andrei Shleifer, and Robert W. Vishny. 1992. "The Structure and Performance of the Money Management Industry." *Brookings Papers on Economic Activity: Microeconomics 1992*: 339–92.

Lakshmanasamy, T. 1989. "Old Age, Risk, Security and Children: An Empirical Evidence from Rural India." *Indian Journal of Economics* 70 (276): 51–67.

——. 1991. "Intergenerational Transfers and Wealth Accumulation: Motivations for Saving and the Effect of Annuities." *Indian Journal of Economics* 71 (283): 465–84.

Laslett, Peter. 1989. "The Demographic Scene: An Overview." In Eekelaar and Pearl (1989).

Lazear, Edward. 1982. "Severance Pay, Pensions, and Efficient Mobility." National Bureau of Economic Research Working Paper 854, Cambridge, Mass.

Lazear, Edward, and Robert Moore. 1987. "Pensions and Turnover." In Bodie, Shoven, and Wise (1987).

Lee, Maw Lin, and She-Wen Chao. 1988. "Effects of Social Security on Personal Saving." *Economic Letters* 28: 365–68.

Lee, Ronald, and Shelley Lapkoff. 1988. "Intergenerational Flows of Time and Goods: Consequences of Slowing Population Growth." *Journal of Political Economy* 96 (3): 618–51.

Lee, Ronald, W. Arthur, and Gerry Rodgers, eds. 1988. *Economics of Changing Age Distributions in Developed Countries.* Oxford: Clarendon Press.

Leff, Mark, 1987. "Historical Perspective on Old-Age Insurance: The State of the Art on the Art of the State." In Edward Berkowitz, ed., *Social Security after Fifty: Successes and Failures.* New York: Greenwood Press.

Leibenstein, Harvey. 1957. *Economic Backwardness and Economic Growth.* New York: John Wiley.

——. 1975. "The Economic Theory of Fertility Decline." *Quarterly Journal of Economics* 89: 1–31.

Leimer, Dean, and S. Lesnoy. 1982. "Social Security and Private Saving: New Time-Series Evidence." *Journal of Political Economy* 90: 606–42.

Leimer, Dean, and Peter Petri. 1981. "Cohort-Specific Effects of Social Security Policy." *National Tax Journal* 34 (1): 9–28.

Lim, Chong Yah. 1986. "Report of the Central Provident Fund Study Group." *Singapore Economic Review* 31 (1): 11–107.

Lindert, Peter H. 1980. "Child Costs and Economic Development." In R. S. Easterlin, ed., *Population and Economic Change in Developing Countries.* Chicago: University of Chicago Press.

——. 1983. "Changing Costs and Benefits of Having Children." In R. A. Bulatao and R. D. Lee, eds., *Determinants of Fertility in Developing Countries.* New York: Academic Press.

Liu, Lillian. 1991. "Social Security for State-Sector Workers in the People's Republic of China: The Reform Decade and Beyond." *Social Security Bulletin* 54 (10): 2–16.

Lloyd-Sherlock, Peter. 1992. "Social Insurance Reform in an Ageing World: The Case of Latin America." London School of Economics Development Research Program (August).

Loewy, M. 1988. "Equilibrium Policy in an Overlapping Generations Economy." *Journal of Monetary Economics* 22 (3): 485–99.

Lok, C. C., and M. R. Lok. 1985. "A Note on Social Security and Private Savings in Singapore." *Public Finance*, 299–304.

Lora, E., Hernando Zuleta, and Loredana Helmsdorff. 1992. "Viabilidad Macroeconomica y Financiera de un Sistema Privado de Pensiones." *Coyuntura Economica* 22 (1): 75–95.

Luzadis, Rebecca, and Olivia Mitchell. 1990. "Explaining Pension Dynamics." *Journal of Human Resources* 26 (4): 679–703.

McCormic, Barry, and Gordon Hughs. 1984. "The Influence of Pensions on Job Mobility." *Journal of Public Economics* 23: 183–206.

McGreevey, William. 1990. *Social Security in Latin America: Issues and Options for the World Bank.* Discussion Paper 110. World Bank, Population, Health, and Nutrition Department, Washington, D.C.

Mackenzie, G. A. 1988. "Social Security Issues in Developing Countries: The Latin America Experience." *IMF Staff Papers* 35 (3): 496–522.

Maddison, Angus. 1987. "Growth and Slowdown in Advanced Capitalist Economies: Techniques of Quantitative Assessment." *Journal of Economic Literature* 25: 649–98.

Marlow, Michael, and Mark W. Crain. 1990. "The Causal Relationship between Social Security and the Federal Budget." In Weaver (1990).

Marmer, T. R., and J. L. Marshall. 1988. *Social Security: Beyond the Rhetoric.* Princeton, N.J.: Princeton University Press.

Marquez, Gustavo. 1992. "El Seguro Social en Venezuela." Banco Interamericano de Desarrollo, Washington, D.C.

Martin, Linda. 1990. "Changing Intergenerational Family Relations in East Asia." *The Annals* 510: 102–14.

Martin, Linda, and Samuel Preston, eds. 1994. *Demography of Aging.* Washington, D.C.: National Academy Press.

Mason, Andrew, and others. 1993. "Saving in Thailand." East-West Center Working Paper, Honolulu.

Mauritius, Government of. 1987. *Statistical Yearbook of Mauritius.*

Mazumdar, Dipak. 1994. "Wages in Africa." World Bank, Africa Regional Office, Office of the Chief Economist, Washington, D.C.

Mesa-Lago, Carmelo. 1989. *Ascent to Bankruptcy: Financing Social Security in Latin America.* Pittsburgh: University of Pittsburgh Press.

——. 1991a. *Portfolio Performance of Selected Social Security Institutes in Latin America.* Discussion Paper 139. World Bank, Washington, D.C.

——. 1991b. *Social Security and Prospects for Equity in Latin America.* Discussion Paper 140. World Bank, Washington, D.C.

Mesa-Lago, Carmelo, ed. 1985. *The Crisis of Social Security and Health Care: Latin American Experiences and Lessons.* Pittsburgh: University of Pittsburgh Press.

Mesa-Lago, Carmelo, Maria Cruz-Saco, and Lorena Zamalloa. 1990. "Determinantes de los Costos y la Cobertura del Seguro-Seguridad Social. Una Comparacion Internacional Enfocada en la America Latina." *El Trimestre Economico* 57 (225): 27–57.

Meyer, Charles, and Nancy Wolff. 1987. "Intercohort and Intracohort Redistribution under the Old-Age Insurance: The 1962–1972 Retirement Cohorts." *Public Finance Quarterly* 15 (3): 259–81.

Mitchell, B. R. 1982. *International Historical Statistics: Asia and Africa.* New York: New York University Press.

——. 1983. *International Historical Statistics: The Americas and Australasia.* Detroit: Gale Research Company.

——. 1990. *International Historical Statistics: Europe 1750–1988.* 3d ed. New York: Stockton Press.

Mitchell, Deborah. 1992. *Income Transfers in Ten Welfare States.* Aldershot, United Kingdom: Avebury.

——. 1993. "Income Security for Old Age: Evidence for Eight OECD Countries." Australian National University Research School of Social Sciences.

Mitchell, Olivia S. 1982. "Fringe Benefits and Labor Mobility." *Journal of Human Resources* 17: 286–98.

——. 1983. "Fringe Benefits and the Cost of Changing Jobs." *Industrial and Labor Relations Review* 37: 70–78.

——. 1994. "Retirement Systems in Developed and Developing Countries: Institutional Features, Economic Effects, and Lessons for Economies in Transition." In A. Van Adames, E. King, and Z. Tzannatos, eds., *Labor Market Policies for Managing the Social Costs of Economic Adjustment.* Washington, D.C.: World Bank.

Mitchell, Olivia S., and Ping Lung Hsin. 1994a. "Managing Public Sector Pensions." In John Shoven and Sylvester Schieber, eds., *Public Policy toward Pensions.* New York: Twentieth Century Fund.

——. 1994b. "The Political Economy of Public Pensions: Pension Funding, Governance, and Fiscal Stress." In P. Arrau and K. Schmidt-Hebbel, eds., *Revista de Análisis Económico: Special Issue on Pension Systems and Reform.*

Mitchell, Olivia S., and Rebecca A. Luzadis. 1988. "Firm-Level Policy toward Older Workers." *Industrial and Labor Relations Review* 12: 100–08.

Mitchell, Olivia S., and Robert Smith. 1992. "Public Sector Pensions: Benefits, Funding and Unionization." *Industrial Relations Research Association Papers and Proceedings.* 126–33.

——. Forthcoming. "Public Sector Pension Funding." *Review of Economics and Statistics.*

Mitchell, Olivia S., Annika Sundén, Ping Lung Hsin, and G. Reid. 1994. "An International Appraisal of Social Security Administration Costs." World Bank, Latin America and the Caribbean Regional Office, Technical Department, Public Sector Management Division, Washington, D.C.

Modigliani, F. 1988. "The Role of Intergenerational Transfers and Life-Cycle Saving in the Accumulation of Wealth." *Journal of Economic Perspectives* 2 (2): 15–40.

Modigliani, F., and R. Hemming, eds. 1983. *The Determinants of National Savings and Wealth.* London: Macmillan.

Modigliani, F., and A. Sterling. 1983. "The Determinants of Private Saving with Special Reference to the Role of Social Security—Cross-Country Tests." In Modigliani and Hemming (1983).

Moffitt, Robert. 1983. "An Economic Model of Welfare Stigma." *American Economic Review* 73 (5): 1023–35.

——. 1984. "Trends in Social Security Wealth by Cohort." In Marilyn Moon, ed., *Economic Transfers in the United States.* Chicago: National Bureau of Economic Research.

Munnell, Alicia H. 1974. "The Impact of Social Security on Personal Savings." *National Tax Journal* 27: 553–67.

———. 1982. *The Economics of Private Pensions.* Washington, D.C.: Brookings Institution.

Munnell, Alicia, and C. N. Ernsberger. 1989. "Public Pension Surpluses and National Saving: Foreign Experience." *New England Economic Review* 0 (0): 16–38.

Munnell, Alicia, and Frederick Yohn. 1992. "What Is the Impact of Pensions on Savings?" In Bodie and Munnell (1992).

Murray, Christopher, R. Govindaraj, and G. Chellaraj. 1993. "Global Domestic Expenditures on Health." Harvard University, Center for Population and Development Studies, Cambridge, Mass.

Myers, Robert. 1993a. "Chile's Social Security Reform after Ten Years." *Benefits Quarterly.*

———. 1993b. *Social Security.* Philadelphia: Pension Research Council.

Myles, John. 1989. *Old Age in the Welfare State: The Political Economy of Public Pensions.* Lawrence, Kan.: University Press of Kansas.

Nair, Sobha B., and Martin B. Tracy. 1989. "Pensions for Women in the Third World: A Case Study of Kerala, India." *International Journal of Contemporary Sociology* 26: 175–87.

Navarro, Vicente. 1991. "Race or Class or Race and Class: Growing Mortality Differentials in the United States." *International Journal of Health Services* 21 (2): 229–35.

Neher, Philip. 1977. "Peasants, Procreation and Pensions." *American Economic Review* 61 (3): 380–89.

Nelissen, Jan. 1987. "The Redistributive Impact of the General Old Age Pensions Act on Lifetime Income in the Netherlands." *European Economic Review* 31 (7): 1419–41.

Netherlands, Ministry of Social Affairs and Employment. 1990. *Social Security in the Netherlands.* Deventer: Kluwer Law and Taxation Publishers.

Nordic Countries Statistical Secretariat. Various Years. *Social Security in the Nordic Countries.* Stockholm: Nordic Statistical Secretariat.

Novos, Ian E. 1989. "Social Security Wealth and Wealth Accumulation: Further Microeconomic Evidence." *Review of Economics and Statistics* 71 (1) 167–71.

Nugent, Jeffrey B. 1985. "The Old Age Security Motive for Fertility." *Population and Development Review* 11: 75–97.

Nugent, Jeffrey B., and Thomas Gillaspy. 1983. "Old Age Pensions and Fertility in Rural Areas of Less Developed Countries: Some Evidence from Mexico." *Economic Development and Cultural Change* 31: 809–29.

OECD (Organization for Economic Cooperation and Development). 1988a. *Ageing Population: The Social Policy Implications.* Paris.

———. 1988b. *Reforming Public Pensions.* Paris.

———. 1988c. *Switzerland, Economic Survey 1987–88.* Paris.

———. 1992. *Private Pensions and Public Policy.* Paris.

Okonkwo, U. 1975. *Intragenerational Equity under Social Security.* Washington, D.C.: International Monetary Fund.

Oliviera, Francisco, M. H. da T. Henriques, and K. I. Beltrao. 1987. "The Brazilian Social Security System: Coverage and Constraints." *International Social Security Review* 4: 373–85.

Orazem, Peter, and Milan Vodopivec. 1994. "Winners and Losers in Transition: Returns to Education, Experience, and Gender in Slovenia." World Bank, Policy Research Department, Washington, D.C.

Palacios, Robert. 1994a. "International Patterns of Public Pension Coverage." Working paper. World Bank, Policy Research Department, Washington, D.C.

———. 1994b. "Averting the Old Age Crisis: Technical Annex." World Bank, Policy Research Department, Washington, D.C.

———. 1994c. "Life Cycle of a Pay-as-You-Go Pension Scheme." World Bank, Policy Research Department, Washington, D.C.

Palmer, J., T. Smeeding, and B. Torrey, eds. 1988. *The Vulnerable.* Washington, D.C.: Urban Institute Press.

Pan American Health Organization. 1989a. *Mid-life and Older Women in Latin America and the Caribbean.* Washington, D.C.

———. 1989b. *A Profile of the Elderly in Argentina.* Washington, D.C.

———. 1989c. *A Profile of the Elderly in Guyana.* Washington, D.C.

———. 1989d. *A Profile of the Elderly in Trinidad and Tobago.* Washington, D.C.

———. 1990a. *A Profile of the Elderly in Chile.* Washington, D.C.

———. 1990b. *A Profile of the Elderly in Costa Rica.* Washington, D.C.

Pappas, G., S. Queen, W. Hadden, and Gail Fisher. 1993. "The Increasing Disparity in Mortality between Socioeconomic Groups in the United States, 1960 and 1986." *Journal of the American Medical Association* 329 (2): 103–09.

Pathak, J. D. 1978. *Our Elderly.* Bombay, India: Medical Research Center.

Patton, Carl V. 1978. "The Politics of Social Security." In Michael J Boskin, ed., *The Crisis in Social Security: Problems and Prospects.* San Francisco: Institute for Contemporary Studies.

Pellechio, Anthony. 1979. "Estimation of Labor Supply over Kinked Budget Constraints: Some New Econo-

metric Methodology." National Bureau of Economic Research Working Paper 387. Cambridge, Mass.

———. 1981. "Social Security and the Decision to Retire." National Bureau of Economic Research Working Paper 734. Cambridge, Mass.

Pesando, James. 1991. "The Multiple Roles of Private Pensions: Effect on Savings, Capital Markets, and Labour Market Decisions." Presented at the OECD Conference on Private Pensions and Public Policy. Paris.

Pestieau, Pierre. 1991. "Private Pensions and Public Policy: The Distribution of Private Pension Benefits: How Fair Is It?" University of Liege, Department of Economics, Belgium.

Petersen, Jorn-Hendrik. 1986. "Three Precursors of Modern Theories of Old-Age Pensions: A Contribution to the History of Social Policy Doctrines." *History of Political Economy* 18 (3): 405–17.

———. 1991. "A Reply to My Commentators." *History of Political Economy* 23 (1): 87–92.

Peterson, Ray. 1961. "The Coming Din of Inequity." *Journal of the American Medical Association* (April 8): 118–26.

Petkov, Krastyu, and Doukhomir Minev. 1989. "Work and Income of the Bulgarian Pensioner." *International Social Security Review* 1 (2): 70–86.

Petrei, A. H., ed. 1987. "El Gasto Publico Social y Sus Efectos Distributivos." Programa de Estudios Conjuntos Sobre Integracíon Economíca Latino Americana, Rio de Janeiro, Brazil.

Piggott, John, and David Knox. 1993. "Contemporary Issues in Australian Superannuation—A Conference Summary." Superannuation Economics Research Group Research Paper Series 12. University of New South Wales, Australia.

Porket, J. L. 1980. "Inequalities in Eastern Europe: The Case of Old Age Pensioners." Papers in East European Economics No. 64. St. Anthony's College, Oxford.

Provida (Administrativo de Fondos de Pensiones). 1993. *Informe Annual.* Chile.

Psacharopoulos, George. 1993. "Returns to Investment in Education: A Global Update." Working Paper WPS1067. World Bank, Policy Research Department, Washington, D.C.

Psacharopoulos, George, Samuel Morley, Ariel Fiszbein, Haeduck Lee, and Bill Wood. 1993. "Poverty and Income Distribution in Latin America: The Story of the 1980s." World Bank, Human Resources Division, Washington, D.C.

Queisser, Monika. 1991. "Social Security Systems in South East Asia: Indonesia, the Philippines and Singapore." *International Social Security Review* 44: 121–35.

Quinn, Joseph. 1977. "Microeconomic Determinants of Early Retirement: A Cross-Sectional View of White Married Men." *Journal of Human Resources* 12: 329–46.

Quinn, Joseph, R. Burkhauser, and D. Myers. 1990. *Passing the Torch: The Influence of Economic Incentives on Work and Retirement.* Kalamazoo, Mich.: W. E. Upjohn Institute.

Ramos, Luiz. 1992. "Family Support for Elderly People in São Paulo, Brazil." In Kendig, Hashimoto, and Coppard, eds. (1992).

Rashid, Mansoora. 1993. "Financing the Polish Social Security System: A Simulation Model and Results from Two Experiments." World Bank, Europe and Central Asia–Country Department II, Human Resources Operations Division, Washington, D.C.

Ravallion, Martin. 1992. "Poverty Comparisons: A Guide to Concepts and Methods." Living Standards Measurement Study Working Paper No. 88. World Bank, Policy Research Department, Poverty and Human Resources Division, Washington, D.C.

Reichel, Klaus-Walter. 1989. "Growth in France's Social Security System Impairs Work Incentives and Com-petitiveness: Staff Study and Outline for Reforms." International Monetary Fund, Washington, D.C.

Reimers, Cordelia K. W. 1977. "The Timing of Retirement of American Men." Dissertation. Columbia University, Department of Economics, New York.

Reisen, Helmut. 1994. "On the Wealth of Nations and Retirees." OECD Development Centre. Paris.

Rofman, Rafael. 1993a. "Diferencias de Mortalidad Adulta en Argentina." Centro de Estudios de Poblacion. Buenos Aires, Argentina.

——. 1993b. "Social Security and Income Distribution: Mortality and Equity in Pension Plans." Dissertation. University of California at Berkeley.

——. 1994. "La Reforma Previsional en Argentina: Que Podemos Esperar?" Centro de Estudios de Poblacion. Buenos Aires, Argentina.

Rosa, Jean-Jacques, ed. 1982. *The World Crisis in Social Security.* San Francisco: Institute for Contemporary Studies.

Ross, Christine, Sheldon Danziger, and Eugene Smolensky. 1985. "The Level and Trend of Poverty in the United States, 1939–1979." IRP Discussion Paper. University of Wisconsin, Madison.

Rowntree, B., and G. R. Lavers. 1951. *Poverty and the Welfare State.* London: Longmans, Green and Co.

Samuelson, Paul. 1958. "An Exact Consumption Loan Model with or without the Social Contrivance of Money." *Journal of Political Economy* 66 (6): 467–82.

——. 1985. "The Federal Civil Service Retirement System: An Analysis of Its Financial Condition and the Current Reform Proposals: Comment." In Wise (1985).

Sanderson, Warren, and Jee-Peng Tan. 1994. "Population in Asia." Regional and Sectoral Studies Series. World Bank, Education and Social Policy Department, Washington, D.C.

Schieber, Sylvester. 1989. "A History of the Evolution of Employer Sponsored Pension Plans, Provisions, and Regulations in the United States." Wyatt Company, Washington, D.C.

Schiller, Bradley, and Randall Weiss. 1979. "The Impact of Private Pensions on Firm Attachment." *Review of Economics and Statistics* (August): 369–80.

Schioppa, Fiorella Padoa. 1990. "Undesirable Redistributions in the Retirement Public Pension Schemes: The Italian Case Study." Discussion Paper 463. Centre for Economic Policy Research, London.

Schmähl, Winfried. 1988. "The Public Old Age Pension System in Germany." Friedrich Ebert Foundation.

Schmähl, Winfried, and Stephen Bohm. 1993. "Occupational Pension Schemes in the Private and Public Sector in the Federal Republic of Germany—An Overview." *Ageing and World* 11 (3).

Schmidt-Hebbel, Klaus, Steven Webb, and Ginacarlo Corsetti. 1992. "Household Saving in Developing Countries: First Cross-Country Evidence." *World Bank Economic Review* 6 (3): 529–47.

Schulz, James. 1992. "Economic Support in Old Age: The Role of Social Insurance in Developing Countries." Presented at the 24th General Assembly of the International Social Security Association.

Schulz, James, and others. 1991. *Economics of Population Aging: The "Graying" of Australia, Japan and the US.* New York: Auburn House.

Schwarz, Anita. 1992a. "Basic Parameters of Mandatory Retirement Savings Schemes." World Bank, Country Economics Department, Financial Policy Division, Washington, D.C.

——. 1992b. "Policy Issues in Pension Guarantees." World Bank, Country Economics Department, Financial Policy Division, Washington, D.C.

——. 1994. "The Trade-Off between Redistribution and Savings in Alternative Pension Systems." World Bank, Country Economics Department, Financial Policy Division, Washington, D.C.

Setapa, Sabariah. 1993. "Old Age Support and Security in Malaysia." Thesis. University of California at Berkeley.

Siegel, Jeremy. 1992. "The Real Rate of Interest from 1800–1990." *Journal of Monetary Economics* 29: 227–52.

Sjoblom, Kriss. 1985. "Voting for Social Security." *Public Choice* 45: 225–40.

Smallhout, James. 1993. "Avoiding the Next Guaranteed Bailout: Reforms for the Pension Insurance Program." *Brookings Review* 11 (2): 12–5.

Smeeding, Timothy M. 1990. "Meaning of Retirement: Gross National Patterns and Trends." Working Paper 51. Luxembourg Income Study. Luxembourg.

——. 1991. "Cross National Patterns of Retirement and Poverty among Men and Women in the 1980s: Full Stop or Gradual Withdrawal?" Luxembourg Income Study. Luxembourg.

——. 1992. "Why the US Antipoverty System Doesn't Work Well." *Challenge* (January–February): 30–5.

Smith, Alasdair. 1982. "Intergenerational Transfers as Social Insurance." *Journal of Public Economics* 19: 97–106.

South Africa, Government of. 1992. *Mouton Report.* Johannesburg.

Spivak, Avia, and Larry Summers. 1982. "The Adequacy of Savings." *American Economic Review* 72 (5): 1056–69.

Stahlberg, Ann-Charlotte. 1989. "Redistribution Effects of Social Policy in a Lifetime Analytical Framework." In Gustaffson and Klevmarken (1989).

Steuerle, C., and Jon Bakija. 1994. *Retooling Social Security for the 21st Century: Right and Wrong Approaches to Reform.* Washington, D.C.: Urban Institute Press.

Superintendencia de AFPs (Banco Central de Chile). 1993. *Informe Anual.* Santiago, Chile: Banco Central de Chile.

Szalchman, Raquel, and Andras Uthoff. 1992. "Sistema de Pensiones en America Latina: Diagnostico y Alternativas de Reform." Comision Economica para America Latina, Santiago, Chile.

Tabellini, Guido. 1992. "A Positive Theory of Social Security." University of Brescia, Italy.

Takayama, Noriyuki. 1990. "How Much Do Public Pensions Discourage Personal Saving and Induce Early Retirement in Japan?" *Hitotsubashi Journal of Economics* 31 (2): 87–103.

Thompson, Lawrence. 1983. "The Social Security Reform Debate." *Journal of Economic Literature* 21 (3): 1425–56.

Thomson, David. 1989. "The Elderly in an Urban Industrial Society: England, 1750 to the Present." In Eekelaar and Pearl (1989).

Tokman, Victor. 1992. *Beyond Regulation: The Informal Economy in Latin America.* Boulder, Colo.: Rienner.

Townley, P. G. C. 1981. "Public Choice and the Social Insurance Paradox: A Note." *Canadian Journal of Economics* 14: 712–17.

Tracy, Martin B., and Paul Adams. 1989. "Age of First Pension Award under Social Security: Pattern in Eight Industrial Countries, 1960–1986." *Social Security Review* 4 (42): 447–61.

Tracy, Martin B., and F. Pampel. 1991. *International Handbook on Old-Age Insurance.* Westport, Conn.: Greenwood Press.

Turner, John. 1993a. "Contracting Out in Japan." U.S. Department of Labor, Washington, D.C.

———. 1993b. *Pension Policy for a Mobile Labor Force.* Kalamazoo, Mich.: W. E. Upjohn Institute.

Turner, J., and D. Beller. 1989. *Trends in Pensions* (annual). Washington, D.C.: U.S. Department of Labor.

———. 1992. *Trends in Pensions* (annual). Washington, D.C.: U.S. Department of Labor.

Turner, John, and Lorna Dailey. 1991. *Pension Policy: An International Perspective.* Washington, D.C.: U.S. Department of Labor.

United Kingdom. 1899. "The Aged Deserving Poor." Report presented at the United Kingdom Parliament meeting, London.

United Nations. 1985. *The World Aging Situation: Strategies and Policies.* New York.

———. 1992a. *Demographic Causes and Economic Consequences of Population Aging.* New York: Economic Commission for Europe.

———. 1992b. *Demographic Yearbook.* New York.

U.S. Bureau of the Census. Various years. *Current Population Reports Series P-60* (annual). Washington, D.C.

U.S. Department of Commerce. 1993. *An Aging World II.* Washington, D.C.

U.S. Social Security Administration. 1993. *Social Security Programs throughout the World—1991.* Washington, D.C.

———. Various years. *Social Security Bulletin* (annual). Washington, D.C.

Valdés-Prieto, Salvador. 1993. "Administrative Costs in the Chilean Pension System: Evidence from an International Comparison." World Bank, Policy Research Department, Washington, D.C.

————. 1994. "Distributive Concerns When Substituting for a Pay-as-You-Go Scheme with a Fully Funded Pension System." *Revista de Análisis Económico* 9 (1): 77–103.

Valdés-Prieto, Salvador, and Rudrigo Cifuentes, 1993. "Credit Constraints and Pensions." Manuscript. Catholic University of Chile, Santiago.

van de Walle, Dominique, Martin Ravallion, and Madhur Gautam. 1994. "How Well Does the Social Safety Net Work? The Incidence of Cash Benefits in Hungary 1987–1989." World Bank, Policy Research Department, Washington, D.C.

Van der Noord, Paul, and Richard Herd. 1993. "Pension Liabilities in the Seven Major Economies." Working Paper. OECD Economics Department, Paris.

Veall, Michael. 1986. "Public Pensions as Optimal Social Contracts." *Journal of Public Economics* 31 (2): 237–51.

Verbon, Harrie. 1988. *The Evolution of Public Pension Schemes.* London: Springer-Verlag.

————. 1990. "Transfers to the Old, Government Debt and Demographic Change." *Journal of Population Economics* 3 (2): 89–104.

Vittas, Dimitri. 1992. "Contractual Savings and Emerging Securities Markets." Policy Research Working Paper 858. World Bank, Policy Research Department, Washington, D.C.

————. 1993a. "Options for Pension Reform in Tunisia." Policy Research Working Paper 1154. World Bank, Policy Research Department, Washington, D.C.

————. 1993b. "The Simple(r) Algebra of Pension Plans." Policy Research Working Paper 1145. World Bank, Policy Research Department, Washington, D.C.

————. 1993c. "Swiss Chilanpore: The Way Forward for Pension Reform?" Policy Research Working Paper

1093. World Bank, Policy Research Department, Washington, D.C.

————. 1994a. "The Argentine Pension Reform and its Relevance for Eastern Europe." World Bank, Financial Sector Development Department, Washington, D.C.

————. 1994b. "Policy Issues in Contractual Savings in South Africa." World Bank, Financial Sector Development Department, Washington, D.C.

Vittas, Dimitri, and Augusto Iglesias. 1992. "The Rationale and Performance of Personal Pension Plans in Chile." Policy Research Working Paper 867. World Bank, Policy Research Department, Washington, D.C.

Vittas, Dimitri, and Michael Skully. 1991. "Overview of Contractual Savings Institutions." Policy Research Working Paper 605. World Bank, Policy Research Department, Washington, D.C.

Vlassoff, C. 1990. "The Value of Sons in an Indian Village: How Widows See It." *Population Studies* 44: 5–20.

Vlassoff, M., and C. Vlassoff. 1980. "Old Age Security and the Utility of Children in Rural India." *Population Studies* 34: 487–89.

von Benda-Beckmann, F., K. von Benda-Beckmann, E. Casino, F. Hirtz, and H. Zacher, eds. 1988. *Between Kinship and the State: Social Security and Law in Developing Countries.* Providence, R.I.: Foris Publications.

von Furstenburg, George. 1979. *Social Security versus Private Saving.* Cambridge, Mass.: Ballinger.

von Weizsacker, Robert. 1990. "Population Aging and Social Security: A Politico-Economic Model of State Pension Financing." *Public Finance* 45 (3): 491–509.

Vukovich, Gabriella. 1991. "Population Aging in Hungary: Selected Aspects." CICRED (Committee for International Cooperation in National Research in Demography), Paris.

Wachter, Susan. 1988a. *Private and Public Provision of Retirement Insurance.* Lexington, Mass.: Heath Lexington Books.

———. 1988b. *Social Security and Private Pensions: Providing for Retirement in the Twenty-first Century.* Lexington, Mass: Heath Lexington Books.

Wagner, Gert. 1991. "La Seguridad Social y el Programa de Pension Minima Garantizada." *Estudios de Economia* 18 (1): 35–89.

Walker, A., J. Alber, and Anne-Marie Guillemard. 1993. "Older People in Europe: Social and Economic Policies." Commission of European Communities, Social Affairs Directorate, Paris.

Wallich, Christine. 1982. "Savings Mobilization through Social Security: The Experience of Chile during 1916–1977." Staff Working Paper Series 553. World Bank, Washington, D.C.

Warlick, Jennifer. 1982. "Participation of the Aged in SSI." *Journal of Human Resources* 17: 236–60.

Weaver, Carolyn. 1982. *The Crisis in Social Security: Economic and Political Origins.* Durham, N.C.: Duke University Press.

———. 1993. "Guarantees of Private Pension Benefits: Current Problems and Likely Future Prospects." American Enterprise Institute, Washington, D.C.

Weaver, Carolyn, ed. 1990. *Social Security's Looming Surpluses: Prospects and Implications.* Washington, D.C.: American Enterprise Institute Press.

Williamson, Nancy. 1976. *Sons or Daughters: A Cross-Cultural Survey of Parental Preferences.* Beverly Hills, Calif.: Sage Publications.

Williamson, Samuel. 1992. "U.S. and Canadian Pensions before 1930: A Historical Perspective." In Turner and Beller (1992).

Wise, David. 1990. *Economics of Aging.* Chicago: University of Chicago Press.

Wise, David, ed. 1985. *Pensions, Labor, and Individual Choice.* Chicago: University of Chicago Press for the National Bureau of Economic Research.

Wolf, Douglas, and Frank Levy. 1984. "Pension Coverage, Pension Vesting and the Distribution of Job Tenure." In Aaron and Burtless (1984).

Wolff, Edward, ed. 1987. *International Comparisons of the Distribution of Household Wealth.* Oxford: Oxford University Press.

World Bank. 1990. "China: Reforming Social Security in a Socialist Economy." World Bank, Country Operations Division, China Department, Asia Regional Office, Washington, D.C.

———. 1991a. *Ecuador: Public Sector Reforms for Growth in the Era of Declining Oil Output.* Washington, D.C.

———. 1991b. *Lessons of Tax Reform.* Washington, D.C.

———. 1992a. "Philippines, Capital Market Study." World Bank, Industry and Energy Division, East Asia and Pacific Region, Washington, D.C.

———. 1992b. "Poland: Income Support and the Social Safety Net: Policies for the Transition." World Bank, Europe and Central Asia Regional Office, Washington, D.C.

———. 1992c. *Social Indicators of Development 1991–1992.* Baltimore: Johns Hopkins University Press.

———. 1992d. *World Development Report 1992: Development and the Environment.* New York: Oxford University Press.

———. 1993. "The Turkish Pension System." Washington, D.C.

———. 1994a. "The Brazilian Social Security." World Bank, Latin America and the Caribbean Department, Country Operations Division, Washington, D.C.

——. 1994b. *Uruguay: The Private Sector*. World Bank, Latin America and the Caribbean Department, Country Operations Division, Washington, D.C.

Yagi, Tadashi. 1990. "Why Are Annuity Systems Used to Redistribute Income?" *Economic Studies Quarterly* 41 (2): 134–54.

Yamada, Tetsuji, Tadashi Yamada, and Guoen Liu. 1992. "Interdependency of Personal Savings and Labour Force Participation of the Elderly, and Social Security Wealth: A Time Series Analysis." *Applied Economics* 24: 379–88.

Yumiba, Yoshihiro. 1990. "Japan: Private Pension Statistics." Presented at the International Conference on Private Pension Policy and Statistical Analysis. Paris.

Zabalza, A., C. Pissarides, and M. Barton. 1980. "Social Security and the Choice between Full-Time Work, Part-Time Work and Retirement." *Journal of Public Economics* 14: 245–76.

Zambia, National Provident Fund of. Various years. *Annual Report*. Zambia.

Zedlewski, S., and Jack Meyer. 1989. *Toward Ending Poverty among the Elderly and Disabled through SSI Reform*. Washington, D.C.: Urban Institute.

For Further Reading

Full bibliographic information for the works that follow is given in the Bibliography. For further reading on the following topics, see:

History of public pension systems: Aaron, Pechman, and Taussig (1968); Atkinson (1991a, 1991b); Burns (1944); Esping-Andersen (1990); Gordon (1988); Graebner (1980); Johnson (1985); Kohler and Zacher (1982); Leff (1987); Petersen (1986, 1991); Rowntree and Lavers (1951); United Kingdom (1899); Verbon (1988); Weaver (1982).

History of occupational pensions: Dobbin (1992); Esping-Andersen (1990); Graebner (1980); Hannah (1986); Schieber (1989).

Poverty among the elderly: Cangping (1991); Deaton and Paxson (1991); Dreze (1990); Förster (1993); Fox (1994); Gaiha and Kazmi (1982); Palmer, Smeeding, and Torrey (1988); Steuerle and Bakija (1994); Warlick (1982).

Comparison of administrative costs of pensions: Acuña and Iglesias (1992); James and Palacios (1994); Sundén and Mitchell (1994); Turner and Beller (1989); Valdés-Prieto (1993).

Distributive effects of public pension schemes: Aaron (1977, 1982); Aaron, Pechman, and Taussig (1968); Auerbach and Kotlikoff (1987); Boskin, Kotlikoff, Puffert, and Shoven (1987); Brittain (1972); Burkhauser and Warlick (1981); Creedy, Disney, and Whitehouse (1992); Feldstein and Samwick (1992); Fernandez Riva (1992); Hurd and Shoven (1985); Leimer and Petri (1981); Meyer and Wolff (1987); Moffitt (1983, 1984); Nelissen (1987); Petrei (1987); Schioppa (1990); Schwarz (1994); Smeeding (1991); Stahlberg (1989); Steuerle and Bakija (1994); Valdés-Prieto (1994).

The political economy of public pension schemes: Browning (1975); Cukierman and Meltzer (1989); Hansson and Stuart (1989); Hu (1982); Loewy (1988); Patton (1978); Sjoblom (1985); Tabellini (1992); Townley (1981); Verbon (1988).

The effects of pensions on labor supply: Blinder, Gordon, and Wise (1980); Bodie and Munnell (1992); Boskin (1977); Boskin and Hurd (1978); Burkhauser (1980); Burtless and Moffitt (1984); Diamond and Hausman (1984); Fields and Mitchell (1984a); Gustman and Steinmeier (1984); Hamermesh (1984); Ippolito (1990); Kahn (1988); Kotlikoff (1979); Pellechio (1979, 1981); Quinn (1977); Quinn, Burkhauser, and Myers (1990); Reimers (1977); Zabalza, Pissarides, and Barton (1980).

The impact of pensions on labor mobility: Allen, Clark, and McDermed (1988, 1993); Bartel and Borjas (1977); Bodie and Munnell (1992); Bulow (1981, 1982); Even and Macpherson (1990); Gustman and Steinmeir (1987, 1989, 1990); Ippolito (1986, 1991); Kotlikoff and Wise (1987a, 1987b, 1989); Lazear (1982); Lazear and Moore (1987); McCormic and Hughs (1984); O. Mitchell (1982, 1983); Schiller and Weiss (1979); Wolf and Levy (1984).

The impact of pensions on saving and capital markets:
Atkinson (1987); Auerbach and Kotlikoff (1990); Auerbach and others (1989); Barro (1974); Barro and Mac-Donald (1979); Bernheim and Levin (1989); Blinder, Gordon, and Wise (1983); Boyle and Murray (1979); Carmichael and Hawtrey (1981); Darby (1979); Diamond and Hausman (1984); Feldstein (1974, 1977, 1978, 1980, 1982, 1983); Feldstein and Pellechio (1979); Gokhale, Kotlikoff, and Sabelhaus (1994); King and Dicks-Mireaux (1982); Kopits and Gotur (1980); Koskela and Viren (1983); Kotlikoff (1979, 1989b); Kotlikoff, Shoven, and Spivak (1989); Lee and Chao (1988); Leimer and Lesnoy (1982); Modigliani and Sterling (1983); Munnell (1974, 1982); Novos (1989); Takayama (1990); Yamada, Yamada, and Liu (1992).

Pay-as-you-go pension financing: Aaron (1966); Arrau (1990); Arrau and Schmidt-Hebbel (1993); Auerbach, Gokhale, and Kotlikoff (1994); Auerbach and Kotlikoff (1984); Barro (1974); Bernheim (1987); Blanchet and Kessler (1991); Bos and Cnossen (1992); Breyer (1989); Brunner (1990); Brunner and Wickstrom (1991); Carmichael (1982); Diamond (1977); Greene (1974); Hansson and Stuart (1989); Homburg (1990); Lee and Lapkoff (1988); Samuelson (1958); Smith (1982); Veall (1986); Verbon (1988, 1990).

Rationale for government intervention: Aaron (1966); Aaron (1982); Barr (1992); Buchanan (1968); Diamond (1977); James (1992); Kotlikoff (1987); Kotlikoff, Spivak, and Summers (1982); Samuelson (1958).

Data Notes

A full description of the data sources and methodologies used in this report are presented in the Technical Annex (Palacios 1994b). The data are also available on diskette. This note presents a brief summary.

Demographic and labor force data. Historical demographic data were adapted from *International Historical Statistics: Asia and Africa* (B. R. Mitchell 1982), *International Historical Statistics: The Americas and Australasia* (B. R. Mitchell 1983), and *International Historical Statistics: Europe 1750–1988* (B. R. Mitchell 1990).

Demographic estimates for 1990 and projections from 2000 to 2150 are from the World Bank's population data base and were generated using the STARS program.

Data for labor force participation by age group were generally taken from the ILO's *Yearbook of Labour Statistics* (various years). The size of the labor force was taken in most cases from the World Bank's *Social Indicators of Development 1991–1992* (1992).

Pension spending. In this study, pension spending is defined as old age, retirement, survivors', death and invalidity, and disability payments based on past contribution records and noncontributory, universal flat, or means-tested programs specifically targeting the old. In-kind services such as housing and medical care and poverty assistance not based on age are not included. Data are for years between 1985 and 1993. The sources and years of data in the spending and receipts tables often differ.

Most data come from the ILO's *The Cost of Social Security*. Only the pension part of total social security expenditures is included. The data are collected through an in-

ternational survey conducted by the ILO every few years. Most data for the OECD countries are based on expenditures on nonhealth spending on the aged as furnished by the OECD in Paris. These data, which cover the twenty-four OECD countries, are based on Eurostat data for the European Economic Community countries as well as individual country sources collected by the OECD. The most recent year for most OECD countries was between 1988 and 1990.

In addition to these publications, country-specific sources such as statistical yearbooks and annual reports of administering agencies were used, along with internal World Bank reports.

Pension revenues. *Revenues* here refer to combined employer-employee payroll taxes, income from the investment of pension reserves, and direct and indirect government subsidies. The data are taken from the ILO's *The Cost of Social Security* and exclude nonpension programs such as medical care, family allowances, and so forth. Revenues separated by destination (such as pensions) are not available as often as benefit spending, and countries where the separation was not available were not included. The surplus is defined as payroll taxes for pensions plus income from capital minus cash benefits. Government subsidies are excluded from revenues when calculating the surplus.

Coverage and system dependency rates. *Coverage ratio* is defined here as the number of workers actively contributing to a publicly mandated old age or retirement scheme that pays a lump sum or annuitized pension, the value of which is a function of past contributions or earnings, divided by the estimated labor force. The labor force was normally defined as the percentage of persons ages 15 to 64 who were economically active, whether employed or unemployed.

Data on contributors were taken from many sources, including annual reports of the administering agencies, unpublished data from the ILO, and internal World Bank studies. In some cases, estimates were made in order to reconcile data on multiple schemes from different years. Methodology and sources are discussed in the Technical Annex (Palacios 1994b).

Estimates of the labor force were usually taken from the World Bank's *Social Indicators of Development.* In cases where data on the labor force and the number of contributors were not available for the same year, interpolations or extrapolations were used in order to compute the coverage ratio.

System support and dependency ratios refer to the unadjusted ratio of active contributors to persons receiving old age, survivors', or invalidity pensions in the same year. The breakdown of the pensioner population into these three categories will vary by country and is not taken into account here.

Public pension scheme characteristics. Data were adapted from *Social Security Programs Throughout the World, 1991,* published by the U.S. Social Security Administration in 1993. All data refer to the country's main pension scheme. Design features vary among different pension schemes in the same country. Schemes were categorized by benefit type based on whether the majority of pension spending was known to be on contribution-related, provident, universal flat, or means-tested pensions. Qualifying conditions and contribution rates vary across pension schemes within the country. They also will vary by factors such as wage level, industry, and work conditions within the main pension scheme itself. Normal retirement ages may differ significantly from average effective retirement ages. Comparisons should made with caution and with a more detailed analysis of each scheme, depending on the purpose of the analysis.

Pension reserves and investment returns. Two kinds of investment returns were listed for publicly managed schemes. For defined contribution schemes or provident funds, investment returns represent the nominal rates of return credited to members' accounts, after expenses, adjusted for changes in the consumer price index. For defined benefit schemes, investment returns were defined as the nominal gross returns earned by invested assets adjusted for changes in the consumer price index. For all public schemes, the annual real returns are simple, not compounded, returns.

Real returns on equities and government bonds and private pension fund returns are based on simulated results from *The Structure, Regulation, and Performance of Pension Funds in Nine Industrial Countries* (E. P. Davis 1993). These simulations applied average returns by financial asset type in each country in each year to the known portfolio distribution of assets of the pension sector.

Administrative costs. Administrative costs are those related to the old age, survivors', and invalidity pension system. These costs are taken from the ILO's *The Cost of Social Security* (1992) and unpublished data from the fourteenth ILO Costs of Social Security survey (in progress). Other sources include statistical yearbooks from administering agencies. See James and Palacios (1994) for further details.

Other indicators. Gross domestic product and government spending in country currency were taken from the IMF's *International Financial Statistics* (various years). Inflation estimates and exchange rates are also taken from the same source.